300 YEARS

Kitchen collectibles

2nd EDITION

by
LINDA CAMPBELL FRANKLIN

photographed by
DAVID ARKY

Please!
Turn to the last page for newsletter information.

OVER 3500 SEPARATE PRICE LISTINGS

OVER 800 PICTURES ILLUSTRATING
MORE THAN 2000 ITEMS

ISBN 0-89689-041-4

BOOKS AMERICANA
INC

i

Many thanks to all my
enthusiastic friends and to
my fabulous family

ACKNOWLEDGEMENTS

Acknowledgments are about as carefully read as Prefaces and Forewords, but they are just as important. Without the people and institutions listed below, this book would have been on a back burner still! A hip! hip! hooray! for everyone, please.

First, I want to honor the late Archie and Myra Keillor for introducing me to the wide world of kitchen tools. I could never have thanked them enough in a hundred years. Then, many thanks to: my photographer and friend, David Arky; my parents, Mary Mac and Robert Franklin; my editor and publisher, Dan Alexander; Paul Persoff, who photographed items in the Keillor Collection; my collectors and friends Meryle Evans, Vernagene Vogelzang, Evelyn Welch, Robert Carr, Marion Levy, Karol Atkinson, Susan Kistler, Howard Templeton, Carol Merrill, Lar Hothem, Bruce Barber, James Trice, Brother Timothy Diener, Darwin Urffer, John and Evelyn Kuhlman, Marilyn Hodgkiss, Linda Fishbeck, Allen Sitomer, Phyllis and Jim Moffet, the Steed Collection, and the Disshuls. Also to designer Larry Zim of Zim-Lerner, Inc., Industrial & Residential Design, NYC. Also to Kyle Husfloen, Editor of **The Antique Trader**. Special thanks to Bob Cahn, The Primitive Man, dealer and discoverer of kitchen antiques in Carmel, NY. I'm also indebted to dealers Georgia G. Levett of Levett's Antiques in Camden, Maine, to Bonnie Barnes of Anteek Corner in Waynesboro, Virginia, to Arkie's Antiques in Chillicothe, Missouri, Al and Nacy Schlegel of Willow Hollow Antiques of Penacook, New Hampshire, Bill and Esther Neyer of Birchland Antiques in Landisville, Pennsylvania, and The Jorgensens of The 1685 Mill House in Wells, Maine. I am also indebted to General Electric, Sunbeam, Hobart, Rival Manufacturing, and public relations people at other kitchenwares corporations.

Very special thanks go to Anne M. Serio, Museum Specialist, Division of Domestic Life, National Museum of American History, Smithsonian Institution, for helping me find more wonderful pictures to add to this edition. As a representative of the many thousands of kitchen collectors around the country, I am forever grateful for the opportunity to see the parts of the Smithsonian's glorious collection, stored in its cellars. cellars.

More thanks go to Sylvia Franklin at Christie, Manson and Woods International in New York and to Ginger Sawyer at Robert W. Skinner Inc. in Bolton, Massachusetts — both auction houses that frequently offer kitchen related pieces.

Thanks too to The Metropolitan Museum of Art, Elisha
Whittelsey Collection.

Finally, the biggest hooray for collectors, dealers,
museums, friends, fans, book dealers, scholars, dilettantes and
everyone who helped put the spirit into this book! i'll be back.
back.

TABLE OF CONTENTS

FOREWORD

A lot has happened in the kitchen collecting world in the last two years, since the first edition' of this book was published. Many new books — most of them on specialized subject areas — have come out, and this is a healthy sign of interest. At least two offer evidence that there's a growing market for more modern kitchen collectibles: Jane Celehar's **Kitchens and Gadgets** and Don Fredgant's **Electrical Collectibles**. As Fredgant says so well, the coming of the electronic age has given a collectors' cachet to electrical gadgets, not all of them that old.

As a general rule, the tendency is still for the oldest things to be valued the highest, and the most recent things the least. It's hard not to equate the patina and aura of age with high value. There's a certain respectful distance we feel when we handle the 18th and early 19th century things that scores of other long-gone hands have touched. Also, the more unfamiliar or peculiar a shape or function, the more enthralling is the object. If I were stronger, I'd forebear from mentioning him, but the beatific if unbeautiful E.T. is an example of that way of thinking.

There are roughly three ways to look at anything: 1) with awe, because it can never be possessed or understood; 2) with disdain, because, understood or not, you're sure you wouldn't want it even if you were paid; and 3) matter-of-factly, non-judgmentally. Some people would view a diamond with awe, a plastic tulip with disdain, and a ballpoint pen with no feelings at all.

I strive toward the ideal of trying to look at everything without judging it instantly. Allow some awe: even a plastic tulip has its own inherent fascination, if you think about how the design was adapted from nature, how the thing was manufactured, how it was assembled.

Unbiased consideration, coupled with careful choosing, is a good way to insure some interesting collections in the future.

In 1982, the **Wall Street Journal** carried a fascinating article entitled "Believe It or Not: Some Appliances Endure for Decades." People all over the country boast of venerable toasters, vacuum cleaners, beaters, washing machines and refrigerators that perform as stolidly and reliably today as they did when new — 20, 40, even 50 years ago! One man had a 1928 refrigerator that had exposed workings and wiring, so in 1933 he decided to trade it in for a new one, the now famed G.E. monitor-top. Don't you wonder what he's got in his kitchen cupboards?

Late in 1982, the National Housewares Manufacturers Association announced a survey of the attitudes and buying habits of American consumers toward houseware products including cookware, kitchen tools and gadgets, small electric appliances and barwares. I bet they're going to be told some very interesting things, especially about how "they just don't make things the way they used to." The loving attachment that thousands of people have toward old kitchen things, whether they consider themselves collectors or not, is bound to relate to their feelings about the new.

One of the reasons for doing a price guide is that, for the writer, it becomes an excuse for exploring, and for other collectors it becomes a sort of skeletal inventory or sketchy map of the frontiers. Once you know that something exists, like El Dorado — even if you've never seen it — you gotta look, because it might fit into your puzzle. I have heard from many people since the first edition came out. So, reportedly, have Karol Atkinson and Dr. Marion Levy, who wrote articles on pot scrapers and apple parers, respectively, for the book. Consequently, I'm trying to set up a file or clearing house of names of collectors, dealers and curators of kitchen things. Early in 1984, I'd like to start a newsletter for these people, if the response warrants it. If you have ideas or information for me, please write me at Post Office Box 383, Murray Hill Station, New York City, N.Y. 10016.

Rather than retelling the reasons for first, doing this book back in 1980, I offer the original Foreword in slightly edited form.

The Original Foreword

This is my second book on collecting kitchen utensils, gadgets and implements. The first, **From Hearth to Cookstove,** House of Collectibles, was published first in 1976. It reflected my enthusiasms and biases at the time. It took years of work, and I'm still proud of it, but there have been influences on my philosophy of collecting which are expressed in this new guide. I'm even less conservative than I was then!

First of all, the tight confines of my present living quarters (a single 350-square foot room) has meant that I can't actively collect anything larger than a postcard. In fact, paper collecting — the ephemera of everyday life — is now a major interest, and that's reflected in the "Related Collectibles" section of this book. My long-suffering, though proud, parents, who live in a house with a full and filled basement, have undertaken the storage of my collection of kitchen things. This is not to say that I'm no longer looking at kitchenwares — continually pricing things, adding them to the collection in my mind, even on occasion buying somethng. I still go to auctions and flea markets; I still avidly search the ads and articles in collectors' newspapers such as **Antique Trader, Ohio Antiques Review,** the **New York-Pennsylvania Collector, The Newtown Bee's Arts & Antiques Weekly**, and the very sane and wonderful **M.A.D.** — the **Maine Antique Digest.** All the great collecting magazines help keep me up to date too.

The major change in my thinking concerns dates and arbitrary time limits. In **Hearth to Cookstove,** I felt that the wonderful labor-saving devices of the late 19th and early 20th centuries had been sadly neglected and ignored by collectors and antiques critics. I became — and still am — an apologist for humor, whimsy, fantasy, foolishness and inventive genius. Also for cheap materials, clumsy construction. . .all of it, because it all fit into the bigger picture. My friends who were seriously into antiques booed and bah-ed. My egalitarian stance meant some lost sales for the book — Colonial Williamsburg, for example, refused to stock the book in its heavily-trafficked bookstore because of the late things. That snobbish attitude still confounds me. There was a practical reason for including the later things, however; when I started collecting, back in the early 1960s, my pocketbook dictated my choices in kitchen collectibles. The prodigious output of the period from about 1860 to 1930 suited me very well, and still does. Possibly because I had been an art student, there was a rather bohemian reverse snobbishness in me — toward the staid and rather forbidding hearth implements. But I didn't know then what I know now: all of it is remarkable.

I have, to put it simply, become stimulated by the continuum of human inventive genius. I couldn't possibly decree that the output of one period is superior to another. Everything fits together too wonderfully.

That, then, is my aim in this book — to encourage you to collect anything that appeals to you personally. Remember that tomorrow's antique is today's brand new product. You'll see pictures in this book of what I think are the "classics" of the second half of the 20th century. I propose that you consider the new appliances, gadgets, utensils and implements being sold right now in dimestores, department stores, in specialty kitchen equipment shops and through specialized mail order catalogs. (One paper thing I collect now, by the way, is today's catalogs — everything from a Macy's Cellar catalog to one from Williams Sonoma.)

It's obvious that I'm a generalist, perhaps even a dilettante. I know a little about a lot, a lot about a little. My own desire to interrelate everything is not superior to another's desire to learn everything possible about one thing, from A & J implement handles to ice cream molds. Fortunately, there's not only room for all of us, there's a need for all of us too.

EXPLANATION OF THE ORGANIZATION

Arghh or Ahhh. Either you can't find something or you can. Organizing a book like this is a real challenge, and fortunately I find it satisfying to categorize and arrange information. Maybe that comes from being the child of librarians!

I thought a lot about how to divide up the numerous utensils and gadgets to make them accessible to users of the book. I decided against strictly alphabetizing everything because if you don't know what something is you'd have to search the whole book to find it. The chances are greater that you have some inkling of what an item does, so the book is arranged by function rather than by materials or age. There are a few arguably arbitrary exceptions, but I made those because it somehow seemed right: Coffee and Tea stuff together, Electrical Appliances together, etc.

There were many flaws in the organization of the first edition, all of which I hope have been corrected in this new edition. I'll welcome suggestions for the third. The biggest improvement is the addition of a thorough index.

The greatest proportion of kitchen collectibles falls into a preparation category: cleaning and cutting up or mashing the food, mixing it with other ingredients, forming it into some shape. Then there are all the tools used in handling the food for cooling, measuring it. Then the cooking itself — the stoves and the utensils; canning, freezing, drying the food. Then some way to open and close the cans, bottles and jars food is put up in. Then more containers — for the storage of food or utensils, and bigger items of furniture. Of course all these things have to be cared for, so there's a section for cleaning and sharpening. The next special section is high voltage: electrical appliances used in preparing or storing food. Another way to have arranged each of those items would be by function — it is intriguing, as you'll see in one picture in the book, to see how a manual and an electric version of the same thing look next to each other.

Especially fun for me is the section for collectibles related to cookery — items in the shapes of utensils, intriguing things found in the kitchen but not really for cooking, salesmen's samples. Following that is a short section of toy cookery collectibles.

Three new sections involve a closely-related family of items — all the tools and appliances used for household chores besides cooking. I will amplify this section greatly in the third edition, and would appreciate hearing from collectors with suggestions or with knowledge of certain areas. Following are sections for related collectibles and for toy household appliances.

Next come the paper things: trade catalogs and store catalogs, cookbooks, various kinds of paper ephemera related to cookery.

Fitted in, as logically as possible throughout the book, are articles especially written or adapted for this book. There are several new articles in this edition that I hope will spur you on to new fields.

I hope you find it easy as pie to use the second edition of **300 Years of Kitchen Collectibles.** But I also hope you'll allow yourself to get lost browsing through all the sections.

NOTE ON PRICES

The same old caveat you always hear holds true when using a price guide: buyer beware. In a relatively new field like kitchen collectibles, where new finds are being discovered all the time, it is very hard to really set the market value of something. Auctions and recorded prices tend to set market values, and prices can go down as well as up. Utensils and hearth tools from the 18th and early 19th centuries have a fairly sturdy market value, and compilers of auction catalogs are often able to estimate prices quite accurately, especially on high ticket items. But for the thousands of things that rarely if ever appear at auction or get catalogued, both the seller and the buyer tend to use gut feelings and imagination in setting prices. I guess the greatest disadvantage to a price guide is that some sellers — with no consideration for their own market context — simply choose the highest price and back it up saying "It's in the book." How many times have you tried to argue with "the book"? On the other hand, the big advantage is that if the book's writer plays fair, you've got a fairly sensible guide at your side and some valuable clues to things you never suspected existed.

The prices in this book were gathered from many, many sources: at flea markets, antique shows, yard sales, dealer shops, country auctions and big city auctions, advertisements, other collectors' advice. Wide variations are attributable to place, time and opportunity.

Wide price variances are also attributable to dealer philosophies and collector whims. Many times throughout the book you will find something listed with a price range — sometimes the range is small, sometimes fairly large. Then, there'll be another listing for the same item, with a price much, much higher. A price guide must serve a reportorial function as well as an editorial — or advisory — one. Those reported high prices are either a price being asked by a dealer or paid by a collector.

Another reason for wide variations in price is regional pride or chauvinism. An Iowa collector will pay, for example, more for Iowa egg separators than will someone from Georgia, even if the supply in Iowa is much more abundant. So the rules of supply and demand have many intricacies in the collector market. Yellow wood knobs may mean an extra $2.00 to some collectors; brass undoubtedly means a lot to dealers, and — by inference — collectors. The "A & J" mark is worth bucks to some; unmarked and homemade mysteries mean a lot to others.

PREPARATION

I'm gonna pit, core, stone, peel, cut and slice,
I'm gonna chop, grate, grind, crush, mash and dice,
I'm a kitchen-full of tools not a Cuisinart. . .
And oh, boy, am I nice!

PIT TO DICE

There are two fundamentals of food preparation that underlie this category. First, the removal of inedible portions (pits, stones, stems and skins in the case of fruits and vegetables, and bones, gristle, skin, and offal, in the case of animals, fish or fowl). Second, the division of the edible portions into smaller pieces for various purposes. Some of the most popular and enchanting kitchen collectibles fall into this category — including apple parers, chopping knives and nutmeg graters. As soon as Moses Coates invented a mechanical apple parer, back about 1803, Americans had their first mini-production lines. Apple bees, with friends and neighbors gathered together with assorted apple parers, all working as fast as possible to peel and slice apples for drying, must have been joyful and pleasant occasions. I don't know why, it makes me think of the Marx Brothers — I wish they'd made a movie placed in a farm community of the 1840's or '50s. Wouldn't it be fun?

Until about 1850, most apple parers were handmade of wood, and had wooden, cast iron or brass gears — often borrowed from other farm machinery and adapted, as were cranks and handles and clamps. These homemade parers usually did not "gear up." That is, one revolution of the crank meant one revolution of the apple. This relative inefficiency of energy was corrected when parers of cast iron were mass produced. Then, one turn of the crank often meant several turns for the apple. In addition, some of these new patented parers would core, quarter or slice the apple after paring it, and push it off the fork too!

Another fascinating collecting area in the preparation category is graters. Ranging from early 18th century sheet iron graters, with roughly punched holes forming the sharp grating surface, to the useful multi-surface graters from this century, there is something for everyone. The most popular specialty in graters is nutmeg graters. Some collectors buy nothing else —

homemade ones and patented ones, ingenious little machines that hold the nutmeg against the grating surface with springs to save fingertips and knuckles, silver pocket graters carried by traveling gentry. My connoisseurship is still quite satsified by the Edgar nutmeg grater; it's tops in my opinion. I'll never forget the thrill I felt years ago when I found one at the Englishtown Flea Market in New Jersey, after hours of trudging from table to table. Marked $12, I got it for $10, and — without question — got a bargain. They're often marked as high as $70 now, although I'd love for you all to find one much cheaper.

Implements for grinding, crushing and mashing are used in the most basic and ancient of food preparation techniques. After cooking itself, grinding or mashing is probably the oldest culinary trick. Somehow those ancient ancestors of ours had to reduce seeds and grains into something which, when cooked with liquid, would form a portable food. Viewed from here, surrounded by Pepperidge Farm bread and hotdog buns, it seems an amazing feat of imagination for those people to realize that they could create a wonderful food — bread — by grinding grains and mixing it with a liquid, and then baking it. It's interesting to try to imagine yourself in the same situation, knowing nothing and having to go on intuition alone.

For many collectors, nutcrackers are the most interesting subgroup of collectibles. Many varieties have been made. Putting a nut between a rock and a hard place is obviously the first or earliest resort, and during the 19th century a number of different styles of nut anvils and small nut-cracking hammers did the work. But the ones we're most familiar with are based on one of two mechanical systems: the screwed press or the levered jaw. The latter is particularly well-suited to wild and whimsical designs taking off on the theme of animal or human jaws. What I'd like most, should I decide to form a collection of nutcrackers, is a kennel full of the various dog's-body crackers whose tails are the levers that move the jaws up and down. Many figural nutcrackers are German or Tyrolean, and some are found on the handle end of gadget walking sticks or canes.

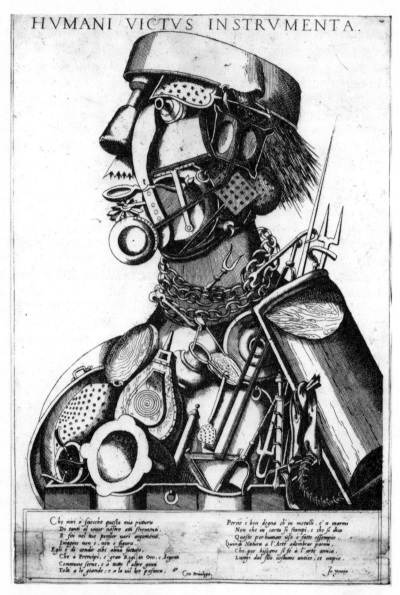

"Instruments of Human Sustenance: Cooking," etching by Circle of Guiseppe Archimboldo, 1569. Part of the verse translates as "This is not an image, this is not a figure. It is the noble makings in the art of cooking." Courtesy of the Metropolitan Museum of Art, Elisha Whittelsey Collection, The Elisha Whittelsey Fund, and Harris Brisbane Dick Fund, by exchange, 1977.

Thrift Shop Window in New York, two views. It doesn't happen often (enough), but this kind of display sets a collector's heart beating. Not the tin "melon" pudding mold (top) and the cast aluminum cake turner (bottom). The cake turner was the magnet that drew four or five people to stand in line before opening, hoping to get it. I got in liine, and was first, at 6 a.m. that day . . . the shop opened at 9!

Apple corer, tin with wood knob handle,
"The Gem Apple Corer," blade
inside allows core to be removed
without going all the way through
the apple, c. 1890 .... $6.00 to $12.00
Apple corer and parer combined, tin
and wood, 2-part: corer fits into
handle of broad-blade parer,
"Dandy," pat'd 1913 .... $9.00 to $12.00
Apple corer, tin with wood handle,
"Boye Needle Company," pat'd 1916 ....3.00 to $5.00
Apple corer, iron with wood handle,
"Boye Needle Company," pat'd 1916 .... $2.00
Apple corer, all tin with tubular T-handle,
6" long .... $7.00 to $12.00
Apple corer and peeler combined, heavy
tin, "Real-A-Peel," Tarrson
Company, Chicago, pat'd 1937,
5" long .... $4.00 to $7.00
Apple corer, homemade of bone $8.00
Apple parer, cast iron, "The Thompson,"
New England Butt Company, pat'd
1877, quarter-circle gear rack,
pares, cores, segments, very rare .... $75.00 to $100.00
Apple parer, cast iron, "White Mountain
Turntable '98," Goodell Company,
pat'd May 26, 1898, screw clamps
to table .... $38.00 to $50.00
Apple parer, cast iron with wood fork
handle, "Goodell Company,"
pat'd 1884, semicircular gear rack ...... $22.00 to $30.00
Apple parer, cast iron, C.L. Hudson,
"Little Star," pat'd 1885 .... $26.00 to $32.00
Apple parer, cast iron, C.L. Hudson,
"Rocking Table," pat'd 1882 .... $22.00 to $30.00

Brown Betty Pudding

"Take a cup of grated bread crumbs, two cups
fine-chopped tart apples, ½ cup brown sugar, teaspoon
cinnamon, one tablespoon butter, cut into bits.

Butter a deep pudding dish, and put a layer of apples
on the bottom; then sprinkle with sugar, cinnamon and

butter, and cover with bread crumbs. Put in another layer of apples, and proceed as before until ingredients have been used, having a crumb layer last. Cover the dish and bake for three-quarters of an hour in moderate oven, then remove the cover and brown the top. Serve with sugar and cream."
Kitchen Companion, Maria Parloa, 1887

Apple parer, cast iron, Reading
  Hardware, pat'd 1868, 1875, 1877,
  1878 .... $22.00 to $35.00

NOTE: White Mountain Freezer Inc., Winchendon, MA 01475, manufacturers two apple parers of cast iron: the "Reading Style" — based on the famous one pat'd in 1878 and made in Reading Pennsylvania, and the very simple lathe style "White Mountain" parer, corer and spiral slicer, made by the Goodell Company 100 years ago. Both are enameled green, and have red wooden handles, and retail, respectively, for about $40.00 and $23.00.

Apple parer, cast iron, Lockley &
  Howland, "Turntable," pat'd 1856,
  clamps to table, an early patent .... $22.00 to $46.00
Apple parer, all wood with iron fork,
  bench type, 25" long, bench 17"
  high, c. 1830s, '40s .... $280.00 to $330.00
Apple parer, Pennsylvania German
  painted wood, straddle type, iron
  gear, wood crank, 3-color paint,
  29" long .... $100.00 to $175.00
Apple parer, walnut with iron prong,
  straddle type, c. 1850s .... $80.00 to $120.00
Apple parer, wood, handcarved, strap-
  to-leg type with remnants of original
  leather strapping, very primitive .... $65.00 to $90.00
Apple parer, light-colored wood,
  probably Shaker, clamps to table
  top $130.00
Apple parer, maple, probably
  Shaker, table model $255.00

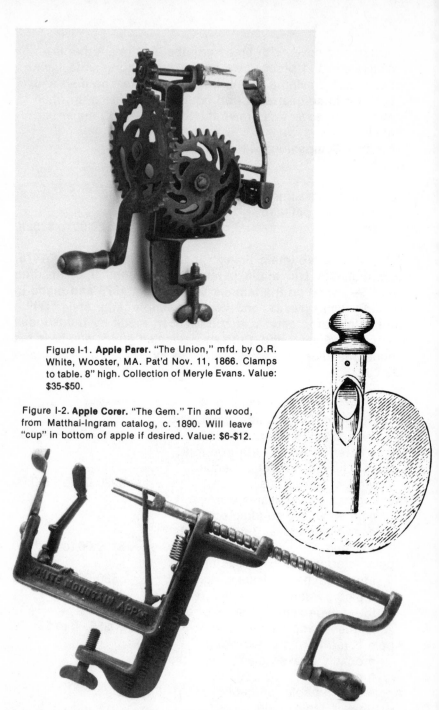

Figure I-1. **Apple Parer**. "The Union," mfd. by O.R. White, Wooster, MA. Pat'd Nov. 11, 1866. Clamps to table. 8" high. Collection of Meryle Evans. Value: $35-$50.

Figure I-2. **Apple Corer.** "The Gem." Tin and wood, from Matthai-Ingram catalog, c. 1890. Will leave "cup" in bottom of apple if desired. Value: $6-$12.

Figure I-3. **Apple Parer.** "White Mountain, Goodell Co., Antrim, NH. 1880s-1900. 6½" high x 11" long. Cast iron. Collection of Robert Franklin. Value: $38-$50.

14

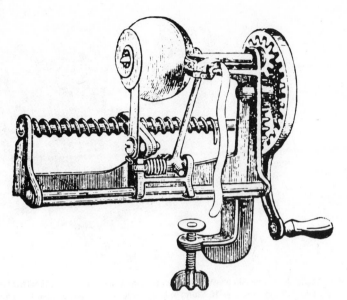

Figure I-4. **Apple Parer and Corer.** Cast iron. Lathe type. From F.A. Walker catalog, 1880s. Value: $20-$35.

Figure I-5. **Apple Parer.** "Bonanza," mfd. by Goodell Co. Large size for hotel or bakery. Collection of Robert D. Franklin. Value: $40-$50.

Figure I-6. **Apple Corer and Slicer.** Wood and cast iron. Marked only "PATENTED" on half-circle of iron. 19th century. 13" long x 6½" wide x 7" high. Formerly in the Keillor Collection. Value: $60-$100.

Figure I-7. **Apple Parer.** Homemade wood, with large tray to hold pared apples? This is what I think the late Archie Keillor, collector nonpareil, told me, but after 10 years of finding chair seats harder and harder I think the "tray" may actually have been made to hold a large cushion, and that this is therefore a straddle parer! 26" long x 9" wide x 7½" high. 19th century. Formerly in the Keillor Collection. Value: $150-$220.

Figure I-8. **Apple Parer.** Homemade wood, with iron crank and fork. Clamps like a bench-vise to table; runs with cord or leather belt. 19th century. 10" long x 3½" wide x 18" high. Formerly in the Keillor Collection. Value: $90-$140.

Figure I-10. **Apple Parer.** Homemade clamp-on style. Tiger maple and iron. Each wooden gear tooth fitted separately — could be easily replaced. 19th century. 9½" long x 9¾" high. Formerly in the Keillor Collection. Value: $130-$200.

Figure I-9. **Apple Parer.** Homemade straddle type, turned walnut, with beautifully shaped seat and well-turned pieces. Worked with leather belt to drive fork. 19th century. 27" long x 7¼" wide x 8" high. Formerly in the Keillor Collection. Value: $120-$175.

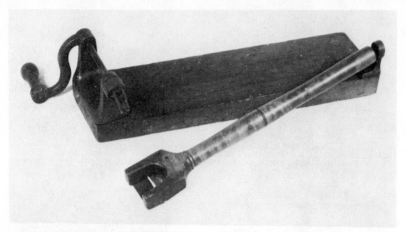

Figure I-11. **Apple Parer.** Tiger maple blade arm, cast iron crank and crank frame. Homemade, early 19th century. 12" long x 3 1/8" wide x 3" high. Formerly in the Keillor Collection. Value: $100-$150.

Figure I-12. **Apple Parer Bench.** Homemade, all wood, with wooden sawtooth gears. Early 19th century. 26½" long x 8" wide x 24" high. Formerly in the Keillor Collection. Value: $120-$180.

Figure I-13. **Apple Parer.** Homemade, wood, with pegged gear. Early 19th century straddle parer. 23" long x 5½" wide x 11" high. Formerly in the Keillor Collection. Value: $100-$150.

Figure I-14. **Apple Parer.** Homemade, wood, with pegged gear. Early 19th century, 22" long x 12" high. Formerly in the Keillor Collection. Value: $100-$150.

Figure I-15. **Apple Parer.** All wood with leather strap to strap it to bench. Cast iron crank is on other side of large gear wheel. Early 19th century. 14½" long x 9½" wide x 10" high. Formerly in the Keillor Collection. Value: $120-$180.

Figure I-16. **Apple Parer.** Homemade wooden parer, with wood gears, iron fork and crank, slicing wire between gears, leather strap to fix to bench. Cutter is hand-held. 19th century. 15" long x 9½" wide x 10" high. Collection of Meryle Evans. Value: $90-$125.

Figure I-17. **Apple Parer.** Homemade knee-held apple parer, with curved body to hold between your knees; attached "shaver" blade and ungeared fork/prong. Light-colored wood, perhaps maple. 19th century. 9¼" long x 6" high. Collection of Meryle Evans. Value: $75-$95.

Figure I-18. **Apple Parer.** Homemade wooden type, painted red, meant to be clamped to bench or table. Mid-19th century. Author's collection. Value: $65-$80.

Apple parer, cherry wood, bench type
with 3-legged bench, iron fork and
peeler, 12" high sans legs, 29"
long, American 19th century $160.00

Apple parer, cast iron, Scott,
pat'd 1868 .... $60.00

Apple parer, Keen Kutter $60.00

Apple parer, cast iron, "Little Star,"
clamps to table $28.00

Apple parer, cast iron, Reading
Hardware, missing wooden crank knob $40.00

NOTE: At a New England country auction in 1982, a number of homemade wooden apple parers, of various types — straddle, clamp, bench, sold for under $100.00. The first one I ever bought, about 1973, cost only $10 — with the original red buttermilk paint. This was at a fancy antique show in New York. I believe that often the biggest bargains in antiques or collectibles are the undocumented homemade pieces, precisely because they can't be catalogued and listed and therefore their market value is more or less up to the collector. But, in several other — here unmentioned — fields, I've managed to get in on the ground level, only to find myself priced out of the field within five or six years.

Apple segmenter, tin with wooden
handles, hand-held, quarters and
cores the apple with one push,
c. 1880 .... $16.00 to $24.00

Apple segmenter, cast iron with tin
blades, Rollman Mfg. Co., cuts 12
segments and cores apple, hand-
held, c. 1880 .... $20.00 to $25.00

Apple segmenter, cast iron, cuts 8
segments, screw clamps to table,
pat'd 1869 .... $24.00 to $32.00

Apple slicer, wood and iron, 42" long
with six slicing blades. Apple fits
onto prong, which is mounted to a
sliding piece of wood. The apple is
pushed through the slicing blades.
Very primitive $130.00

Figure I-19. **Apple Parer.** "Landers, Frary & Clark," pat'd 1873. Picture courtesy of The Smithsonian Institution, Museum of History and Technology.

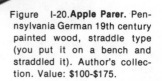

Figure I-20. **Apple Parer.** Pennsylvania German 19th century painted wood, straddle type (you put it on a bench and straddled it). Author's collection. Value: $100-$175.

Figure I-21. **Apple Parer.** The "'78," mfd. by Reading Hardware Co., PA, pat'd 1878. Cast iron. Author's collection. Value: $22-$35.

Figure I-23. **Apple Segmenter and Corer.** Cast iron, tin. Marked only with patent date, February 10, 1869. 10" high x 7" wide. Author's collection. Value: $35-$55.

Figure I-22. **Apple Quarterer & Corer.** All tin. 19th century. 4¾" high, could cut 5" diameter apple. Collection of Meryle Evans. Value: $16-$24.

The following is adapted from an article which appeared in **The Antique Trader**, October 24, 1979. Many of you will have seen it, but I feel that it is such a good study of mechanical apple parers that it should be printed again. The original article, which appears in the **Trader's** annual articles for the year 1979, has several more parers pictured.

THERE'S FASCINATION IN APPLE PARERS
By Marion Levy

"An apple peeler!! You must be kidding!" That was my reaction to the antique dealer's identification of the queer item I had picked up from the "your choice 50 cents table." (It must have been in the 1950s at that price.) I took it home and would show it to visitors as an amusing "Rube Goldberg — what's it." One evening one of my guests commented, "My grandmother had an apple peeler, but it had gears." Imagine! More than one kind of apple peeler! And so began my quest in the antiques shops and flea markets for more of these curiosities. It was not long before I realized that far from being a "gag," apple parers were an important item in the 19th century kitchen and that they were the subject of many patents and the specialty of a number of manufacturers, each of whom tried to outdo the other in sales features. It was at this point when the engineer in me took over from the antiquarian and I began to see each parer as a step in the mechanics of peeling apples rather than as a group of antique kitchen aids.

The first thing I did was classify the parers into "home-made" or "manufactured." If I had been interested in variety rather than evolution I most certainly would have concentrated on the former, as each one was distinctive, showing the ingenuity and craftsmanship of its maker. The designs were often taken from a farmer's magazine article or copied, with embellishment, from one his neighbor had built. But for evolution one had to examine the manufactured product, for here ingenuity paid off in increased sales and hoped-for profits.

Between 1803, when the first patent was issued to Moses Coates of Downings Field, Pennsylvania (Figure AP-1), to the turn of the century, about a hundred and fifty patents were issued pertaining to apple parers. The first manufactured apple parer, and nearly all of the home-made ones, consisted simply of an axle with a crank on one end and fork to hold the apple on the other, plus a knife blade on a hinged arm that could be guided over the apple as the crank was turned. Figure AP-2 is typical of these simple hand-guided parers. Its similarity to the first patent drawing is evident. This was the starting point, the progenitor, of all the rest.   25

From the simplest form the next step naturally was to speed up the process by adding gearing or pulleys. Figure AP-3 is a very early geared parer that became quite popular in New England in the early 1820s. Figure AP-4, on the other hand, used pulleys to increase the speed, with the added feature of coring and quartering the peeled apple. It was nearly all wood (including the threaded posts and nuts) and sold in fair quantities in Indiana and Ohio.

One of the most interesting of the hand-guided apple parers is the M. S. Ault (Figure AP-5), patented in 1855; though it has a very low patent number, 13,894, it had quite advanced ideas. With the fork in position, the apple can be pared by turning the crank and guiding the spring-loaded knife over the apple. By releasing the catch next to the fork, you may rotate the fork through 90 degrees. This disengages the gear that formerly turned the fork, making it possible to turn the fork by the small hand crank, while the six cutting blades on the flywheel chop the apple into small chips. The extra knob in the center of the small crank is a "push-off" to eject the core.

Probably (meaning open to further study) the first practical apple parer with the blade being guided over the apple mechanically was the Sargent & Foster (Figure AP-6). On the shaft, between the crank and the fork, is a spiral which meshes with a large gear, this turns another gear, which is notable for having a space where five or six teeth have been omitted. Meshing with this partly-toothed gear is a geared quadrant which guides a knife blade in a semi-circle over the apple. The knife arm, which rides in a long slot, is held against the apple by a spring. When the geared quadrant, which is also under spring tension, reaches the gap in the partly-toothed gear, the teeth no longer mesh and the whole arm assembly snaps back to the starting position. The pared apple is removed by hand.

Now you can begin to see evolution. The Sargent & Foster model turned the apple once for each turn of the crank. J. D. Seagrave (Figure AP-7) produced one shortly thereafter that geared the fork for faster action and patented the swiveling knife arm that keeps the blade tangent to the paring surface. It showed further consideration for the users by moving the fork forward to make loading and unloading more convenient.

In the 1850s, ideas for apple parers began to proliferate and they were developed along several rather definitive avenues of approach. Four basic classifications evolved which may well be designated as: **turntable, quick return, geared segment** and

lathe. Within each classification there were subdivisions with identifiable trends and variations, each with its merits and limitations. First, consider the "turntable" classification. We will use Figure AP-8 as an example. This was the first of a series by Lockey & Howland, patented December 16, 1856. By this time all apple parer action begins with the knife arm in the position shown; the blade pressed against the apple by spring tension. As the crank is turned, the apple is rotated rapidly and the "turntable" which carries the knife arm makes a complete circle. During the first half of the cycle, the knife pares the apple. By the time it has reached the opposite end of the apple, the paring is complete and a cam beneath the turntable lifts the knife arm away from the apple. The turntable continues to rotate in the same direction, without the knife being in contact with the apple. Just before the knife arm passes beneath the fork shaft, the pared apple is removed, and a new apple is put on. As cranking is resumed, the knife arm passes beneath the fork, the cam releases the knife so the blade makes contact with the apple and the next paring cycle begins. The characteristic of all **turntable** parers is that the knife arm travel through a 360 degree cycle.

An improved version has an automatic "push-off." When the knife arm is three-quarters of the way around, a projection on the edge of the turntable makes contact with the lower end of a lever which causes a "push-off" to perform its function.

It is obvious that the peels, juices and shavings falling on the turntable and gears must have caused frequent clogging and aggravation. Whether the covered turntable manufactured by Harbster Brothers Co. Foundry, and sold through their subsidiary, Reading Hardware Works (Figure AP-9), or the Penn Hardware Co. model with the turntable in the vertical plane came first can only be conjectured, but in any event both approaches were successful in solving the problem of peels and juice.

Another improvement that was added was a "blossom cutter," an auxiliary knife that removed the little growth at the bottom of the apple. Most were simple additions to a standard model.

Probably the most popular apple parer of its time was the Reading Hardware Co. '78 (Figure AP-10), an impressive model, aesthetically and mechanically the pride of the trade. The gears were on top, out of the way, protected by an artistically-decorated bronzed cover that readily distinguished it from all others. The mechanism was canted at an angle to improve visibility and insure that the parings would fall into a bucket on the floor. Besides a "push-off" and "Blossom cutter," the '78 featured an "anti-reverse" pawl that prevented it from being turned backward and damaging the cams and followers a not uncommon occurence. Just to give you an idea of the value of money in those days, the '78 was listed in the Sears Roebuck catalog of 1897 for 75 cents.

Somewhat alike in appearance to the **turntable**, but mechanically different, were the **quick return** apple parers, typified by the Gold Medal. The knife of a **quick return** type pares the apple in the first 180 degrees of travel, but instead of continuing around the circle in the same direction, as is the case with the **turntable** type, it lifts off the pared apple and returns to the starting point over the same path. Various other interesting mechanical movements were employed to obtain the return action. One of these is the Harbster Brothers No. 2B, which used a double set of gears. Although actually the Sargent & Foster (Figure AP-6 is technically a **quick return** type, it seems that many of the later models might have evolved out of the necessity of avoiding the Lockey & Howland **turntable** patents. In any event, the quick return principle did speed up action and offered other advantages.

The **geared segment** type is a novel adaptation of the **quick return** that generally substitutes a handle for a crank. Basically, the design employs a curved gear rack that is stationary, and the geared fork is moved in a semi-circle by a handle, as it pares and ejects the apple. Figure AP-11 is typical of the **geared segment** although there were several variations of this principle that were fairly successful. One in particular, Figure AP-11, known as the Thompson Parer, manufactured by the New England Butt Co. and patented in 1877, combined a turntable with a geared quadrant plus a six-blade slicer. It pared, cored, cut the apple into six segments and ejected the core, all in one back-and-forth movement of the handle. Judging by its rarity, the Thompson never achieved the financial rewards for its inventor that the mechanical ingenuity merited.

Although the last to be described in this article, the **lathe** types were by no means the least important. Because of their simplicity and low cost, combined with the several very desirable functions they performed, they ultimately outsold all of the others. The fact of the matter is that one model, the White Mountain, is still being produced today (about $25.00 now versus 40 cents in 1897). Figure AP-12, one of the earliest and simplest of the **lathe** type, illustrates the basic principles and benefits of this design. A shaft with a crank on one end and a fork on the other is supported by fixed bearings, just like a simple lathe. Between the bearings, the shaft has a spiral thread which engages an arm that is attached to a sliding carriage. Mounted on the carriage is the paring knife and an inverted "L"-shaped coring and slicing blade. The action starts with the carriage in the extreme left hand position, with the arm disengaged from the spiral. The arm and carriage and all the parts on it lie flat and out of the way for loading. The apple is impaled on the fork (blossom end first, they recommend) and the arm is lifted and engaged with the spiral, through the "U" bend in the horizontal wire guard. As you turn the crank, the arm is held against the spiral by the wire guard and the whole carriage moved toward the fork. The knife arm is spring-loaded so that the blade will follow the contour as it peels the apple, and the blade is semi-circular in shape so that a cutting edge is always tangent to the surface of the apple. The vertical slicer blade cuts the pared portion in a continuous spiral, while the "L"-shaped end of the blade cuts out the core. When the paring and slicing of the apple is completed, the arm reaches the righthand "U" of the wire guard and drops through the opening. You can now slide the spirally-slided apple off the core, take a single cut with a knife halfway through the apple and — voila! — you have a whole handful of thin rings, perfect for drying. Later production models, titled "Bay State", incorporated a gear drive, a core push-off and a table clamp, and were also made in larger sizes for commercial use.

In the Bay State the apple stays in a fixed position and the paring knife and slicer move toward the apple. The reverse of this is true of a whole line of **lathe** parer-slicers typified by the Little Star (Figure AP-13). In this arrangement the corer-slicer blade is rigidly attached to the frame, and the parer arm can swivel to follow the contour of the apple, but in a fixed position on the frame. The apple moves toward the corer-slicer rather than vice versa. The threaded shaft with the crank on one end and the fork on the other, slides back and forth in the bearings. When the pawl, pivoted on the rear bearing support, is down, it engages the thread and advances the shaft and fork toward the knives as the crank is turned. Again the apple is pared, cored and spiral-sliced. At the end of the forward movement the "S" shaped bulge of the crank handle knocks the pawl up, and the shaft can be drawn to the right. The shape of the slicer blade being as it is, pushes the sliced apple off of the core, and as you continue to pull the shaft to the right, the rider strips off the core.

29

Almost all of the apple parers described here have been intended for home or farm use and typify the basic classifications. However, there are dozens of intriguing variations in each class and a whole group of larger and more sophisticated models for institutional and commercial use, but that is another story.

This hobby, apple parer collecting, creates a number of peripheral interests. The personal characteristics of the inventors are often revealed in their methods of viewing and solving the problems that presented themselves. For example, there was the pessimist; his design pared in both directions for fear that he would not get it all done the first time; and the iconoclast, who did everything just the opposite from the way others did. Delving into the patents becomes an extended project, not so much as to what you learn about apple parers, but because of the fascination of reading about the other crazy gadgets described on either side and beyond the object of your initial interest. Then there is the problem of photography — trying to work out a practical way to eliminate internal and external shadows so that a real gear does not mesh with a phantom. Or getting into long distance correspondence with fellow apple parer enthusiasts as to why you think this model antedates another because of minor variations in production details. Apple paring may be no big deal today when you buy apple sauce in jars, when one hardly ever hears of apple butter, pies are store bought and Hawaiian Punch is more popular than apple cider, but in the olden days, come fall and apple-picking time, you had to work fast to get them all peeled and cooked, or dried, for they were going to be a prominent part of the coming winter's diet. Anything that would speed the paring and slicing was greatly appreciated by the entire family. But to me it's not what it did but how it did it.

A self-addressed stamped envelope to me, Mr. Marion Levy, at 16000 South Woodland Road, Cleveland, Ohio 44120, will get a reply to anyone with an interest in apple parers.

Editor's note: The Moses Coates drawing [Figure AP-1] was published in The Domestic Encyclopedia, by Anthony Willich, 1803-04, **a book which undoubtedly was in the library of many rural men who wished to have a reference source for answers to all the problems they had in practical matters and useful arts.**

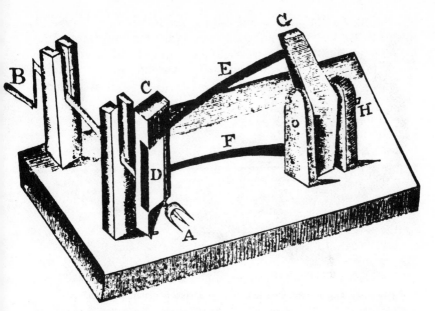

Figure AP-1. **Apple Parer.** Moses Coates, pat'd 1803. From **The Domestic Encyclopedia**, by Anthony Willich, 1804.

Figure AP-2. **Apple Parer.** Homemade, c. 1810. Picture of this and following 12 parers all courtesy of Dr. Marion Levy.

Figure AP-3. **Apple Parer.** Geared pulley type. New England, c. 1820s.

Figure AP-4. **Apple Parer.** All wood. Pulley type. Cores and quarters as well as pares.

Figure AP-5. **Apple Parer.** "M.S. Ault," pat'd 1855.

Figure AP-6. **Apple Parer.** "Sargent & Foster," mid-19th century.

Figure AP-7. **Apple Parer.** "J.D. Seagrave," mid-19th century.

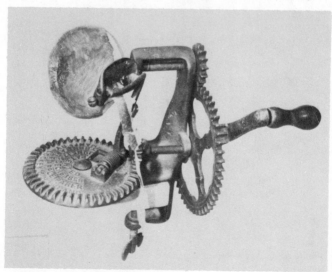

Figure AP-8. **Apple Parer.** "Lockey & Howland," pat'd 1856.

Figure AP-9. **Apple Parer.** "Harbster Brothers Co. Foundry," pat'd 1868.

Figure AP-10. **Apple Parer.** Geared quadrant.

Figure AP-11. **Apple Parer.** "Thompson Parer," mfd. by New England Butt Co., pat'd August 14, 1877.

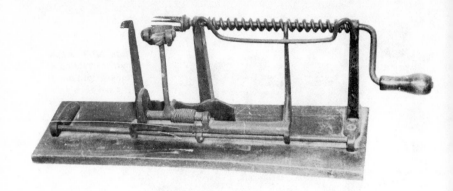

Figure AP-12. **Apple Parer.** Lathe type.

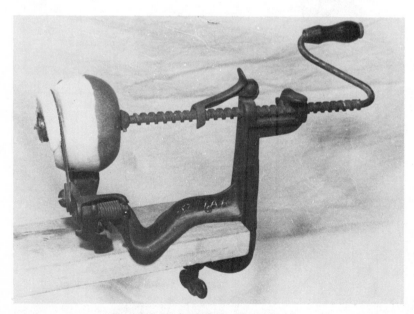

Figure AP-13. **Apple Parer.** "Little Star."

36

Bean slicer and pea sheller combination, cast iron with interchangeable rollers of iron and rubber, screw clamps to table, 12" high $25.00

Bean slicer and pea sheller, cast iron, "Vaughn's," screw clamps to table, green wood handle $35.00

Bean slicer, pea sheller, cast iron $12.00

Bean slicer, cast iron with ornate design, japanned with dark brown and bronze, beans are fed into hopper and pass between two rollers to be sliced. Screw clamps to table, 6½" high .... $35.00 to $40.00

Beetle, wood, has 6 short points on business end .... $12.00 to $15.00

Beetle, meat fret or pounder, turned wood, all one piece, with mushroom shaped pestle at end of handle, 10" long .... $12.00 to $15.00

Beetle, turned wood, 2-piece, with handle that screws into large head, slight dryness check, 9" long $8.00

Beetle, walnut, turned of one piece of wood $10.00

Beetle, turned wood with soft patina, unusually long: 23", a couple of small chips $40.00

Beetle, turned wood, 8" of length turned with narrow rows of ridges, like a cracker roller or cookie rolling pin, 5½" turned handle. Unusual $26.00

See also: Potato masher for wire and wood types.

Bread fork, carved wood handle with wheat sheaf on one side and the words "Manners Makyth Man" on the other .... $28.00 to $35.00

Bread fork, carved wooden handle says "Bread," 3-prong, broad silver-plated fork, very handsome $85.00

Bread grater, heavy tinned sheet iron, slightly curved grating surface with coarse punched holes fairly close

together, wooden handle, early
19th century $65.00
Bread grater, tin, large punched cylinder
with coarse grating surface, fixed
and braced handle, 10" long $16.00
Bread knife, carved wooden handle
with "Bread", carbon steel blade,
quite worn but nice patina .... $18.00 to $25.00
Bread knife, plain wood handle, carbon
steel blade, truncated tip, "Climax,"
13¼" long, late 19th century .... $8.00 to $12.00
Bread knife, wooden handle, carbon
steel blade, "Tip-Top," pointed tip,
15" long, late 19th century .... $8.00 to $12.00
Bread knife, wooden handle, carbon
steel blade, "Victoria," American
Cutlery Company, truncated blade
tip, 14¾" long, late 19th century .... $8.00 to $12.00
Bread knife, wooden handle, "Victor" $4.00
Bread knife, carved wooden handle with
"Bread" engraved on carbon steel
blade (a real bargain!) $6.00
Bread knife, wooden handle with wheat
sheaf carved on it, carbon steel
blade $28.00
Bread knife, "Bread" carved on wooden
handle, Sheffield blade .... $40.00 to $45.00
Bread knife, wheat carved on handle,
blade marked "Alexander E. Foulis" $64.00
Bread knife, "Bread" carved on handle,
carbon steel blade .... $46.00 to $49.00
Bread knife, wheat sheaf carved on
handle, 11½" long $36.00
Bread knife, primitive leaf carved on
handle, 11½" long $36.00
Bread knife, "Want Not" carved on
handle, 12" long $36.00
Bread knife, flower and leaves carved
on handle, 12" long $36.00
Bread knife, wheat carved on handle,
unusually short knife, only 8" long,
very worn, but nevertheless $35.00

Figure I-24. **Bean Slicer.** Japanned iron, dark brown and bronze finish. Very ornate casting. Feed beans into hopper at top. 19th century. 6½" high. Collection of Meryle Evans. Value: $35-$40.

Figure I-25. **Bread Slicing Box.** Heavily varnished wood, like a mitre box. Holds loaf and the slots guide the knife. 19th century. 13½" long x 5¾" high. Collection of Meryle Evans. Value: $25-$50.

Figure I-26. **Beetle.** Turned from one piece of wood. 19th century. Author's collection. Value: $8-$12.

Figure I-27. **Berry Press.** Wood platform (shown here resting on blocks, just for the picture) and foller with tinned iron saucepan-shaped berry holder, perforated on the bottom. 19th century. 11¾" high x 26½" long. Picture courtesy of the National Museum of American History, Smithsonian Institution.

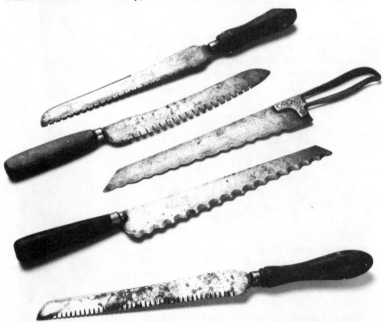

Figure I-28. **Bread and Cake Knives.** C. 1890s. Value: $6-$12.

40

Bread knife and matching board, wheat
   carved on bread knife handle and
   board, words "Bread Knife" engraved
   on steel blade $85.00

**NOTE: One dealer I talked to said that knife and board blanks
were sold for people to carve themselves. This seems a reasonable assumption — especially after you've seen several dozen of
the knives and boards. The technique for cutting the raised
block letters of the words is basic but the results are often
strikingly different, especially in spacing and size. Mottoes
relating to bread abound the world over — ranging from jokes to
blessings — so it is possible that this kind of carving is a
tradition, at least in some countries. I have never found a
document to back up this dealer's assertion, but would
appreciate hearing from anyone who knows of such a document
[catalog or whatever] or who knows firsthand, perhaps through
a family member, of this practice.**

Bread knife, advertising knife marked
   "The Pride of Brooklyn, McGarvey's
   Home Made Bread," $12.00
Bread knife, black wooden handle,
   Ontario Knife Co., 13" long $7.00

**See also: Cake knife. Some can be used for both, but the basic
rule is that the more widely spaced serrations or scallops are
on cake knives, the narrower spaced are bread.**

Bread rasp, heavy wrought iron with
   wood handle, very rough chiseled
   teeth. Shaped like a mason's trowel
   for sidewalk work, early 1800s or
   late 1700s, very rare .... $35.00 to $50.00
Butcher knife, handmade brass and
   wood handle, carbon steel blade,
   quite heavy, 12" long .... $10.00 to $15.00
Butcher knife, homemade, large steel
   blade and walnut handles with
   brass rivets, 14" long $5.00
Cabbage or kraut cutter box grater,
   worn and silky wood with steel
   blade, box 26" long, 19th century .... $20.00 to $30.00

Figure I-28. **Cabbage or Slaw Cutters.** Both walnut and iron, probably Pennsylvania German. One with heart cut-out dated "1883," 18½" long. One with tulip cut-out and arched end (which may have fitted more comfortably against hip or leg while grating) is not dated and is 19" long. Picture courtesy of the National Museum of American History, Smithsonian Institution.

Figure I-29. **Cabbage or Kraut Cutter.** Wood and porcelain handle on heavily-sprung lid (foller), cast iron hinge, steel cutting blade. Sweep of blade in holder is 17"; 13" high. 19th century. Collection of Meryle Evans. Value: $50-$75.

42

Figure I-30. **Cheese Grater.** Wood and punched tin. Stick hard cheese on short prongs, reassemble 2 parts and swivel back and forth. 6½" long. Collection of Meryle Evans. Value: $20-$30.

Cabbage cutter box grater, wood with
 steel blade, 22" long, box well made
 and looks handmade $45.00
Cabbage cutter, simple wood board
 with blade, 12¼" wide x 34½"
 long, worn $12.00
Cabbage cutter, 2 blades, "The
 Indianapolis Kraut Cutter," pat'd
 1905, mfg. by Tucker & Dorsey $45.00
Cabbage cutter, walnut, 3 blades,
 marked "Disston & Morss,
 Philadelphia," 24" long x 9" wide $43.00
Cabbage cutter, walnut, one adjustable
 steel blade, cast iron handle,
 marked "Brady, Lancaster, Penn.,"
 pat'd March 9, 1880, 25" long x
 7¾" wide $75.00
Cabbage cutter, simple wood board
 with guides and one adjustable
 knife, marked "Tucker & Dorsey
 Mfg. Co. $12.00
Cabbage cutter, wood, handmade
 with pegged construction, box
 grater with one very worn blade,
 30" long $38.00
Cake knife, blue glass, c. 1930s $12.00

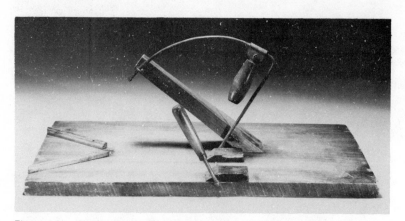

Figure I-31. **Cherry Pitter.** Homemade wood and iron. Very unusual to find homemade cherry pitters. 8" high x 20" long. 19th century American. This could be worked on a slight slant . . . the cherries funneled toward the pitting hole by the wooden wedge. Picture courtesy of the National Museum of American History, Smithsonian Institution.

Figure I-32. **Cherry Pitter.** Cast iron, 3-legged. Pat'd Nov. 17, 1863. Picture courtesy of The Smithsonian Institution, Museum of History and Technology.

Cake knife, green glass, "DUR-X',
flower and leaf design on handle,
in original box, Design patent
#112059 (1938), 9" long, also
used for fruit $20.00
Cake knife, clear glass, "Cryst-O-Lite,"
8½" long $9.00
Cake knife, carbon steel blade with
cast iron handle, "Clauss,"
Fremont, Ohio $10.00
Cake knife, carbon steel blade, "Christy" ...... $6.00 to $10.00
Cake knife, steel blade, cast iron
handle, "Christy", pat'd 1889, 1891 .... $8.00 to $10.00
Carving set, carbon steel, Keen Kutter,
knife, fork and sharpening steel .... $150.00 to $175.00

**NOTE: I remarked in the first edition that this seemed an
incredible amount of money for something so simple, but I had
seen two sets advertised. I still find it incredible, and would like
to hear from anyone who can explain why the price is so high.**
Cherry pitter or stoner, cast iron,
Goodell Co., Antrim, New
Hampshire, pat'd 1886, pits 2
cherries at a time .... $25.00 to $40.00
Cherry pitter, cast iron, Goodell Co.,
clamps to table $36.00
Cherry pitter, cast iron, Enterprise #16 .... $14.00 to $35.00
Cherry pitter, cast iron, with tinned
finish, Enterprise #2, Enterprise
Mfg. Co., pat'd 1903, clamps to
table, cherries are fed into the
hopper, a crank rubs them against
a ridge plate which splits them and
removes pits, price varies widely .... $12.00 to $40.00
Cherry stoner, cast iron, Enterprise
#17, adjusts for different sized
cherries .... $30.00 to $45.00
Cherry stoner, cast iron, "The Family
Cherry Stoner," Goodell Co.,
double trough, lever action, clamps
to table, c. 1895 .... $30.00 to $50.00
Cherry pitter, cast iron, "Home Cherry
Stoner," pat'd 1917, screw clamps
to table .... $22.00 to $25.00

Cherry pitter, tinned cast iron, "New
   Standard No. 50," New Standard
   Hardware Works, screw clamps
   to table, lever action, c. 1900 .... $20.00 to $35.00
Cherry stoner, cast iron, "New Standard
   Cherry Stoner No. 75," .... $20.00 to $35.00
Cherry pitter, cast iron, "New Standard
   No. 75," patent applied for, 12" high $32.00

**NOTE: A cherry pitter similar in style to the one-cherry New
Standard of the turn-of-the-century, is being made — also of
tinned cast iron — by the White Mountain Freezer Inc.,
Winchendon, MA 01475. It retails for about $34.00.**

Cherry pitter, cast iron, "New Britain" $45.00
Cherry pitter, cast iron, "Rollman Mfg.
   Co.," screw clamp $36.00
Cherry pitter, cast iron, "Rollman," 14"
   long, screw clamp $35.00
Cherry pitter, cast iron, "New Standard",
   10" H, this one was advertised for
   an outrageous and unexplained $150.00
Cherry pitter, cast iron, 4-legs, dated 1866 .... $45.00
Cherry pitter, cast iron, "Scott Mfg.
   Co.," 3 legs mounted to board $22.00
Cherry pitter, cast iron with nickel
   plate, "New Standard No. 50,"
   Mount Joy, Penn., patent pending,
   red wood handle and punched
   leather insert to hold cherries firmly $30.00
Cherry pitter, cast iron, "New Standard
   No. 50," and even missing the
   hopper it was marked at $30.00
Cherry pitter, cast metal, not a well-
   made version of the Rollman, screw
   clamps, one cherry at a time $15.00
Cherry pitter, tinned cast iron (?),
   plunger with a spring, one cherry
   at a time $28.00
Cherry pitter, "Rollman" double plunger,
   painted turquoise $30.00
Cherry pitter, cast iron, Enterprise,
   pat'd April 24, 1883, screw clamps $22.00

NOTE: The trend seems to be that even for cherry pitters that are not very unusual or old for the prices to be edging up. Used to be, most cherry pitters were about $18.00 to about $23.00. Now the range seems to be about $22.00 on up to over $40.00, although obviously there are many less than that. A brand new cherry pitter, styled exactly like the old Enterprise stoner, is being manufactured — not, I hasten to add, to fool collectors, but for use. It is clearly marked [cast into the body] "CHOP-RITE Pottstown U.S.A." Just five or six years ago it sold for about $13.00 to $16.00, but I don't know what the retail price is now.

Chocolate grater, tin, square holder for
    chocolate, 7½" long, "The Edgar,"
    turn-of-century. I've never seen one
    of these, but it appeared, along with
    the famed Edgar nutmeg grater, in
    the W.B. Belknap & Company
    Wholesale Hardware catalog of
    November 29, 1901. I wonder if
    sometimes it's not mistaken for
    some other kind of grater? Given
    the high prices of the nutmeg grater,
    I'd imagine this to go for at least
    $35, but the fact that it's possibly
    unique in the field of chocolate
    graters might diminish its value in
    some collectors' minds.
Chopping bowl, wood, painted red on
    the outside, oblong, 22½" long,
    almost surely mid- or early 19th
    century $220.00
Chopping bowl, wood with old red paint,
    oblong and quite large: 25" long x
    17" wide, American 19th century.
    Sold at 1982 auction; estimated at
    $100 to $200, but sold for $300.00
Chopping bowl, handcarved wood, nice
    patina, 25" long x 10½" wide x 4"
    deep, mid-19th century $45.00
Chopping knife, cast iron handle with
    cast steel blade shaped like a baby's
    bottom . . . hence its name, "Double
    Action," pat'd 1892 .... $6.00 to $10.00

47

Figure I-33. **Cherry Pitter.** Homemade wood, iron hinge, nails to punch out pits. Does 20 cherries at a time; slide out the cherry carrier drawer, fit with cherries, insert into box, fit the "foller" or follower into body of pitter, push out 20 pits. Pull out hinged drawer and dump the pitted cherries into bowl. Pits fall out underneath. Much more fun, but probably much more time-consuming than using a Family Cherry Stoner, 2 at a time! 19th century. 6¼" high x 6¼" long x 5¾" wide. Collection of Meryle Evans. Value: $100-$160.

Figure I-34. **Cherry Pitter.** Heavily nickel plated iron. New Standard Corp., Mount Joy, PA, patents pending. All parts numbered, therefore replaceable with stock parts. Nifty action: you feed it cherries with your left hand, and the platform that holds 4 cherries moves around to lie under the punch. 19th century. 10¼" high. Collection of Meryle Evans. Value: $50-$65.

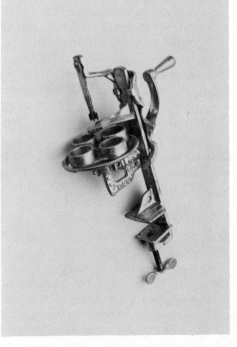

Figure I-35. **Cherry Pitter.** "Duke," Reading Hardware Co. Patent pending. This one very unusual. Very strong action. The swiveling hinge just above the clamp seems to function as a shock absorber while pitter is in operation. 19th century. 11" long not including wooden handle. Collection of Meryle Evans. Value: $40-$50.

Figure I-36. **Cherry Pitter.** "New Standard," Mt. Joy, PA. Patent pending. Nickel-plated cast iron with red wood handle and punched leather insert to make firmer punch. This one. c. 1920s-40s. Photographed at Bonnie Barnes' Anteek Corner, Waynesboro, VA. Value: $30.

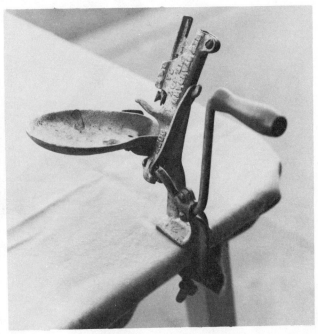

Figure I-37. **Cherry Pitter.**
"New Standard," not plated.
Lying beside it is the leather
insert. This one missing the
cherry hopper, but probably
earlier than plated one. Photographed at Bonnie Barnes' Anteek Corner, Waynesboro, VA.
Value: $30.

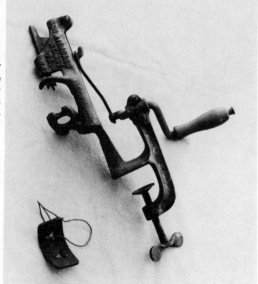

Figure I-38. **Cherry Pitter.**
"New Standard, No. 50." c.
1900. 10" high. Collection
Robert D. Franklin. Value: $20-
$35.

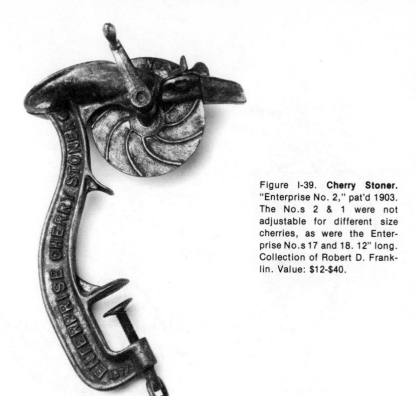

Figure I-39. **Cherry Stoner.** "Enterprise No. 2," pat'd 1903. The No.s 2 & 1 were not adjustable for different size cherries, as were the Enterprise No.s 17 and 18. 12" long. Collection of Robert D. Franklin. Value: $12-$40.

Figure I-40. **Cherry Stoner.** "The Family Cherry Stoner." Goodell Co., Antrim, NH, c. 1895. 8" high. Collection of Robert D. Franklin. Value: $30-$50.

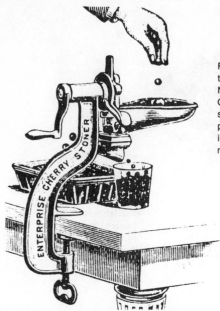

Figure I-41. **Cherry Stoner.** Enterprise No. 12, c. 1880. "The New Cherry Stoner, tinned. Our new Stoner is intended for stoning Cherries with the least possible cutting or disfiguring." Cost then: $1.00. Value now: $30-$50.

Figure I-42. **Cherry Stoner.** "Perfection." Pat'd. This picture appeared in an F. W. Seastrand catalog, c. 1912. "It fits the hand. Seeds and stems at the same time — no other seeder will do this. For the housewife who has long desired an article to take the place of the hand, at the same time permitting the same degree of care in selecting the fruit." C. 1890-1910. Value: $4-$8.

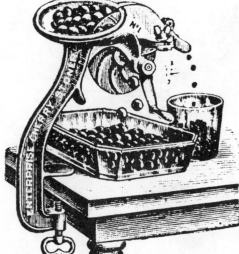

Figure I-43. **Cherry Stoner.** Enterprise No. 1, No. 2. (The No. 1 was japanned and cost 60 cents, the No. 2 was tinned and cost 75 cents.) "It can be adjusted by thumb screws to adapt it to the different sizes of cherry stones." C. 1880-1890. Value: $12-$40.

Figure I-44. **Chopping Knife.** Steel blades and cast iron handle. Marked "N.R.S. & Co. Groton, N.Y., No. 20", pat'd May 2, 1893. 5½" high. Picture courtesy of the National Museum of American History, Smithsonian Institution.

Figure I-45. **Chopping Knife.** Wrought iron with wood handle. C. 1800. Author's collection. Value: $25-$40.

Figure I-46. **Chopping Knife & Cutting Board.** Forged iron and wood, knife with trotting horse and turned wood "tail." 7" high x 14¼" long. Estimated to sell at 1982 Seymour auction for $400-$600. Realized price: $550. Picture courtesy of Christie, Manson & Woods International Inc.

Figure I-47. **Chopping Knives.** Left, hand-forged iron with wood handle, early 19th century. Top right, commercially manufactured. Bottom, hand-forged, mid-1800s. One on left is 8" high with 9¼" long blade. Collection of Meryle Evans. Value: $65-$95 for one on left; $22-$45 for others.

54

Figure I-49. **Chopping Knives.** Commercially made iron and wood. One at top worth the most. Author's collection. Value: $7-$15.

Figure I-50. **Chopping Knives.** Double-bladed rocker style. c. 1900. Author's collection. Value: $12-$18.

55

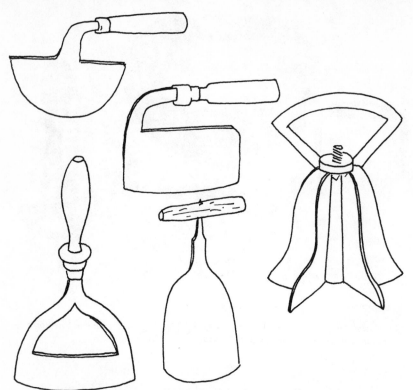

Figure I-51. **Chopping Knives.** Clockwise, starting top left: First two are wrought iron with wood handles in the "tiller style", early 1800s. Value $55-$85. Extreme right is patented steel chopper with 6 blades that can be unscrewed for sharpening or cleaning. Pat'd 1906. Value $8-$15. Lower middle is wrought iron, T-handle of wood, late 18th or early 19th century. Value $40-$65. Bottom left is iron with brass ferrule and nicely turned wood handle. Value $30-$45. The most expensive choppers are either the 18th or early 19th century ones with interesting hand wrought details or the more intricate late 19th century, especially those with fancy shapes.

Chopping knife, cast steel, J.B. Foote
    Foundry, quadrant handle screws
    to six "buttress"-like blades, pat'd
    1906, this one really does a job! .... $8.00 to $15.00
Chopping knife, stainless steel with
    wood handle, "A & J," painted
    handle, four blades, c. 1925 .... $7.00 to $13.00
Chopping knife, stainless steel with
    wood ball handle, "Androck", 2
    bell-shaped, open-cut blades set
    at right angles .... $5.00 to $8.00
Chopping knife, stainless steel, Foley
    Chopper, pat'd 1938, triple blades
    with spring action .... $8.00 to $12.00

Chopping knife, steel with upside down
"Y" shaped double tang attached
to wooden handle, deep double
rocker blades with truncated ends .... $12.00 to $18.00
Chopping knife, nickeled steel, tubular
handle, rocker blade, c. 1910 .... $6.00 to $12.00
Chopping knife, iron with wood "tiller"
handle (just imagine the tiller of a
small sailboat to get an idea of the
shape and angle), 6½" blade with
fat rounded end, 19th century .... $18.00 to $22.00
Chopping knife, cast steel and wood,
with rocker blade, large fat handle
that fits comfortably in hand, late
1800s .... $10.00 to $12.00
Chopping knife, iron with "woven"
basketwork steel handle (like those
heat-dissipating stove-lid lifter
handles), rosettes at rivet point,
rocker blade, c. 1870s-'80s .... $12.00 to $18.00
Chopping knife, steel with wooden
handle, blade pivots — one end
makes scalloped cuts, the other is
strictly a chopper, 19th century,
unusual .... $18.00 to $25.00
Chopping knife, "Universal" by L. & F.
Co., cast steel blade with wood
handle $18.00
Chopping knife, stainless steel with
green-painted cast iron handle,
Acme Mfg. Co., two 5½" x 2½" blades $6.00
Chopping knife, cast iron handle,
double crossed blades, "N.R.S.
& Co. #40," pat'd May 2, 1893,
made in Groton, NY, 5½" high $12.00
Chopping knife, stainless steel triple-
bladed, wood handle, spring action,
Foley $5.00
Chopping knife, steel blade with
enameled cast iron handle, 2-tang
and very stately, c. 1910 .... $10.00

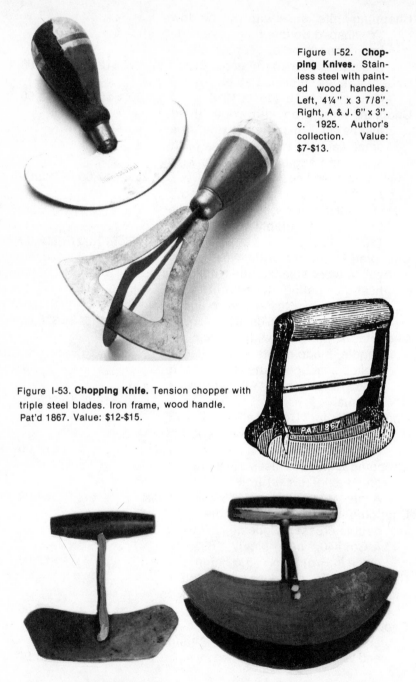

Figure I-52. **Chopping Knives.** Stainless steel with painted wood handles. Left, 4¼" x 3 7/8". Right, A & J. 6" x 3". c. 1925. Author's collection. Value: $7-$13.

Figure I-53. **Chopping Knife.** Tension chopper with triple steel blades. Iron frame, wood handle. Pat'd 1867. Value: $12-$15.

PAT. 1867

Figure I-54. **Chopping Knives.** Iron with wood handles. 19th century. Picture courtesy of Lar Hothem. Value: $12-$18.

58

Figure I-55. **Chopping or Mincing Knives.** Nickel-plated blades with green, yellow or red painted knob handles. From Androck catalog, 1936. Value: $4-$6.

Figure I-56. **Cleaver Combination Tool.** Also a meat tenderizer, bottle opener, meat scorer, bone sawer (?), hammer, and can opener. 19th century. 14¼" long, including hanging ring. Located by the Primitive Man, Bob Cahn, Carmel, NY. His evaluation: $45-$65.

Figure I-57. **Coconut Grater.** Hand-crafted from variety of parts. Cast iron bolt probably went through hole in table top. Brass handle with steel knob, heavy sheet metal serrated blades to shred the coconut. You'd work by holding a half-coconut with grater blade inside, then turn handle. Quite possibly English for colonial use — perhaps Jamaica. Mid 19th century. 7" high. Located by the Primitive Man, Bob Cahn, Carmel, NY. His evaluation: $75.

Figure I-58. **Corer and Doughnut Cutter Combination.** All tin. c. 1905. Value: $8-$15. (See listing under FORM, SHAPE, MOLD)

Figure I-59. **Cutters or Corers in Box.** For vegetables. Tin in tin box, hinged conical lid. From F.A. Walker catalog, 1870s. Value: $18-$20.

Figure I-61. **Food Chopper.** "Universal No. 0," Landers, Frary & Clark, pat'd 1897/1900. Value: $125-$20. Picture courtesy of The Smithsonian Institution, Museum of History and Technology.

Figure I-60. **Food Chopper.** "Universal No. 1" from Landers, Frary & Clark catalog. Came in 4 sizes: 00-small family; 1-regular family; 2-large family; 3-hotel or market. Cast iron, nickel plated. Value: $15-$22.

Figure I-62. **Corn Grater.** Nicely made of wood with iron grater. 19th century. 11¾" long x 4½" high, including 4 cute little legs. Collection of Meryle Evans. Value: $75-$100.

Chopping knife, made of one piece of steel . . . the cylindrical rolled-up handle formed from the top of the blade, no cutout for fingerhold, 5" long blade, 4½" high $10.00

Chopping knife, hand-forged, long blade and long tang attached to wooden handle, 19th century $18.00

Chopping knife, 2-tang straight bottom blade, snug-to-the-hand turned wood handle, marked "Brades Co.", 6" wide $40.00

Chopping knife, hand-forged iron, 1-tang attaches crescent blade to crude wood handle, 7½" wide $45.00

Chopping knife, steel rocker blade with a fat knob handle at each end, 9½" wide, marked only "9" $35.00

NOTE: The above has continued in production, although the more modern ones have stainless steel blades. Look carefully before you pay over $12.00 or so, unless you're simply buying one to use in cooking.

Chopping knife, hand-forged crescent
blade, bentwood handle, 6" long $65.00
Chopping knife, hinged and mounted
on wooden cutting board, 16½"
long x 11" wide, wood handle,
early 19th century $175.00

NOTE: Sometimes this type is described by dealers and in ads as a "tobacco cutter."

Old-Fashioned Bubble & Squeak

"Cut from boiled plain or corned beef, slices sufficient for your family. Chop cold boiled cabbage, spinach or Brussels sprouts to make one pint. Put a tablespoon of butter into a saucepan; add one sliced onion; cook slowly until tender; add the cabbage, a palatable seasoning of salt and pepper, and stand on the back of the stove to slowly heat. Dip the slices of meat into melted drippings or butter, and broil quickly. Dish them at once on a heated platter, cover over the cabbage, and serve. To make bubble and squeak still more appetizing and sightly, cover it with tomato sauce, or serve with it chopped tomatoes which have been seasoned with salt, pepper, oil and lemon juice."
Mrs. St. T. Rorer, in "Ladies Home Journal," March 1899

Chopping knife, hand-forged steel with
turned wood handle, nicely shaped
cut-out for hand, almost like the
top of a valentine, straight-bottom
blade $28.00
Chopping knife, iron blade curved
around like a croissant or sleeping
dog, triple tangs leading to a single-
shank T-handle, 6¾" high $30.00
Chopping knife, iron with cast iron
handle, 2-tang rocker blade,
illegible mark, c. 1890 .... $5.00
Chopping knife, hand-forged iron
blade, beautiful arrow-tipped
tang, turned wooden handle $30.00

Chopping knife, steel blade with
carved wooden 2-tang handle,
marked "Henry Disston" $9.00
Chopping knife, half-circle iron blade,
the top, non-cutting edge, fancifully
scalloped like waves, riveted to
fancy carved wooden handle rather
like a saw handle, early- to mid-19th
century, 6½" wide x 8½" high $85.00
Chopping knife, iron blade, very fat
and curved, with unusual brass
tang and fat cigar-shaped T-handle
grip $45.00
Chopping knife, hand-wrought iron
blade with two extra long tangs,
attached to a thick, slightly carved
wood handle, 5" wide x 6½" high,
early 19th century $35.00
Chopping knife, cast steel blade, cast
iron shank and turned wood T-
handle, blade is lightly rocked,
with very high rounded "shoulders"
to the blade, marked "S.H.F.
Bingham," 5½" wide x 7" high,
very nice $17.00
Chopping knife, hand-forged iron,
curved blade with unusually shaped
shoulders leading to single shank
and turned wood T-handle, mid-19th
century $26.00

NOTE: As a general rule, the hand-
forged choppers, many with lovely
shapes and nice turned handles in
worn wood finish, are more expensive
than the patented manufactured
ones. They are often quite reasonable,
and offer the collector who wants
early pieces to get started without
a whole lot of money. A very nice
collection can be made of late 18th
and early 19th century hand-wrought
choppers, most from .... $20.00 to $50.00

Cleaver, steel blade marked with a steer
and "Wm. Beatty & Sons, Chester,
Penn.", 6" long $15.00
Cleaver, hand-forged iron blade ending
in upturned "genie shoe" curl, late
18th century, very handsome $45.00
Cleaver, tool steel with wood handle,
12¼" long, late 19th century .... $16.00 to $22.00
Cleaver, iron blade with wood handle,
8" long blade, 15½" overall length $8.50
Cleaver, carbon steel blade, iron handle
with room for fingers, very simple,
even crude, 13" long $10.00
Cleaver and tenderizer, combo tool,
cast iron handle, marked "Tenda-Cleve" $8.00

Coffee grinder: see Coffee, Tea & Chocolate

Cucumber slicer, silver and ivory, very
small, made by famous colonial
American silversmith, Hester
Bateman, dated 1775 .... $1,400.00
Egg slicer, cast aluminum and wire,
with base that holds egg, and
hinged wire slicer top, Bloomfield
Industries, Chicago, c. 1935, 4" x 4" ..... $10.00 to $12.00
Egg slicer, sheet aluminum and hinged
wire slicer, very cheap construction,
but nifty, 5" long x 2¾" wide .... $5.00 to $8.00
Fish scaler, cast iron, "C.D. Kenny",
19th century $20.00
Flour grinder or mill, "Arcade", with
original painted finish and decal,
c. 1920 .... $85.00
Food grinder, chopper or mill, cast iron
with graniteware hopper and wooden
foller or pusher, 1880s .... $40.00 to $45.00
Food mill, cast iron, "Keen Kutter #11,"
pat'd May 29, 1906, mfd. by E.C.
Simmons, screw clamps to table,
9½" high $25.00
Food mill, "Keen Kutter #10" $6.50

Figure I-63. **Food Press.** Tinned iron in cast iron frame, painted black. Includes 3 grades of inserts — fine to coarse. Marked "Little Field's," pat'd June 16, 1868. 7½" high. Picture courtesy of the National Museum of American History, Smithsonian Institution.

This invention is a real little treasure.—*Public Ledger, Phila.*

Philadelphia Cooking School,
1525 CHESTNUT STREET.
MR. C. F. HENIS:
Dear Sir: A few days ago some one left one of your patent Fruit and Vegetable Presses at my school, on trial. I used it to-day for the first, and find it the best thing of the kind I have ever used. Would you be kind enough to write me where they can be purchased.
Respectfully yours,
(Mrs.) S. L. RORER,
4, 22, '84.   *Principal.*

Figure I-64. **Fruit and Vegetable Press.** "Henis," Charles F. Henis Co., Philadelphia, PA, pat'd 188-? Used to mash potatoes and other cooked vegetables, for "Pressing the juice from grapes," "straining the hulls from oat-meal mush," etc. Picture from advertisement, 1884. Value: $7-$9.

Figure I-65. **Fruit Press.** (Two views.) Enterprise Mfg. Co., pat'd 1879. These views are from **The Enterprising Housekeeper,** 1881. Value: $40-$55.

Figure I-66. **Fruit Press.** "Enterprise," Philadelphia. Pat'd September 30, 1879. Cast iron with wood handle. From bottom of clamp to top of hopper 12" high x 11" long. Collection of Meryle Evans. Value: $40-$55.

Food mill, "Keen Kutter #10," cast iron
  with wood handle, screw clamps,
  pat'd May 15, 1904 .... $22.50
Food mill, cast iron, "Eveready #55,"
  screw clamp, 8" high $20.00
Food mill, cast iron, "Rollman Food
  Chopper No. 12," Rollman Mfg. Co. $10.00
Food mill, cast iron, "Winchester" $40.00
Food mill, cast iron, wood knob on
  crank handle, "Universal No. 2,"
  Pat'd October 12, 1897, April 18,
  1899 and 1900. Screw clamps, only
  one blade $10.00

Food mill, cast iron with wood handle,
2 cutters — one of which reverses
coarse to fine, other is marked
"Universal Bread Crumber," Universal,
pat'd 1897 and 1899, so earlier than
preceding mill, nice to have special
bread blade $23.00
Food mill, cast iron, "Chipaway Food
Grinder," screw clamps $5.00
Food mill, tin, wood foller, "Edith",
made in Germany $22.50
Food mill, marked "#7, O-V-B" (Our
very best), Pat'd May 17, 1904,
mfd. by Hibbard, Spencer, Bartlett
& Co., 8" high, screw clamps to table $18.00
Food mill, cast iron in original cardboard
box, "Universal No. 2," very unusual
to find box .... only $8.00
Food mill, sheet iron and wood, with
wrought handle, extremely fine
handmade, early (late 18th century)
food grinder, with various adjustments.
Mounting board 16½" long, hopper
4" deep $280.00
Food mill, "Acme Rotary Mincer,"
1935, in original box, with great
red Bakelite handle $15.00
Grape press, cast iron with tin reservoir
and wood foller (or pusher),
"Little Field's," pat'd 1868 .... $25.00 to $40.00
Grater, brass semi-cylinder with iron
handle, 14" long, early 1800s,
possibly English (the brass is a
clue) .... $85.00 to $100.00
Grater, tin and wire, "All-in-One," 3
grating surfaces plus a slicer,
10 5/8" long, c. 1940 .... $4.00 to $8.00
Grater, tin and wire, Half is a woven
wire mesh, the other half is machine-
punched tin, "Kitchen Novelty
company," made in Germany, 12½"
long, c. 1890s .... $8.00 to $12.00

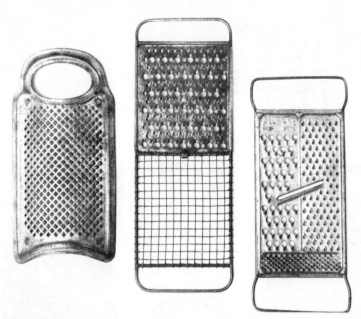

Figure I-67. **Graters.** left: 9½" long, c. 1910. Middle: 12½" long, made in Germany for Kitchen Novelty Co., Atlantic City, NJ, c. 1895. Right: "All-in-One," c. 1940. Values: $3-$12.

Grater, tin and wire, "Ekco," 2 grating
surfaces, a slicer, and a Saratoga
(French fry) slicer, 10½" long .... $7.00 to $10.00
Grater, punched tin, wide tin strap
handle, rounded off rectangle,
held rather like a curry comb, 4¼"
long, turn-of-the-century or later .... $4.00 to $7.00
Grater, punched tin, wide tin strap
handle, oval in shape, otherwise
much like above, "Bromwell's
Greater-Grater . . . Easy to use . . .
Grates Rapidly . . . Safe and
Sanitary for all grating purposes"
(so says the original paper label
on this one .... $4.00 to $8.00
Grater, pierced tin cylinder with strap
handle, fine and medium grating
surfaces, pat'd 1901, 7½" high .... $10.00 to $15.00
Grater, stamped and punched tin, c.
1910, 9½" long .... $7.00 to $9.00

Figure I-68. **Grater.** Mechanical geared revolving grater, mfd. by Enos Stimson, pat'd August 14, 1866. Collection of Marilyn Hodgkiss. Value: $25-$35.

Figure I-69. **Graters.** Punched tin, all c. 1900. Tall one is 16" high; small strap-handled one is 4¼" long. Author's collection. Value: $4-$15.

Grater, tin cylinder wtih three surface
grades, early 1900s, 9¼" high .... $8.00 to $15.00
Grater, tin with wood handle, circular
grating area, late 19th century, 7"
long .... $15.00 to $20.00
Grater, pierced copper mounted to
board, 22" long, homemade and
probably from the mid-19th century $58.00
Grater, tin, "Gilmore" pat'd 1897 .... $3.50

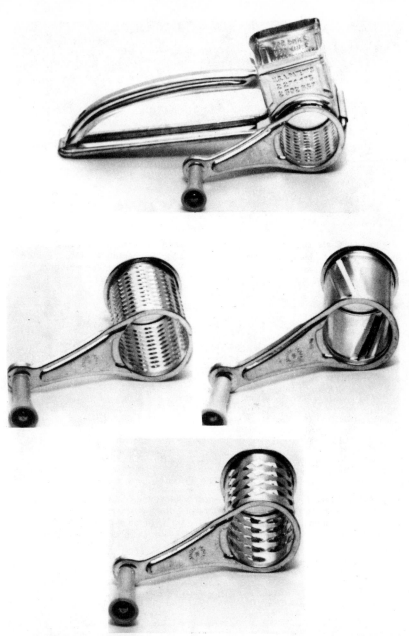

Figure I-70. **Grater, modern classic.** Mouli Manufacturing, imported from France. This familiar gadget was first imported in America right after WWII by Joseph Markala, retired US Navy Commander. Markala started Mouli Mfg. to distribute gadgets manufactured by Moulinex of France. One unusual feature of this grater is that the various slicing, julienne, grater drums can be positioned for right-or left-handed use! Stainless steel and plastic.

Figure I-71. **Grater.** Box style, of wood and punched tin, with porcelain knob. Could be hung from wall. Most likely homemade. 15" long. 19th century American. Picture courtesy of the National Museum of American History, Smithsonian Institution.

Figure I-72. **Grater** (Two views.) "H.P. Arthur's Vegetable Grater," pat'd October 8, 1867, stenciled on top. All wood with metal grater drum, wood hoop and foller, wood handle. Top latches on and lifts off for cleaning. 13¾" to top of hopper; 19" to top of fulcrum of handle/lever. Frame is 13" long x 6" wide. Collection of Meryle Evans. Value: $75-$110.

Figure I-73. **Revolving Grater.** Very similar to the Enos Stimson one from 1867. This picture from **Practical Housekeeping,** published in 1881. Value: $25-$35.

72

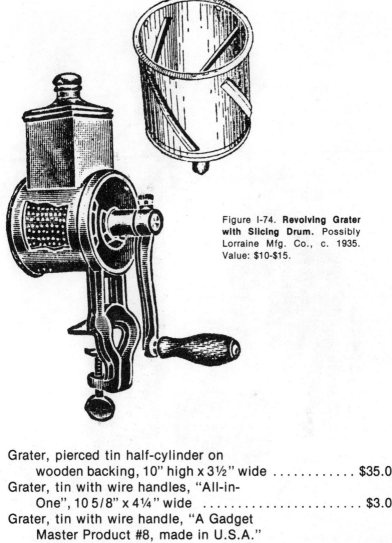

Figure I-74. **Revolving Grater with Slicing Drum.** Possibly Lorraine Mfg. Co., c. 1935. Value: $10-$15.

Grater, pierced tin half-cylinder on
    wooden backing, 10" high x 3½" wide $35.00
Grater, tin with wire handles, "All-in-
    One", 10 5/8" x 4¼" wide $3.00
Grater, tin with wire handle, "A Gadget
    Master Product #8, made in U.S.A."
    10" long x 7" wide $6.50
Grater, tin, mechanical, with three
    grating discs that insert in frame
    and slide back and forth to slice,
    fine grate or coarse grate, "Safety
    Veg-E-Grater" mfd. by Knapp-
    Monarch Mfg. Co., 12½" long $15.00
Grater, revolving, "Lorraine Metal Mfg.,"
    wooden handle painted green,
    screw clamps to table, 8½" high $23.00

73

Figure I-75. **Revolving Graters.** Right: Lorraine Metal Mfg. Co., cast iron, tin and wood. 8½" high. c. 1935. Left: unmarked, possibly Lorraine. Tin and wood. has 3 drums in different coarsenesses. C. 1935. Author's collection. Value: $8-$23.

Grater, revolving, tin and wood, very
simple with knobless crank, three
grating drums, 6½" high $20.00
Grater, revolving, wood with a tin drum,
the box being rectangular with a lid
that lifts to reveal grating drum.
Two drawers below, 9½" high x

9¼" long, late 1700s, early 1800s,
American. Estimated to sell at
auction in 1982 for between $150
and $175 — this is a rare and interesting
piece — but it made only $50.00

New England Hasty Pudding,
or Stir-About

"Boil three quarts of water in an iron pot; mix a pint of Indian meal in cold water, and make it thin enough to pour easily; when the water boils, pour it in; stir well with a wooden stick kept for this purpose; it takes about an hour to boil; salt to your taste; stir in dry meal to make it thick enough, beating it all the time. Eat with milk or molasses, or butter and sugar."
Domestic Cookery, Elizabeth E. Lea, 1859

Hasty Pudding Sauce

1 cup hot milk
1 cup sugar
2 eggs
1 tablespoon butter

Stir the butter into the boiling milk, add the sugar, and pour this on the beaten eggs. Return to the custard kettle and stir until it begins to thicken. Flavor with vanilla, adding, if you like, nutmeg, and set in hot, not boiling, water till needed.
House & Home, a Complete House-Wife's Guide, Marion Harland, 1889

Grater, revolving, tin, cast iron and
    wood, "BME No. 620," screw
    clamps to table, 13" high, c. 1930s ...... $12.00 to $14.00
Grater, revolving, tin, wood and nickel-
    plated metal, three grating drums:
    coarse, fine, medium, screw clamps
    to table, c. 1925 .... $7.00 to $12.00
Grater, revolving, tin and cast iron,
    very heavy duty large size, clamps
    to table, c. 1880 .... $12.00 to $18.00

Grater, revolving, cast iron and tin,
    large grating drum, very elegant
    cast iron wheel, Enos Stimson,
    pat'd August 14, 1866, 10½" high,
    terrific .... $25.00 to $40.00
Gristmill, for corn, cast iron, Arcade,
    screw clamps to table $35.00

NOTE: A brand new tinned cast iron mill, for "cereal or flour," is sold by the White Mountain Freezer Company. It has a large hopper, screw clamps to table, and has a natural light-colored wooden crank handle. It doesn't look as old-fashioned as other White Mountain mills, but could easily be mistaken. The suggested retail is about $63.00, so it's unlikely that you'll be finding one in an antique shop. [Winchendon, MA 01475.]

Figure I-76. **Herb Crusher or Spice Mill.** Cast iron with stained or stove-blacked wooden handles. 19th century, probably not American. 17" long with 7" diameter wheel. Collection of Meryle Evans. Value: $100-$150.

Figure I-77. **Herb Grinder or Mill.** All wood. 19th century, possibly European, even Asian. 12½" long x 5" high. Formerly in the Keillor Collection. Value: $90-$120.

Herb boat or grinder, cast iron with
      bootjack base, rolling cast iron
      pestle, 18" long, early 19th century $110.00
Herb boat or grinder, cast iron footed
      iron boat, rolling pestle with two
      wooden handles, 26" long, 19th
      century $170.00
Herb masher, turned maple with small
      head carved with concentric circles,
      7" long (like a small-headed beetle) ...... $35.00 to $40.00
Herb mill, japanned tin, sheet iron
      hopper, wooden drawer below and
      small wooden handle on crank, 7" high $76.00
Huller or pin-feather picker, tin, "Nip-
      it," pat'd 1906 .... $1.00 to $3,00
Ice crushers, shavers, etc.: see section on Chilling & Freezing
Juicer, aluminum and painted tin,
      10½" high, flimsy but cute as R2-D2!
      "Handy Andy," mfd. by the H.A.
      Specialty Company, Inc., pat'd
      July 23, 1935, although on the market
      for about five years before that.
      Came with red or green painted
      base (saw one adv'd in 1982 for
      $57.50 but) .... $15.00 to $32.00
Juicer, cast aluminum, chromed and
      painted iron, "Juice-O-Mat," Rival
      Mfg. Co., pat'd 1937, 7 7/8" high .... $12.00 to $20.00
Juicer, aluminum with wooden knob,
      "The Speedo Super Juicer," mfd.
      by Central States Mfg. Co., c. 1930,
      5¼" high, wall bracket is usually
      missing, but this juicer is a really
      terrific gadget for today's kitchens .... $5.00 to $12.00
Juicer, cast metal and aluminum, 10"
      high, very unusual and handsome
      . . . on four widespread legs, side
      crank, hopper and reamer at top,
      Universal, by Landers Frary & Clark .... $9.00 to $15.00
Juicer, sheet metal with green finish
      wooden knob, triple extractor,
      with three reamers, for grapefruit,
      oranges, lemons and for tomatoes.
      Screw clamps to table, c. 1931 .... $4.00 to $9.00

77

Figure I-78. **Juicer and Reamers.** Aluminum. Big one is the funny "Handy Andy," this one with **red**-painted base. 10½" high x 6 7/8" diameter. Author's collection. Values: Handy Andy $15-$32; others $2-$5.

See also: Reamers

Kitchen saw, carbon steel with turned
wood handle, Keen Kutter, 13½" long   . . . $10.00 to $15.00

Kitchen saw, adjustable carbon steel
blade in cast aluminum frame,
"Always Sharp," Charles Wohr,
15¾" long, very attractive . . . . $12.00 to $16.00
Kitchen saw and cake knife combo,
carbon steel with wood handle,
"Victor," American Cutlery Co.,
the saw is the top edge, the scalloped
cake knife along the bottom . . . . $7.00 to $12.00
Lemon reamer, maple, well-carved,
7¼" long $22.50
Lemon reamer, wood, 9" long,
grooved end . . . . $18.00 to $20.00
Lemon reamer, maple, possibly
Shaker, 10½" long $35.00

**NOTE: A very well-carved wooden reamer, with deep grooves
and a small delicate rounded point and well-shaped handle, 7"
long, was being manufactured during the 1970s, and probably
still is, to sell for about $7.00. It is so well made and attractive,
that it could easily be mistaken for an earlier reamer.**

Lemon squeezer, cast iron, hinged . . . . $10.00 to $15.00
Lemon squeezer, cast iron with glass
insert, "Williams," late 19th century . . . . . $28.00 to $40.00
Lemon squeezer, maple, hinged "male"
and "female" halves, 1870s, 10¾"
long . . . . $22.00 to $32.00
Lemon squeezer, maple wtih porcelain
insert, 8½" long . . . . $25.00 to $28.00
Lemon squeezer, japanned cast iron
with separate, heavily-tinned cup
which can be used separately as a
reamer, "American Queen," c. 1906 . . . . . . $18.00 to $25.00
Lemon squeezer, wood, footed table
top model, Shaker? $150.00
Lemon squeezer, iron, 8½" long with
2½" diameter cup and bowl $6.00
Lemon squeezer, cast iron, "Pearl" $18.00
Lemon squeezer, wood, hinged 2-part
with handles . . . . $30.00 to $45.00
Lemon squeezer, iron with porcelain
liner, patent applied for in 1888 . . . . $45.00

(No Model.)

J. H. COX.
LEMON GRATER.

No. 462,626.   Patented Nov. 3, 1891.

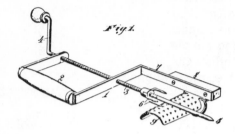

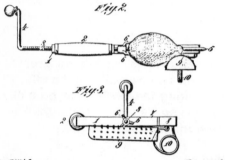

Witnesses.
Phil Emitt
Dennis Sumly.

Inventor.
Jennie H. Cox.
By
James La Norris
Atty.

Figure I-79. **Lemon Grater Patent Drawing.** Pat'd November 3, 1891 by Jennie H. Cox, of Winfield, KS. Iron frame with wood grips and punctured tin grating surface.

Figure I-80.   **Knife.** Painted wood handle, c. 1930s, 40s. Author's collection. Value: $8-$12.

Figure I-81. **Lemon Squeezer.** Wood with turned handles. 1880s. 10¾" long. Picture courtesy of Lar Hothem. Value: $22-$32.

80

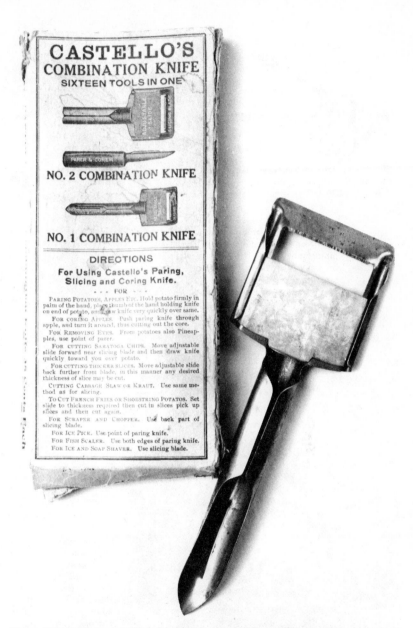

Figure I-82. **Knife, Parer & Corer Combination Tool.** Mfd. by Castello, 1913. Author's Collection. Value: $10-$14.

Figure I-83. **Lemon Squeezer.** Japanned cast metal frame with tin cup, c. 1880s. Value: $18-$25.

Figure I-84. **Lemon Squeezer and Slicer.** Cast iron mounted on wood. Rack and pinion movement. Missing porcelain (?) or glass (?) reamer insert. Probably for restaurant use. No marks. 12" high. Photographed at Bonnie Barnes' Anteek Corner, Waynesboro, VA. Value: $55.

Figure I-85. **Lemon Squeezer.** Wood with heavily tinned insert. 19th century. Picture courtesy of the National Museum of American History, Smithsonian Institution.

Figure I-86. **Lemon Squeezer.** Plated cast iron, hinged hand-held press. 19th century. 7¼" long. Picture courtesy of the National Museum of American History, Smithsonian Institution.

Figure I-87. **Masticator.** Iron and wood. Pre-1895. Picture courtesy of The Smithsonian Institution, Museum of History and Technology.

Lemon squeezer, cast iron, 4-legged, rack & pinion movement, cuts lemon then squeezes it, 12" high, 19th century, very unusual, but useful? $55.00

Lemon squeezer, "Diamond Point," pat'd July 10, 1888 .... $28.00

Lemon or lime squeezer, heavy cast aluminum, marked "Acid & Rust Free," 6½" long, works like pliers .... $10.00 to $12.00

Lemon and lime squeezer, zinc-plated iron, "Vaughn Co.," Chicago, IL, 6" long $10.00

Lemon and lime squeezer, cast white metal, "Quick & Easy," 6" long $4.00

Lime squeezer, maple, turned handles, almost looks hand-carved, 9" long, c. 1910, dealer suggested it might be a bartender's squeezer $38.00

Figure I-88. **Lemon Reamer.** Lathe-turned and carved wood, c. 1870s-1890s. 6½" long. Collection of Meryle Evans. Value: $18-$22.

Figure I-89. **Lime and Lemon Squeezer.** Zinc-plated iron. Mfd. by Vaughn Co., Chicago. C. 1930s. 6" long. Collection of Mary Mac and Robert Franklin. Value: $10-$12.

Masticator: See Meat Tenderizer

Meat chopper, galvanized metal, "The Home No. 1," screw clamps to table, 1890s .... $16.00 to $22.00

Meat chopper, cast iron, tin hopper on wood base, "Athol Machine Co.," pat'd 1865, fabulous-looking cranked machine that has a revolving hopper with wood liner. Wonderful coordination, and great fun to use, this is extremely desirable .... $125.00 to $175.00

Meat chopper, cast iron gears and
　　frame, wood tub .... $60.00 to $85.00
Meat chopper or grinder, nickeled iron,
　　"The Little Giant" No. 205, height
　　of hopper and grinder is adjustable,
　　screw clamps to table, 1890s .... $15.00 to $28.00
Meat grinder, "Universal No. 00,"
　　Landers, Frary & Clark .... $12.00 to $15.00
Meat grinder, "Winchester" $55.00
Meat grinder, cast iron, "Keen Kutter,"
　　dated 1906 .... $8.00
Meat grinder, same $9.00
Meat grinder, same $15.00
Meat grinder, same $25.00
Meat grinder and juicer, cast iron,
　　marked "No. 1," and Canadian
　　patent date of 1901 .... $12.00
Meat grinder, cast metal painted red,
　　with white enameled hopper interior,
　　"Aalwerke #5" and "R AALEN",
　　wooden crank handle, only one
　　blade: medium/coarse, 9" high $25.00
Meat grinder, cast metal, white
　　porcelainized hopper, "Harras
　　No. 52" $48.00
Meat grinder, cast iron, Sargent & Co.,
　　pat'd March 8, 1892, screw clamps,
　　large size $25.00
Meat grinders . . . simple metal ones
　　with one blade, dulled tin or zinc
　　finish, smallish in size .... $5.00 to $12.00
Meat and food chopper, galvanized
　　iron, Steinfeld, pat'd 1904, screw
　　clamps to table .... $8.00 to $12.00

**NOTE: A cast iron meat grinder, the Universal No. 3, is still
being sold.**

Meat press/juicer, cast iron, "Columbia,"
　　mfd. by Landers, Frary & Clark,
　　late 19th century .... $25.00 to $30.00

Figure I-90. **Meat Chopper or Hasher.** Cast iron, tin, painted wood. Pat'd by Leroy Starrett, mfd. by Athol Machine Co., Athol Depot, Mass. Pat'd May 23, 1865. 16" long x 7" wide x 13½" high. Adjustable blades, reciprocating gear turns the hopper around for thorough chopping. All in all, this has to be the neatest gadget in the kitchen collectible world. Collection of Meryle Evans. Value: $125-$175.

Meat and cheese press, cast iron with
    tin hopper, brown finish with
    yellow stenciling, "Starretts,"
    pat'd 1873, 9" high $35.00
Meat and cheese press, cast iron frame
    with heavy tin liner, "Starretts,"
    yellow stenciling on brown finish,
    9" long, 7½" high, pat'd 1873 . . . . $28.00
Meat and fruit press, nickeled-brass
    with wood foller, Wilder's, pat'd 1906 . . . . $28.00 to $35.00

NOTE: I can just see what'll happen. One of those brass-and-flash dealers finds this Wilder's press and takes it down to the brass, buffs it and puts it out for $100.00. Will you go for it? ALSO NOTE: A new cast iron meat, fruit and cheese press and sausage stuffer combo, with an 8-quart capacity, is being made now by the Chop-Rite Manufacturing Company of Pottstown, Pennsylvania. Very well made and very useful, for about $140.00 retail!!

Figure I-91. **Meat Chopper.** Athol Machine Co., pat'd 1865. This cut from the F.A. Walker catalog, 1870s. Value: $125 -$175.

Figure I-92. **Meat Chopper.** From **Treasure-House of Knowledge,** by Henry Scammel, 1890. The description in the book reads "This little machine is indispensable in every family where sausage and mince pies are favorite dishes. It does its work perfectly and with great rapidity. Men who can buy mowing machines and hay forks cannot afford to let their wives work away in the kitchen with old-fashioned implements when better ones are to be had at a small outlay of money. If any husband refuses to buy it, let the wife cut off his supply of hash and sausages on trial, and then take severer means afterward if necessary." Uh oh!

Figure I-93. **Meat Juice Press.** "Columbia," Landers, Frary & Clark. Late 1800s. Meat juice, by the way, was for soups, gravies and especially invalids. Picture courtesy of The Smithsonian Institution, Museum of History and Technology. Value: $35-$45.

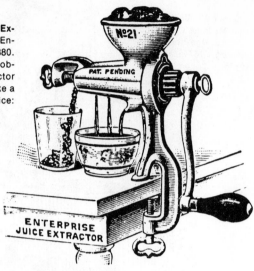

Figure I-94. **Meat Juice Extractor.** Enterprise No. 21, Enterprise Mfg. Co., c. 1880. Tinned cast iron. This is obviously also a juice extractor — it says so, but it looks like a meat grinder. Original price: $2.50. Value now: $15-$25.

Figure I-95. **Meat Grinder.** Cherry wood box with iron gear and crank. Screws to table top. Trunk-shaped, lid with chamfered edges and square aperture opening to grinding mechanism, steel blades. 8½" high x 13" long x 9" deep. Estimated at 1983 Linden sale between $80-$120. Actual price: $198. Picture courtesy of Christie, Manson & Woods International Inc.

Meat pounder, cast iron with grid of
  tiny pyramids, 7½" long, late
  19th century, early 20th .... $13.00 to $15.00
Meat tenderer, cast iron, pat'd 1892,
  rocks on 20 pointed and lethal teeth ..... $12.00 to $20.00
Meat tenderizer and ax, nickeled-
  steel with wood handle, Tyler Mfg.
  Co., pat'd 1922, 10" long .... $8.00 to $12.00

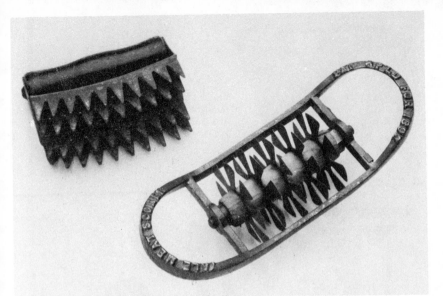

Figure I-96. **Meat Tenderizers.** Top: galvanized tin with wood handle. 4½" long. 19th century. Collection of Meryle Evans. Bottom: cast iron frame, wooden rod, very sharp steel blades. "Yale Meat Scorer," patent applied for 1892. 8¼" long. Located by the Primitive Man, Bob Cahn. Carmel, NY. Value, top: $15-$25. Cahn's evaluation of bottom: $75-$95.

Figure I-97. **Meat Tenderizers.** Left is a lawn-roller style with wood roller, wire handle. 12" long x 9½" wide. Small one has iron blades and a wood handle. 9" long. 19th century. Collection of Meryle Evans. Value: $15-$22.

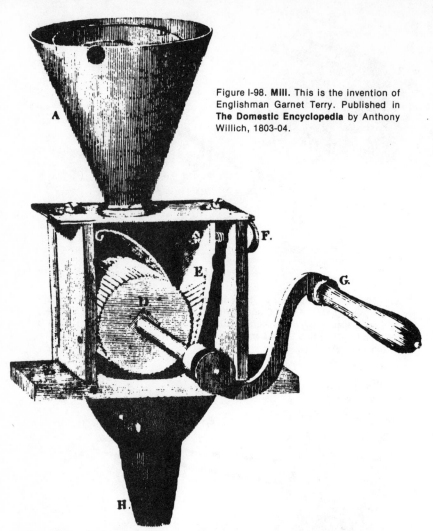

Figure I-98. **Mill.** This is the invention of Englishman Garnet Terry. Published in **The Domestic Encyclopedia** by Anthony Willich, 1803-04.

See also: Beetles

Meat and food slicer, cast metal,
General, cranks $27.00
Meat and food slicer, tin with wood
handle, "Dandy" $8.00
Meat and food slicer, "Eagle", screw
clamps to table $6.00
Meat and food slicer, cast iron with
painted frame and decals, Enterprise,
dated 1881, handsome and good-
sized, for stores $65.00

Figure I-99. **MIll.** Heavy wood box, iron gears, counterweighted cast iron balance wheel, the revolving wooden drum has square nails driven into it. The only place to feed in food is a little "mouse hole" in front. No signs of use. No marks. 8" high x 7½" long x 5½" wide. Looks mid-19th century, but what exactly is it? Collection of Meryle Evans. Value: $75-$95.

Mortar and pestle, brass, probably a
    pharmacist's item $45.00
Mortar and pestle, heavy white ceramic
    with wood-handled pestle, 6" diameter ... $20.00 to $30.00

NOTE: Brand new white ceramic mortar/pestle sets are being made now. If you can put an old one and one of the new ones next to each other, you'll see the difference. Generally, the new ones aren't quite as heavy, often they are glazed, and the wooden handles to the pestles don't seem to fit quite as snugly and neatly.

Mortar and pestle, lignum vitae, 7"
    high, beautiful markings and patina $135.00
Mortar and pestle, lignum vitae, turned
    with a great pedestal base, 7¾" high
    x 4" diameter, early 19th century $125.00

Figure I-100. **Mortar and Pestle.** Well-carved wood painted with red buttermilk paint. 7" high x 4½" diameter. Pestle is 9" long. 19th century. Collection of Meryle Evans. Value: $50-$65.

Figure I-101. **Mortar and Pestle.** Burl mortar with 2 pestles. 7" high. American 19th century. Picture courtesy of Christie, Manson & Woods International Inc. Realized price of $308 included barrel churn and rimmed funnel, shown elsewhere in this book.

Mortar and pestle, lignum vitae, slight check in pestle, 7" high x 5 3/8" diameter $125.00

Mortar and pestle, wood with turned base, 13½" high $65.00

Mortar and pestle, turned maple with footed mortar, some dry checks in mortar, 7" high $60.00

Mortar and pestle, cast iron, 7" high x 6¾" diameter $58.00

Mortar and pestle, cast iron, flared rim to mortar, 6¾" high x 6¾" diameter, not kitchen item $35.00

Mortar and pestle, cast iron, 8" high x 9" diameter $60.00

Noodle cutter, tin and wire, handheld, 10 blades, made in Germany .... $7.00 to $8.00

Noodle cutter, metal with turned wood handles, dated 1932 .... $6.00

Figure I-102. **Mortar and Pestle.** Stoneware. 19th century. Collection of Mary Mac Franklin. Value: $22-$30.

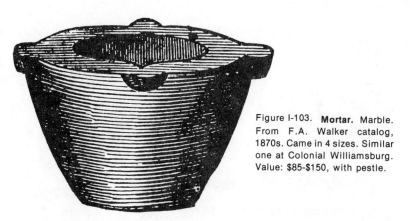

Figure I-103. **Mortar.** Marble. From F.A. Walker catalog, 1870s. Came in 4 sizes. Similar one at Colonial Williamsburg. Value: $85-$150, with pestle.

Nutcracker, brass, crocodile shape, 8" long .... $20.00 to $25.00

Nutcracker, brass, rooster shape, 20th century .... $10.00 to $15.00

Nutcracker, cast iron, "Home," pat'd 1915, long lever operates it, screws to table top .... $22.00 to $28.00

Nutcracker, cast iron, handheld pliers type, the handles flip around axis to accommodate another size nut .... $8.00 to $10.00

Figure I-104. **Nutcracker.** Cast and machined brass in shape of ship's wheel. Wooden base. 4¼" high. 20th century. Collection of Meryle Evans. Value: $12-$20.

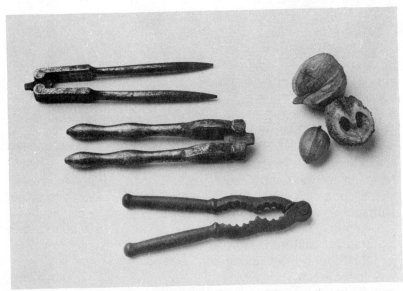

Figure I-105. **Nutcrackers.** Top: steel, 5½" long; middle: silver-plated iron, 5¼" long, flips to other side for smaller nuts; bottom: cast iron, 51/8" long. All 1890s. Author's collection. Value: $8-$12.

Figure I-106. **Nutcracker.** Nickel-plated iron. Pat'd 1863. Made in England. 8¾" long. Author's collection. Value: $25-$45.

Figure I-107. **Nutcracker.** Cast iron. From F.A. Walker catalog, 1870s. Value: $20-$30.

Nutcracker, silver-plated iron, same
    type as above but more decorative .... $10.00 to $12.00
Nutcracker, cast iron, "knee warmer"
    type — curved to fit on your leg
    with small cavity to hold nuts,
    used with a hammer, early 19th
    century .... $20.00 to $30.00
Nutcracker, nickeled iron, dog with
    long tail lever, nut is cracked in
    dog's jaws. Several versions of
    this exist, including one in brass,
    most are .... $25.00 to $45.00

Figure I-108. **Nutmeg Graters.** Left: nickel-plated cast iron, tin, wood grip and crank handle. 3¾" long, c. 1880. Right: wood, tin and wire. Long piece is wood and has remains of paper label. This is the "Common Sense" grater, pat'd July 23, 1867. Picture courtesy of the National Museum of American History, Smithsonian Institution.

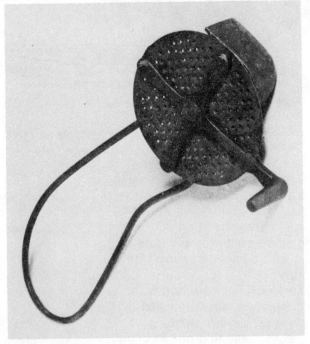

Figure I-109. **Nutmeg Grater.** Tin, wire and cast iron. pat'd March 9, 1886. 7" long. Collection of Marilyn Hodgkiss. Value: $40-$75.

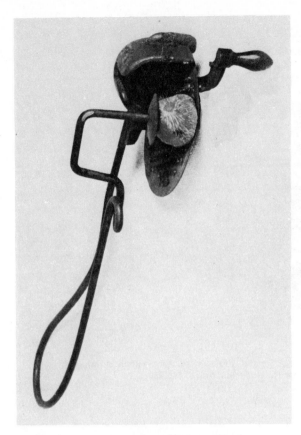

Figure I-110. **Nutmeg Grater.** Tin and wire. Simple crank, and the springy wire holds nutmeg in place against grater. 7" long, c. 1880s. Collection of Marilyn Hodgkiss. Value: $35-$75.

Nutcracker, cast iron, dog shape, marked "Dog Tray Nut Cracker" on the base; "Harper Supply Co., North Chicago" on bottom. "Tray" refers probably to Stephen Collins Foster's song, "Old Dog Tray," written in the middle of the 19th century. 13" long $30.00

Nutcracker, cast iron, dog with lever tail, adv'd for $125.00

Nutcracker, cast iron, St. Bernard, large size $50.00

Nutcracker, cast iron, in shape of squirrel — tail is the lever .... $7.50 to $8.50

NOTE: I've seen these for up to $30.00, but the preceding listing, taken from ad, represents a much lower evaluation.

Figure I-111. **Nutmeg Grater.** Tin and wire with spring-held plate for nut. 6¼" long, c. 1880s. Collection of Marilyn Hodgkiss. Value: $45-$80.

Nutcracker, cast iron, "Perfection," pat'd 1889, clamps to table, looks like a small bench vise $22.00

Nutcracker, "Perfection Nut Cracker Co., Texas," pat'd 1914 .... $14.00 to $28.00

Nutcracker, nickeled iron, "Ideal," fits in palm, T-handle or looped handle (depending on model) screws a pressure plate against nut. 5" long when fully extended .... $6.00 to $10.00

Nutcracker, cast iron, "Home," pat'd 1915 .... $10.00

Nutcracker, cast iron, "The Hamilton," table top vise $8.00

Nutcracker, wood, carved as bawdy lady $10.00

Nutcracker, wood, carved as head of bearded man with skull cap, typical European 19th century figural $95.00

Figure I-112. **Nutmeg Grater.** Tin and wire with wood presser and knob. Spring-loaded. Only 3½" long. 1880s. Collection of Marilyn Hodgkiss. Value: $45-$80.

Figure I-113. **Nutmeg Graters.** Punched tin "coffin style." Late 19th century, early 20th. Picture courtesy of Lar Hothem. Value: $8-$15.

Figure I-114. **Nutmeg Grater.** The "Edgar," pat'd August 18, 1891. Tin, wire and natural varnished wood. The Smithsonian's Edgar has green-painted knob and handle. 5 7/8" long. Author's collection. Value: $38-$70.

Nutcracker, cast iron, eagle head (nut
goes in beak), on primitive 4-
legged base, 7" long, 19th century
very unusual and underpriced, I think, at $35.00
Nutcracker, nickel-plated metal rachet
mechanism and lever, black-enameled
metal tray, "Krag's Whole Kernel
Nut Cracker," n.d. (c. 1930s) in
original orange and black cardboard
box, 6" long $30.00
Nutcracker and 6 picks, nickel-plated
fitted in wooden box, c. 1910 .... $8.00
Nutcracker bowl, wood with cast iron
central "anvil," and 8" iron hammer $20.00
Nut grinder, green-painted metal,
"Lorraine Metal Mfg. Co., turn-
of-century $22.00
Nut grinder, cast iron and tin, "Climax" $35.00
Nutmeg grater, silver and tin, a gent's
grater, meant to be carried around,
bottom is hinged to hold nutmegs,
marked "Phipps & Robinson," and
dated 1811 .... $1,950.00
Nutmeg grater, tin with wood handle,
"Common Sense," pat'd July 23,
1867, still has original paper label $150.00
Nutmeg grater, tin and wood, black
knob-held round grating surface,
with spring-loaded crank that holds
nutmeg, patent applied for $85.00
Nutmeg grater, carved wood and ivory,
lid — which holds a nutmeg —
screws onto grater part, early 19th
century grater meant to be carried
in a pocket .... $30.00 to $45.00
Nutmeg grater, tin and wire, curved
quadrant grating surface, spring-
loaded nutmeg holder moves over
grater, 5" long, late 19th century .... $20.00 to $30.00
Nutmeg grater tin and wood,
homemade, paddle shape with
semi-cylindrical punched tin arched
grating surface, 4" long .... $12.00 to $20.00

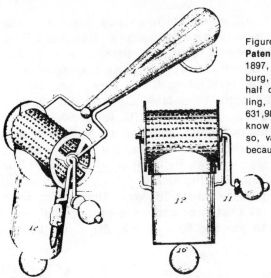

Figure I-115. **Nutmeg Grater Patent Drawing.** Filed April 13, 1897, by John W. Hart, Pittsburg, Kansas, assignor of one-half of William J. Kaemmerling, same place. Serial No. 631,985. (No model.) I don't know if it were ever made . . . if so, value would be $65-$100 because of scarcity.

Nutmeg grater, wire, tin and wood,
    "The Edgar," pat'd 1891, 1896,
    5 7/8" long. This is going up
    amazingly in price, at least on the
    East Coast. I paid $10 in about
    1973. By the late '70s they were
    about $18.00. By 1980 they were
    going between $20.00 and $30.00.
    By 1982, the price range is . . . . $38.00 to $70.00
    Several seen at Brimfield (Mas-
    sachusetts) in the fall of 1982,
    were $45.00, $53.00, $60.00 and
    $70.00. Argghh.

Nutmeg grater, tin, spring-
    loaded, c. 1890, 6¼" long . . . . $20.00 to $30.00
Nutmeg grater, tin, spring-loaded,
    "The Boye," . . . . $45.00 to $55.00
Nutmeg grater, tin with sliding cover,
    "Acme Nut Grater" . . . . $40.00 to $45.00
Nutmeg grater, cast iron, pat'd 1870 . . . . $98.00
Nutmeg grater, wood and tin, "The
    Little Rhody," with paper label
    still attached . . . . $34.00 to 48.00

NOTE: While the small rather coffin-shaped non-mechanical nutmeg graters/holders, such as the hanging "Bee Brand," still go for $8.00, $12.00, even $15.00, the mechanical ones have been getting higher prices year-by-year since the grand Keillor auction back in 1976, in Wading River, New York. At that auction, a young collector from New England bid on every nutmeg grater in the sale, paying over $100 for some — just to get the nucleus for his collection. Never would he have such an opportunity again, granted, but it demonstrates the special pressures and inducements at an auction — pressures that often have a lasting effect on the market prices. My advice still is to attempt to find these things for less. That seems to go without saying, but for a patented and mass-produced object, it seems alien to me to pay $85.00 or more. Am I just being a prude?

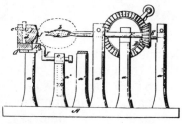

Figure I-117. **Peach Parer Patent Drawing.** Pat'd December 27, 1859 by Mary E. Hermans for her deceased husband, the inventor, Alva Hermans, Henderson, TX. I'd love to know the story behind that one! Wood with cast iron. Unusual feature was the flexibility of the tines that pierced the peach. but circumnavigated the peach's pit.

Figure I-116. **Pasta Maker.** "Titantonio Mfg. Co., Cleveland OH, pat'd February 13, 1906, March 2, 1920. Cast iron, tin and wood; roller attachment, "Zigzag #6", is iron, tin and has white rubber around axle. Pasta maker is screwed to wood which would be clamped to table top for operation. 7" high, 7" wide. Author's collection. Value: $45-$65.

Pea sheller, cast iron, "Acme," screw
  clamps to table, c. 1880s . . . . $25.00 to $35.00

Bonnie Barnes, a dealer (Antique Corner, 280 N. Commerce Street, Waynesboro, VA) who carries a large number of old kitchen things, tells a firsthand story that gives us a glimpse of the inventive spirit behind many of these 19th century inventions we collect. When she was a child, her grandfather tried to figure out a good way to shell peas because they grew so many on their farm. Finally he thought of putting the peas through the wringers of an old-fashioned hand-cranked washing machine. Soon as you'd put the end of the pea pod in and turned the crank, it would force all the air inside the pod toward the end, and the pod would burst open and the peas came out just fine. Trouble was, they came out everywhere! The family tried spreading sheets around the floor underneath the washing machine, but it was an ill-fated idea.

Peach parer, cast iron, Sinclair Scott
    Co., Baltimore, c. 1880, screw
    clamps to table, 10" long .... $30.00 to $60.00

NOTE: In the American Agriculturist, June 1872, a peach parer is pictured and discussed. I've never seen one, that I know, but here's the quote: "A continuous and urgent inquiry for a machine for Paring Peaches, has been ringing in our ears from all Peach-growing sections, for the past five years, and in response to this universal appeal, the manufacturers of the Lightning & Turn-Table Apple Parers have at last succeeded in obtaining and securing a device for Holding and Paring Peaches, which is as practical and economical as the Apple Parer, and cannot fail to come into immediate and general use. They pare apples too, as well as any Apple-Parer." This peach parer, which resembles very closely the apple parer advertised by F.A. Walker in the early 1870s, and depicted in Figure 31, page 6, of my From Hearth To Cookstove, was supposedly introduced first in county fairs in the fall of 1869, where they won several prizes. There were at least two earlier peach parers, Ward's Peach Parer and Cutting Machine, pat'd 1851, and Alva Hermans' parer, pat'd 1859.

Peanut shucker, wood, two part mill
    with 19" diameter grinding surfaces,
    which can be turned on an axle by
    means of a fancy-turned handle-
    bar like handle. Extremely unusual and inventive
    solution to the pesky problem of

how to get the shucks off peanuts.
This piece, probably mid-19th
century, was sold during 1982 by
dealer Helen Cranston Burley, Old
Chesterfield Inn, Chesterfield, NH
03443 for $295.00

Pepper grinder, cast iron, wall-mounted
side mill, c. 1900 .... $16.00 to $20.00

Pineapple eyesnips, iron, scissor-
action, pat'd 1901 .... $12.00 to $16.00

Poppyseed grinder, green-painted
cast iron, spun brass hopper,
"Standard," c. 1890s, 9¼" high,
screw clamps to table .... $28.00 to $40.00

Poppyseed grinder, green-painted
iron, screw clamps, "Kosmos" $48.00

Potato french-fry cutter, tin cylinder
with a cutting frame (like a tic-tac-toe
game) that cuts 25 french fries or
"Saratoga's. "Silver's Sure-Cut"
embossed on side. 4" high $18.00

Potato masher, nickeled iron with
thick wood handle, 7" long .... $8.00 to $12.00

Potato masher, nickeled iron, 8¾" long .... $8.00 to $12.00

Potato masher, heavy twisted wire
with wood handle, very large hotel
or restaurant size, 22½" long $22.00

Potato masher, zigzagging wire masher,
long wooden handle, another
commercial size (or large farm?),
22" long $30.00

Potato mashers, wire and wood, various
designs from a flat spiraled head to
a wire grid to a slightly rocking set
of 8 fingers to a crisscross of
loosely strung wires, an
enormous variety, most about 8"
to 10" tall .... $8.00 to $14.00

Potato peeler, tin with gritty composition
that literally sands off the peeling;
looks like a little tart pan with
crimped edges, strap handle,
"Hamlinite Peeler," pat'd 1920,
4½" long, most are about $10.00

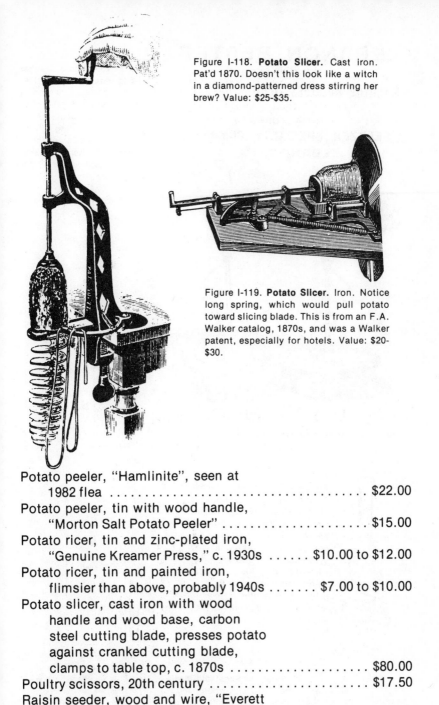

Figure I-118. **Potato Slicer.** Cast iron. Pat'd 1870. Doesn't this look like a witch in a diamond-patterned dress stirring her brew? Value: $25-$35.

Figure I-119. **Potato Slicer.** Iron. Notice long spring, which would pull potato toward slicing blade. This is from an F.A. Walker catalog, 1870s, and was a Walker patent, especially for hotels. Value: $20-$30.

Potato peeler, "Hamlinite", seen at
  1982 flea $22.00
Potato peeler, tin with wood handle,
  "Morton Salt Potato Peeler" $15.00
Potato ricer, tin and zinc-plated iron,
  "Genuine Kreamer Press," c. 1930s ...... $10.00 to $12.00
Potato ricer, tin and painted iron,
  flimsier than above, probably 1940s .... $7.00 to $10.00
Potato slicer, cast iron with wood
  handle and wood base, carbon
  steel cutting blade, presses potato
  against cranked cutting blade,
  clamps to table top, c. 1870s $80.00
Poultry scissors, 20th century $17.50
Raisin seeder, wood and wire, "Everett
  Co.," 7 wires set into one-piece
  knob and block, 3 1/8" high, 1880s ...... $10.00 to $15.00

LEBANON BEATER
~~> FOR <~~
Mashing Potatoes, Beating Eggs, Etc.

MANUFACTURED BY
SELTZER SPECIALTY COMPANY,
LEBANON, PA.

EGGS   **POTATOES**

For sale by all dealers.

Figure I-120. **Potato Masher and Egg Beater.** Wire, steel and wood handle.d "Lebanon Beater," mfd. by Seltzer Specialty Co., Lebanon, PA, c. 1880s, "patent pending." From one of many differently-backed trade cards. Masher value: $15-$20; Trade card value: $1.50-$2.00

Figure I-121. **Potato Masher Patent Drawing.** Pat'd April 12, 1892 by Charles Spicer Apple, who — as far as I know — never invented anything for apples or spice. Apple resided in Bellaire, OH. Spring steel wire with wood handle. Apple suggested that rattan, rubber, celluloid or other "elastic material" would work as well as wire!

Figure I-122. **Potato or Vegetable Masher.** Heavy tinned wire with wood handle. 22½" long. 19th or early 20th century. Photographed at Bonnie Barnes' Anteek Corner, Waynesboro, VA. Value: $22.

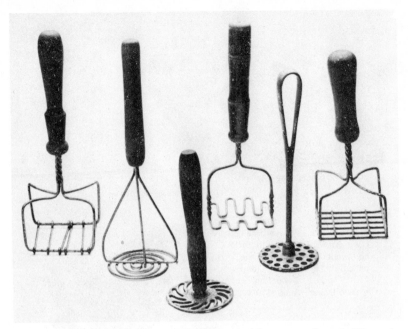

Figure I-123. **Mashers.** for Cooked Root Vegetables, Potatoes or Squash. Wire and wood; two are nickeled iron. All 1890s to 1930s. 6" to 10" in height. Author's collection. Value: $8-$14.

Figure I-124. **Potato Masher or Pastry Blender.** Nickeled iron with wood handle. 1915-1940s. 9½" long. Author's collection. Value: $8-$12.

Figure I-125. **Potato Peeler.** (Two views.) Tin with grit composition. "Hamlinite," pat'd July 20, 1920. 4½" long x 2¼" wide. Collection of Meryle Evans. Value: $10-$22.

Figure I-126. **Potato Ricer.** Japanned iron handles, tin body. "Genuine Kreamer Press," c. 1930. 11" long. Picture courtesy of Lar Hothem. Value: $10-$12.

108

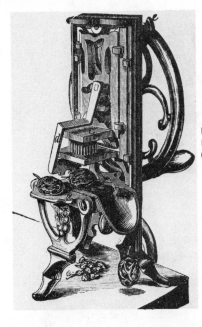

Figure I-127. **Raisin Seeder.** Cast iron. From F.A. Walker catalog, 1870s. Only 6½" high. Value: $75-$120.

Raisin seeder, nickeled-cast iron, rubber rollers, Enterprise Mfg. Co., #36, "Wet the Raisins" cast in surface, pat'd 1895, screw clamps to table, 11" long . . . . $20.00 to $35.00

Raisin seeder, cast iron, wire and rubber, "Lightning," pat'd 1895, 1898, 7¼" high, screw clamps to table, not so elegant as the Enterprise . . . $12.00 to $25.00

Raisin seeder, cast iron, beautifully cast with grapes and leaves, 3-legged, probably imported from France, sits on table, 6½" high, c. 1870 . . . . $75.00 to $120.00

Raisin seeder, like above only nickel-plated. Perhaps later . . . . $60.00 to $75.00

Raisin seeder, cast iron, "Gem," mfd. in Auburn, Maine $35.00

Raisin seeder, "Improved Gem" $30.00

Raisin seeder, cast iron, "EZY Raisin seeder," Pat'd May 21, 1899, "Scald the Raisins" cast into frame, 5" high exclusive of wingnut, clamps to table . . . . $30.00 to $45.00

Figure I-128. **Raisin Seeders.** Top right is nickel-plated cast iron, like one shown in catalog cut from 1870s. 6½" high. Bottom left is the "Everett," patent applied for, but dating from the 1890s, and much advertised in old **Ladies Home Journals.** Wire with wood handle, and wood body. 3 1/8" high. Both courtesy of the Meryle Evans Collection. Value: cast iron, $100-$150; "Everett," $22-$30. Top left: Cast iron with an 8-wire seeder. Pat'd May 7, 1895. 4 legs. Bottom right: cast metal, "EZY Raisin Seeder," pat'd May 21, 1899. "Scald the Raisins" cast into other side. Clamps to table. 5" high. Both located by the Primitive Man, Bob Cahn, Carmel, NY. His evaluation, in order: $185-$225; $185-$225. (Cahn's evaluation of the cast iron at top: $225-$295.)

Reamer, green Depression glass	$15.00 to $43.00
Reamer, amber glass	$25.00
Reamer and pitcher, "Good Morning"	$18.00
Reamer and pitcher, figural, with 4 juice cups	$30.00
Reamer, clear glass, "Sunkist Fruit Growers Exchange"	$26.00
Reamer, duck figural	$30.00
Reamer, spun aluminum with small ear handle	$6.00 to $8.00
Reamer, painted china, clown head	$25.00 to $35.00

NOTE: These prices are very approximate. Many people collect nothing but reamers, particularly the figural china and glass ones, and they are amazingly colorful and varied . . . clowns, swans, camels, oranges . . . splendid!

Figure I-129. **Raisin and Grape Seeder.** What! it won't peel the grapes too? "Enterprise No. 36," pat'd 1895. Larger size, No. 38, for bakers and hotels. Tinned cast iron. Notice the Enterprise says "Wet the Raisins." Value: $20-$35.

Figure I-130. **Raisin Seeder.** Cast iron with nickel plating, rubber roller. "Enterprise Mfg. Co., Philadelphia." Pat'd April 2, August 20, 1895. 11" high. Collection of Robert D. Franklin. Value: $20-$35.

NOTE: Most sausage grinders are also stuffers, but the reverse is less likely to be true.

Sausage grinder, iron, hangs on wall,
    pat'd 1885, 27" long .... $25.00 to $32.00
Sausage grinder, iron, "Keen Kutter" .... $7.00 to $12.00
Sausage grinder, cast iron, "Keen Kutter" $40.00
Sausage grinder, galvanized iron,
    "Enterprise No. 5," Landers,
    Frary & Clark .... $12.00 to $18.00
Sausage grinder, cast iron, "O.V.B.
    No. 8" $6.00
Sausage grinder, cast iron, pig shape,
    long lever, late 19th century .... $20.00 to $35.00
Sausage grinder, all wood, mid-19th
    century $150.00

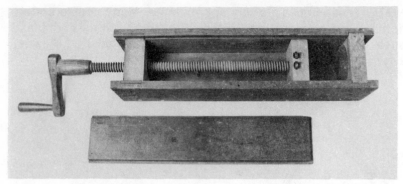

Figure I-131. **Sausage Stuffer.** Handmade, all wood, lid at left. Box 25" high x 5¾" square. Crank, measured from top of screw to top of handle, is 8". 19th century. Author's collection. Value: $100-$135.

Sausage grinder/stuffer, wood and wrought
    iron with tin gun, platform made
    to bridge two chairs or tables, 30"
    lever worked up and down — like
    a water pump — to stuff casings $95.00
Sausage stuffer, pieced tin with wood
    foller, 21" long, end of 19th century . . . . . . $25.00 to $30.00
Sausage stuffer, tin and cast iron,
    "Angers Perfect No. 1 Filler,"
    Sargent & Co., pat'd 1898, mounts
    to table top, spring-loaded lever
    action, shaped like an urn, sort of . . . . $30.00 to $40.00
Sausage stuffer, tin cone, cast iron
    base, c. 1880 . . . . $18.00
Sausage stuffer, tin with maple plunger,
    worked either with two people, or
    was held with plunger against
    belly, different size casing funnels
    attached by bayonet closing at
    end, each part 18" long $65.00
Sausage stuffer, tin and wood, "P.S.
    & W. Co., No. 112," hand-cranked,
    screw clamps to table $35.00
Sausage stuffer, handmade wood box
    with wood gears, sliding cover,
    19th century, 30" long . . . . $70.00 to $90.00

See also: Meat and Food Grinders.

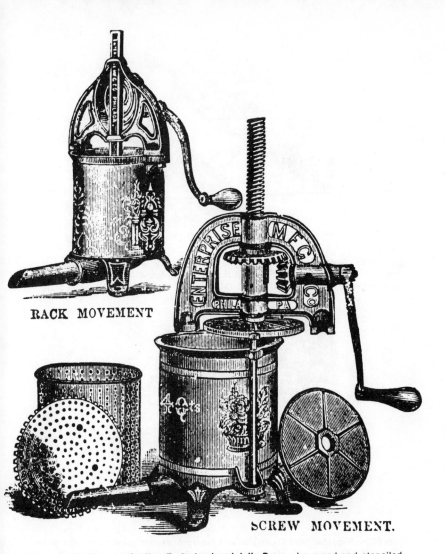

RACK MOVEMENT

SCREW MOVEMENT.

Figure I-132. **Sausage Stuffer, Fruit, Lard and Jelly Press.** Japanned and stenciled tin with cast iron. Enterprise Mfg. Co., Pat'd July 11, 1876. As you can see from the catalog picture, it came with two kinds of movements: screw and rack-and-pinion. Value: $45-$65.

Strawberry huller, nickel-plated spring
    steel, "Spee-Dee Strawberry huller" .... $2.00 to $4.00
Strawberry huller, "Berry Huller," with
    stamped strawberry design $2.00
Sugar nippers, iron, hand held, very
    simple, 19th century .... $40.00 to $60.00
Sugar nippers, steel mounted on
    wood base, 10" long, 19th century .... $45.00 to $60.00

Figure I-133. **Sausage Stuffers.** Tin and wood. Above left is 29½" long, with plunger/foller all the way in. It takes different casing-funnel sizes. Other is 19½" long, plunger all the way in. 1870s-80s. Collection of Meryle Evans. Value: $35-$75.

Figure I-134. **Slicer for Root Vegetables and Potatoes.** Japanned cast iron. Clamps to table. 4 cutting blades. 19th century. 10½" long. Collection of Meryle Evans. Value: $45-$65.

Sugar nippers, heavy wrought iron
     mounted on wood, brass ferrule
     on unusual wood handle, early
     1800s, (don't underestimate the
     power of a touch of brass to add
     some bucks to the price of kitchen
     things . . . this is why dealers are
     always removing plating and
     puffing and buffing) $145.00

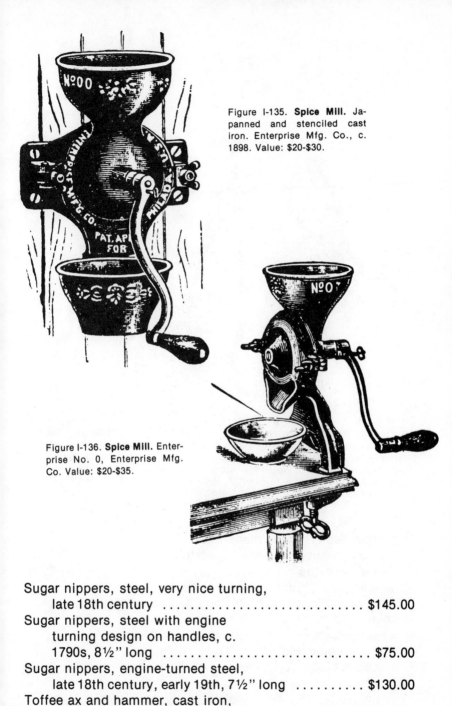

Figure I-135. **Spice Mill.** Japanned and stenciled cast iron. Enterprise Mfg. Co., c. 1898. Value: $20-$30.

Figure I-136. **Spice Mill.** Enterprise No. 0, Enterprise Mfg. Co. Value: $20-$35.

Sugar nippers, steel, very nice turning,
    late 18th century $145.00
Sugar nippers, steel with engine
    turning design on handles, c.
    1790s, 8½" long $75.00
Sugar nippers, engine-turned steel,
    late 18th century, early 19th, 7½" long $130.00
Toffee ax and hammer, cast iron,
    "For Toffee" cast into surface,
    7 3/8" long, very unusual .... $25.00 to $40.00

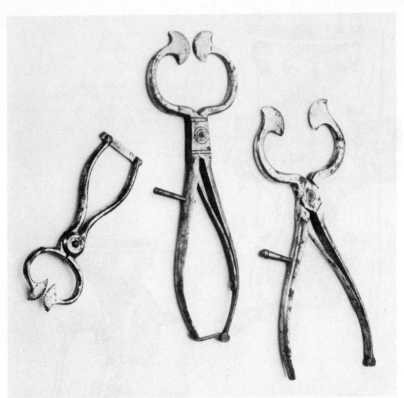

Figure I-137. **Sugar Nippers.** Miniature on left, with serrated cutting blades, 5" long; Middle: engine-turned concentric circles around where pin-pivot is, finger guard, 8¾" long; similar one on right, brighter steel, missing catch but has finger guard, 8" long. All steel and sharp, these were used to nip, or peck away at, molded cones of sugar in the 18th and early to mid-19th century. Some nippers are mounted on a board. Collection of Meryle Evans. Value: $75-$130.

Vegetable peeler, metal blade with
    wood handle, hand-held, "Morton
    Salt" on blade $5.00
Vegetable parer, knife & corer combo,
    tin, Costello, 1913, 8 7/8" long .... $10.00 to $14.00
Vegetable parer, corer & slicer combo,
    nickeled steel, wood handle set
    at 45-degree angle to bullet-
    shaped blade, "Universal", c. 1900 .... $7.00
Vegetable slicer, cast iron and tin,
    "Enterprise No. 49," revolving
    cylinder moves all kinds of
    vegetables over the blade, 16" high ...... $60.00 to $75.00

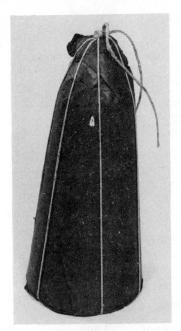

Figure I-138. **Sugar Cone.** Wrapped in blue paper with cord. This one actually is from Belgium, but it is quite similar to the paper wrapped cones made during the early 19th century in America. Sugar nippers were used to nip away at the sugar cones. Picture courtesy of the National Museum of American History, Smithsonian Institution.

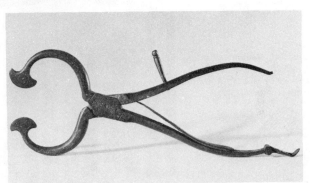

Figure I-139. **Sugar Nippers.** Iron with spring steel. Shown here upside down — the thumb guard would rest on the table surface in use. Early 19th or late 18th century. Probably American. 8¾" long. Picture courtesy of the National Museum of American History, Smithsonian Institution.

Vegetable slicer, deep fluted tin blade
   with wire handle, c. 1900, not
      mechanical .... $5.00 to $10.00
Vegetable slicer, steel, large wood
   handle and press bar, pat'd 1900, nifty ... $45.00 to $55.00
Vegetable slicer, "Universal,"
   turn-of-century .... $22.00 to $28.00

Figure I-140. **Vegetable Chopper.** Glass with tin and steel lid, spring action cutter, wood block inside jar. 20th century. Author's collection. Value: $6-$12.

Figure I-141. **Vegetable Cutter.** Corrugated tin with wire. Makes fancy slices. Author's collection. Value: $5-$10.

Figure I-142. **Combination Tool.** From Montgomery Ward catalog, c. 1910. Description reads "This unique culinary device (patented 1906) is the latest and best invention yet devised. It is inexpensive and useful in many ways. It is practically the best corn grater ever invented. For taking scales off of fish or scraping or cleaning vegetables it can not be excelled. It is the first and only pineapple shredder ever placed on the market. Has hardwood handle and is nickel-plated. Its deserving merit will place it first among the kitchen utensils. Our special price for this little wonder 20 cents. Postage 5 cents extra." Value now: $5-$10.

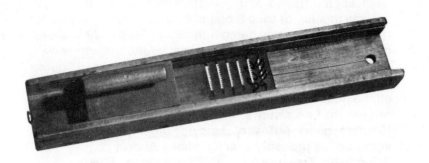

Figure I-143. **Vegetable Shredder or Corn Grater.** Wood and steel. Catawissa Specialty Mfg. Co., pat'd 1898. Picture courtesy of The Smithsonian Institution, Museum of History and Technology.

Figure I-144. **Vegetable Scorer.** The Smithsonian records identify this as a vegetable scorer, but I don't know why you'd want to do that. It seems possible to me that it might well be a device for chipping ice. It is only 3" high, which is one clue. Perhaps used to grate corn. Does anyone know? Tin, strap handle, c. 1880s, marked "F.A. Walker, Boston," which means it was either mfd. by them or imported by them. Picture courtesy of the National Museum of American History, Smithsonian Institution.

Chutney Sauce

Sour apples (pared and cored), tomatoes, brown sugar, sultana raisins, of each 3 pounds; common salt, 4 ounces; red chillies and powdered ginger, of each, 29 ounces; garlic and shallots, of each 1 ounce; pound the whole well; add, of strong vinegar, 3 quarts; lemon juice, 1 quart; digest, with frequent agitation, for a month; pour off nearly all the liquor, and bottle it. Use for fish or meat, either hot or cold, to flavor stews, etc.
[Sounds good but very spicy! "Digest, with frequent agitation" is probably exactly what you do.]
Scammell's Treasure-House of Knowledge, 1891

Rusks

In cold weather, to make up two-and-a-half quarts of flour, mix into a paste with one pint of boiling water; two tablespoonsfuls of sugar; three of flour; and two large Irish potatoes boiled and mashed smooth; in the evening make up dough with this sponge; add three well-beaten eggs; three-quarter pound sugar; one-half pint fresh milk; set it away in a covered vessel, leaving plenty of room to swell; next morning work into the risen dough, which should not be stiff, one-quarter-pound of butter and lard mixed; make into rolls or biscuits; let the dough rise for the second time; flavor with two grated nutmegs or one-half ounce of pounded stick cinnamon; when very light, bake in a quick, steady oven till of a pretty brown color; glaze with the yolk of an egg, and sprinkle with powdered sugar.
Scammell's Treasure-House of Knowledge, 1891

MIX, BEAT, STIR, CHURN & BLEND

How to mix it all up together? My long-time favorites among all the kitchen gadgets are the eggbeaters. Could anyone not fall under their fascination? They look like dancers, twirling and spinning. An eggbeater is star, in fact, of a short Dada surrealist film called "Ballet Mechanique," made years ago by

Marcel Duchamp, one of the leading Dadaists. See if your local library has a copy; I guarantee you'll love it. The charm of eggbeaters comes from their movement, but even at rest, their curved blades and small waists and waiting arms promise the dance to come.

To my eye, everything else seems comparatively pedestrian. For example, except for the small Dazey glass churns, most churns hide their activity in barrel bodies; mixing spoons — even when beautifully formed — look the same at rest and in use, although I wouldn't want to give away any of them! Who knows, by the third edition, I may find a new affection creeping up on me!

Batter pitcher, Rockingham flintware,
    yellow and brown .... $100.00 to $135.00
Batter pitcher, stoneware with yellow
    glaze, wire bail handle with wooden grip .. $70.00 to $90.00
Beaten biscuit machine, wood, table
    top model, c. 1860s $155.00
Beaten biscuit machine, cast iron with
    nickel-plated rollers, J.A. DeMuth,
    St. Joseph, Missouri, cast iron
    base with marble top, overall height
    approximately 44", c. 1890 .... $250.00 to $500.00

NOTE: I've seen only one of these ever. It belongs to a friend in Virginia, and she's been making beaten biscuits for her famous parties for years. I used to think that someday at a flea market or even a yard sale that I'd find one; the seller wouldn't know what it was . . . would sell it as an old washing machine attachment or something. Finally, back in the late 1970s, I saw a tiny ad in "The Antique Trader" miscellaneous for sale classifieds for a beaten biscuit machine . . . for about $350.00. Too much for me, though I believe the machine is worth it. In the last edition, I put the price range between $250.00 and $500.00, based entirely on my personal opinion. Nothing has turned up since then, and I've not seen another for sale anywhere. But you may be the lucky person of 1983 who finds one, perhaps for a take-it-away $10.00 at a swap meet or Saturday morning flea market. My whole-hearted, biscuit-lovin' advice is: buy it! P.S. Just after completing this section I heard from a Texas collector, Linda Fishbeck, who did indeed find one! And she says to tell you that by "breaking it down" into three parts, U.P.S. shipped it to her in Texas!

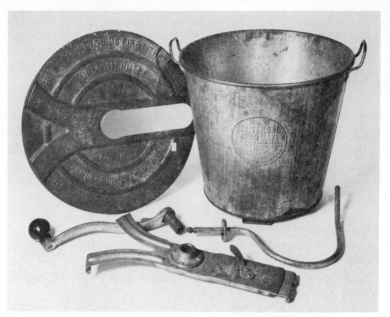

Figure II-1. **Bread Maker.** Tin and iron. "Universal No. 8," Landers, Frary & Clark, New Britain, CT, 1904. Stamped on lid are the directions: "Put in all liquids first - then flour - turn 3 minutes - raise in pail - after raising turn until dough forms a ball - take off cross piece - lift out dough with kneader." 11 7/8" high. Picture courtesy of the National Nuseum of American History, Smithsonian Insititution.

Figure II-2. **Bread Mixer.** "Universal No. 4," Landers, Frary & Clark, c. 1910-1920. Value: $20-$50.

Figure II-3. **Butter Worker.** Table top model, bentwood holder for butter and worker, wooden frame, wooden gears, iron handle, 13½" high x 9" x 8" square. 19th century. Collection of Meryle Evans. Value: $120-$150.

Beater jars, the next group of listings, were new to me in 1981. They are straight-sided crock-like ceramic jars, approximately 6" high x 4½" diameter. They were ideal for inserting an eggbeater, being taller than wide. The most popular ones seem to be those made by various Red Wing [Minnesota] potteries. At least in the Midwest, Red Wing pottery pieces in general are extremely popular. Red Wing beater jars come in various finishes: blue band, gray line [grayish white with blue and red bands], saffron yellow-ware, etc.

Beater jar, Red Wing blue band,
    advertising $54.00
Beater jar, Red Wing, "Red Wing
    Beater Jar, Eggs, Cream Salad
    Dressing" $60.00
Beater jar, Red Wing, "Cream Eggs
    Salad Dressing," $75.00
Beater jar, gray line, advertising $57.00
Beater jar, yellow ware, marked
    "Foremost Dairies" $30.00
Beater jar, marked "Parkersburg, Iowa" $60.00
Beater jar, blue and white design,
    advertises "Wesson Oil" $20.00
Beater jar, blue striped grayish
    stoneware, marked "E.C. Reed,
    North English, Iowa" $65.00
Beater jar, blue and white stripes with
    eggbeater $35.00
Bread maker, tin pail and iron frame,
    "Universal No. 4," Landers, Frary
    & Clark, cranked snaky kneaders
    are fitted to lid, pail clamps to
    table, turn-of-century to 1920 .... $20.00 to $50.00
Bread maker, same as above, with
    original paper label .... add about $6.00
Bread maker, tin and cast iron,
    "Universal No. 44," Landers,
    Frary & Clark, clamps to table or
    shelf edge, lid is level with
    tabletop, turn-of-century .... $20.00 to $35.00
Bread maker, "Universal No. 2," very
    simple, never had a lid, clamps to
    table .... $12.00 to $18.00

Bread maker, "Universal No. 4," dated
    1904 .... $50.00
Butter worker, wood, corrugated
    swinging arm, shows wear, small
    home size .... $45.00 to $60.00-
Butter worker, wood, blue paint remains
    on outside, 30" trough and two
    corrugated rollers, on skeletal frame $125.00

**NOTE: The blue paint of the above is worth more than money.
Please don't have such things refinished.**

Cake mixer, tin with cast iron gears,
    crank and frame or stand, "American
    Machine Co.," pat'd 1873, screw
    clamps to table .... $25.00 to $35.00
Cake spoon, tin and wire, marked
    "Saltmans Improved Royal Rumford
    Cake Mixer and Cream Whip,"
    long slots in bowl of spoon, pat'd 1908 .... $7.00 to $11.00
Churn, brown stoneware, 6-gallon size .... $45.00 to $60.00
Churn, pottery, Catawba Valley, NC $260.00
Churn, pottery, possibly Hewell from
    Gillesville, GA $175.00

NOTE: All three of the above are without lids or dashers.

Churn, Red Wing stoneware, 5-gallon $40.00
Churn, Red Wing stoneware, small
    crack, with lid $42.00
Churn, Red Wing stoneware, 6-gallon
    size, lid $120.00
Churn, white stoneware with blue, #3,
    wood cover and dasher $86.00
Churn, Red Wing, 2-gallon size with
    handles, lid and dasher complete,
    dated 1915 .... $175.00
Churn, same $250.00
Churn, wood with heavy tin bandings,
    handforged nails, dasher type, 1870s $350.00
Churn, barrel construction with tapered
    sides, one stave is elongated to
    become handle, original or at least
    old red paint, dasher style, 18½"

Figure II-4. **Implements and Utensils in a 19th century Candy Kitchen,** as depicted on a real photo post card, c. 1905. Note candy thermometer in copper or brass kettle in foreground, the stoneware crocks holding ingredients, the array of tools lying on the wooden table, the scale to measure ingredients, and the sieve hanging top center. Author's collection. Card's value: $18-$22.

high, New England, late 18th or
early 19th century, estimated to
go at 1982 auction for $150 to $200,
actually brought $325.00

Churn, barrel style, blue buttermilk
paint and great patina, wide lapped
band at top, 4 iron bands, 25"
high, 11" diameter at top, 1870-1880s $285.00

Churn, with elongated handle stave,
4-fingered wooden hoops, 12" high
late 18th century, early 19th century $415.00

Churn, bentwood with rose maling
painted decoration, 4-gallon size,
dated 1882, Wapa Koneta, OH $250.00

Churn, White Cedar cylinder, No. 1,
8-gallon size $90.00

Churn, barrel construction, very large $275.00

Churn, "White Cedar" cylinder churn,
4 gallons $75.00

Churn, wood drum with red stenciling
and cow, ... $55.00

Churn, wood drum with red stenciling
and cow design, 13" high, missing
dasher/paddle $65.00

Figure II-5. **Cylinder Churn.** Montgomery Ward catalog, c. 1895-1900. Depending on size, value: $45-$75.

Churn, cylinder, Shaker: Canterbury,
    from Londonderry, NH, beautifully
    shaped, nice patina $325.00
Churn, wood with grayish green
    original paint, Shaker $170.00
Churn, wood rocking style, original or
    old red milk paint, Shaker $200.00
Churn, glass and wood, Dazey Churn
    Co., table top, 1 quart size $45.00
Churn, glass and wood, Dazey #60,
    pat'd February 14, 1922 .... $32.00
Churn, glass and wood, Dazey #60,
    small chip $37.50
Churn, glass and wood, Dazey #20,
    pat'd 1922 .... $30.00
Churn, tin in cast iron frame, square
    body with flywheel $32.00
Churn, same as above but larger,
    dated 1907 .... $50.00
Churn, glass, metal and wood, Dazey
    4-quart size, missing paper label $40.00

NOTE: Oddly enough, for something washed so often, usually the Dazey glass churns are found with the labels.

Figure II-6. **Churn.** The "Premier" Two Minute Butter Machine, Culinary Mfg. Co., c. 1910. Value: $30-$40.

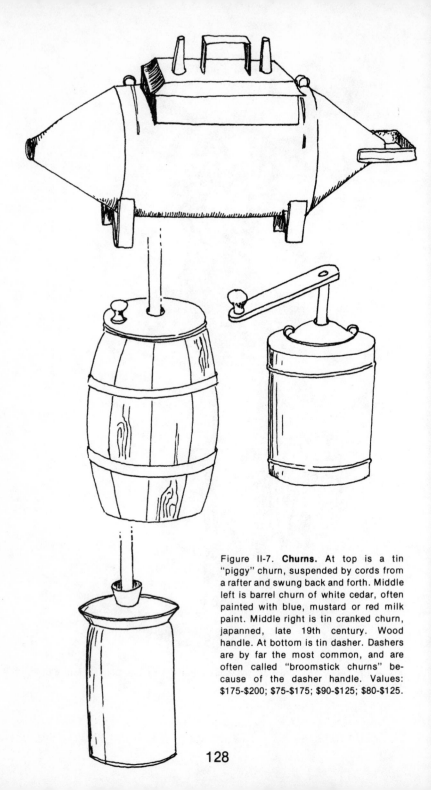

Figure II-7. **Churns.** At top is a tin "piggy" churn, suspended by cords from a rafter and swung back and forth. Middle left is barrel churn of white cedar, often painted with blue, mustard or red milk paint. Middle right is tin cranked churn, japanned, late 19th century. Wood handle. At bottom is tin dasher. Dashers are by far the most common, and are often called "broomstick churns" because of the dasher handle. Values: $175-$200; $75-$175; $90-$125; $80-$125.

Churn, glass, metal and wood, 1 quart
   size, paper label says "Dandy
   Deluxe Churn, designed by J.P.
   Dazey, Jr., Mfd. by Taylor Brothers
   Churn & Mfg. Co., St. Louis."
   Domed metal top, painted white,
   shaped like fat igloo; red wood
   crank handle, 1940s? simpler in
   style than earlier Dazeys $27.50
Churn, wood, cream colored paint,
   pat'd December 18, 1877, 18" high
   with 12" gear wheel above that,
   wooden top $75.00
Churn, glass barrel, embossed cow on
   front and back with words "Use
   with Gem Dairy Electric Churn,",
   mfd. by Douglas, missing cover $25.00
Churn, same, 2-gallon size, 21¾" high
   with cover, wire bail handle $65.00
Churn, tin with wood paddle, "Connfaut
   Can Co.," 40-quart size, 21½" high $135.00
Churn, tin, small 9" cylinder $35.00
Churn, tin cylinder with wood dasher
   and crank handle, a 4-footed
   cream whip churn, 8" x 6" x 4½" $85.00
Churn, tin with wood top, container
   12" square x 14" high, 4 short legs,
   Dazey Churn Co. $65.00
Churn, tin in iron frame, shaped like
   a barrel .... $85.00 to $100.00
Churn, saltglaze stoneware with
   wooden dasher and lid, "Love &
   Fields Pottery, Dallas, Texas" .... $75.00 to $80.00
Churn, cedar with brass bands, dasher
   style $80.00
Churn, rocker style, all wood including
   paddles and crank, blue buttermilk
   paint, 30" high $165.00
Churn, redware with dark olive-green
   glaze, turned wood dasher, made
   in North Carolina, 19th century $375.00
Churn, wood with iron hoops, iron
   crank, "Diamond Balance," named
   for its diamond-shaped box body,
   pat'd 1889, 1891, 10-gallon size .... $40.00 to $65.00

Figure II-8. **Sheep-Powered Cream-Separator.** Wood and iron. Vermont Farm Machinery Co., Montgomery Ward, c. 1895-1900. Value: $125-$200, but there'd be few takers.

Churn, wood, dog-powered, 2-part
    with painted churn body $350.00
Churn, glass 1-gallon jar, cast iron
    gears and round wood perforated
    paddle blades, "The Premier Two
    Minute Butter Machine," Culinary
    Mfg. Co., turn-of-century .... $30.00 to $40.00
Cream separator, "Royal Blue, Jr.",
    table top model $40.00

Figure II-9. **Churn.** Diamond Balance, pat'd May 28, 1889. Various sizes from one to 60 gallons. Value: $45-$65.

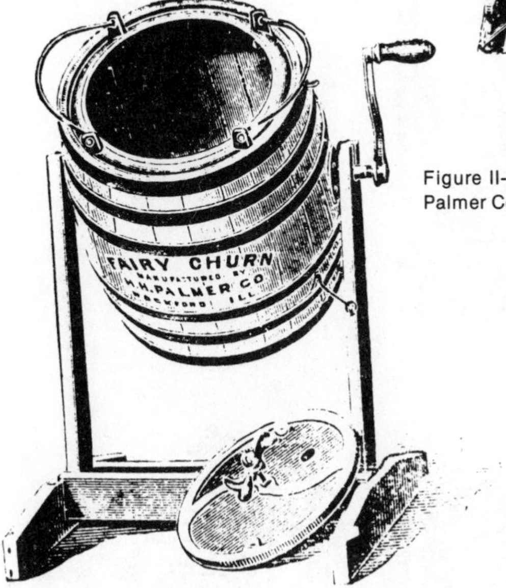

Figure II-10. **Churn.** "Fairy Churn," N.H. Palmer Co., c. 1890-1900. Value: $30-$75.

Figure II-11. **Churn.** Small turned wood churn, only 13 1/8" high. American 19th century. Picture courtesy of Christie, Manson & Woods International Inc. Price of $308 at 1983 Linden sale included burl mortar and rimmed funnel shown elsewhere in this book.

Figure II-12. **Churn.** "Dazey," pat'd December 18, 1877. Metal body painted cream color, natural wood top, cast iron gears and crank. 18" high with 12" wheel on top of that. Value: $65-$85.

Figure II-13. **Cream Separator and Churn.** Two-dog power. Montgomery Ward, c. 1895-1900. Farm machinery collectors would want this one a lot more than the average kitchen collector. Value: maybe $125-$200. From the original ad: "The illustration above shows how the double dog power can be used in operating a cream separator; when the separator is not in use and you desire to churn connect it to tumbling rod sent with machine. A corn sheller, fan mill or sawing machine can be connected by belt for balance wheel. Separators require a high gear and for this purpose we recommend our steel pulley, 3½" x 36 inches, this we can furnish at $6.00 extra. If iron coupling rod and coupling as shown in illustration is desired to connect and run cream separator, we can furnish them at $3.00 extra.

132

Figure II-14. **Cocktail Shaker.** Stainless steel with wood handle in bell shape. 11" high. 20th century. Author's collection. Value: $15-$20.

Cream separator, tin with wooden
legs, works by gravity, marked
"Marvel" $15.00

Cream whip, stainless steel and wood,
"Turbine," by Androck, 1936 .... $10.00 to $20.00

Cream whip, tin and cast iron, "Fries,"
side crank, 8" high on 4 little
legs, c. 1890 .... $25.00 to $32.00

Cream whip and egg beater, glass and
stainless steel, Androck, lid,
beaters, and crank all in one, 1930s ...... $10.00 to $14.00

Cream whip and egg beater, tin with
wire handle, "Lightning," pat'd 1868 ..... $18.00 to $23.00

Dough bowl, primitively carved oak,
18" long, 9½" wide, early (?) 19th
century $45.00

Dough bowl, carved wood, fairly
smooth patina, 24" long by 10" wide $50.00

133

Figure II- 15. **Cocktail Shaker Set.** Chrome rocket ship with 4 cups, footed cup, lemon reamer, 4 spoons and shaker that fit inside. It is marked simply "Made in Germany." 12" high. Believed to have been made in the 1930s . . . do you know? Photograph by Leslie Harris, courtesy of The Greenwich Auction Room, Ltd., NYC. Estimated to sell at 1983 auction between $300-$400. Realized: $500.

Figure II-16. **Dough Mixer.** Double layer of bent wood, nailed construction. Cast iron crank wood knob, iron blade. This fits in crook of arm, held against body. you really need some body English to make it do its thing. 5" high x 10" diameter. Collection of Meryle Evans. Value: $75-$95.

Figure II-17. **Eggbeaters.** Cyclone at left, pat'd 1901, $12-$22; Taplin "Light Running" at center, pat'd 1908, $8-$12; at right, $8-$12. Author's collection.

Dough mixer and kneader, tin and cast
iron, "Universal," Landers, Frary
& Clark, shallow pan with sloped
sides, above which is mounted
the frame and paddles, 1880s to 90s ..... $35.00 to $48.00

Drink mixer, see Mixer, drink

"Better the family wait for the omelet than the omelet wait
for the family." — **Eggs, by Anna Barrows, 1890**

Egg whip, tin, C.A. Chapman's "The
Van Deusen Egg Whip" .... $10.00 to $14.00
Eggbeater, iron and wire, "A & J,"
pat'd 1923, 11" long .... $9.00 to $15.00
Eggbeater, green wood T-handle and
knob, A & J, "High Speed Super
Center Drive Beater", patent #
2,049,727 (1936), 11½" long .... $7.00 to $12.00
Eggbeater, red wood handle and knob,
same as above .... $8.00 to $12.00
Eggbeater, with three beaters worked
from one crank, "Master Beater"
made by Aurelius Brothers,
Braham, Minnesota .... $18.00 to $25.00
Eggbeater, heavy stamped metal, 3
fold-flat heart-shaped beater
blades, "Minute Maid," mfd. by
Henderson Company, Seattle,
Washington .... $18.00 to $25.00
Eggbeater, iron, "Ladd" .... $6.00 to $10.00
Eggbeater or cream whip, stamped
metal and wire, "Cassady-Fairbanks
Mfg. Co.," c. 1930 .... $12.00 to $18.00
Eggbeater, tin, "Turbine," wood
handle, 12¼" long .... $3.00 to $18.00
Eggbeater, cast and stamped aluminum
marked either "Aluminum Beauty"
or "Aluminum Beauty Beater VIKO
Instant Whip," mfd. by Ullman
Aluminum, pat'd April 20, 1920,
10 3/8" long .... $12.00 to $22.00

**The "Aluminum Beauty" truly is a beauty, and works better
than any eggbeater I've ever tried.**

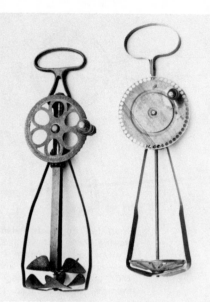

Figure II-18. **Eggbeaters.** Left: Lyon Egg Beater & Cream Whip, No. 2, Albany, NY, pat'd September 7, 1887, iron and tin, 10" long; right: Turbine Egg Beater, Cassidy-Fairbank Mfg. Co., Chicago, IL, "patent allowed," c. 1900. Collection of Meryle Evans. Value: $15-$22.

Figure II-19. **Eggbeaters.** Left to right: "The NECO," M.P. Hougen, Minneapolis, patent pending; "WHIPPIT" Cream & Egg Beater, Duro Metal Products Co., Chicago Pat. #1,705,639, white and teal blue marbling on handle, 2 slotted dished dashers, 13½" long; "Dunlap's Sanitary Silver Blade Cream & Egg Whip, Casey-Hudson Co., distributors, pat'd 1906-1916. "Quik-Whip," patent pending, nickel plated, 11" long, unusual action because you fit top knob in palm, use forefinger to pull up on spring-tension hook then release. Author's collection. Value: $8-$15.

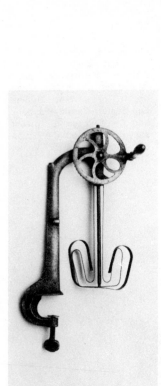

Figure II-20. **Egg Beater Patent Drawing**. Pat'd April 19, 1853 by James F. and Edwin P. Monroe, (Fitchburg, MA and NYC), prolific kitchen gadget inventors. Screw-clamped to table or shelf edge above mixing bowl. Patent claimed it could also be used to mix paint!

Figure II-21. **Eggbeater.** Clamp on, no marks or date. Nickel plated tin, 10" long. Dashers removable. Collection of Meryle Evans. Value: $25-$40.

Figure II-22. **Eggbeater.** Homemade, machined brass and wire. 19th century. 9¼" long. Charming modest little back and forth movement of dashers. Author's collection. This one hard to evaluate because you either think one-of-a-kind handmade things are worth more than patented items or you don't. I like 'em best, and paid $95 for this in early 1983. Patented beaters from same dealer were much higher.

138

Figure II-23. **Eggbeaters.** Top: Holt's Egg Beater, pat'd August 22, 1899, iron and tin, 12½" long. Has the so-called "flare dasher." Bottom left: Holt's Pat'd Flare Dasher Egg Beater, NY, iron and tin, 8¾" long, side handle; right: same name but much less flair! Not so well made. Same length. Collection of Meryle Evans. Values: top, $20-$35. Bottom two, $22-$38.

"There are two objects in beating eggs; to mingle the two parts of the egg, and to incorporate air with it.

"For custards, etc., the first is all that is required. For cakes more beating is necessary to accomplish the latter.

"A variety of beaters are in the market, all doing the work in a more or less perfect way. But many of the best cooks, except for a large quantity of eggs, prefer a knife or fork or simple whip to the more elaborate machines." — **Eggs, by Anna Barrows, 1906**

Eggbeater, nickeled-steel, tin, wire,
"Whipwell," pat'd March 23, 1920,
May 2, 1921, 11" long .... $12.00 to $15.00
Eggbeater, cast iron and tin, "Light
Running," Taplin Mfg. Co., pat'd
November 24, 1908, 12¼" long .... $8.00 to $12.00
Eggbeater, cast iron or nickel-plated
iron, perforated tin blades,
"Cyclone," pat'd 6/25/1901 and
7/16/1901, either 11½" or 11¾" long .... $12.00 to $22.00
Eggbeater, cast iron and tin, Dover
No. 14, hotel size, clamps to
shelf above bowl, 17" long, c. 1890 ...... $22.00 to $28.00
Eggbeater, cast iron with tin blades,
Dover, pat'd in 1880 but made for
at least 40 years! .... $10.00 to $18.00
Eggbeater, cast iron with tin blades,
"Taplin's Dover Pattern Improved,"
pat'd 1903 .... $8.00 to $18.00
Eggbeater, chromed steel with wood
T-handle, "Ladd Ball Bearing,"
late 1920s .... $7.00 to $12.00
Eggbeater, spiral-coiled wire and cast
iron, "Easy Egg Beater" — the
four spokes of the crank wheel
have E-A-S-Y cast into the design
1890s .... $12.00 to $22.00
Eggbeater and cream whip, wire, "The
Up To Date Egg & Cream Whip,"
pat'd 190-?, works on the
Archimedean screw principle .... $8.00 to $12.00
Eggbeater, cast iron and wire, top part
and wheel very like the old Dover,
the bottom is a semi-circular
frame with a wire "oar" that goes
back and forth, very unusual, c. 1910 ..... $20.00 to $35.00
Eggbeater, stamped metal and wire,
nickel plated, "Ram Beater Patent,"
bottle-shaped frame for beater
blades or "wings" — wire forms
back-and-forth hairpin curves,
very handsome sculpture, 12" long ...... $30.00 to $40.00

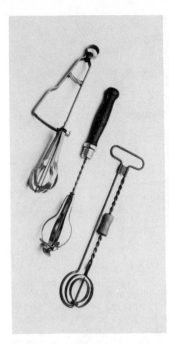

Figure II-24. **Eggbeaters.** Above left: "One Hand 'WIP,'" by Eagle Precision Mfg. Co., chrome and red plastic, squeeze action, black wood handle on one, 13¾" long; "Bryant's Patent," no date, 12 7/8" long on other with cute little wood knob moved up and down. Collection of Meryle Evans. Value: $7-$22.

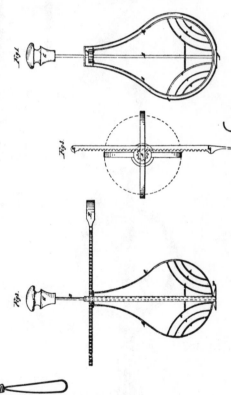

Figure II-25. **Egg Beater Patent Drawing.** Pat'd July 7, 1863 by Timothy Earle, then of Smithfield, RI, who invented a number of eggbeaters over a long period.

Figure II-26. **Egg Beater Patent Drawing.** Pat'd April 12, 1892 by Howard M. Brittain, of Martin's Creek, PA. Wire with wood handle. The action is the same idea as the aboriginal bow drill fire-starting tool: the beater sits firmly in the bowl, gripped and held in place by the vertical handle, while the horizontal wire drill bow and its spooled cord is moved back and forth to turn the beaters this way, then that.

141

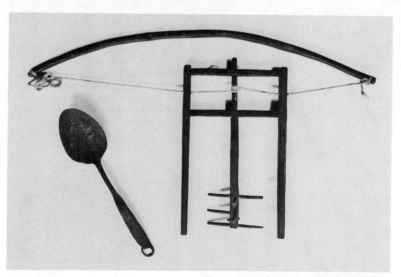

Figure II-27. **Eggbeater and Spoon.** Bow drill beater that works by sawing the bow back and forth. The cord, which passes through two small holes in the support frame, turns the beater first one way, then the other. 19th century. The wrought iron mixing spoon is late 18th or very early 19th century. Rattail handle. Picture courtesy of the National Museum of American History, Smithsonian Institution.

Figure II-28. **Eggbeater.** Dover. Cast iron and tinned iron. C. 1880-1910. 10¼" long. Author's collection. Value: $12-$30.

142

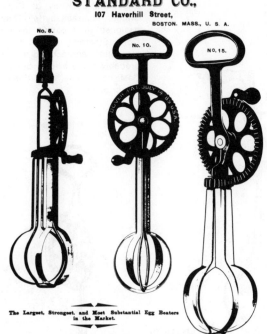

New Enlarged
DOVER EGG BEATER,
(Manufactured by)
STANDARD CO.,
107 Haverhill Street,
BOSTON. MASS., U. S. A.

No. 5.

No. 10.

NO. 15.

The Largest, Strongest, and Most Substantial Egg Beaters in the Market.

Figure II-29. **Eggbeaters.** Dover, Standard Co., c. 1885-1900. Picture is from old Dover flyer. Value of flyer: $12-$15; Value of beaters: $12-$30.

Eggbeater, chrome and red plastic, with one-hand squeeze action, "One Hand WIP", Eagle Precision Mfg. Co., 12½" long, mid-20th century .... $7.00 to $14.00

Eggbeater, stamped metal, with cup cover, "A & J," pat'd 1923, 12" high, this is quite common, and without the accompanying bowl usually sells for from .... $7.00 to $12.00

Eggbeater, "A & J" beater with detachable lid, green glass beater bowl with four squat thick feet, bowl embossed "Patent Applied for," standard A & J beater dated October 9, 1923 .... $22.00 to $30.00

Eggbeater, A & J "Big Bingo" #7, knob handle, very small diameter blade "balloon" $6.00

143

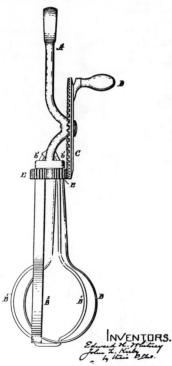

(No Model.)　　　　　　　　2 Sheets—Sheet 1.

E. H. WHITNEY & J. L. KIRBY.
EGG BEATER.

No. 463,818.　　　　　　Patented Nov. 24, 1891.

Figure II-30. **Egg Beater Patent Drawing.** Pat'd November 24, 1891 by Edward H. Whitney and John L. Kirby of Cambridge, Massachusetts. They assigned their patent to the Dover Stamping Co. of Boston, who manufactured it and probably made a lotta bucks. Cast iron frame with tinned beater blades.

WITNESSES.

INVENTORS.

Figure II-31. **Eggbeater.** Illustration from F.A. Walker catalog, 1870s. Value: $15-$25.

Eggbeater, egg-shaped knob handle, "A & J," pat'd Oct. 9, 1923, 11" long $7.00

Eggbeater, green-painted handle, A & J "High Speed Super Center Drive Beater," 12" long $8.00

Eggbeater, painted wood handle, wire rings at bottom, Archimedean screw action, made in England, 11" long .... $5.00 to $15.00

Eggbeater, tin and wood, "Turbine" by Androck, also marked "Lutz File Company," 13½" long $12.00

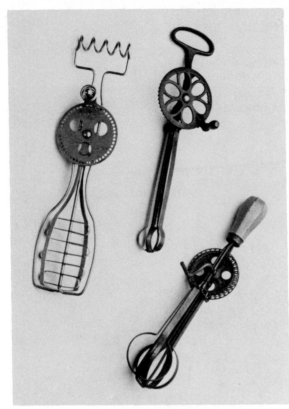

Figure II-32. **Eggbeaters.** Left to right: "Ram Beater" with wiggly finger-hold grip, chrome plate, 12" long; middle with teeny dashers, Dover, 11 3/8" long, iron and tin; lower right, "Whip Well," pat'd 1920, yellow wood handle, 11" long. First two, collection of Meryle Evans. Bottom, Author's collection. Value: $12-$22.

Eggbeater, "Silver New Egg Beater"
with glass jar, jar 3¼" square x
7" high, marked in various measures
on different sides, plus the great
Brooklyn Bridge with words
"Silvers Brooklyn" around the
bridge, a great one for the Brooklyn
Bridge's Centennial in 1983! . . . . $28.00 to $35.00
Eggbeater, cast iron, wire and tin,
"The Hill" on the cast iron wheel,
pat'd 1901, very unusual . . . . $35.00 to $45.00
Eggbeater, "Holt's Dover" eggbeater
and creamwhip, 1899 . . . . $22.00
Eggbeater or cream whip, 2 slotted
and slightly-dished dashers at
bottom, one above the other,
wooden handle painted teal &
white marbleized, "WHIPPIT,"

145

mfd. by Duro Metal Products Co.,
Chicago, Pat'd 1929 (#1,705,639),
13½" long .... $8.00 to $15.00
Eggbeater or cream whip, 3-leaf clover
dasher at bottom, wooden handle
and knob, "The NECO," mfd. by
M.A. Hougen, Minneapolis,
patent pending .... $8.00 to $15.00

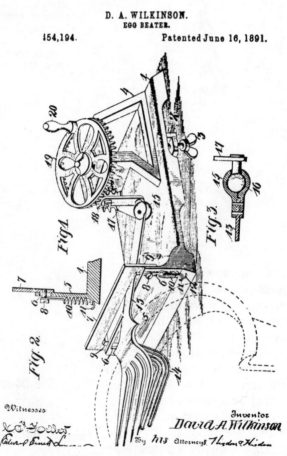

Figure II-33. **Eggbeater Patent Drawing.** From the **Official Gazette,** 1891. David A. Wilkinson, St. Louis, MO. Would love to find this, but don't know if it was ever mf'd.

Figure II-34. **Larding Needles.** Brass and steel. From F.A. Walker catalog, 1870s. Value: $16-$20.

Figure II-35. **Marshmallow Beater.** "V.F.M." No. 17, pat'd December 22, 1914. heavy tin box, strange drumwheel with tiny shingled blades all over it. Peaked roof. Box is 5" high x 8" long x 5¼" wide. Collection of Meryle Evans. Value: $28-$45.

Figure II-36. **Mayonaise Mixer and Cream Whip.** White porcelain bowl, tin top, single tin dasher with 4 holes cut in it, wood-handled crank. Beautiful footed bowl. Funnel hole for making mayo. Bowl is 4" high. 19th century. Collection of Meryle Evans. Value: $25-$35.

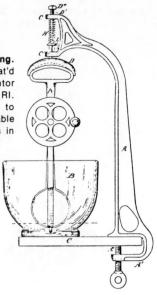

Figure II-37. **Egg Beater Patent Drawing.** An "apparatus for beating eggs" pat'd March 2, 1880, by the prolific inventor Timothy Earle, then of Valley Falls, RI. Cast iron frame that screw-clamps to table edge, with beater that's detachable from frame. Special feature is recess in center of bowl.

Eggbeater or cream whip, single bent
    dasher, oblong in shape, "Dunlap's
    Sanitary Silver Blade Cream &
    Egg Whip," Casey Hudson Co.
    distributers, "No Splash or Waste,"
    pat'd 1906, 1916 .... $8.00 to $15.00
Egg whips/whisks, tinned wire, 1890s
    to present, unless really unusual,
    most are between .... $2.00 to $8.00

Flour sifter: see next category, Separate, Strain, Sift, Etc.

Larding needles in case, steel and
    japanned tin, 9½" long, late 19th
    century. These are in this mixing
    category because larding needles
    are used to lard in, or in effect
    mix in, fat to lean meat .... $16.00 to $20.00

Moonshine

Beat the whites of 6 eggs into a very stiff froth; then add gradually 6 tablespoonfuls of powdered sugar, beating for not less than 15 minutes; then beat in 1 heaping tablespoonful of preserved peaches, cut in tiny bits; serve, pour in each saucer some rich cream sweetened and flavored with vanilla; on the cream place a liberal portion of the moonshine.

Scammell's Treasure-House of Knowledge, 1891

Mixer, liquid, wire with wood handle,
"A & J," Archimedean screw
action, small pivoting "foot"
seats it steady in bowl or jar,
12½" high .... $10.00 to $12.00

Mixer, drink, metal shaker with lid,
"Ovaltine" $18.00

Mixer, drink or malted milk, aluminum
container with lid, "Thompson's
Double Malted," 7" high $4.00

Mixer, drink or liquid, glass jar with
tin lid, spiral tin whipper,
Archimedean screw action, pat'd
3/30/15, 16" high $15.00

Mixer, stirrer, silverplated coil with
handle, "Holmes, Edwards" dated 1889 .... $12.00

Mixer, drink or liquid, wire, "Horlick's,"
9¼" long .... $8.00 to $12.00

Mixer, liquid or eggs, glass and
nickeled iron, "Even Full, New
Keystone Beater," Culinary
Utilities Co., late 1920s, rectangular
jar holds 1 quart .... $15.00 to $18.00

Mixer, liquid or eggs, green glass
"Root Mason" jar, cast iron and
tin screw-on lid and gears, wire
beater blades, Standard
Specialty Co., pat'd 1907. The
beater actually looks very like a
Dover. I've not seen another of this ...... $22.00 to $30.00

Figure II-38. **Mayonaise Mixers.** Left: "Universal Mayonaise Mixer & Cream Whip Whipper," Landers, Frary & Clark, patent applied for. Nickeled iron top, nickel plated dashers with long-fingers, lid has swivel cover for oil hole. 2½-3 cup capacity, approx. 9 3/8" high. 19th century. Right: "S & S Hutchinson," NY. Patent applied for, 19th century. Footed glass bowl with built-in oil funnel. Standard eggbeater blades. 9¾" high. Collection of Meryle Evans. Value: $25-$40.

Mixer, liquid or eggs, glass jar 8" high,
    beaters are wire and resemble
    abstract human hands, works on
    Archimedean screw principle,
    pat'd 1915 .... $16.00 to $22.00

See also: Electric Collectibles

Mixing bowls, green Depression glass,
    nesting set of 4 .... $28.00
Mixing bowl, yellow ware with white
    glaze, 8" diameter $16.00
Mixing bowl, blue enameled tin, 7"
    diameter .... $10.00 to $13.00

Mixing bowl, yellow earthenware with
    green sponge design, range from
    quite small to 14" diameter .... $25.00 to $100.00
    (Small is not necessarily cheapest.)
Mixing bowl, yellow ware with brown
    bands, 9" diameter $20.00
Mixing bowl, Red Wing spongeware,
    nesting set of 3 .... $200.00
Mixing bowl, decorated china, with
    cottage scene, girl and flowers,
    9" diameter $20.00
Mixing bowl, Red Wing, saffron spatter $35.00
Mixing bowl, green with pink & blue
    stripes, "Oven Ware," early 20th
    century, 14" diameter $45.00
Mixing bowl, pumpkin-colored "Oven
    Ware," 7" diameter $10.00
Mixing bowl, Red Wing spongeware,
    11" diameter $130.00
Mixing bowl, blue & rust spatter
    decoration, advertises "Boyne's
    Grocery, West Union, Iowa" $50.00
Mixing bowl, spongeware, brown &
    nice small size, 5½" diameter $35.00
Mixing bowl, graniteware, yellow &
    white marbelized, 9½" diameter $23.00
Mixing bowl, blue, rust & cream
    spongeware, 6" diameter $38.00
Mixing bowl, Ohio Pottery, advertises
    "It pays to mix with Thoren Brothers
    Rock City and Rock Grove, Illinois"
    on inside, 8" diameter x 6" deep,
    very unusual piece $50.00
Mixing bowl, spongeware in blue, rust
    & gray, 6 panels, 8" diameter $48.00
Mixing spoon, tin and wood, "Ideal,"
    pat'd March, 1908 .... $12.00 to $18.00
Mixing spoons, slotted tin, look like
    kitty litter scoops, still made very
    much the same .... $1.00 to $5.00
Mixing spoons, tin, advertising
    "Rumford Baking Powder" $4.00

Figure II-39. **Mixers.** Left: "The New Keystone Beater." Different types of measures embossed on each side of glass jar: "Even Full One Quart or Standard Measuring Cups" (working load is 3 cups), "Coffee Cups Full" on another side, "Pound Flour, ½ pound, ¼ pound, and "Sifted Even Full Whole Pound," on last side is liquid measures — 4 oz. to 16 oz. Cast iron lid with decorative scalloped edge, cast iron wheels, wire blades. Collection of Meryle Evans. Value: $22-$35. Right: "E.Z. Mixer," Registered 1902, pat'd June 30, 1093. 32 oz. 13" high. Cast iron top with flat pad for pressing against with heel of hand while mixing. No marks cast into metal. Lid has oil funnel hole. Courtesy of the Steed Collection. Located by the Primitive Man, Bob Cahn, Carmel, NY. His evaluation: $95-$125.

Figure II-40. **Eggbeaters and Liquid Makers.** Left: A & J, pat'd 1923; right "AD," pat'd 1915, Archimedean screw principle. Value: $12-$22.

Figure II-41. **Eggbeater and Liquid Mixer.** New Keystone Beater, "Even Full." Compare with older, scalloped-top Even Full. Mf'd by Culinary Utilities Co., c. 1929. Value: $15-$22.

Mixing spoons, tin with wood
    handles, 1910 to 1930s, depending
    on style and color of handle,
    and desire of collector .... $4.00 to $10.00
Mixing spoon, tin and iron, "Rumford
    Baking Powder," 10¼" long $8.00

Figure II-42. **Mixers, Beaters.** Left bottom: electric "Challenge," mf'd by CEM Co., Tyre Avub (??). Simple single dasher blade, works perfectly, even hums, 3 cup capacity, 8½" high, 110-120 volts. Author's collection. Value: $10-$12. Right top: "Ladd Beater#1," United Royalties Corp., pat'd July 7, 1908, Feb. 2, 1915. Beaters like all Ladd eggbeaters, and can be dismantled from lid. 13" high. Collection of Meryle Evans. Value $25-$35.

Figure II-43. **Mixer.** "Jones Wonder Mixer," c. 1910. Tin, iron and glass. Value: $10-$15.

154

Figure II-44. **Eggbeaters & Measuring Cup Sets.** Pint size. From A & J (Edward Katzinger) catalog, 1940. Value: $15-$25.

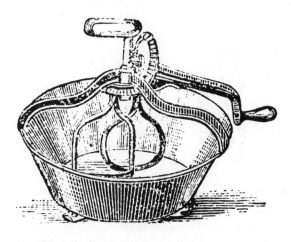

Figure II-45. **Mixing Machine.** Cast iron and tin. Illustration from 1881 cookbook, but this is probably 1860s or 1870s. Value: $25-$40.

Figure II-46. **Mixers and Spiral Egg Whisk.** Left: Horlick's drink mixer, c. 1910; A & J, pat'd 1907; The Up To Date Egg and Cream Whip, 190-; wire egg whisk, common from 1880s-1930; pretty example made in England, no mfr. name. All but whisk work on Archimedean screw principle. Value: $8-$18.

156

Figure II-47. **Mixing Spoons.** The skeletal "Ideal," pat'd March 9, 1908, at center. Other two, 1920s-30s. Value: $12-$18 for Ideal; others, $4-$10.

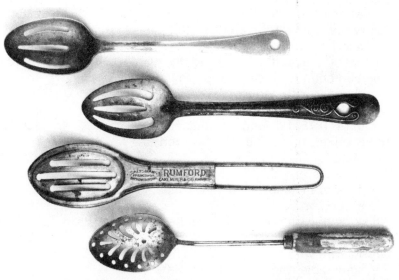

Figure II-48. **Slotted Spoons, or Cake Mixers.** Tin, tin and wire, tinned steel and wood. Top three are c. 1900, the Rumford's advertising one probably worth the most. Bottom is 1930s-40s. Author's collection. Value: $4-$8.

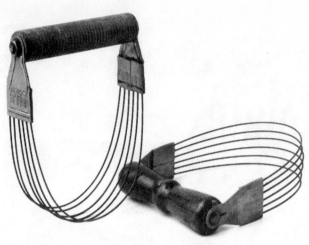

Figure II-49. **Pastry Blenders.** Wire, steel and wood. Both Androck, pat'd 1929. Author's collection. Value: $4-$8.

Pastry blender, heavy nickeled-iron
 wood handle, 9¼" long .... $5.00 to $8.00
Pastry blender, wire, stainless steel
 and turned wood grip, Androck,
 pat'd 1929, handles vary slightly .... $4.00 to $8.00
Syllabub churn or cream whip, tin
 cylinder with conical beater/dasher
 inside, wood T-handle, pat'd
 9/14/1875, 12" long x 4" diameter $36.00
Toddy mixer, glass and metal, "Toddy
 Man" $9.00
Whisk, brass $40.00
Whisk, wire in "snowshoe" flat shape,
 9" long $6.00
Whisk, wire with coiled wire handle,
 14" long $9.00
Whisk, wire with wood handle and
 adjustable ring for changing flare
 of wings, ring attached to handle,
 1880s or so $14.00

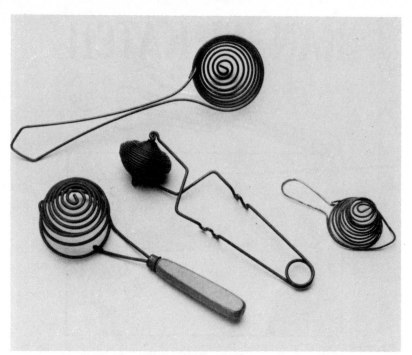

Figure II-50. **Whips, Whisks & Egg Lifters.** All of spiraled springy wire. The most unusual is the one with the squeeze action . . . you work it rapidly and it makes the wires go in and out, rather like an accordian! One with green wood handle, is possibly Edlund. Miniature is 4¼" long; longest is 9¼" long. Collection of Meryle Evans. Value: $6-$10.

Figure II-51. **Whisk.** Wire with wood handle. Loop, seen in position near end. adjustable so that flare of whisk could be increased or decreased. 1870s-1890 or so. 8" long. Collection of Meryle Evans. Value: $12-$18.

KAN-U-KATCH

Figure II-52. **Whisk or Whatsit?** This "KAN-U-KATCH" is a good example of something which might easily be mistaken for a kitchen collectible — wire with a spring release and wood handle, it looks very much like a whisk, but it's really a toy for tossing balls, c. 1916. I'd be very interested in having readers send me other **confusables.**

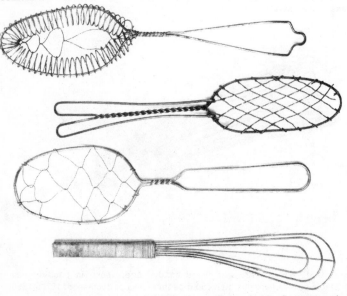

Figure II-53. **Whisks.** Top three variations on twisted wire theme. Bottom, probably European. Middle two are oldest . . . c. 1880s. Author's collection. Value: $6-$12.

SEPARATE, STRAIN, SIFT, DREDGE & FUNNEL

This preparation category encompasses all the implements that assist the cook either by allowing the smaller particles of food stuff to be retained (in a sieve, colander, skimmer, etc.), or for larger particles to be pushed through some kind of screen or holey surface in order that the smaller particles thereby created be scattered, aerated, or more readily mixed. (But for potato ricers, see the grind, mash category.)

Colanders, both foot-fast and foot-loose, are among the most popular utensils in this category. Collectors can find them in a wide variety of forms made of heavy tin, aluminum, wire, enameled iron, ceramic, even — from modern times — plastic. A single colander is a thing of great beauty, probably because it speaks so eloquently of its function, but a collection of different colanders — each with its particular tattoo of holes — is really wonderful.

Cheese drainers, which are really molds, pose a problem in categorization for me. They look so much like colanders, but they function like molds. However, I believe that since they have two functions: first to drain, second to hold the shape, that they should go here.

Bean sizing sieve: See under MEASURE

Cheese drainer/mold, tin with two
    strap handles, has a cheese ladder
    with it, late 19th century .... $45.00 to $60.00
Cheese drainer/mold, punched tin
    cup with two strap handles, 4"
    high x 4" diameter, 19th century $50.00
Cheese drainer/mold, copper, heart-
    shaped, 3 short feet, probably
    imported, 19th century? $225.00
Cheese drainer/mold, pierced tin,
    heart-shaped with 3 short feet,
    probably Pennsylvania-German,
    this one is 19th century .... $65.00 to $100.00

NOTE OF CAUTION: This is very desirable because of its shape and Pennsylvania German origin. It is widely reproduced — not for the purpose of fakery — and is sold in all kinds of gift shops all over the country. The "country look" in new kitchens has encouraged this. Study the drainer you find carefully, looking for signs of more modern, less careful [or too perfect] construction.

Cheese drainer, natural wood with arrow-shaped slats leading from square base up to round hooped top rim. So-called "Windsor-style," early 19th century, 9½" diameter x 5" deep $325.00

Cheese drainer/basket, rather limp basketry, 10" diameter, 4" deep $130.00

Cheese basket/mold, beautiful weave forming 6-pointed stars, 15" diameter, 3" deep, 19th century $225.00

Cheese basket/drainer, similar to above but with well-defined bottom, 12½" diameter x 4" deep $185.00

Cheese basket/drainer, similar to above but with much larger interstices, traces of blue paint $200.00

Cheese basket/drainer, round rim with two handles, fairly tightly-woven sides leading to square bottom, 12½" diameter x 6" deep, 19th century $225.00

Cheese strainer, pieced tin with strap handles, possible Shaker, 19th century $95.00

Colander, sheet iron in good condition, 10" diameter $30.00

Colander, sheet iron, very large with good-size holes, crudely-soldered foot ring, 14" diameter, quite imposing if primitive $12.00

Colander, mottled green graniteware, strap handles, 10" diameter $11.00

Colander, gray graniteware, footed, 11" diameter $10.00

Figure III-1. **Colanders.** (Two pictures.) Perforated tin. Both "foot fast" style, which means ring foot is soldered fast to the colander body. Late 19th century. Collection of Mary Mac Franklin. Value: $15-$25.

Colander, aqua enamelware with a few
   chips, 11" diameter $14.00
Colander, pieced tin, footed, ear
   handles, 12" diameter, c. 1890 to 1910 ... $12.00 to $20.00
Colander, gray graniteware, 11"
   diameter, c. 1890 .... $15.00 to $18.00

Figure III-2. **Colander.** Foot fast style, from Matthai-Ingram catalog, c. 1890. Value: $15-$20.

Figure III-3. **Colander.** Tin. Foot loose — unsoldered. From Matthai-Ingram catalog, c. 1890. Value: $15-$22.

Figure III-4. **Colander.** Tin with tubular handle. 1870s-80s. Photograph courtesy of Lar Hothem. Value: $20-$30.

Figure III-5. **Colander.** Tin with saucepan style handle, and strap support for resting within a pan. Spelled "cullender" in the Matthai-Ingram catalog, c. 1890, from which this picture comes. Nine sizes from 5" x 2½" to 1" x 5". Value: $10-$15.

Figure III-6. **Colander Strainer.** Wire, mesh, stainless steel, 8" diameter mesh bowl is removable. 5½" high. Green wood handles. From Androck catalog, 1936. Value: $8-$12.

164

Figure III-7. **Cream Cheese Mold.** Tin with little feet. From Matthai-Ingram catalog, c. 1890. Value: $8-$15.

Figure III-8. **Flour Sifter.** Tin, mesh and iron crank. Scoop shaped. "Earnshaw's Patent." From F.A. Walker catalog, 1870s. Value: $30-$50.

Colander, stamped tin, foot loose —
    therefore hard to find, because
    unattached foot rings soon
    become lost, 13" diameter,
    turn-of-century .... $18.00 to $22.00
Colander, wire mesh in tin and wire
    frame, wood ear handles,
    Androck, 1936 .... $8.00 to $15.00
Draining pan for sink, royal blue &
    white enamelware, 12" diameter .... $12.00 to $18.00
Draining pan, white enamelware,
    triangular to fit into corner of
    sink, three short legs .... $8.00 to $15.00

For dish drainers, see section on washing.

Dredger, for ground cinnamon, glass
    and tin, with one side flat to fit
    against back of stove shelf. Looks
    a wee bit like a fire hydrant in
    shape! 6" high .... $12.00 to $18.00
Dredger, for flour, tin, a cup with
    handle and close-fit but not
    screwed-on pierced, domed lid,
    c. 1880s .... $8.00 to $15.00

Dredger, for flour, heavy tin, footed
like a goblet, domed pierced lid,
late 19th century, nifty .... $15.00 to $18.00
Dredger, for flour, japanned (asphaltum)
tin with small handle, domed lid,
4" high, late 19th century $25.00
Dredger, milk glass with metal screw-on
lid, "FLOUR" painted on
side, 4½" high x 2½" diameter $10.00
Dredger, tin with double lid, inside
one is pierced shaker top. "Steele's
Dredge Box," mfd. in New Haven,
CT, Pat'd December 27, 1870,
3¼" high x 2" diameter $10.00
Egg separator, aluminum, large
ear handles, c. 1915 .... $4.00 to $7.00
Egg separator, white graniteware,
single thumb handle .... $6.00 to $10.00
Egg separator, tin, "Do You Know
Kemo?" stamped in rim .... $6.00 to $8.00
Egg separator, tin, advertising
stamped in rim .... $6.00 to $8.00
Egg separator, tin, advertises a dairy
3¼" diameter, thumb handle $8.00
Egg separator, "Jewel Stoves &
Ranges," 3 3/8" diameter, prettily-
shaped thumb handle, a bit more
because of stove advertising $12.00

NOTE: Some people specialize in separators stamped with the name and/or motto of egg farmers and dairies in their area. And, of course, are willing to pay a bit more to get what they want than someone from another area.

Flour sifter, tin with double lid (top
and bottom), "Duplex Sifter,"
Uneek Utilities Co., pat'd 1922 .... $12.00 to $20.00
Flour sifter, double-end tin with yellow
wood handle, "KWIK" $15.00
Flour sifter, tin with double lids,
5-cup size, yellow wood handle $30.00
Flour sifter, tin, mug style with side
crank, "H. & Hodges," 6½" high $5.00

Figure III-9. **Flour Scoop and Sifter.** Tinned sheet iron with iron crank and woven wire mesh. Strap handle. Marked "Earnshaw's Patent, July 25, 1865." 8½" high. Picture courtesy of the National Museum of American History, Smithsonian Institution.

Flour sifter, tin and wire mesh, "Banner
    Sifter #15," saucepan style with
    tubular tin handle and wire crank $18.00
Flour sifter, tin, Bromwell, 3-cup size $2.00

NOTE: Bromwell, of Saranac, Michigan, claims to be "The Oldest Housewares Company in America, "in business since 1819." They offer a nice range of flour sifters — shakers, crankers and squeezers — pretty much indistinguishable from ones they made 50 years ago.

Flour sifter, tin with side crank,
    "Standard," pat'd October 15,
    1918, 7" high $6.00
Flour sifter, wooden with metal crank,
    in the shape of a bin, crank in
    side, marked "Tilden's Patent,
    Mar. 28, 1865" $145.00

Figure III-10. **Dredge Box.** Japanned tin with domed lid. From F.A. Walker catalog, 1870s. Value: $10-$15.

Figure III-11. **Flour Sifters.** Both double-ended, for doing the double sifting for cakes. Left: Duplex Sifter, light turquoise wood handle, 6¾" high, holds 5 cups. Author's collection. Right: Bromwell's Multiple, patent pending. Meduim green wood handle. This one works by shaking back and forth in one hand. 7" high. Collection of Meryle Evans. Value of either: $15-$20.

Flour sifter, wooden with brushes and
   screen, a commercial size No. 100,
   mfd. by J.H. Day & co. $125.00
Flour sifter, tin, squeeze handle type,
   "Foley" $10.00

Figure III-12. **Flour Sifters**. Left: cheap tin saucepan style, woven mesh. 9¼" long, turn-of-century. Author's collection. Value: $6-$11. Right: Tin with perforated mesh bottom, spring tension dasher. This one clamps to shelf. 6" high. Collection of Meryle Evans. Value: $20-$30.

Figure III-13. **Flour Sifter.** Heavy tin, perforated tin mesh, iron crank handle turns paddles on inside against the mesh "Eddy's Patent," April 20, 1880. 14¾" high x 8¼" diameter. Collection of Meryle Evans. Value: $30-$55.

Figure III-14. **Toy Flour Sifter.** Tinned sheet iron stamped in relief on side: "HUNTER'S-TOY-SIFTER (pat. May 16 71 - Apr. 7 74) BUY A BIG ONE." Only 2¼" high. In the January 1889 issue of **Ladies Home Journal** was an ad for the Hunter Sifter. " . . . combines 12 kitchen utensils in one. It is a Mixer, Scoop, Measure, Weigher, Dredger, Rice Washer, Starch, Tomato, Wine, and Fruit Strainer. It is the most useful kitchen utensil made . . . A toy sifter, the size of the above cut (which was actually 1¼" high), which shows how the large sifter works, and which will afford amusement to any little girl, will be sent free to anyone who will mention where this advertisement was seen, and enclose 2 cents for postage to The Fred J. Meyers Mfg. Co., Covington, Kentucky." Can you imagine it? Only two cents!! Picture courtesy of the National Museum of American History, Smithsonian Institution.

Figure III-15. **Flour Sifters.** Left: Savory Sifter, 1910-1920s. Right: Hunter's Sifter, mfd. by The Fred J. Meyers Mfg. Co., pat'd August 5, 1879, by Jacob Hunter of Cincinnati. Crank is in tubular handle. Author's collection. Value for Savory: $8-$12. For Hunter's: $15-$25.

Figure III-16. **Flour Sifter.** Wood on little legs, woven screen sifter, leather sifter blades. "Tilden's Universal," pat'd March 28, 1863. 11¾" high x 9½" long x 7¾" wide. Collection of Meryle Evans. Value: $50-$70.

Figure III-17. **Flour Sifter.** Wood with 2 wooden roller blades and screen bottom. Comes apart so you can clean. c. 1860s. Body stands on little pointed legs 8¾" high, approx. 10½" x 9" space for pan underneath. Rocker action, similar to rocker churns. Collection of Meryle Evans. Value: $50-$75.

Figure III-18. **Flour Sifter.** Wood with very fine perforated metal sifter screen, metal handle. Extended frame so you can rest it on top of bowl or dough box. Mystery is: You can't get the blades out, so how do you clean it? Box: 6" high x 6½" x 5½" square. 19th century. Collection of Meryle Evans. Value: $40-$65.

Figure III-19. **Flour Sifter.** Tin and cast iron. 2 paddles on inside, woven wire mesh. Cast iron handle. 19th century. 10" high x 7½" diameter. Collection of Meryle Evans. Value: $40-$60.

Flour sifter, tin, green wood handle
    and crank knob, "Bromwell" $5.00
Flour sifter, tin enameled yellow,
    side crank, "Bromwell" $12.00
Flour sifter, from Hoosier cabinet $55.00

NOTE: There is a place to get sifters for these old cabinets. The Dahlquists [Country Store Antiques, 618 49th Avenue, N.W., Puyallup, Washington 98371] write "We located the company that had the dies from the old Sellers flour and sugar bins. We are national distributors for the sifters and sugars for antique shops and buyers."

Flour sifter, tin, "Autumn Leaf" flour $18.00
Flour sifter, wood, "Blood's Improved
    Flour Sifter," pat'd 1861 .... $80.00 to $90.00
Flour sifter, wooden, dated 1861
    (probably Blood's) $95.00
Flour sifter, tin with wire and screen
    mesh, very simple .... $6.00 to $8.00
Flour sifter, tin, screening, spiral wire
    with wooden knob, looks like a
    saucepan, c. 1910 .... $6.00 to $11.00

Figure III-20. **Funnels.** Aluminum. Top one is regular funnel and bottom is wide-mouthed canning jar funnel. From Montgomery Ward catalog, 1895. Value: $5-$7.

Aluminum

Figure III-21. **Funnel.** Enameled ware, with lip for resting in coffee maker. Held cloth filter. Called a "percolator funnel." From Matthai-Ingram catalog, c. 1890. Value: $12-$18.

Figure III-22. **Funnel.** Turned wood, with lip. 5¼" long. Sold at Linden sale in 1983 in lot with churn and burl mortar for $308. Picture courtesy of Christie, Manson & Woods International Inc.

Flour sifter, tin, "Earnshaw's" shaped
   like a big angular scoop, side
   crank, pat'd 1866, rare .... $30.00 to $50.00
Flour sifter, tin and wire, "Hunter's
   Sifter," Fred J. Meyers Mfg. Co.,
   pat'd 1879, tubular handle with
   the crank in the handle, 11¼"
   high, really neat .... $15.00 to $25.00
Funnel, enamelware, white, small size .... $5.00 to $10.00
Funnel, copper with tinned inside,
   tapers from 6½" diameter down
   to 2", late 19th century .... $25.00 to $30.00

**NOTE: This is lovely, but it's the kind of item that brings a much
higher price when it's been polished and buffed by the dealer.
Such a nice "decorator's piece" is the line . . . but you shouldn't
have to pay their Brasso bill! I know I sound crazed on the
subject of buffed brass and copper sometimes, but on the other
hand, if a dealer has a copper coffee pot, just retinned on the
inside, that I'm willing to pay for . . . tinning is about $1.00 a
square inch. By the way, the old-fashioned way to polish copper
was to keep a little saucer of sour milk by the stove for wiping
the copper pot.**

Funnel, brewers', copper with wire
   hanging loop, Eastern Bottlers
   Supply Co., 11" long x 9¼"
   diameter at top, c. 1880s. Unusual
   for its size, tho' not strictly "kitchen" .... $45.00 to $55.00
Funnel, gray graniteware, loop handle,
   5" deep .... $12.00 to $18.00
Funnel, spun aluminum, ring handle,
   small mouth, 1940s? .... $5.00 to $7.00
Funnel, glass, probably laboratory
   equipment $6.00
Funnel, porcelain, meant for fruit jar
   filling (funnel has wide mouth,
   but doesn't taper that much. All
   canning funnels had to be able to
   be sterilized $9.00
Funnel, cider, carved from one piece
   of wood, 21" x 8" oblong, 3"
   deep, early to mid 19th century $95.00

Funnel, cider, carved from hunk of
   wood, 18" x 8½" oblong, 3½"
   deep with 1" hole in center of
   "bowl," early 19th century $268.00
Funnel, cider, carved from one piece
   of wood, 20" x 8½" oblong, 4"
   deep, second quarter of 19th
   century, probably $100.00

NOTE: These are very unusual, often primitive pieces meant to fit across the top of a cider keg. Price ranges considerably, not so much because one is that much nicer than another, but depending on the marketplace. A few cider funnels have dates or initials carved in them, adding to the value.

Funnel, white enamelware, large size $15.00
Funnel, maple sap, hand-carved
   maple, early 1800s .... $75.00 to $100.00
Funnel, maple sap, wood with iron
   band, very large .... $80.00 to $120.00
Funnel, maple sap, barrel construction
   with iron band, 12" deep, 11½"
   diameter, 6" long cylindrical funnel $240.00
Gravy strainer, tin and mesh, cylindrical
   or tubular handle with ring hanger,
   6 7/8" diameter, c. 1890s .... $10.00 to $15.00
Kettle water pourer, pierced tin and
   wire, pat'd 1898, 16" long x 10"
   wide, used to strain contents of
   preserve kettle when pouring from it ..... $12.00 to $15.00
Lard skimmer, heavy tin, 10" long $8.00
Maple sugar skimmer, galvanized
   pierced tin cup with wooden
   handle, 55" long, quite beautiful .... $55.00 to $70.00
Sieve, tin with brass screen, tapered
   from 9½" diameter down to 2½",
   turn-of-century .... $8.00 to $15.00
Sieve, horsehair and wood, fastened
   with copper nails, Shaker
   manufacture, 6" diameter $125.00
Sieve, horsehair in wood frame, white
   hair, 9" diameter, 4" deep,
   probably Shaker $50.00

Figure III-23. **Jelly Bag.** Unseamed strip of heavy coarse crash cloth, probably linen or linen/cotton. 2 metal rings holding to 2 wooden "jump rope" like handles. Put very liquid jelly in cloth, hold handles and twist to squeeze out excess liquid. Fully extended: 24" long. 19th century. Marvelous used color. Collection of Meryle Evans. Value: $50-$65.

Figure III-24. **Jelly Bag Strainers.** "Cloth held by removable rim, easily renewed. Fits into metal frame, which fits any size bowl. 6" and 9" diameter. FromAndrock catalog, 1936. Value: $6-$8 (bowl not included).

Figure III-25. **Funnel Dipper Combination.** Tin, with 6 parts that fit in in various ways to serve as funnel, sifter, dredger, measure, ladle, etc. c. 1890s. Author's collection. Value: $15-$20.

Sieve, horsehair, 4½" diameter, Shaker $105.00
Sieve, horsehair, 4½" diameter in
    two-fingered frame, Shaker $55.00

NOTE: If you ever find a horsehair sieve with a "plaid" or checker pattern, woven from white and black hairs, you've got a find, worth at least half again as much as the plain.

Sieves, perforated tin, look like gold
    miners' pans — shallow with
    slightly sloped sides, varying
    coarseness to perforations, late
    19th century .... $7.00 to $18.00
Sieve, screening in wood frame, 12"
    diameter $18.00
Sieve, tin, 2-part sieve, like a ricer, the
    concave part, the cup, has the
    holes, the "presser" is convex,
    tubular tin handle with loop for
    hanging, very odd and attractive.
    Have only seen one $35.00
Skimmer, brass with wrought iron
    handle, 12½" long, early 19th century $245.00

Figure III-26. **Strainer**. Enamelware. 19th century, early 20th very small. Author's collection. Value: $8-$10.

Skimmer, perforated enameled tin,
    "Cream City Ware," c. 1890 .... $8.00 to $10.00
Skimmer, pierced and engraved brass
    pan, 22" long $650.00
Skimmer, pierced brass, marked
    "W.R. Boston" on handle, 23" long $1200.00
Skimmer, for cream, tin $4.50
Skimmer, yellow spatter enamelware,
    brown handle $25.00
Skimmer, for cream, shallow carved
    wood — rather like a shell,
    finger hold cut into short handle $48.00
Skimmer, iron with brass trim,
    coffin-shaped handle, spoon
    quite pear-shaped, the fat pear
    bottom attached to handle, 12" long $65.00
Skimmer, tin bowl with iron handle,
    18" long $32.00
Skimmer, tin bowl with long turned
    wood handle, 21" long $85.00
Skimmer, blue graniteware $24.00
Skimmer, gray graniteware $23.00

Figure III-27. **Strainers.** Top one, "Forbes Quality Coffee," stamped in tin; other wire mesh, tin and wood. Both turn-of-century. Value: $6-$10 for tin; $3-$7 for wire.

Skimmer, wrought iron, big bowl,
  relatively short handle looped at
  end for hanging, late 18th or early
  19th century, 9½" long $68.00
Skimmer, for sorghum, perforated tin
  with 48" wood handle $42.00
Skimmer, for sorghum, perforated tin
  with 47" wood handle $22.00
Skimmer, for sorghum, tin with 48"
  long handle, very primitive $60.00
Skimmer, for sorghum, tin with
  lightly-carved wooden handle 50" long $62.00
Skimmer, brass bowl with iron handle,
  28" long, early 19th century, very
  nice looking, as are most of the
  two-metal skimmers and other
  implements $95.00
Spout strainer, tin and wire, 2"
  diameter, c. 1890s .... $12.00 to $15.00
Strainer, blue graniteware with white
  inside, 2 handles .... $20.00 to $25.00
Strainer, pierced tin, handmade, 11"
  diameter .... $20.00 to $30.00
Strainer, white enamelware, wire
  mesh, turn-of-century, 10" diameter ..... $20.00 to $23.00

Strainer, wire with wood handle,
    bowl made up of concentric rings
    of wire, almost round .... $12.00 to $18.00
Strainer, brown marbleized
    graniteware, 8" diameter $26.00
Strainer, blue graniteware $25.00
Strainer, gray graniteware, tab footed,
    7½" diameter $14.00
Strainer, dark blue & white speckled
    graniteware, hook on rim for hanging $24.00
Strainer, gray graniteware, tab footed
    7¾" diameter $14.00
Strainer, for milk, tin with brass mesh,
    meant to fit into milk can top,
    10¼" diameter $13.00
Strainer, pierced tin, conical bowl,
    tubular tin handle with ring loop
    for hanging, 8½" diameter, 17"
    overall length, very attractive and simple $38.00
Strainer, tin with brass screen, like
    a funnel, 7" high $5.00
Strainer, tin with wood handle, "Ajax,"
    5" long $5.00
Strainer, tin with wood handle, "Ajax,"
    8" long $9.00

PREPARATION

FORM, MOLD, SHAPE & DECORATE

I am late coming to the things in this category, although molds and cutters and related things have been extremely popular with other collectors for years. It's almost as if my attention was taken entirely by eggbeaters, and molds and other shaping implements have had to wait for my attention to wander. If you are a general collector like me, you will probably experience this sort of delayed reaction too. One unanswerable but rather nagging question raised is "Gadz! How many fabulous molds or jaggers (or whatever is now striking your fancy) have I passed by without seeing over the years?"

This category is very interesting because some of the tools are so ingenious (like the bird nest fryer below, or the julien cutter or some of the pastry jaggers), and because others are so revealing of the imaginativeness of cooks, who have probably been gussying up food since the first patty. Some, such as the butter hands, don't suggest their function or the result of using them. Others, like the large gingerbread man cookie cutters, could be figured out by a person who had never seen one. Many people collect nothing but butter prints and molds, or pewter ice cream molds, others collect more broadly. I think a very interesting collection could be made of cookie cutters, especially by continuing to add contemporary cutters each year. Cutters are made to represent current fads and characters from TV. Old standbys, like Santa, Easter Bunny, Christmas Tree or Halloween Pumpkin holiday symbols, are redesigned all the time, offering the collector many fascinating interpretations. My advice to those who collect modern pieces is to save examples of the packaging — boxes, labels, cardboard backs, as well as instruction sheets. Blister packs are bulky, but one of them, in some interesting molded form, would be a good documentary accompaniment to the tool itself.

Barley sugar mold, cast iron, 3 eagles
design .... $40.00 to $60.00
Barley sugar mold, pewter, design
is a clipper ship, 4½" x 5" .... $40.00 to $50.00
Bird nest fryer, tin and wire mesh,
Androck, double nesting mesh
bowls with long wire handle, 1930s .... $7.00 to $10.00

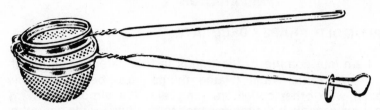

Figure IV-1. **Bird Nest Fryer.** Tinned wire and mesh. "Used for molding cooked noodles or riced potatoes into shape of a bird's nest, and frying them in the mold" itself. Coated with tin. Each came with booklet of recipes; that would add a lot of value. From Androck catalog, 1936. Value: $7-$10.

Biscuit cutter, tin with wire finger
loop, "White Lily Flour Has No
Equal," Metal Specialty Mfg. Co.,
1910 to 1915 .... $4.00 to $6.00
Biscuit cutter, stamped tin with fixed
loop handle, Matthai-Ingram, c. 1890s ..... $4.00 to $6.00
Biscuit cutter, tin, stamped "Rumford"
on top of tubular handle
and around top of cutter itself,
turn-of-century, 4½" high .... $6.00 to $9.00
Biscuit cutter, aluminum with red
wood knob, 2¾" diameter $3.50
Biscuit cutter, carved wood with knob
handle, 19th century, and this
one priced a bit low at $5.00
Biscuit or cookie cutter, aluminum
wire handle, rolling type that cuts
multiples, very simple .... $7.00 to $15.00
Biscuit or cookie cutter, same as
above only marked with advertising
slogan .... $8.00 to $15.00
Biscuit cutter, tin with scalloped or
fluted edge, strap handle .... $5.00 to $8.00
Biscuit or cracker cutter, heavy tin
with nail-like prickers inside,
mfd. by Fries, 2" diameter .... $7.00 to $10.00
Border mold: see Ring Mold under Food Mold category
Bouche iron, cast iron with wood
handle, fluted .... $10.00 to $12.00
Bread board, wood (usually maple),
round with carved motto along
edge, good condition with all
letters clear .... $28.00 to $50.00

Figure IV-2. **Pastry Cutter Combination Tool**. Tin and wire. This great little tool has 4 parts: the wire handle with a dough scraper at one end, and 3 rolling cutters. One makes scalloped edged biscuits (or cookies), one makes squares — biscuits or crackers, one makes simple rounds. Pat'd by the Feldt Mfg. Co., Jamestown, NY. Cutters — 3" to 4" wide. 19th century. Picture courtesy of the National Museum of American History, Smithsonian Institution.

Figure IV-3. **Cutters.** Left: tin biscuit cutter, rolls out 4 biscuits with each revolution of wheel, wire handle. 8¾" long. 19th, early 20th century. Author's collection. Value: $12-$18. Above: roll cutter, to cut dough into rolls, from mennonite boarding house, Olley Valley, PA. Makes 14 rolls each revolution. 11" long, rolls, 5" long. Collections of Meryle Evans. Value: $15-$25.

Figure IV-4. **Biscuit Cutters.** Left: Tin, stamped "White Lily Flour Has No Equal," 19th century, early 20th. Value: $4-$6; middle: advertises "Loella-the Finest Butter in America" also "Gold Seal Flour." Aluminum and wire. Author's collection. Value: $7-$15. Right: scalloped cutter with strap handle, tin. Value: $5-$8.

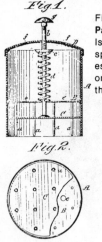

Figure IV-5. **Biscuit-Cutter and Sticker Patent Drawing.** Pat'd July 20, 1880 by Isaac W. Lincoln, of St. Joseph, MO. Tin, spring-action cutter that pricked holes — especially good for cracker-like biscuits or beaten biscuits — at the same time, then ejected dough onto pan.

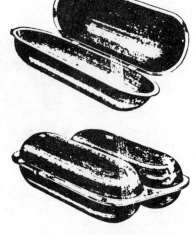

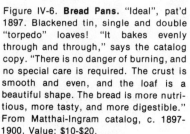

Figure IV-6. **Bread Pans.** "Ideal", pat'd 1897. Blackened tin, single and double "torpedo" loaves! "It bakes evenly through and through," says the catalog copy. "There is no danger of burning, and no special care is required. The crust is smooth and even, and the loaf is a beautiful shape. The bread is more nutritious, more tasty, and more digestible." From Matthai-Ingram catalog, c. 1897-1900. Value: $10-$20.

Figure IV-7. **Bread Pan.** "ideal," blackened tin, hinged lid. Single loaf. Pat'd 1897. Collection of Robert D. Franklin. Value: $10-$20.

Figure IV-8. **Butter Print.** Many of the molds on these pages are from the fine collection of James E. Trice, who wrote **Butter Molds: An Identification & Value Guide, Collector Books, 1980.** Rarest and most valuable are the eagle, cows, rabbit. Values: $65-$300.

Bread board, same only somewhat
worn, with some letters too worn
to read clearly .... $20.00 to $28.00
Bread board, same, very badly worn,
most of motto obliterated .... $7.00 to $15.00

NOTE: See also in the "Cutting" category under bread knives.

Bread board, maple, round with motto
"Our Daily Bread" carved around
border, with matching knife .... $45.00 to $65.00
Bread board (or plate), maple, "Staff
of Life" plus a wheat sheaf carved
on border $38.00
Bread board, maple, "Bread"
carved on border, 9½" diameter $50.00
Bread pan, blackened tin, shaped like
a blimp or a huge cigar!, "Ideal",
1897, one loaf size $18.00
Bread pan, blackened tin, Ideal,
double loaf, side by side tubes .... $10.00 to $20.00
Bread pan, blackened tin, four compartments .. $15.00 to 22.00
Bread pan, cast iron, hinged pans,
dated 1879 .... $26.00
Brush, pastry, turned wood and real
bristles, Shaker attribution, 8¼" long $80.00
Butter hands or paddles, corrugated
maple, 8" long, well-made and
somewhat smooth from use .... $10.00 to $20.00
Butter hands, corrugated wood with
beautiful patina, well-shaped
handles, 9" long $55.00
Butter hands, corrugated wood, 8"
long x 4" wide, worn, but nice
because of unusual width $12.00
Butter hands, corrugated wood, each
approximately 8½" long x 3" wide
but handles enough different in
width and shape to indicate they
may be mismatched, but this is
not unusual, and may even be
some slim proof that they aren't new! $16.00

NOTE: Nice wooden butter hands are still being made.

Butter molds, barrel type, maple or
walnut with pewter bands, various
fruit, nut and geometric designs .... $85.00 to $120.00
Butter mold, plunger type, wood, 4"
square, rosette design .... $70.00 to $75.00

Figure IV-9. **Butter Prints.** (Two pictures.) Rayed flower with dandelion like leaves, and acorn branch. Collection and photographs, James E. Trice.

Figure IV-10. **Butter Prints.** (Two pictures.) Above, "Demilune" print of primitive cow and tree. Bottom, another primitive cow print, with piecrust border. 19th century. Collection and photographs, James E. Trice.

Figure IV-11. **Butter Prints.** (Two pictures.) Lollipop style — for obvious reasons. Simple geometrics. Pennsylvania German, probably. 19th century. Collection and photographs, James E. Trice.

Figure IV-12. **Butter Prints.** (Two pictures.) Flower and acorn. 19th century. Collection and photographs, James E. Trice.

Figure IV-13. **Butter Print.** Leaping rabbit, piecrust border. Very unusual and nice. 19th century. Collection and photograph, James E. Trice.

Figure IV-14. **Butter Stamp.** Unusual oval with eagle standing on globe with open beak. Criss-cross border design. Initials "E" and "M" flank figure. Handle is chipped. American, 19th century. 5½" long x 3" wide. Estimated: $400-$500. Realized: $350. Picture courtesy of Robert W. Skinner Inc., Auctioneers, Bolton, MA.

Butter mold, cylinder type, wood with
pewter bands, simple flower &
leaf design .... $70.00 to $85.00
Butter mold, hexagonal cylinder with
pewter bands, incised cow, 3"
diameter x 4½" high, American
19th century, estimated $300/$400
at '82 auction $100.00
Butter mold, plunger & cylinder, 3½"
diameter, design of sheaf of wheat
with leaves in border $18.00
Butter mold, cylinder, 3½" diameter,
swan with rope border $25.00
Butter mold, plunger/cylinder in
hexagonal form, simple thistle design $58.00
Butter mold, plunger type, ½ lb. size,
deep-carved goose (possibly
swan?), 3¾" diameter $150.00
Butter mold, dovetailed construction,
brass clips, 2-piece with no pattern $11.00
Butter mold, maple 3-piece, carved cow $120.00
Butter mold, 5 lb. box $22.00
Butter mold box, divided into 8 small
squares with leaf designs $100.00
Butter molds, machine-made, dove-
tailed box types, simple designs .... $22.00 to $45.00
Butter mold, 1 lb. size with removable
sides, design is sheaf of wheat
and a flower $45.00
Butter mold, 1 lb. size, simple swan $52.00
Butter mold, glass with wooden
plunger handle, 4½" diameter,
cow print, this one old .... $45.00 to $65.00

**NOTE: This glass plunger mold is being reproduced now, and is
sold all over the country — both in a cow and swan design. Look
for signs of wear along bottom edge of glass and on wooden
handle for age. Old molds are also a bit heavier.**

Butter mold, box style, hinged ½ lb. size $30.00
Butter mold, dovetailed with brass
clasps, 1 lb. size, simple machine-
carved flowers $32.00

Butter mold, plunger type, 3-piece,
    very small size, fruit (pomegranate?)
    design $36.00
Butter mold, cylinder, fern pattern $40.00
Butter press, handmade, acorn design $58.00
Butter mold, dovetailed box,
    double strawberry design .... $60.00 to $75.00
Butter mold, box in 2 lb. size, makes 8
    mini prints of flowers and fruit .... $75.00 to $110.00
Butter mold, plunger type, machine-
    carved wheat sheaf, 7" high .... $65.00 to $75.00
Butter mold, wood and nickeled-brass
    hardware, 2-piece rectangular
    box, imprints "JERSEY" .... $85.00 to $95.00
Butter mold, wood, 2-piece, round
    print of acorns above a leafy
    branch, piecrust edge, 5" diameter ...... $70.00 to $90.00
Butter mold, wood, very small,
    marked "Munsing" $18.00
Butter mold, wood, box style, makes
    four 4-petaled flowers and four
    8-pointed stars, marked "Porter
    Blanchards Son's Co., Nashua,
    N.H." .... $100.00 to $115.00
Butter print, single 4-petal flower $50.00
Butter print/stamp, flower design
    with ring border, 2⅔" diameter $65.00
Butter stamp, deep-carved cow $150.00
Butter stamp, nicely carved cow $145.00
Butter print, cow with sunburst
    border, 4¼" diameter $200.00
Butter print, carving of strawberries
    with leaves and a flower, 4¾" diameter $145.00
Butter stamp, acorns and 2 oaks
    leaves, 4" diameter $85.00
Butter stamp, primitive rope border
    design around three fat-petaled flowers $65.00
Butter print, deep-cut pineapple
    design, 4¼" diameter $72.00
Butter print, for single pat, rose and
    leaves, 1 7/8" diameter $95.00
Butter print, for single pat, snowflake
    design, 1 7/8" diameter $85.00

Figure IV-15. **Butter Stamp.** Deep-carved cow with serrated edge. American 19th century. 3½" diameter. Estimated to go at recent auction for $200-$300. Realized: $150. Picture courtesy of Robert W. Skinner Inc., Auctioneers, Bolton, MA.

Figure IV-16. **Butter Stamp.** Described by the auction house as "highly stylized eagle." I can see the arrows, gripped in claws, but cannot see head of eagle. American 19th century. 3½" diameter. Estimated: $300-$400, but didn't sell. Picture courtesy of Robert W. Skinner, Inc., Auctioneers, Bolton, MA.

Butter stamp, for single pat, 3 very finely-carved designs of a 3-leaf clover, a thistle and a rose, only 1¾" diameter $100.00

Butter stamp, unusual double-sided, design of a vase of flowers, and on other side, a dove, 3¼" diameter $180.00

Butter stamp, small carved eagle with an 8-sided star, 2¾" diameter. American 19th century, estimated to sell at 1982 auction for $250-$350 .... $125.00

Figure IV-17. **Butter Stamp.** Deer with stylized leaves and corn plant — which he may have been eating! American 19th century, 4" diameter. Estimated to sell for $300-$400. Realized: $275. Picture courtesy of Robert W. Skinner Inc., Auctioneers, Bolton, MA.

Butter stamp, incised eagle with
    branch in beak, 3½" diameter,
    American 19th century, estimated
    at '82 auction to go for $250/$350 .... $200.00
Butter stamp, deeply carved cow with
    leaves, 4¼" diameter, American
    19th century, estimated $200/$300 .... $100.00

Hard to tell why the above sold for so much less than they were estimated at.

Butter stamp, handcarved, thistle design ..... $40.00 to $75.00
Butter stamp, very fine incised sheep design $160.00
Butter stamp, "lollipop" style, large
    size, stylized flowers and geometric
    border .... $160.00 to $190.00
Butter stamp, lollipop style, carved
    with 6-petal flower, serrated
    border, elongated shield-shaped
    handle ending in heart, 10" long,
    from Maine sold at Julia's Antique
    Barn, Fairfield Maine, in 1982 for
    a whopping but not undeserved $685.00

195

Figure IV-18. **Butter Stamp.** Anchor fouled with line. Minor cracks and handle missing, 3 3/8" diameter. American 19th century. Estimated at $350-$450 because of desirable subject and nice carving, but crack and missing handle did it in. Realized only: $75. Picture courtesy of Robert W. Skinner Inc., Auctioneers, Bolton, Ma.

Figure IV-19. **Butter Stamp.** Scallop shell with double border. 3½" diameter, American 19th century. Estimated between $250-$350. Realized $100. Picture courtesy of Robert W. Skinner Inc., Auctioneers, Bolton, MA.

Figure IV-20. **Butter Stamp.** Lovely design of bluebird on leafy branch. 3" diameter. American 19th century. Estimated: $200-$300. Realized: $225. Picture courtesy of Robert W. Skinner Inc., Auctioneers, Bolton, MA.

Figure IV-21. **Butter Stamp.** Incised pelican standing on one leg. American 19th century, 3¼" diameter. Estimated: $350-$450. Realized: $175. Picture courtesy of Robert W. skinner Inc., Auctioneers, Bolton, MA.

Figure IV-22. **Butter Stamp.** Dentil-carved heart within a wreath of laurel. Seen behind is a drying stand for the stamp. Pennsylvania German, 19th century. Print: 4" diameter, stand: 5" diameter. Very simple but attractive. Estimated: $500-$600. Realized: $200. Picture courtesy of Robert W. Skinner Inc., Auctioneers, Bolton, MA.

Figure IV-23. **Butter Stamp.** Standing grouse. American 19th century, 3¼" diameter. Estimated: $300-$400. Realized: $300. Picture courtesy of Robert W. Skinner Inc., Auctioneers, Bolton, MA.

Figure IV-24. **Butter Stamp.** Deeply carved ram with flowers. American 19th century, 4¼" diameter. Estimated: $400-$500. Realized: $350. Picture courtesy of Robert W. Skinner Inc., Auctioneers, Bolton, MA.

Figure IV-25. **Butter Stamp.** Demilune stamp with pineapple — symbol of hospitality. 19th century. 7¼" wide x 4" high. Estimated between $250-$350, but for some reason didn't sell. Really a lovely piece. Picture courtesy of Robert W. Skinner Inc., Auctioneers, Bolton, MA.

Figure IV-26. **Butter Stamp.** Small deeply carved ewe, only 2 7/8" diameter. American 19th century. Small crack. Estimated: $300-$400. Realized: $275. Picture courtesy of Robert W. Skinner Inc., Auctioneers, Bolton, MA.

Figure IV-27. **Butter Stamp.** Eagle on branch with star above head. Piecrust edge. "A.F. Thompson. New York" carved within border. Cracked and repaired. 4½" diameter, 19th century American. Estimated: $400-$500, but didn't sell. Picture courtesy of Robert W. Skinner Inc., Auctioneers, Bolton, MA.

Butter print, knob handle, handcarved
"Crow's Foot" design, 3" diameter $55.00
Butter stamp, with knob handle,
well-cut cow with folk art pointy
legs, ears and horns . . . . $225.00 to $275.00
Butter stamp, handcarved cow at
barnyard gate, piecrust border . . . . $225.00 to $250.00

Figure IV-28. **Butter Prints.** Eagle motif, finely carved. One is mounted on an old butter paddle. Stamp is 3 5/8" diameter; other is 3¾" diameter. 19th century. Estimated at 1980 Brooke sale between $400-$600. Realized $260. Shield body eagle, 4¾" diameter, was not sold. Picture courtesy of Christie, Manson & Woods International Inc.

Figure IV-28. **Butter Hands.** Corrugated maple. Also called "Scotch Hands." Author's collection. Value: $12-$15.

Figure IV-29. **Butter Mold.** Wood and iron. This press made a pound block of butter. 5¾" long x 3 5/8" wide. 19th century. Picture courtesy of the National Museum of American History, Smithsonian Institution.

Butter print, knob handle,
    handcarved eagle, 5" diameter $195.00
Butter print, handcarved 6-point
    snowflake, very short knob
    handle, 4" diameter $95.00
Butter stamp and butter paddle
    combined, one piece of wood,
    handcarved, the stamp has a cow
    and 2 acorns, paddle 14" long
    overall, stamp 4" diameter,
    American 19th century. Estimated
    to go at auction in 1982 for
    $600/$800 because of its rarity
    and interest. Sold for $500.00

NOTE: Maine Antique Digest reported in July 1982 what they think "is probably a record" price for a buttermold . . . $800 for a beautifully deep-carved print of an eagle with shield body, and the words "JAMES HOFMAN - SHIP BUILDER" around the border. Do you know of a higher price?

For other butter paddles [without stamps] see the "TURN, RETRIEVE, SPOON & LIFT" category further on.

Butter slicer, nickel plated iron,
    porcelainized cast iron base,
     "Elgin #48," Cleveland
     Faucet Co., pat'd December 31,
     1901 in Canada, September 1911
     in U.S.A., quarters a pound butter
     block, then slices into pats,
     probably for hotel or restaurant
     use. 8½" long x 8½" high $32.00

Figure IV-30. **Butter Mold.** Carved wood in five parts with holding pegs. Simple star design. Marked with stylized flowers and initials "H.Y." Block made is 3 3/8" x 2" x 2¾" deep. Some people say this is a maple sugar mold. Can you set me straight for sure? Collection of Meryle Evans. Value: $85-$125.

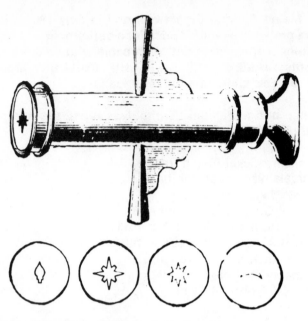

Figure IV-31. **Butter Press or Jumble Mold.** Tin with wood plunger. Various fancy-holed inserts. From F.A. Walker catalog, c. 1870s. Value: $18-$28.

Figure IV-32. **Butter Slicer.** "Elgin No. 48" Cleveland Faucet Co., pat'd December 31, 1901 in Canada, September 1911 in U.S.A. Porcelainized cast iron base, nickel-plated cutter frame, wire blades. This would quarter a pound block of butter then slice it into pats . . . for restaurant use. 8½" long x 8½" high. Photographed at Bonnie Barnes' Anteek Corner, Waynesboro, VA. Value: $45-$55.

Cake decorations, set of 4 Beatles
 figures, in original 1965 package $9.00
Cake decoration/candle holders,
 painted iron flowers $25.00
Cake decorator/frosting tubes, tin, 8
 various heads $20.00
Cake decorator set, "Ateco," pat'd
 1925, in box with 12 tubes and
 instruction book. Still being
 mfd., but if old .... $15.00 to $20.00
Cake mold, cast iron, lamb $35.00
Cake mold, cast iron, sitting rabbit $555.00

Franklin Cake, An Old Time Thanksgiving Dainty

Mix together a pint of molasses and a half-pint milk in
which cut up a half-pound butter. Warm just enough to
melt butter, and stir in six ounces of brown sugar, adding
three tablespoons of ginger, one tablespoon powdered
cinnamon, one teaspoon powdered cloves, and a grated
nutmeg. Beat seven eggs very light, and stir them
gradually into the mixture, in turn with a pound and two
ounces sifted flour. Add the grated peel and juice of two
lemons. Stir very hard. Put in buttered tins and bake in a
moderate oven."
From "The Home-Maker" magazine, November 1889

Cake mold, cast iron, Krum Kake,
 mfd. by Andreason, Minneapolis $45.00
Cake mold, redware, 2-piece sitting
 (horizontal) rabbit, mid-19th century $180.00
Cake mold, tubed redware with yellow
 glaze, marked "John Bell,
 Waynesboro," 19th century $190.00
Cake mold, redware, Turk's head, 7¾"
 diameter $75.00
Cake mold, creamware, Turk's head
 with spout or tube, 9" diameter $38.00
Cake mold, cast iron, sitting
 lamb, #866, 9" long $85.00
Cake mold, cast aluminum but heavy,
 vertical sitting rabbit, 10" high $26.00
Cake mold, cast iron, lamb .... $30.00 to $50.00

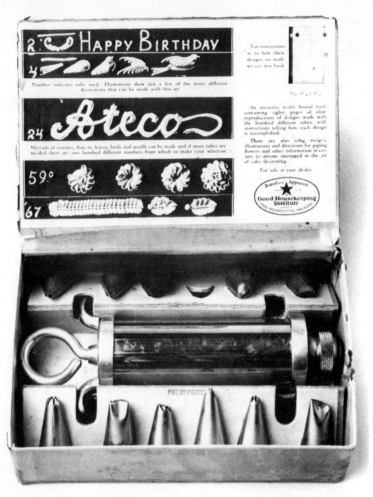

Figure IV-33. **Cake Decorating Set.** Ateco, pat'd 1925. Complete with instruction booklet and various size tubes for frosting. Original box. Value: $15-$20.

Cake mold, cast iron, Santa Claus,
    mfd. by Griswold $125.00
Cake pan, cast iron, old Bundt (new
    ones are aluminum with Teflon) $35.00
Cake pan, tin, angel cake with tube
    and handles, "Vanity Co." $14.00
Cake pan, blackened tin, octagonal
    with tube, 13" diameter, 19th century $35.00
Cake pan, tin, tubed angel food,
    "Swans Down Cake Flour" .... $8.00 to $10.00

Cake pan, tin, adv'g "George
    Urban Milling Co., Buffalo, N.Y. $25.00
Cake pan, tin, adv'g "Calumet Baking
    Powder" .... $7.00 to $9.00
Cake pan, tin, "Swan's Down Angel
    Food Cake" .... $10.00 to $12.00
Cake pan, blackened tin, tubed and
    with scalloped edge, 8" diameter,
    late 19th century .... $10.00 to $20.00
Cake pan, stamped tin, Turk's head
    tubed, 9" diameter .... $10.00 to $15.00
Cake pans (two), tin in colorful card-
    board box, "Kate Smith's Bake-A-
    Cake Kit," with recipes, 9" pans .... $12.00 to $25.00

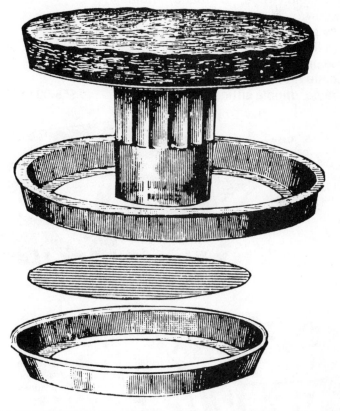

Figure IV-34. **Cake Mold.** Tin in 4 parts. Makes either spouted or tubed cake like angel food, or regular cake. "Perfection." 19th century. Value: $7-$12.

Cake pan, aqua and white graniteware
   spouted for angel food cake, 9"
   diameter .... $18.00 to $25.00
Candy mold, pewter, seated dogs $35.00
Candy mold, tin, sitting rabbit .... $12.00 to $18.00
Candy mold, tin, standing rabbit,
   6" high .... $12.00 to $18.00
Candy mold, tin, double seated
   rabbits, only 4" high .... $18.00 to $25.00
Candy mold, pewter, pair of eagles .... $45.00 to $55.00

Cheese basket or drainer: see section on "Separate, Strain & Sift"

Cheese mold, wood, 10" round, prints
   a cow $55.00
Cheese press, oak and maple, stands
   on floor, large $55.00
Cheese press, oak, fancier legs, 38" high $62.00
Chocolate mold, heavy leaded tin, iron
   frame, double sitting-up rabbits .... $58.00 to $65.00

Figure IV-35. **Cake Mold.** Tin, octagon tubed shape. Came in several sizes from 2 to 6 quarts. From Matthai-Ingram catalog, c. 1890. Value: $8-$15.

Figure IV-36. **Spouted Turban Mold.** Tin. Came in 2, 4, 5 and 6 quart sizes. From Matthai-Ingram catalog, c. 1890. Value: $15-$20.

Figure IV-37. **Kugelhopf Spouted Mold,** two views. Tin. Collection of Mary Mac Franklin. Value: $25-$35.

Chocolate mold, heavy metal, 6 Santa
   Clauses .... $35.00 to $48.00
Chocolate mold, tin, running rabbit,
   marked "Brandt's" .... $15.00 to $18,00
Chocolate mold, tin, standing rabbit,
   6" high .... $18.00 to $25.00

Figure IV-38. **Cake Mold.** Brown-glazed earthenware. 19th century American. Spouted with handle. 9½" diameter x 3 1/8" high. Formerly in the Keillor Collection. Value: $120-$145.

Figure IV-39. **Mold for Cake.** Tin, 12 pieces forming heart. Each piece of cake apparently the same size, so no fights at Valentine parties! Also came in floral crosses, rounds, diamonds, and horn of plenty. From F.A. Walker catalog, 1870s. Value: $15-$22.

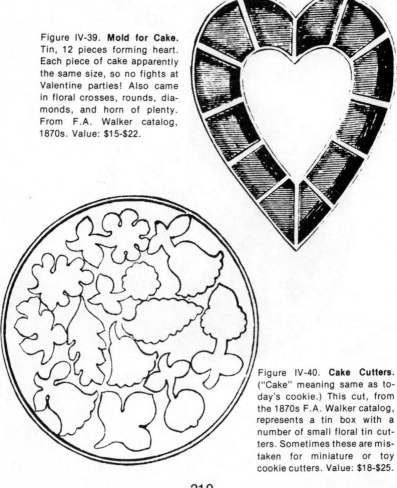

Figure IV-40. **Cake Cutters.** ("Cake" meaning same as today's cookie.) This cut, from the 1870s F.A. Walker catalog, represents a tin box with a number of small floral tin cutters. Sometimes these are mistaken for miniature or toy cookie cutters. Value: $18-$25.

210

Figure IV-41. **Chocolate Mold.** Heavy tin, standing Santa Claus. Late 19th or early 20th century. 7" high. Picture courtesy of the National Museum of American History, Smithsonian Institution.

Figure IV-42. **Chocolate Mold.** Cast metal, with heavy tinning. "AUERBACH" and letters of alphabet. 12" x 6" x ¾" thick and makes chocolate wafers 3/16" thick. We shot the back side, not the mold side. Collection of Meryle Evans. Value: $50.

Figure IV-43. **Chocolate Mold.** Heavy tin. Makes 3 monkeys, but they are not "hear no evil, speak no evil, see no evil," nor "eat no evil!" 7" long x 3¾" high. Collection of Meryle Evans. Value: $45-$65.

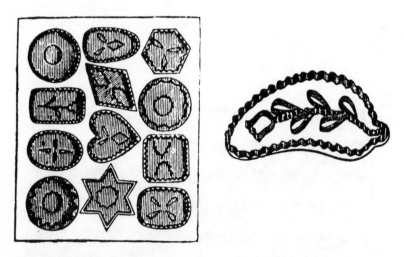

Figure IV-44. **Cookie Cutters.** Tin. Picture from **Scammel's Treasure-House of Knowledge,** 1891. Book states "These two engravings show a few of the many designs in cake cutters made of tin, to give fancy forms to cakes. They may be had of all house furnishing stores, and are among the luxuries of the kitchen — very nice where they can be afforded, and they are not very costly. The effect is pretty when different or even a single fancy form is used." Value: $8-$15 each.

Chocolate mold, heavy tin, rooster, 3
hinged sections, 10" high $43.00
Chocolate mold, tin, a pair of rabbits
(one is bigger) with an Easter basket ..... $30.00 to $42.00
Chocolate mold, tin, standing rabbit
with a basket "back pack," 8½" high ..... $25.00 to $32.00
Chocolate mold, tin, 2" rabbit $13.00
Chocolate mold, tin, standing rabbit,
7" high $26.00
Chocolate mold, pewter, a child with cat $45.00
Chocolate mold, pewter, turkey, hinge
and clamp .... $30.00 to $42.00
Cookie cutter (also often referred to as
"cake cutter"), tin, flatback style,
eagle with spread wings, 6¼"
wide, late 19th century .... $35.00 to $50.00
Cookie cutter, tin, flatback, makes a
tobacco pipe(!) shaped cookie,
for Father's Day? 5½" long .... $35.00 to $45.00

Figure IV-45. **Cookie Cutter.** Heart-in-hand, the working side. Tin, with strap handle. 19th century. Picture courtesy of the National Museum of American History, Smithsonian Institution.

Figure IV-46. **Cookie Cutter.** Handmade tin, 19th century. Famous Shaker "heart in hand." Very small. Courtesy of The Smithsonian Institution, Museum of History and Technology.

NOTE: The Smithsonian's wonderful hand-and-heart cutter has been adapted and made by hand by tinsmiths Bill and Bob Cukla. The original is only 2¾" long, but the modern one [about $12.00 from the Smithsonian] is much larger . . . 5" high x 3½" wide.

Cookie cutter, tin, flatback, simple fish $22.00
Cookie cutter, tin, strap handle, Santa
     Claus, 9" high, along with a tin
     Christmas tree cutter, both $225.00
Cookie cutter, tin, flatback, wonderful
     profile of full figure of Uncle Sam,
     with tail coat and high hat, 12½" high $160.00
Cookie cutter, tin, flatback, very
     primitive standing man with hat,
     8½" high, I loved this one at $98.00
Cookie cutter, tin, flatback with
     several small "release" or air
     holes, simple chick $12.00
Cookie cutter, tin, flatback with strap
     handle, a running dog . . . very
     like a Scottie, 4½" long x 3" wide $20.00
Cookie cutter, tin, Santa Claus without
     much appeal, 20th century, 3½" high $5.00
Cookie cutter, tin, flatback, small
     distelfink, 3" long $8.50

Figure IV-47. **Cookie Cutters.** Tin and tin and wood. Top left is mid-19th century fluted or corrugated tin with two holes to facilitate removal of dough. Top right is crudely-shaped woman's form in long dress, nailed to wooden back. Mid-19th century. Middle left looks homemade, but I have seen several quite similar — described variously as "preacher with book" and "Uncle Sam." It is nearly a foot high. Middle right is a partially corrugated eagle soldered to scrap tin, trimmed roughly to size. c. 1840s-1870s. At bottom is a Pennsylvania German **distelfink** — their popular finch form. Values: $20-$25; $60-$90; $100-$150; $45-$65; $20-$28.

215

Figure IV-48. **Cookie Cutters.** Light blue plastic with fine details. "Stanley Rome Products." 1950s-60s. 5" Santa; 4½" Xmas tree. Author's collection. Value: $.50-$1.50 each.

Figure IV-49. **Cookie Cutter.** Tin horse on rough-trimmed back. From Montgomery Ward catalog, c. 1895. Came in assorted animal forms. Cost 4 cents back then. Value now: $6-$10.

Figure IV-50. **Cookie Cutters.** Gingerbread Boys. Left: tin, fairly recent manufacture, 8" high; right: aluminum, 1940s, 5¾" high. Author's collection. Value: $1.50-$3.00

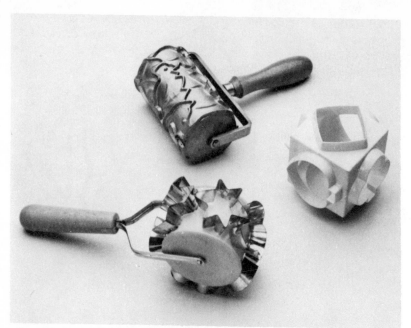

Figure IV-51. **Cookie Cutters.** Multi-pattern. Plastic cube at right is EKCO, 4 bridge club motifs: heart, spade, diamond, club, plus half moon and star. 3½" square. 1980. Top rolling cutter: heavy cast metal drum, many interlocking designs, bird on branch, elf, bear, another bird, bell, rabbit, chicken, chick, Xmas tree with star on top. Natural finish wood handle. 7¾" long. No marks. 1960s-1980. Bottom: rolling mold, yellow plastic drum on which are a molded cross, 4-pointed star, odd shamrock, circle, heart and a whatsit. yellow wood handle. Marked "Made in Hong Kong." Recent manufacture. 9¾" long. Author's collection. Value: $2-$5.

Cookie cutters, tin, flatback, various animals as follows:

nice eagle, 4½" wide	$36.00
eagle, boring, 4" wide	$20.00
simple ax, 5" long	$40.00
running horse, 7½" long	$45.00
rooster, 5½" high	$22.00
chicken, 5" high	$28.00
Small, simple woman with long skirt, no arms	$38.00
horse on platform (at auction?), 6" long	$28.00
rather big distelfink, 5½" high	$34.00
horse's head, 4½" high	$55.00
odd-looking ax	$22.00
small auto, 4½" long	$35.00
simple pitcher, 4½" high	$45.00
standing woman (this one with arms)	$22.00
standing man, 7" high	$28.00
chicken, definitely 20th century	$5.00

NOTE: Most of the cookie cutters on the previous page are just primitive enough to look handmade, if not homemade. Most of the ones with flatbacks don't have a strap handle, and the flatbacks are trimmed irregularly from scrap tin.

Cookie cutter, tin, homemade and
primitive horse with very short,
slightly bent, legs, 7" long, really neat $130.00
Cookie cutter, copper, very plain
geometric female form . . . a
woman in a long dress: small
circle for head, larger circle for
upper body, large triangle for
skirt, no arms, 2 push-out holes,
very nice, 8" high $55.00

Figure IV-52. **Cookie Mold.** Carved wood, great detail. 19th century. Collection of Mary Mac Franklin. Value: $85-$150.

219

Cookie cutter, tin, strap handle, flying bird $12.00
Cookie cutter, tin, strap handle, bird
   on branch, possibly a Pennsylvania
   German distelfink $12.00
Cookie cutter, tin, standing man,
   rather primitive, this type not really
   my idea of a "gingerbread man",
   7" high $40.00
Cookie cutter, tin, flatback, eagle $30.00
Cookie cutter, tin, flatback, daisy-like
   flower $30.00
Cookie cutters, tin, set of four bridge
   cutters: heart, diamond, spade,
   club, in original '30's box $22.00
Cookie cutter, tin, strap handle
   attached to flatback, a chubby
   gingerbread boy $12.00
Cookie cutter, tin, possibly a toy
   because it's only 1½" high, rabbit $7.00
Cookie cutter, tin, simple lion, 20th century .... $8.00 to $12.00
Cookie cutter, tin, "Davis Baking
   Powder," duck $8.00
Cookie cutter, rolling, tin with wire
   handle, has 3 interchangeable
   rolls: diamonds, waffling, swirls,
   mfd. by Guirier, in original box, c. 1930 .... $25.00
Cookie cutter, tin, strap handle,
   Dutchman in wooden shoes and
   wide pantaloons, 4¾" high $22.00
Cookie cutter, tin, daisy with 10 petals,
   3¾" diameter $10.00
Cookie cutter, tin, strap handle, half-moon $5.00
Cookie cutter, tin, Robin Hood flour,
   Maid Marion $8.00
Cookie mold or wafer mold, bird on
   branch with 5 stars, no handles,
   5" x 3½" oval $110.00

**NOTE: Tin cookie cutters were easily made from scrap pieces by
the householder or by traveling tinkers. If you think of all the
special subjects your family is interested in, then imagine how
many many shapes handmade cookie cutters can be expected to
be found in!**

Cookie cutter, tin, Moravian 10-point
    star, 2" diameter .... $12.00 to $15.00
Cookie cutter, tin, fluted edges with
    strap handle, 3" diameter x 5"
    high (including handle) .... $5.00 to $10.00

Cookie molds: see Springerle molds

Cookie press, tin, small cylinder with
    side "wings" used to hold it while
    pressing the plunger. Could be
    fitted with several different pierced
    flat tin plates which expressed
    the cookie dough in fancy shapes.
    Also used as a butter press for
    fancy pats. C. 1870s .... $15.00 to $25.00
Cookie press, tin with wooden plunger,
    star-shaped opening, 10½" long $27.00

Figure IV-53. **Cutting Board.** This beautiful thing is made of slate not wood. Arrow-shaped handle with hole for hanging cord. 17½" diameter. American, early 19th century. Sold for $500. Picture courtesy of Robert W. Skinner Inc., Auctioneers, Bolton, MA.

221

Cookie press, tin with wood plunger,
no handles $20.00
Corn stick pan, cast iron, Wagner
Ware, "Krusty Korn Kobs, Jr.",
well-modeled corn cobs, pat'd
1920, 12½" long .... $12.00 to $22.00
Corn stick mold, cast iron with wire
handles, "Wagner Ware," makes
2 full "cobs" about 5½" long,
c. 1880 .... $12.00 to $18.00
Corn stick mold, same as above only
makes 4 cobs .... $12.00 to $22.00

Figure IV-54. **Cornbread Mold.** "Griswold Crispy Corn Stick Pan," c. 1920s. NOTE: Wagner made one almost identical, called "Krusty Korn Kobs Baking Mold." Wagner also made them in a Tea size — 4 1/8" x 7 1/8", Senior size — 6 7/8" x 13¾"; and Junior size — 5 7/8" x 11 5/8". Picture courtesy of Lar Hothem. Value: $10-$18.

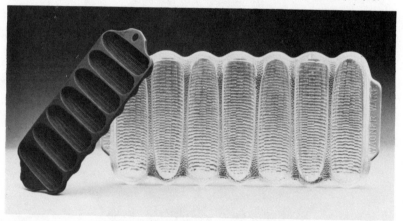

Figure IV-55. **Corn Stick Pans.** Left: cast iron, "Griswold Krispy Cornorwheat Stick Pan #262," Erie, PA. 8½" long x 4 1/8" wide. Makes 7 corn sticks. Right: heavy glass Wagner Ware. 13" long x 6" wide. Makes 7 sticks. Which makes me wonder out loud, why did muffin and roll pans always make odd numbers? Was it a lucky thing? How did you divide uneven numbers? Collection of Meryle Evans. Value of Griswold: $12-$18. Value of Wagner: $20-$35.

Figure IV-56. **Cracker Stamp**. Cast iron, spring steel with wooden block with little 2-pronged "nails" or prickers. With spring load action, this knocks out pricked crackers just short of 2" square. Stamp is 3¾" high. Pat'd December 13, no year marked, I'd say 1870s. Collection of Meryle Evans. Value: $25-$35.

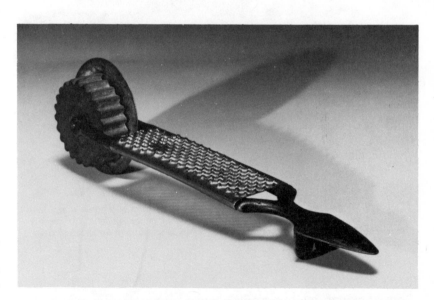

Figure IV-57. **Crimper and Grater Combination Tool.** Tin and wood and cast metal. The grater was probably used for something used in pies — nutmeg most likely. The pointed end may be a can opener or had a pie-making function, perhaps to core or cut an ingredient or to make slashes in the top of a 2-crust pie. 19th century American. 6 7/8" long. Picture courtesy of the National Museum of American History, Smithsonian Institution.

223

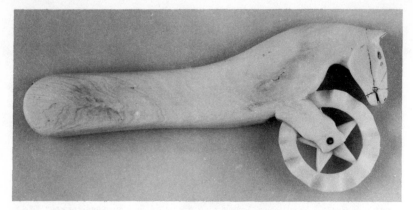

Figure IV-58. **Crimper**. Scrimshaw jagging wheel with horse's head. Early 19th century American. 6" long. Realized at auction: $550. Picture courtesy of Robert W. Skinner Inc., Auctioneers, Bolton, MA.

Figure IV-59. **Crimper.** Scrimshaw piecrust edger in the form of a horse with a fish tail — a sea horse? Notice the nice hearts cut-out in the wheel. 19th century American. 5¾" long. Picture courtesy of the National Museum of American History, Smithsonian Institution.

Corn stick pan, aluminum, Wagner
   Ware "Krusty Korn Kobs," tea
   size, 4 1/8" x 7 1/8" $13.00
Corn stick mold, gray graniteware, small $15.00
Corn stick mold, nickel plated iron,
   Griswold $12.00

NOTE: Iron Craft, of Freedom, New Hampshire, makes a cast iron corn stick pan shaped very much like the Griswold pans, although the cobs do not appear to be quite as well defined. They make three sizes: for 5, 7 and 9 "cobs." Approximately $5.00 to $8.00 retail. By the way, does anyone have a logical reason why all the corn stick molds and muffin pans seem to make odd numbers of sticks or muffins?

NOTE: For convenience, I've called all the following "crimpers," but they go by many names: pastry jagger, pie jagger, or trimmer, jagger, coggling wheel and dough spur, runner or rimmer.

Crimper, turned maple with bone wheel, 4½" long, 19th century	$25.00 to $45.00
Crimper, brass, wheel at one end, curved semi-circle at other, 19th century	$28.00 to $35.00
Crimper, rosewood with porcelain wheel, 19th century	$45.00 to $60.00
Crimper, cast aluminum, 4¾" long, 1920s or '30s	$6.00 to $10.00
Crimper, aluminum, "Juice Tite Pie Sealer," 5½" long	$8.00 to $12.00
Crimper, cast and machined brass, 4½" long	$18.00 to $30.00
Crimper, turned fruitwood with ebony wheel, 4¾" long, c. 1880s	$20.00 to $40.00
Crimper, green and white plastic, 1930s	$8.00 to $20.00
Crimper, handcarved wood, 8" long, c. 1860s or '70s	$25.00 to $45.00
Crimper, wood, 2 different wheels, one at each end, 8" long	$60.00 to $80.00
Crimper, scrimshaw, simple	$225.00 and up
Crimper, scrimshaw, decorative or figural	$350.00 and up

NOTE: At the beautiful, Barbara Johnson collection auction, scrimshaw jaggers, many quite architectural in their carving, one with a fantastically-fluted double wheel [side-by-side like bike wheels] went for fabulous prices . . . from $750.00 to $1700.00! Others, highly ornamental but not figural either, went for $275 [with a broken prong] to $1550.00. At another auction, a number of whale ivory and walrus ivory wheels, none figural, got between $225 and $650.

Figure IV-60. **Crimpers or Pastry Jaggers.** Large wheel is all wood, 19th century, 7" long, homemade? Collection of Meryle Evans. Next is galvanized tin sealer with plain wood handle, 6½" long, late 19th century, homemade. Next is cast aluminum, very cheapo, 4½" long, 20th century; last is Vaughn's Pie Trimmer & Sealer, pat'd May 10, 1921. Aluminum wheel, green wood handle. Author's collection. Value: $8-$20.

Crimper, nickel-plated shank, red
wood handle, aluminum wheel,
"Vaughn's Pie Trimmer & Sealer,"
5½" long .... $8.00 to $10.00
Crimper, brass with unusual straight
handle with slight knob at end, 6"
long, well-priced at $22.00
Crimper, wood with bone wheel,
turned handle, 5" long $28.00
Crimper, iron wheel with turned wood
handle $30.00

226

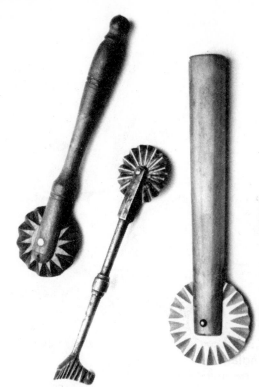

Figure IV-61. **Crimpers or Jaggers.** Left to right: turned wood with ebony-like wheel, 19th century; machined brass, commercially manufactured, 19th century; "ivory plastic and asparagus green plastic handle, c. 1915-1920s. Value, in order: $20-$40, $28-$35, $8-$20.

Crimper, cast iron with wood handle,
    9" long $8.00
Crimper, brass $15.00

NOTE: This price was from an ad. I believe that because of the price, this jagger must be one of the crudely-cast brass crimpers . . . perhaps from India? although I have no evidence of that.

Crimper, iron shaft, brass wheel,
    wood handle, 7½" long $45.00
Crimper, fancily fashioned brass
    wheel with turned wood handle
    and original hang-up ring $125.00
Crimper, carved bone $38.00
Crimper, carved birds'-eye maple $35.00
Crimper, all brass, 9" long, priced
    too high at $88.00

Figure IV-62. **"Four-and-Twenty Blackbirds Baked in a Pie!"** Illustration from 1880's children's magazine, **St. Nicholas.** This nursery rhyme from the early 19th century (?) is what led to **pie birds** — vents for pies made of everything from ceramic to brass. Some collectors specialize in pie birds. Among the ones I've seen: cream color ceramic with pink and green trim, $12; black ceramic, $14; rooster, $12. Other forms, such as black chef, are also referred to as pie "birds".

Crimper, brass shaft, steel wheel,
    wood handle, 9" long $80.00
Crimper, steel handle and brass wheel
    finely made, early 19th century $110.00

NOTE: The Metropolitan Museum of Art, New York, has created in its workshops a beautiful replica of an early 19th century pastry jagger. Made of steel, with a roughly "S" shaped bar, it has at one end a simple bird, and at the other a fishtail. It's 10½" long and sells through their catalog and in their gift shop for about $170.00.

Figure IV-63. **Crimper, Pie Trimmer and Marker.** "This simple little instrument trims off the surplus pie-crust that projects over the plate, and at the same time neatly ornaments the border. It is one of the indispensable conveniences of the kitchen after it has once been used. Pies can be made without it, but if ornamentation does not add to the nutriment, it pleases the eye and aids digestion, and pies are not famous for being the most digestible articles in the world, no matter how carefully made." So says **Scammell's Treasure-House of Knowledge,** 1891.

Figure IV-64. **Crimper.** "The Ideal Pie Cutter and Crimper." From Seastrand catalog, c. 1929. States "You are familiar with the old way of making pies, which necessitates a number of operations, therefore requiring considerable time. Why not save time by using the Ideal Pie Cutter and Crimper? The only perfect pie cutter and crimper on the market. It not only makes a cleaner cut and a neater crimp, but it presses both crusts firmly together, thus preventing the rich juices from boiling over. Price 25 cents." Value: $8-$10.

Cutlet mold, pieced tin, shaped like
    cutlets or big fat commas, 1880s-1900 .... $5.00 to $12.00
Doughnut cutter, stainless steel and
    wood, T-handle, "The Saturn," 1930s ..... $7.00 to $10.00
Doughnut cutter, tin, "Rumford
    Baking Powder," $10.00
Doughnut cutter and apple corer
    combo, tin, corer can be removed
    from cutter, turn-of-century .... $8.00 to $15.00

Figure IV-65. **Cutters.** Two top ones are tin, other is wood. Combination tool — apple corer, doughnut maker, fluted cookie cutter, strainer, 6" long, 3" diameter cup. 19th century. Star shaped cookie cutter, tin, 4" diameter, unusually deep — 3½" to handle, just the cutter itself is 2½" deep. Wooden doughnut cutter, well turned 4½" long x 2 3/8" diameter. 19th century. Collection of Meryle Evans. Value: $12-$22.

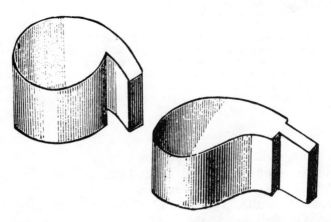

Figure IV-66. **Cutlet Cutters.** Tin. From F.A. Walker catalog, 1870s. Value: $5-$12.

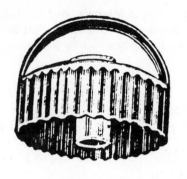

Figure IV-67. **Doughnut Cutter.** Two views. Fluted tin with strap handle, pat'd October 15, 1889. From F.A. Walker catalog, c. 1890. Value: $8-$12.

Doughnut cutter, tin and wire, works
two ways: makes a plain doughnut
or makes scalloped edge cookies,
turn-of-century .... $8.00 to $15.00
Doughnut cutter, tin, strap handle,
1920s to '40s .... $5.00 to $8.00
Doughnut form, iron with wood
handle, "Cloverleaf Doughnut
Form," Ace Co., late 1800s .... $35.00 to $50.00

Ground Rice Flummery

"Boil one quart milk, except that portion which you have reserved to wet a heaping teacup of rice. Stir this in when the milk boils up; put in one teaspoon of salt. When it has thickened, stir in a table spoonful or two of dry ground rice; let it boil up again all around, and take it off the fire as soon as you think the dry rice has become scalded. Have ready a bowl or blancmange mould, wet with a spoonful of milk or cold water, into which pour it. If it is of the right consistency, it will turn out after 15 or 20 minutes in good shape. Eat with sugar and milk or cream. For this and all similar milk preparations, peach leaves are better than any spice. Boil in the milk one-half dozen fresh leaves from the tree. Remember to take them out before you stir in the rice. If you put in too many, they will give a strong flavor to the article."
The Young Housekeepers Friend, Mrs. Cornelius, 1846

Food, Jelly or Blancmange molds. This is the category of molds which come in fancy shapes and were used for dishes that were gelatinized. Aspics, molded desserts, jellies — like the familiar modern cranberry sauce, etc.

Blancmange molds, pair, tin, scalloped
    base with octagonal "lighthouse"
    top, 11½" high, c. 1870s .... $35.00 to $50.00
Blancmange mold, tin, form of
    multiple spires, 8½" high .... $20.00 to $35.00
Blancmange mold, heavy copper with
    tin lining, 6 columnar pieces
    forming mold, 15" high $320.00
Blancmange molds, 8-sided but similar
    to above, only 5" to 6" high .... $350.00 to $450.00
Border mold, copper with heavy tin
    lining, fluted and tubed, 6" deep
    11" diameter $155.00
Border mold, ring mold, tin, marked
    "KREAMER 2," 9½" x 6¼" oval $22.00
Border mold or ring, copper with
    heavy tin lining, geometric oval,
    7" long $185.00
Ring mold, tin, deep molding with
    13 hearts, 8½" diameter $185.00
Ring mold, copper, heavily tinned, oval $275.00
Border mold, tin, scalloped edge with
    plain inside ring, turn-of-century .... $10.00 to $20.00
Border mold, stamped tin, fruit design
    on top, plain sides .... $15.00 to $25.00
Food mold, tubed Turk's head, tin, 9"
    diameter x 7" deep $20.00
Food mold, fluted gray graniteware,
    7" diameter x 2½" high $20.00
Food mold, tin, tubed with 9 sections
    shaped like "Mr. Softee" ice cream
    cones, 9" diameter, hanging ring $175.00
Food mold, tin, old fish shape, 9" long $85.00
Food mold, copper with tin lining,
    oval and tubed, 8" long x 4" deep $135.00
Food molds, copper, tin lined, English,
    5" to 6" long $375.00
Food mold, copper with tin lining,
    corn design $75.00

Food mold, tin, grape design, 2¾" x
    3¼" long $10.00
Food mold, copper with tin lining,
    rose design in top, 7" long x 5" wide $70.00
Food mold, copper with heavy tin
    lining, oval with Cornucopia
    design, 4½" long x 3½" wide x
    1½" deep $42.00
Food mold, copper and tin, thistle design $75.00
Food mold, copper with tin, wheat design $70.00
Food mold, copper rose with tin skirt,
    4" deep x 4" wide x 6½" long $135.00
Food mold, same except corn design $135.00
Food mold, redware, Turk's head,
    orange and brown glaze, 7½"
    diameter, a few flakey chips $55.00
Food mold, brown-glazed ceramic,
    American Centennial mold with
    "1776-1876" molded inside $75.00
Food mold, stoneware, grape bunch design $25.00
Food mold, stoneware, German,
    basket of flowers, 20th century $30.00
Food mold, individual Jell-O mold,
    copper (which is unusual, most
    are aluminum) $15.00
Food molds, individual aluminum
    fluted molds, 4" x 3½", set of 8 .... $12.00

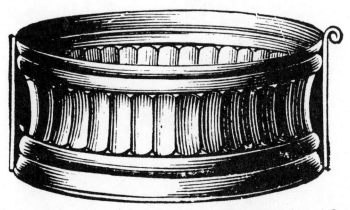

Figure IV-68. **French Pie Mold,** for making pates. Tin, hinged and clamped. Came in 5 sizes: 7", 8", 9", 10" and 12" diameter. From F.A. Walker catalog, 1870s. Walker imported many items of cookware from France. Value: $15-$20.

Food molds, aluminum, 6 fluted
    molds and the wire stacking rack
    for putting them in 'fridge .... $8.00 to $10.00
Jelly mold, stamped tin, shape of
    stack of corn, 1870s .... $18.00 to $30.00
Jelly mold, tin, bunch of grapes, 1870s .... $13.00 to $20.00
Jell-O mold, aluminum, heart-shaped
    with "JELL-O" $12.00
Food mold, copper and tin, ear of corn
    deeply embossed on copper top,
    tin skirt, 5¼" long $135.00
Food mold, tin with wheat design $32.00
Food mold, tin, pineapple design $35.00
Food mold, tin and copper, grape
    bunch embossed deeply in copper,
    top, deep tin skirt, 5½" long $132.00

Figure IV-69. **Grapefruit Corer and double-ended Fruit Baller.** Corer: Turner & Seymour, pat'd 1923. Baller: 1940s, red wood handle. Author's collection. Value: $2-$8.

Food mold, tinned copper, pineapple,
rose or wheat designs, fluted skirts ...... $45.00 to $80.00
Food mold, tin with copper top, rose
design, cathedral arch 1½" skirt,
"J.A. & Co.," pint size, mid 1800s ...... $95.00 to $110.00
Food mold, copper and tin, lion design
on copper top, (bottom), deep tin
skirt, 7" long $200.00
Fritter baker, iron with wood handle,
rather like a small branding iron .... $6.00 to $10.00
Frosting tubes in case, pieced tin, 6
tubes, case 6¼" long, 1970s .... $45.00 to $55.00
Gingerbread mold, wood, rectangular
block carved on one side with a
fish, on the other with a stylized
flower, American, early 19th
century, 3¾" x 10 3/8", estimated
to go at 1982 auction for $125-$175 .... $200.00
See also: Springerle molds.

Figure IV-70. **Ice Cream Molds.** Three-part lily mold, shown completely open, beautiful detailing. 5¼" long, closed up. No marks. Author's collection. Value: $30-$45; 2-part tulip mold, unmarked, and 2-part chrysthanemum. Collection of Meryle Evans. Value: $25-$30.

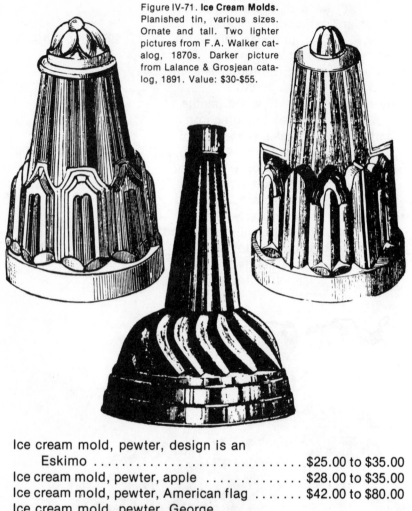

Figure IV-71. **Ice Cream Molds.**
Planished tin, various sizes.
Ornate and tall. Two lighter
pictures from F.A. Walker catalog, 1870s. Darker picture
from Lalance & Grosjean catalog, 1891. Value: $30-$55.

Ice cream mold, pewter, design is an
   Eskimo .... $25.00 to $35.00
Ice cream mold, pewter, apple .... $28.00 to $35.00
Ice cream mold, pewter, American flag .... $42.00 to $80.00
Ice cream mold, pewter, George
   Washington and shield .... $50.00 to $65.00
Ice cream mold, pewter, Washington's
   hatchet, marked "G.W." and "#243" $32.00
Ice cream mold, pewter, Santa Claus, E991 .... $36.00
Ice cream mold, pewter, hinged 2-piece,
   skull & crossbones, #508, 3¾" high $86.00
Ice cream mold, pewter, George
   Washington's bust on a hatchet
   shape, "S. & Co. #336," 3½" wide
   x 4" high $50.00

Figure IV-72. **Ice Cream Molds.** Shown here, a lion and an eagle. Lead, 2-part with clamps. Pictures from F.A. Walker flyer, c. 1880. Value: $65-$75.

Ice cream mold, pewter, 2 fat hearts,
    "LOVE" with flames . . . the
    "Hearts Aflame #300" .... $36.00 to $50.00
Ice cream mold, pewter, banana, #157 .... $30.00
Ice cream mold, pewter, turkey #E650 .... $32.00

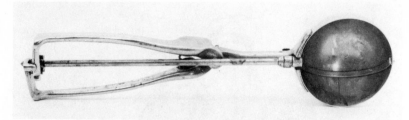

Figure IV-73. **Ice Cream Disher.** Nickeled brass and copper. "Gilchrist No. 30," c. 1930. 10½" long. Squeeze action. Collection of Marilyn Hodgkiss. Value: $20-$28.

Figure IV-74. **Ice Cream Dishers.** Conical one, a "cornet" disher, in the old parlance, with a key-wind, heavy tin. Pat'd 1883 (?), #10, key at top turns the cornet itself, not the scraper inside although the reverse is true on most cornet dishers. Collection of Meryle Evans. Longest disher is a Dover Mfg. Co. #20, with wooden handle, nickel plated disher. This has a leveling cutter that flattens scoop before it comes out. 10½" long. Meryle Evans Collection. Small scoop, 7½" long, is 1950s cast aluminum, from Japan, thumb-lever spring-action prod knocks ice cream out of scoop. Author's collection. Value, in order: $30-$35; $25-$35; $3-$8.

Figure IV-75. **Ice Cream Servers.** Left: one piece cast aluminum, marked "—ESSUS," made in Italy, 1935-1950. 7½" long. Value: $3-$8. Middle: cast aluminum with liquid filler that helps to serve very cold ice cream. Designed by Sherman Kelly, mfd. by Roll Dippers, Inc., this dipper is in the Museum of Modern Art Design Collection, NYC. 7" long. Value: $3-$8. Right: cast aluminum, wood handle, no marks, 8½" long, c. 1940s. Value: $8-$12. All Author's collection.

Ice cream mold, pewter, grape bunch, #S159 .. $30.00 to $45.00
Ice cream mold, grape bunch, #E278 .... $30.00
Ice cream mold, grape bunch, "W. HART" $38.00
Ice cream mold, chick $30.00
Ice cream mold, banana #157 .... $30.00
Ice cream mold, big duck $35.00
Ice cream mold, ear of corn, E219 .... $30.00
Ice cream mold, 3-piece hinged lily, #354 .... $30.00
Ice cream mold, 3-piece hinged lily #472 .... $30.00
Ice cream mold, 3-part calla lily, #210 .... $30.00 to $45.00
Ice cream mold, chrysanthemum, E344 .... $30.00
Ice cream mold, tulip $26.00
Ice cream mold, Odd Fellows Links, #577 .... $27.00
Ice cream mold, tin-washed copper,
    cornucopia, #287 .... $35.00
Ice cream mold, clown head, E1035 .... $40.00
Ice cream mold, potato, hinged 2-part,
    "E. & Co." #244 .... $22.00
Ice cream mold, pewter, 2 fat-bellied
    Kewpie like figures, 9½" high x
    7" wide, marked "T.C. Wygandt Co." $170.00
Ice cream mold, pewter, Masonic symbol $25.00
Ice cream mold, pewter, orange, #357 .... $18.00
Ice cream mold, pewter, cupid, E992 .... $30.00
Ice cream mold, hinged pewter,
    American Indian $30.00
Ice cream mold, pewter, Kewpie E1115 .... $65.00
Ice cream mold, hinged pewter, Miss
    Liberty $30.00
Ice cream mold, pewter, crescent
    moon with face of Sphinx, dated
    1905, "32nd Degree Shriner" $40.00
Ice cream mold, cute and simple
    airplane, "E. & Co." $70.00
Ice cream mold, airplane, #E1132" "E.
    & Co." $36.00
Ice cream mold, pewter, roast turkey,
    S 364 .... $30.00
Ice cream mold, tin, cornucopia, quite
    large $30.00

**NOTE: When looking at ice cream molds, remember that any
damages [holes, small cracks, hinge damage] reduce value**

dramatically. Pewter is fairly soft and easily damaged. Look for really good sound condition and fine interior detail. Interesting shapes or "cult" subjects add value too.

Ice cream scoop, painted cast
    aluminum, ridged handle, Italian
    1940s or '50s, 7½" long .... $6.00 to $12.00
Ice cream scoop, wood handle,
    "Arnold," pat'd 1927 .... $20.00 to $28.00
Ice cream scoop, cast aluminum,
    "Roll Dippers, Inc." 1930s, this is the
    one with the liquid in the handle
    that makes it easy to scoop out
    cold, cold ice cream. It was
    designed by Sherman Kelly and is
    in the Museum of Modern Art's
    design collection .... $10.00 to $13.00
Ice cream disher or server, nickeled-
    brass with wood handle, "Trojan
    No. 16," lever action .... $15.00 to $25.00
Ice cream disher, chrome with Bakelite
    handle, Hamilton Beach .... $20.00 to $30.00
Ice cream server, wood handle, nickel-
    plated brass, thumb control,
    makes ice cream slices, 12½"
    long, Cake Cone Co. .... $30.00 to $50.00
Ice cream server, cast aluminum and
    wood, "Gilchrist 31," 8½" long,
    1930s .... $20.00 to $35.00
Ice cream server, nickeled brass and
    copper, "Gilchrist 30," 10½" long,
    c. 1930 .... $25.00 to $50.00

NOTE: This brings up a real bugabear of mine . . . cast brass dippers that have been stripped of their plating of nickel and buffed from here to Sunday. Then the price goes up and UP. Ads reflect this trend . . . unabashedly saying "brass ice cream scoop" over and over. Such is the power of a golden-glow metal . . . brass glisters like gold, whereas nickel has no glamour at all. I've seen an ordinary server in its original — if somewhat worn — condition for, say, $32.00, and in the next booth at a show, a highly polished stripped one for as high as $68.00. I think this is ridiculous and not a good investment. It's like that awful trend 50 years ago for people to strip early painted furniture down to its "natural state."

Ice cream disher, stainless steel, Icy
  Pi (pronounced "icy pie" but often
  appearing in ads and even on the
  disher itself as the more confusing
  "ICYPI"). Mfd. by Automatic Cone
  Co., this dates to 1929, and makes
  a 4" x 4" slab, as for ice cream
  sandwiches. They sell for as little
  as $25.00 and as much as — at an
  antique show in late '82 — a
  whopping $150.00 . . . but, really . . . . $25.00 to $40.00
Ice cream disher, nickel plated brass,
  very exaggerated finger grip of
  squeeze handle . . . . $55.00 to $75.00
Ice cream disher, Hamilton Beach
  with wooden handle $20.00
Ice cream disher, Hamilton Beach,
  patent #1301055 (or #1361655 —
  either way, 1920), with what looks
  like black hard rubber but is
  probably a Bakelite handle $42.00
Ice cream disher, "Indestructo #4" $28.00
Ice cream scoops, Gilchrist type or
  real Gilchrist, a group of 12, ranging
  from #8 to #24, offered in an ad for $375.00
Ice cream cornet disher, tin, "K.W."
  marked on key, #10, pat'd Nov. 7,
  1905, key rather ornate $32.00
Ice cream cornet disher, unmarked,
  the simplest $35.00
Ice cream cornet disher, large #5, unmarked $38.00
Ice cream cornet disher, simple $34.00

NOTE: Ice cream dishers and servers, at least the ones with
moving parts, have enjoyed a tremendous increase in market
value, but I don't know if this will really hold on. One way the
prices have been raised is by the aforementioned practice of
stripping and buffing. But, there are some extraordinary dishers
around . . . rare and hard to find, but worth looking for. And a
coterie of enthusiasts, with their own association: write Ed
Marks, 1042 Olde Hickory Road, Lancaster, PA 17601. I've got
an idea — they could call themselves the "Coneheads"! Early in
January 1983, another collector, noted particularly for his paper

ephemera collection related to ice cream, announced that he too was interested in starting an association. Perhaps they'll join forces. Write Allan Mellis, 1115 West Montana, Chicago, IL 60614.

While still on the subject of ice cream, you may want to get in touch with Polly and Charles Gaupp at The House of the Clipper Ship, RD 1, 600 Route 6A, East Sandwich, MA 02537, because they put out an excellent ice cream mold price list/catalog, and have reprint copies of trade catalogs of Krauss, Son, and Eppelsheimer & Co. for sale.

Madeline molds, stamped in tin in
    geometric and figural shapes,
    individual sizes, late 19th century .... $15.00 to $30.00

Figure IV-76. **Jelly Molds.** This sampling look like castles, but Walker imported over 40 patterns, including "Prince's Feather," "lion," "Boar's Head," "Thorn Thistle," "Rose," "Shamrock," "Wheat," "Corn," and a variety of animals. "Jelly" by the way refers to a congealed dish, not jelly as in peanut-butter-and . . . From F.A. Walker catalog, c. 1870s-80s. Values: $25-$100.

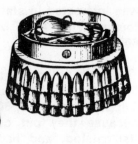

Figure IV-77. **Jelly Molds.** Oval rimmed tin with flower and fruit designs, fluted skirts. Sizes: ½, 1, 1½, 2 pints; 2 quarts. Sampling from F.A. Walker catalog, 1880s. Value: $45-$100.

Maple sugar mold, carved wood, blue
  jay with crest, 5½" x 6¾", 20th century $9.00
Maple sugar mold, handcarved wood
  (maple probably), 2 part, makes 6
  barrel-shaped candies . . . . $95.00 to $100.00
Maple sugar mold, handcarved wood,
  makes a 3-D beaver, 8½" long x
  3¼" high $22.00
Maple sugar mold, leaded tin, "Jaburg
  Bros," prints 12 figures: cornucopia,
  fleur-de-lis, pear, heart, daisy,
  oak leaf, shell, bell, fish, moon,
  flag, auto and strawberry, 6" x 6½" . . . . $125.00 to $150.00
Maple sugar mold, handcarved, long
  and skinny, 42" long, makes 14 2"
  hearts, 19th century $140.00
Maple sugar mold, carved wood,
  squirrel with thick curled tail,
  6½" x 5¼", 20th century $10.00
Maple sugar mold, large house, 19th
  century $100.00
Maple sugar mold, carved wood,
  creates geometric form, 8¾" high $55.00
Maple sugar mold, tin, fluted shallow
  pans, small enough for doll tarts $3.00
Marzipan mold, tin plated, hinged,
  German . . . . $30.00 to $35.00
Marzipan mold, heavy tin plate, 2
  hinged sections, 3" x 3" $28.00
Muffin pan/mold, cast iron, simple,
  makes 12 muffins $10.00

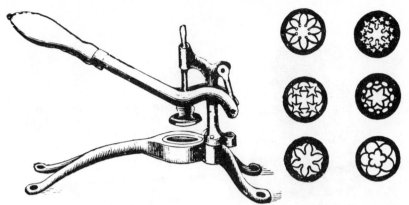

Figure IV-78. **Julien Soup Cutter,** for cutting sliced vegetables to float in clear soups. Cast iron with 20 (6 shown) fancy cutting discs. From F.A. Walker catalog, c. 1890. Value: $30-$40.

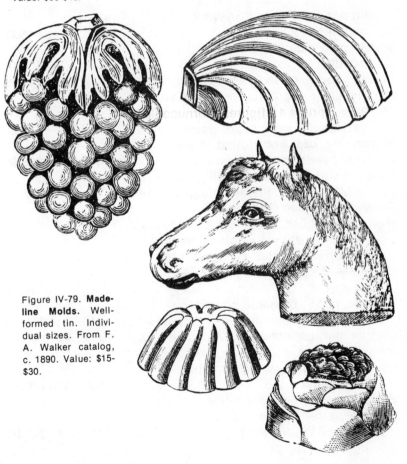

Figure IV-79. **Madeline Molds.** Well-formed tin. Individual sizes. From F. A. Walker catalog, c. 1890. Value: $15-$30.

Figure IV-80. **Mold.** Heavy tin, 3-tiered. 9" high. 19th century. Collection of Meryle Evans. Value: $50-$75.

Muffin pan, cast iron, "Griswold," 11
    muffins .... $12.50 to $15.00
Muffin pan, blue graniteware, good
    condition $36.00
Muffin pan, cast iron, shell design $45.00
Muffin pan, gray graniteware, large size $30.00
Muffin pan, brown & white graniteware
    perfect $32.00
Muffin pan, cast iron, round in shape
    with hearts and stars, unusual .... $10.00 to $15.00
Pastry board, oak covered with tin,
    T. Mills & Bro., Philadelphia, 23" x 14" $75.00
Pastry jagger: see Crimper.
Pie or cake slicer, wire, sets down
    over pie plate (or single layer of
    cake), and creates a guide for the
    knife to cut 8 equal pieces. A
    neat item $9.00
Pie pan, cobalt blue and white
    agateware, 10" diameter .... $10.00 to $15.00
Pie pan, gray graniteware, 10" diameter .... $6.00 to $9.00
Pie pan, stoneware, brown glaze,
    corrugated edge, 9" diameter,
    19th century .... $80.00 to $90.00
Pie pan, cobalt blue and white
    marbleized agateware, white
    inside, 8½" diameter .... $10.00 to $15.00

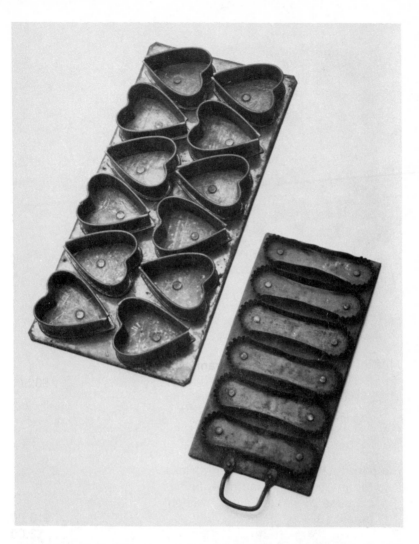

Figure IV-81. **Molds.** Sheet tin, crudely made one makes madelines or Lady Fingers with fluted ends. 6 cups 4¼" long. Mold 9" long exclusive of handle. 19th century, probably homemade. Other makes 12 heart-shaped cookies (?). Sheet tin and blued sheet iron. 13½" long x 6¼" wide. Each heart is 2½" long. 19th century. Collection of Meryle Evans. Value: $28-$40.

Figure IV-82. **Muffin Pans.** Cast iron. Turk's head style makes 12, so does plain cupped pan. Author's collection. Value: $20-$35.

Pie pan, tin, "Presto Self-Rising Cake Flour," but a pie pan ne'ertheless because of slanted sides, design patent 1924 .... $10.00

Pie pan, tin, "Mrs. Smith's" $3.00

Pie pan, tin, "Goldblatt Brothers" $10.00

Pie pan, pale blue & white swirl enamelware, 12" diameter $12.00

Pie pan, turquoise & white swirl enamelware, 12" diameter $15.00

Pie pan/plate (usually the ceramic ones are called "plates") "A Good Apple Pie is the Best of All," Pennsylvania German slipware, 9" diameter $750.00

Figure IV-83. **Muffin Pans.** Unusual scallop shells in circular frame, makes 7, 9" diameter, stamped tin. Other has 7 individual shallow cups riveted together with bent sheet tin strap handle. Honeycomb cups. 9 1/8" diameter. 19th century. Collection of Meryle Evans. Value: $28-$40.

Popover pan, cast iron, Wagner Ware,
     makes 11 popovers in deep (1 7/8")
     slightly slanted-sided cups, 11" long   .... $12.00 to $18.00

NOTE: Iron Craft Inc., of Freedom, New Hampshire, makes quite a credible popover pan — in two sizes: 6 and 11 holes. Cast iron, with 11 cups, but the cups are only 1 3/8" deep [shallower than the old Wagner Ware]. The two "flower petal" cut-outs at each end, presumably serve not only as decorative touches, but also to slightly cool the iron just where a person would pick it up.

Pudding mold, earthenware, spouted
and with a handle, 19th century .... $85.00 to $150.00
Pudding mold, redware with black
glaze, Turk's head design with
spout, widely-canted sides, 11"
diameter, very unusual .... $100.00 to $130.00
Pudding mold, ceramic, glazed and
handpainted, with apple relief
design, fluted sides, 3¾" x 4¾" $20.00
Pudding mold, tin, melon style with
flat lid, 1880s to 1900 .... $20.00 to $30.00
Pudding mold, tin, "Kreamer," melon
style with flat lid, 6½" x 5" $25.00
Pudding mold, gray and cobalt blue
agateware, slope sided, 11" diameter .... $18.00 to $22.00
Pudding mold, gray graniteware,
melon with tin lid, very attractive
and fairly uncommon .... $45.00 to $65.00
Pudding mold, gray graniteware,
spouted Turk's head .... $25.00 to $35.00

Figure IV-84. **Muffin Pan.** Cast iron. W & L Mfg. Co., pat'd 1867. Makes only 11 muffins. Picture courtesy of The Smithsonian Institution, Museum of History and Technology. Value: $20-$35.

Figure IV-85. **Press or Mold — a real Whatsit?** Bentwood and carved wood, possibly mahogany handles. 16" long x 6 7/8" diameter. Practically without a mark or stain, none inside. No drainage holes so it's not for cheese. No bloodstains, so not for meat. All you Westerners . . . is it a tortilla press? Collection of Meryle Evans. Value: $30? $40?

Figure IV-86. **Pudding Mold.** Tin "Melon" shape, with wire handle. Close-fitting lid. Late 19th century. Collection of Mary Mac Franklin. Value: $20-$30.

Figure IV-87. **Pudding Molds,** one shown partly open like smirking jockey. Tin with lids. Left: from Matthai-Ingram catalog, c. 1890; right: from F.A. Walker catalog, c. 1890. Value: $25-$40.

Rice boiler mold, tin, spouted with
  fluted sides, lid, 19th century $45.00
Roll pan, cast iron, makes 12 french
  rolls, dated 1850 .... $22.00
Roll pan, cast iron, "R. & E. Mfg. Co.,
  Pat'd April 5, 1858," 11 shallow
  cups (3¼" diameter x 1" deep) in
  3 rows. Overall dimensions,
  including curved handles at each
  end, 13" long x 8¾" wide $55.00
Rolling pin, glass, cork stopper, c. 1900 ...... $20.00 to $30.00

Figure IV-88. **Rice Boller**. Tin, fluted and tubed with close-fitting lid with strap handle. Make a nice molded rice to turn out on serving platter. Came in three sizes, small, medium, large. From F.A. Walker catalog, 1880s. Value: $28-$40.

Rolling pin, glass with screw-on painted tin lid, 1910 to 1920?, fill this with cold water . . . which was reason for all the glass "bottle" pins .... $15.00 to $22.00

Rolling pin, glass with wooden "axle" and handles, this one **not** a bottle pin, July 28, 1921 .... $25.00 to $45.00

Rolling pin, blown glass, cobalt blue with painted Forget-Me-Nots, 15" long, fabulous $95.00

Rolling pin, blown glass, robin's-egg blue color, a big 29" long, beautiful color $120.00

Rolling pin, freeblown amethyst glass, 2 knob handles, 15½" long, American 19th century, estimated at 1982 auction to go for $75.00/$125.00 .... $90.00

Rolling pin, freeblown amethyst glass, bulbous handles, 15" long, 19th century American $90.00

Rolling pins, marbleized glass, one is swirled cobalt blue and white, the other pink and white, both with knob handles, 17½" long and 16" long, American, mid-19th century, estimated at 1982 auction to go for $150.00/$200.00 for the pair . . . a bargain at $100.00

Figure IV-89. **Roll Pan.** Cast iron. Waterman's 1870s. Makes 8 rolls. Author's collection. Value: $16-$25.

Rolling pin, glass, screw-on metal
cap, cheapest seen, at $8.00
Rolling pin, glass, screw-on metal
cap, 13" long $20.00
Rolling pin, white Nailsea glass, 2
knob handles, 19th century $250.00
Rolling pin, glass with white-painted
screw-on metal cap marked
"ROLL-RITE," 14" long x 2½" diameter $25.00

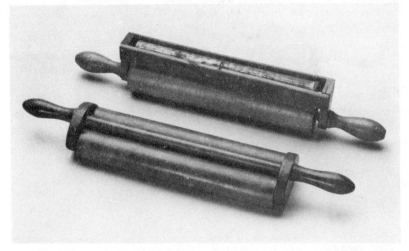

Figure IV-90. **Rolling Pins.** Bottom: double roller, well-formed handles. Twice as smooth pastry? Late 19th century. 20" long. Other is a marvelous roller that carries it's own compartment of dusting flour above in mesh cylinder. This is Harlowe's "Do Not Stick," pat'd December 1903. 20¼" long. Collection of Meryle Evans. Value: $55-$70.

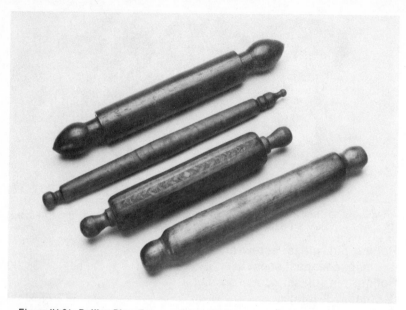

Figure IV-91. **Rolling Pins.** Fancy wooden pins, beautifully carved or turned. The one with variegated wood is possibly a Shaker piece. Notice two different ends on long skinny one — undoubtedly made to order for a cook with very special needs. Variegated wood one: 15¼" long; other, 18½" long. 19th century. Collection of Meryle Evans. Value: $30-$65.

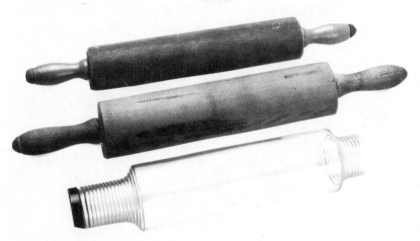

Figure IV-92. **Rolling Pins.** Two wooden ones are made with handles and axle rod. 16¼" long and 18½" long. Glass bottle pin has screw on metal cap, and was meant to be filled with cold water or shaved ice. Many old old pins were glass — they could be chilled, and this makes rolling pastry easier. Turn-of-century date for wood ones, 1930s for glass. Author's collection. Value: $15-$22.

Figure IV-93. **Rolling Pin.** Glazed stoneware roller, non-absorbent and revolves on polished wood handles. "A rolling stone gathers no moss . . . our new rolling pin gathers no dough." Seastrand catalog, c. 1912. Value: $25-$45.

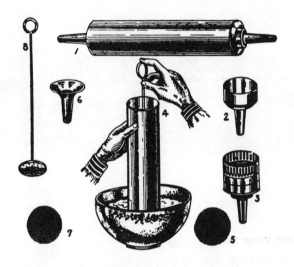

Figure IV-94. **Rolling Pin and Combination Tool**. Tin with everything needed to churn syllabubs, funnel, strain and cut cookies. From Seastrand catalog, c. 1912. Value: $28-$45.

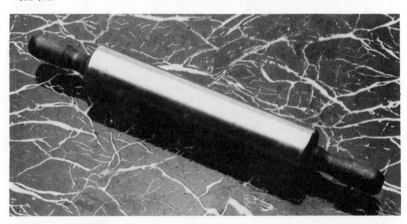

Figure IV-95. **Rolling Pin.** Nickel-plated metal pin with wood handles. Something inside rattles, probably intentional — something like lead shot to make heavier. No marks. 15½" long. Author's collection. Shown here on marbleized enameled stove lid, c. 1920. Value: $12-$18.

255

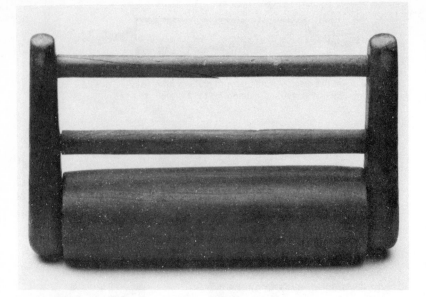

Figure IV-96. **Rolling Pin.** Heavy wood with double-barred handle for a good grip. 11" long x 6¾" high including handle. 19th century. Collection of Meryle Evans. Value: $25-$45.

Rolling pin, freeblown green glass,
   lots of bubbles, 15" long $75.00
Rolling pin, glass, pink & white Nailsea $165.00
Rolling pin, opaline glass, painted
   with ship and prayer decoration $90.00
Rolling pin, Clambroth glass, 19th century $35.00
Rolling pin, red and blue splattered
   glass, handsome $150.00
Rolling pin, hardwood wtih turned
   bone handles, 15" long, 19th
   century, quite handsome $165.00
Rolling pin, one-piece of maple,
   turned with handles, 14" long,
   3½" diameter .... $15.00 to $20.00
Rolling pin, small, possibly a child's
   1920s .... $7.00 to $10.00
Rolling pin, corrugated maple, used to
   crumb crackers or to make fine
   pastry. Sometimes these are
   referred to as "noodle" pins . . .
   I don't know why because they
   couldn't cut noodles, 13" long .... $20.00 to $35.00

Rolling pin, corrugated wood, termed
    in ad "noodle" rolling pin $28.00
Rolling pin, wood, Pennsylvania
    German **draalhus**, I wish I had a
    picture of this one; it's hard to
    describe. At each end, where the
    handles are, are two standing
    carved wood pieces — rather like
    simplified human figures. These
    are connected at top and middle
    with a plane rod and another
    carved rod. 14" long x 5" high,
    including pin and double
    handles, 19th century $150.00
Rolling pin, ridged lengthwise rather
    than around and around the pin,
    carved of one piece of wood, nice
    patina, 14" long $28.00

**NOTE: The next category of rolling pins is fast becoming one of
the most popular subfields in kitchen collecting. These are the
advertising crockery or stoneware pins. In fact, a collector, Bob
Miller, of Roland, Iowa 50236, is compiling a list of known
crockery pins.**

Rolling pin, crockery white with blue
    stripe, "Clarion, Iowa" $135.00
Rolling pin, crockery, brown strip
    with "Perry & Buchanan General
    Merchandise, Quasqueton, Iowa" $160.00
Rolling pin, blue stripe, "Dawson,
    Furniture, Zeigler, Illinois" $160.00
Rolling pin, crockery, "Robert F.
    McAfee, Dealer in Groceries,"
    Augusta, Illinois" $165.00
Rolling pin, brown stripe, "White
    Swan Flour, Garrison, Iowa" $145.00
Rolling pin, "John M. Merriot, Mt.
    Vernon, Iowa" $157.50
Rolling pin, crockery, with handles,
    "Killians, Wahoo, Nebraska" $145.00
Rolling pin, crockery, "Plain View,
    Nebraska" $165.00

257

Rolling pin, crockery, "John H.
  Merritt Quality Groceries, Mount
  Vernon, Iowa" $160.00
Rolling pin, crockery, "J.F. Reily
  Groceries, Hardware, Implements,
  Buggies & Wagons, Seaton, Illinois $175.00
Rolling pin, crockery, blue stripe,
  "Newman Grove, Nebraska" $145.00
Rolling pin, crockery, "Murphyboro,
  Illinois" $145.00
Rolling pin, crockery, wildflower,
  from Milwaukee $165.00
Rolling pin, crockery, brown stripe,
  "Thompson's General Store,
  Grand Junction, Iowa" $140.00
Rolling pin, crockery, blue stripe,
  "Newman Grove, Nebraska" $145.00
Rolling pin, crockery, wildflower,
  "Rodman, Iowa" $145.00
Rolling pin, "Save Your Dough" $110.00
Rolling pin, stoneware with wooden
  handles, motto: "May peace and
  plenty/ Dwell on England
  and shore/ And there remain/ Till
  time shall be no more $250.0
Rolling pin, yellowware $100.0
Rolling pin, yellowware $85.00
Springerle board, hand-carved wood
  carved on both sides, designs
  include angel, pecking chicken
  steam boat, castle and tricorn
  hat, unusual and small $125.00
Springerle cookie mold, machine-
  carved, 4 squares .... $35.00 to $45.00
Springerle mold board, well-carved
  wood, Pennsylvania German
  figures on both sides, 19th century .... $200.00 to $250.00
Springerle cookie board, carved wood,
  5 geometric designs, with a handle
  and a hole for hanging $65.00
Springerle board, carved wood, cherry,
  grapes, sailboat, 5¾" x 3" $120.00

MEASURES.
Copper and brass measures, tin-lined.
One-half to 2-pint size. 19th century.
Collection of Mary Mac Franklin.
Value: $35-$50 each.

CLOCK
Real sheet iron frying pan, ''Cold
Handle'' Acme, N.Y.S. Co.,
copyrighted 1899 by the Pan-
American Exposition Company for
the 1901 fair. Keywound clock with
regulator. 26" long × 13" diameter.
Other souvenirs of this pantastic
pun-opportunity Expo included a
smaller frying pan with a glove decal
inside and clock-and-silver spoons in
the shape of a frying pan. Clock
courtesy of The Larry Zim World
Fairs Collection, New York City.
Value: $400-$600.

MILK JUG.
Blue ombre enamelware. Bail
handle with wood grip. 19th
century. Collection of David
Arky.
Value: $20-$28.

FLOUR CANISTER.
Copper with tin lining. Sifter pan
inside. Collection of Mary Mac
Franklin.
Value: $50-$75.

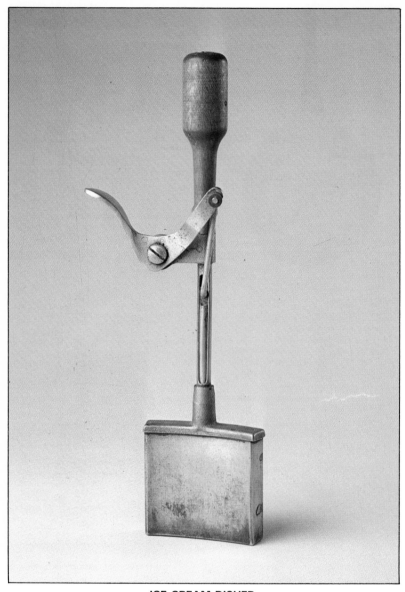

ICE CREAM DISHER.
Nickel plated brass with wood handle. This one makes slices for pie a la mode or ice cream sandwiches. No marks. c. 1930s. 12½″ long. Author's collection.
Value: $30-$50.

NUTMEG GRATER.
The famous wire, tin and wood
"Edgar," pat'd August 18, 1891.
5⅞" long × 5¼" wide. Author's
collection.
Value: $38-$70.

CRIMPERS.
Left: 1930s green and ivory
plastic, **$8-$20**; late 19th century
mass-produced brass, **$28-$35;**
wood and ebony from 19th century, **$25-$40.** Author's collection.

JELLY BAG.
Wood handles
with coarse linen
cloth. Put in the
jelly and wring it
out. 19th cen-
tury. 24" long,
fully extended.
Collection of
Meryle Evans.
Value: $50-$65.

TABLE TOP BUTTER WORKER.
Wooden frame, very gothic looking, with bentwood butter holder. Wooden
gears, iron handle. 19th century American. 13½" high × 9" × 8" square.
Collection of Meryle Evans.
Value: $120-$150.

MILL.
Wood with iron gears and cast iron balance wheel. No marks, no signs of use. 8″ high × 7½″ long × 5½″ wide. 19th century. Collection of Meryle Evans.
Value: $75-$95.

CORN GRATER.
Wood, slightly troughed, with turned legs. Fitted out with grater blades to remove kernels from fresh corn, with dish underneath. 19th century American. 11¾″ long × 4½″ high. Collection of Meryle Evans.
Value: $75-$100.

GRATER.
"H. P. Arthur's Vegetable Grater," pat'd October 8, 1867. All wood with metal grater drum. 13¾" high to top of hopper; frame is 13" × 6" wide.
Collection of Meryle Evans.
Value: $65-$100.

HOMEMADE APPLE PARER.
Red-painted wood, cast iron, steel. Clamped to bench or table. 7" high × 13" long. Early 19th century American. Author's collection.
Value: $65-$80.

CHOPPING KNIFE.
Handforged iron, early 19th or late 18th century. 8″ high × 9¼″ long. Collection of Meryle Evans.
Value: $65-$90.

HOMEMADE APPLE PARER,
Straddle type. Wood painted in possibly Pennsylvania German style in pumpkin and dark green. Iron gears. Author's collection.
Value: $100-$170.

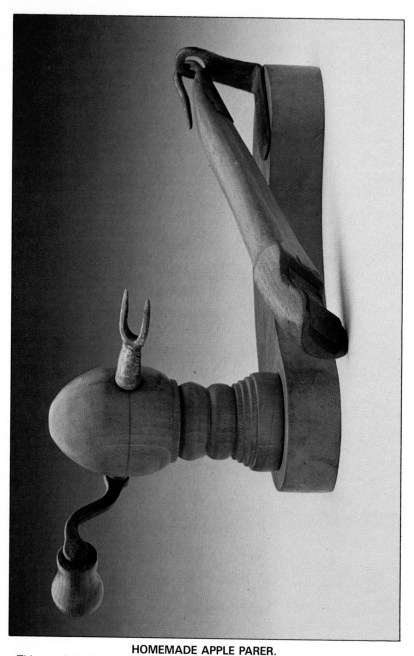

HOMEMADE APPLE PARER.
This one is held between the knees, which accounts for its curved body.
Shaver blade and ungeared prong for apple. American, 19th century. 6″
high × 9¼″ long. Collection of Meryle Evans.
Value: $65-$90.

HOMEMADE APPLE PARER.
Handheld "shaver" type cutter, iron fork, wooden gears, iron crank. This also has an unusual feature—a slicing wire between the gears. American 19th century. 10″ high × 15″ long × 9½″ wide. Collection of Meryle Evans.
Value: $90-$125.

LUNCH BOXES.

Clockwise from top: outstanding graphics of people engaged in a number of sports activities. Stamped ''Metal Package Corp. of New York,'' c. 1920s. 4" high × 7¾" long × 4¾" wide. Excellent condition. **Value: $40.** Next, Mickey Mouse lunch kit, mf'd by Geuder, Paeschke and Frey of Milwaukee, 1935. Earliest known comic character lunch box, certainly one of the most desirable. 4¾" high × 8¼" long × 5" wide. **Value: $100**+. Circus scene box, originally contained candy or cookies. Bottom is stamped ''National Can Co.'' c. 1930. 3⅛" high × 6" long × 3¾" wide. **Value: $35.** Mother Goose characters on a tin that probably originally came filled with candy. Handle is marked ''KIDDYLAND'' and the tin is marked ''Thomas B. Lamb.'' c. 1930. 3¼" high × 4½" long × 3¼" wide. Girls jumping rope and playing with a doll buggy decorate c. 1930 box. Unmarked. 3¾" high × 8¼" long × 5" wide. **Value: $30.** Picture and collection of Robert Carr.

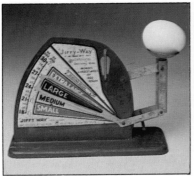

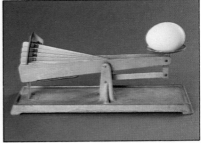

EGG SCALE.
Painted sheet metal. "Jiffy Way," Owatonna, Minnesota, pat'd 1940. 5¾" high × 7⅛" long. Author's collection.
Value: $12-$20.

EGG SCALE.
Sheet and cast aluminum. "Acme Egg Grading Scale," Specialty Mfg. Co., St. Paul, Minnesota, pat'd June 24, 1925. The great thing about this one is the sound—wish you could hear it! 4½" high × 10½" long. Author's collection.
Value: $16-$28.

GRANITEWARE CHILDREN'S PLATES.
At top are two alphabet plates. Brown and white lettering on left, black and white on right, with a clock face for learning to tell time. Right one marked "Made in England, OjE Co." Below is orange and white German plate with little girl singing with the birds. Picture courtesy of Vernagene Vogelzang and Evelyn Welch.
Values: $48, $50, $16.50.

TOY GRANITEWARE WASH SET.
Though they look the same scale as the picture above, these are quite small—the tumbler at bottom right is only 2¼" high. Also included is a bucket, pitcher, bowl, waste chamber pot. Picture courtesy of Vernagene Vogelzang and Evelyn Welch.
Value for set: $235.

GRANITEWARE CUPS AND PIE PANS.
Along the top are various children's mugs and cups. At right is one marked ''Granite Iron Ware.'' White one at center has ''Six and Twenty Blackbirds'' nursery rhyme on it. **Value of cups: $15-$17 each.** Below are pie pans. The blue and whites: **$9 each;** cream and green: **$7.50.** Picture courtesy of Vernagene Vogelzang and Evelyn Welch.

GRANITEWARE COOKING SET FOR CHILDREN.
16 pieces plus two lids, shown on a ''BABY'' range. Picture courtesy of Vernagene Vogelzang and Evelyn Welch.
Value, sans range: $300.

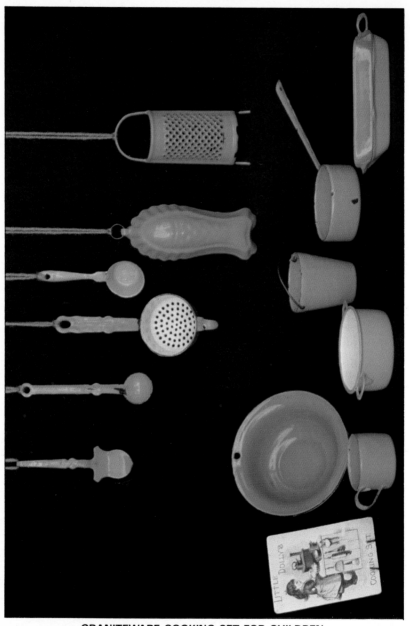

GRANITEWARE COOKING SET FOR CHILDREN.
''Little Dolly's Cooking Set'' with 12 pieces and original card. Picture
courtesy of Vernagene Vogelzang and Evelyn Welch.
Value: $265.

POT SCRAPERS.

Lithographed tin with advertising. Designed to scrape out every crevice and cranny of a pot or kettle. Article on these is found following the CLEAN, SCRUB, WASH...section of this book, written by Karol Atkinson. Pictures courtesy of Karol Atkinson.

EGGBEATER OR MIXER.
Green glass Root Mason jar, cast iron Dover-like beater, tin screw-on lid.
Standard Specialty Co., Milwaukee, Wisconsin, pat'd June 11, 1907 (on
beater). 12″ high × 3⅞″ diameter. Author's collection.
Value: $22-$30.

Figure IV-97. **Tart Sealer.** Cast aluminum with wood knob, spring-loaded action. Tart Master, pat'd 1938. Still being made, only with funny little metal cap knob. Instructions now read: "Roll out a sheet of dough, place small mounds of filling at regular intervals, cover with a second layer and then, with a quick push of plunger, punch out tarts or ravioli." Author's collection. Value: $7-$12.

Springerle cookie board, wormeaten fruitwood, 2 sided, rooster, boar, squirrel and heart on one side, cat, dog, horse and lion on other, 5" x 9", 18th century, or very early 19th, beautiful $550.00

Springerle board, pewter mold mounted to wooden back, 12 rectangular designs of people, plants and animals, unusual, 4½" x 7½" $150.00

Springerle rolling pin, wood, 12 designs in squares, late 19th century, 15" long, not very interesting .... $65.00 to $75.00

Springerle rolling pin, carved maple, 20th century, possibly the '30s .... $25.00 to $30.00

Springerle board, carved pine with heart-shaped flower to make a single small cookie in middle of large board $235.00

Springerle board, birch, carved horse, ram, boar $325.00

Springerle board, carved walnut, large ornate circular design of flowers and birds, from Harman's Bakery of Brunswick, Maine $350.00

NOTE: A modern springerle rolling pin is made with 12 designs in squares, and another in 16 designs, selling very cheaply . . . under $15.00.

Tart sealer, tin and cast aluminum,
with wooden knob handle,
spring-loaded action, "Tart
Master," pat'd 1938 .... $7.00 to $12.00

NOTE: A modern "TARTMASTER" is manufactured almost exactly the same, except that the knob is now a metal cap. The directions read: "Roll out a sheet of dough, place small mounds of filling at regular intervals, cover with a second layer and then, with a quick push of plunger, punch out tarts or ravioli." This was selling in the late '70s, according to a catalog I have, for about $4.00.

Vegetable garnish cutter, metal,
"Acme with original instructions
and envelope .... $4.00 to $6.00
Vegetable or fruit baller, chrome-plated
steel, Turner & Seymour Mfg. Co.,
pat'd 1923 .... $4.00 to $6.00
Wafer iron, cast iron, eagle and shield
design with 16 stars $1000.00
Wafer iron, cast iron, American eagle
and shield with stars, c. 1800 .... $550.00
Wafer iron, cast and forged iron,
shapes a heart wafer, 29½" long $250.00
Wafer iron, cast iron with eagle and shield $300.00
Wafer iron, cast iron with forged long
handles, flower surrounded by
concentric rings, c. 1800 .... $260.00

NOTE: An excellent and dedicated collector, Linda Fishbeck, of Texas, has regretted not buying an iron mold being sold as a "waffle iron" [but probably not — becuase the cast design of a little girl and garden is one both sides]. Has anyone seen one of these round molds and do you know what it is?

Waffle iron, cast iron, "Griswold,"
hearts and stars, 1920 .... $45.00 to $60.00
Waffle iron, cast iron with wrought
handles, diamonds, marked "B &
W Co., Chatham" $125.00
Waffle iron, cast iron, "Wagner," 2
piece with bail handle, 1920 .... $15.00

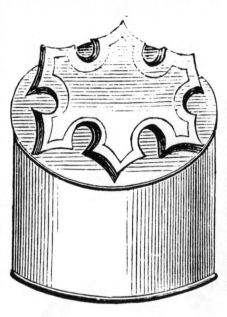

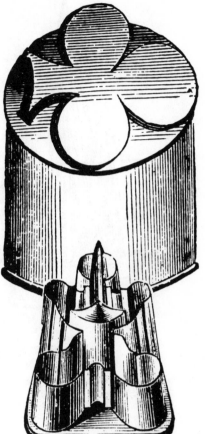

Figure IV-98. **Vegetable Cutters.** (Three pictures.) Tin. The pictures are primitive, but they mean to show that you cut a shamrock or 6-pointed star from a slice of root vegetable. Came in 20 styles — decorations for soup. From F.A. Walker catalog, c. 1890. Value: $15-$20.

Waffle iron, cast iron, "Shapleigh #8"
 with stand $22.00
Waffle iron, cast iron, "National,"
 with stand $22.00
Waffle iron, cast iron, flower, heart,
 diamond, "Francis Buckwalter &
 Co., Boyer's Ford, PA," pat'd
 8/9/10, 2-part with stand $45.00
Waffle iron, cast iron, heart-shaped,
 wood handles $50.00
Waffle iron, cast iron, star in heart $100.00
Waffle iron, cast iron, "Harwi #8" on
 high cast iron stand $22.00
Waffle iron, cast iron, "Griswold,"
 pat'd 1908, on stand $18.00

Figure IV-99. **Vegetable and Rice Mold.** Tin. Meant to make decorative spires of cooked, mashed root veggies or rice. F.A. Walker catalog, c. 1890. Value: $25-$40.

Figure IV-100. **Waffle Iron.** Cast iron, 3-pieces, Majestic Mfg. Co., St. Louis, MO., No. 885M, pat'd 1908. 16" long. Picture courtesy of Lar Hothem. Value: $25-$40.

Figure IV-101. **Waffle Iron.** Cast iron. From 1880s cookbook. Value: $25-$40.

Figure IV-102. **Wafer Irons.** Cast with wrought iron handles. One on left is 27" long x 5½" diameter; one on right, with design of tree, is dated 1785 and has initials "J.W." Picture courtesy of the National Museum of American History, Smithsonian Institution.

Figure IV-103. **Wafer Irons.** Cast iron with wrought iron handles. These were used to make thin crisp cookies called wafers. The very first ones were used to make wafers for communion in churches, and had religious designs. Other early ones, from the 18th century, often had patriotic symbols — eagles and stars. Picture courtesy of the National Museum of American History, Smithsonian Institution.

Waffle iron, cast iron with stand, "Abbott & Lawrence," hearts and diamonds, 8½" long .... $35.00 to $45.00

Waffle iron, cast iron, made for range top with bottom that sets into range eye, late 19th century .... $20.00 to $40.00

Waffle iron, cast iron, "Griswold American No. 8," Griswold Mfg. Co., makes 7¼" diameter waffle, handle is spiraled heavy wire, for quick cooling .... $25.00 to $35.00

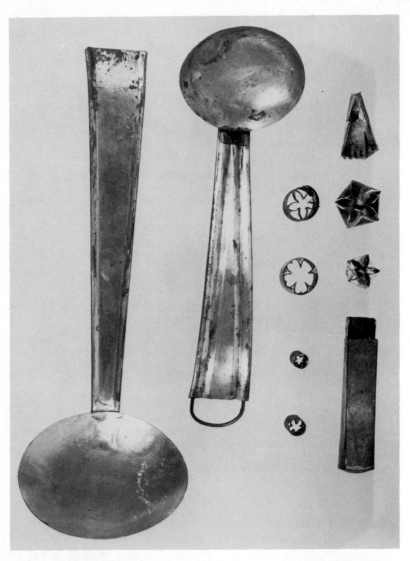

Figure IV-104. **Wax Flower Making Tools.** Tin. This is an example of the kind of thing that is easily confused with a cookery implement. Shown here are dippers for molten wax, plus forms for cutting out the petals. 19th century. Picture courtesy of the National Museum of American History, Smithsonian Institution.

Waffle iron, cast iron, recipe for
  German potato **waffeln** cast in lid,
  very unusual .... $75.00 to $110.00
Waffle iron, cast iron, rectangular,
  makes 3 waffles, c. 1870s .... $35.00 to $45.00
Waffle iron, cast iron, "Wagner Ware",
  pat'd 1925, makes 2 waffles .... $16.00 to $20.00

NOTE: Linda Fishbeck, mentioned above, who is one of a number of enthusiastic "informants" around the country, reports that at least in her Houston area, waffle irons often cost more than $65.00. Maybe they just haven't hit in the Eastern states. I'd like to hear from those of you with what you consider unusual irons . . . drop me a postcard.

HANDLING AND MEASURING

All the kitchen implements and equipment used to handle food, utensils or containers of food, or to measure quantities or weight of food, are in this general category. The canning jar wrenches and holders which fit here, have instead been given their own category, along with other utensils and implements related to putting up food.

HOOK, HANG, RACK, JACK & SPIT: FOR COOKING

Yikes! The above sound positively tortured! But if they **sound** like something from medieval torture chambers, they really do resemble the ancient machines and accoutrements of a dungeon. And most would have been found in a castle kitchen or "hall," or scullery. Cinderella probably had to clean her stepmother's bird trammel, when she wasn't carrying ashes! There is something distinctly Middle Ages about a dog spit, for example, with a specially-bred, short-legged and big-chested dog — called a Turnspit — running for grim death to turn the huge gears that operated a spit burdened with half a sheep or a whole hog. And any of us can imagine peering up into the sooty reaches of an old chimney, seeing silhouetted against a patch of distant blue sky a skeletal smoke jack engine, with scaling wings. Spooky, huh? Well, very few American collectors will ever own either a dog spit or a smoke jack. There were a few in use in America during Colonial times, but most are in museum or restoration collections.

Among the most collectible, if expensive, items in this category are the skewers and skewer racks. Nearly always made of wrought iron, they are endless variations on a theme . . .a two-armed holder, hung with varying lengths of one-eyed skewers.

Many collectors are keen to find as many variations as they can in a category like skewers. Others, as restless and easily distracted as I, collect very broadly. I can't pretend to be an expert in each area of kitchen collecting, although I'm "supposed" to know everything! Instead, I know pretty much about a lot . . . it's all you diligent and scholarly collectors of narrow fields on whom we **all** depend to increase our knowledge of specialties.

Basket spit, wrought iron, complete
with hinges and pulley, late 18th
century, probably English .... $100.00 to $125.00
Bird trammel, wrought iron, 2 hooks,
adjustable from 16" to 23" at
fullest extension, 18th century .... $85.00 to $110.00
Bottle jack mantle clamp, brass, a
simple screw clamp with sliding
jack hook, acorn finial to screw,
late 18th century, very early 19th $150.00
Clock jack, cast, wrought and
machined brass, beautiful scroll
design, 18th century .... $800.00 to $1500.00
Clock jack, brass, 19th century $85.00
Clock jack, brass, signed "John
Linwood," with crown spit $250.00
Clock jack, iron, spoked wheel,
scrolled front plate, arched wall
bracket, 3 gears and spool, 14"
high, late 1700s, early 1800s $650.00
Crane, forged iron, simple with ram's
head tip to tapered bar, 21" long $95.00
Crane, wrought iron, curved bracket,
19" long $40.00
Crane, cast iron $20.00
Cranes, forged iron, pair of standing
cranes with penny feet, T-bar,
35" high, 18th century $350.00
Dangle spit, steel, serpentine,
winglike governor, early 1800s .... $85.00 to $130.00

Figure V-1. **Footman or Trivet.** Pierced
brass and wrought iron with turned wood
handle. Hunting scene and foliage. Probably English, late 18th, early 19th century. 13" high x 13¾" wide x 8 1/8" deep.
Estimated at Seymour sale in 1982 between $300-$500. Realized: $450. Picture
courtesy of Christie, Manson & Woods
International Inc.

Figure V-2. **Footman**. Brass and cast iron. 19th century, probably English. 11¾"
high x 14½" wide x 12½" deep. Collection of Mary Mac Franklin. Value: $200-$300.

Figure V-3. **Footman**. Steel. Early 1800s. 12½" high x 12" wide x 8½" deep.
Collection of Mary Mac Franklin. Value: $130-$165.

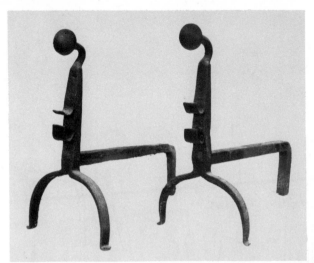

Figure V-4. **Andirons.** Wrought iron. Double spit brackets, and round finials. Probably American, 19th century, 18½" high. Estimated at 1983 Linden sale between $300-$500. Realized: $500. Picture courtesy of Christie, Manson & Woods International Inc.

Figure V-5. **Potato Baking Rack.** Tin with wire handle, c. 1900. Author's collection. Value: $10-$12.

Footman, steel, highly polished steel
front legs, iron back legs, English,
18th century $400.00
Footman, brass, cabriole front legs,
10½" high, probably American,
19th century $150.00
Hake, hand forged iron, "S" hook for
hanging pots or kettles from crane .... $15.00 to $18.00
Hot mat, variegated woods in pinwheel
design, Shaker, 8" diameter (came
in other sizes), 1920s $15.00
Kettle tilter, wrought iron, used to
assist the cook in pouring from a
heavy kettle suspended over a
fire, late 1700s .... $100.00 to $300.00

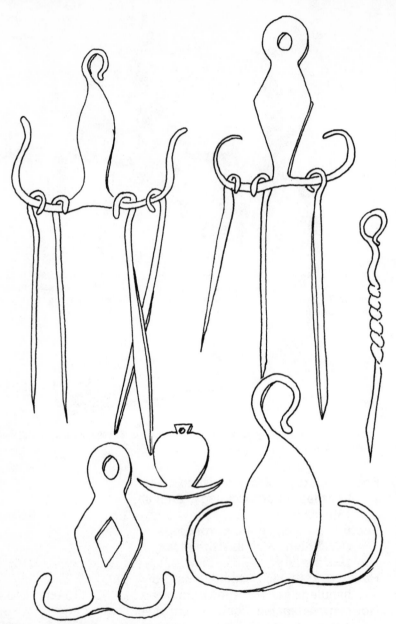

Figure V-6. **Skewer Racks and Skewers.** Wrought iron, 18th and 19th century forms. Almost all skewer holders/racks are similar in form: a diamond or somewhat bulbous shaft with upraised arms. Value depends on age, size and particularly design. Don't worry about a "matched" or "original" set because even in the 18th and early 19th century a set would be built up of various skewers made for specific purposes. Special forms and beautiful detailing, such as extra fine rat-tail loops or twisted iron, add value. Value: $100 and up for racks, $15 and up for individual skewers.

Figure V-7. **Skewer Rack and Skewers.**
Wrought iron, early 1700s. Picture courtesy of The Smithsonian Institution, Museum of History and Technology.

Kettle tilter, hand forged iron, swivel
top with acorn finial, late 1700s $325.00
Kettle tilter, forged iron, swivel ring
and brass knob, 21" long $300.00
Kettle tilter, forged iron, swivel top
and brass knob on handle, 23"
long, c. 1800 .... $400.00
Pot lifter, hand forged iron, swivel hook $22.00
Pot lifter, wrought iron, wooden handle $45.00
Pot pusher, wrought iron, with three
legs and curly handle, 6"
long x 5" high, semi-circle cradles
pot and makes it easy to push
pot steadily, farther in
among the hot coals, 18th century $165.00
Potato baking rack, heavy tin with wire
handle, 6 bent-up projections for
the potatoes, 15¼" long, turn-
of-century .... $10.00 to $12.00
Potato baking rack, steel wire, 8
upright projections, 14" long x 5" wide $5.00
Skewer holder and skewers, wrought
iron, 5 skewers, late 1700s, early
1800s .... $100.00 to $500.00

Figure V-9. **Trivet.** Cast iron with heart motif in center and at end of handle. Dated 1829. 11 3/8" long x 6½" diameter. Picture courtesy of the National Museum of American History, Smithsonian Institution.

Figure V-8. **Trammel.** Wrought iron. Saw-tooth style with crane ring. Early 19th century, probably American. Extension: 45" to 61". Formerly in the Keillor Collection. Value: $75-$110.

Skewer holder and skewers, nicely-
curved arms, 6 various skewers,
late 18th or early 19th century $550.00

Skewer holder and skewers, hand
    forged iron, ring top to boldly
    shaped rack, 18th century $800.00

**NOTE: Provenance and attractiveness are very important in the
pricing of skewer racks and skewers. An extremely plain
example, unexceptional in every way, and relatively "late" would
hardly bring more than $50 to $75. But a good example of an
early Pennsylvania German rack, with skewers, in some unusual
design like a heart, would bring a great deal of money. One or
two cautionary notes: there is no way at all to know if skewers
are original to a particular holder, nor should you expect this.
Blacksmith's marks only identify the maker [or sometimes the
owner]. Also, there's a high probability of finding recently-made
skewer holders and skewers. These have been made, not
necessarily with the intent to deceive, since the early part of this
century. There's no way to tell the difference if someone clever
means to trick you. Best to know and trust the source before
you buy. Some collectors feel that there's a general falling off in
the buying of the simple forged iron early pieces because of the
fact they can be fairly easily reproduced. They go on to say that
perhaps this explains the fast-track approach of later 19th
century patented gadgets, etc., which cost a lot to reproduce
and are therefore not. The cost of molds and the whole casting
process probably means that until antique cast iron things start
selling for $1000 or so, we won't have many reproductions . . . at
least of things with moving parts.**

Spit engine, brass face, wrought iron
    frame, late 18th century $2500.00

**NOTE: Other spit engines from the 1700s or early 1800s are
extremely rare. Expect to pay at least $1600.00.**

Spit, wrought iron with penny feet,
    adjustable vertical spit with
    hooks, 28" high, 18th century $725.00
Spoon rest, stamped aluminum, says
    "Place on kitchen table or range.
    Easy to clean. Unbreakable. Burn
    proof"... $1.00
Trammel, wrought iron, chain with
    long hook, knobbed lugpole
    hook, early 1800s $65.00

Figure V-10. **"The Turnspit."** Illustration from **"Frank Leslie's Boy's & Girl's Weekly,"** August 7, 1869. To quote from the magazine: "Not long since, a wheel in a circular box was brought from an old house to a railroad station in England, with a lot of old trumpery. The other articles attracted little attention, but this puzzled all the group gathered there . . . There were old men and women, too, but none remembered seeing such a thing in use. At last, a blacksmith of a neighboring village said it was a turnspit's wheel, such as he remembered to have seen in use. It seems a hard lot for the dog to be kept at his work for, perhaps, three hours, till the joint was done, and we do not wonder that the custom at last fell into disuse. The dogs themselves often rebelled . . . " Special short-legged and barrel-chested dogs were bred for this purpose, and it is something hard to imagine — thank Heaven — in our more enlightened and animal-loving age.

Trammel, chain, 50" long, early 1800s $40.00
Trammel, chain, strong twisted
    wrought iron hook, 70" long,
    early 19th century $50.00
Trammel, chain, decorative wrought
    iron hook $25.00
Trammel, very heavy chain, 86" long $200.00
Trammel, wrought iron, hook-and-eye,
    adjustable $130.00

Trammel, handwrought iron, sawtooth
    style, 22" to 31" extended, late
    18th century $110.00
Trammel, wrought iron, sawtooth, 56"
    long extended $55.00

NOTE: Most trammels go for under $100; possibly this is because they don't excite much visual interest in people. They were a very important accessory for fireplace cookery, and several would have been found hanging from the crane in early kitchens. Some are very decorative, with scrolling curves and fancifully shaped sawtooth or hook-and-eye elements. These can be expected — at their finest — to go for upwards of $250.00. A good number of the antique trammels for sale in this country today probably just arrived on these shores from England or Europe. But what's the difference if a French trammel got here in 1780 or 1980?

Trivet, brass, stylized thistle design,
    of the type called a "fire bar
    trivet" because it hooked
    onto the fire bar that went between
    two andirons $145.00
Trivet, cast and wrought iron, 3-legged
    hearth style, 10" high, 18th century $250.00
Trivet, wrought iron, round with 3 legs
    and a long handle, 8" diameter x
    6" high with 11" handle $45.00
Trivet, cast iron, "Griswold," for a
    kettle, 12" diameter $15.00
Trivet, cast iron, round, heart
    with rays design, 8" diameter $75.00
Trivets, of the type known as
    "footmen," steel, iron, brass or
    combinations, these resemble
    footstools — usually 4-legged,
    and are meant for keeping food
    or drink hot by the fireplace, more
    often in parlor than kitchen .... $125.00 to $500.00

NOTE: The Metropolitan Museum has created a replica of an early 19th century Pennsylvania heart-shaped trivet of hand-forged iron. It is 6" long and has 3 short legs, and sells for about $18.50.

TURN, RETRIEVE, SPOON & LIFT

In this category are found the implements that help the cook move food or food particles from one utensil to another or from one container to another. There are fuzzy edges to this category definition; for example, I put skimmers into the SEPARATE, STRAIN & SIFT category. The most important — or most widely collected — implement in this category is the cake turner. Possibly second in line is the plate or pie lifter.

Basting spoon, speckled black and
    white agateware, 13" long .... $8.00 to $10.00
Basting spoon, heavy tinned iron,
    deep bowl, 17" long .... $6.00 to $8.00
Bean pot lifter, wire, very simple .... $8.00 to $12.00
Butter fork, wood, "Mrs. Bragg's
    Butter Fork" as sold in late 19th
    century Montgomery Ward
    catalogs, looks rather like an Afro comb .. $10.00 to $15.00
Butter paddle, wire blade with
    maple handle, 8¾" long .... $15.00 to $18.00
Butter paddle, maple, 14" long with
    hole in handle end $13.00
Butter paddle, wood, shaped like a
    thick, slightly scooped ping-pong
    paddle, 9" long, 5¼" diameter $12.00
Butter paddle, carved wood with very
    shallow bowl and short crook-
    necked handle $35.00

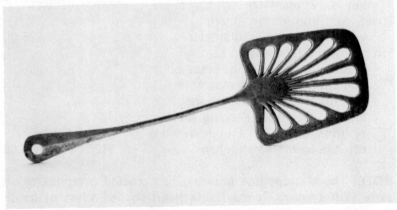

Figure VI-I. **Cake Turner.** Cast aluminum. Marked "Royal Bra—, Made in Germany." 12" long. 1930s. Author's collection. Value: $10-$18.

NOTE: For butter hands, used for shaping butter, look under the FORM, MOLD, SHAPE & DECORATE category.

Cake server, tin and wire, handle
    embossed "Rumford, the
    Wholesome Baking Powder" . . . . $7.00 to $12.00

NOTE: The following are cake turners — often called "spatulas" today, although this is technically incorrect. A [pan]cake turner has a blade which is usually not much longer than it is wide, it is usually about 4" to 4½" wide, and it is also usually slotted or pierced. A spatula is rather like a flexible dinner knife — the blade is long and slender and rounded on the end. A cake turner is, of course, often used for flipping food other than flapjacks: fried eggs, grilled cheese sandwiches, crabcakes or sliced summer squash. Many people specialize in the cake turners of the A & J Company/ Edward Katzinger Company [now EKCO]. Androck products are another popular specialty. Another sort of specialty is possible too . . . mechanical cake turners that do the flipping for you! Yet another kind is designed so that the blade can be used in closed [single] or open [triple] spread position.

Cake turner, cast aluminum, "Royal
    Brand," made in Germany, 12½" long . . . . $10.00 to $18.00
Cake turner, tin with wire, "Coradon,"
    3 blades that fan out when you
    pull thumb release, 12½" long,
    pat'd 1936 . . . . $10.00 to $15.00
Cake turner, steel and wood, "A & J,"
    13¼" long, 1930s . . . . $6.00 to $12.00
Cake turner, tin and wire, handle
    snakes off at end — an elegant
    solution to heat dispersal
    problem, 14¾" long, c. 1910 . . . . $10.00 to $15.00
Cake turner, tin and green wood,
    blade is stamped with ridges to
    add rigidity and perforated with
    highly decorative pattern of holes
    reminiscent of Pennsylvania
    German heart, 11¾" long . . . . $6.00 to $9.00
Cake turner, tin with wood handle,
    odd near-round blade, no
    perforations, quite rigid, early 1900s . . . . . . $7.00 to $10.00

Figure VI-2. **Dipper and Butter Paddle.** The dipper is a dried gourd, the paddle is carved from wood. 19th century. Picture courtesy of the National Museum of American History, Smithsonian Institution.

Cake turner, tin with nickel-plated
wire handle, heart-shaped hole
near riveted hoint of handle and
blade, c. 1900, 10¾" long, possibly
mfd. by Pilgrim Novelty Co. .... $6.00 to $10.00
Cake turner, same as above but
embossed/stamped "Rumford
Baking Powder" .... $7.00 to $12.00
Cake turner, tin with wire shank, blue
& ivory painted wood handle, "A
& J," late 1930s (?) $4.00
Cake turner, tin with wood handle,
"Androck" $1.50

NOTE: The last two listings were seen at a flea market in early 1983. Prices seem very cheap, when I saw so many cake turners over $10.00.

Candy scoop, japanned tin, small
with tubular handle, late
1800s, early 1900s .... $8.00 to $15.00
Candy scoop, brass, 8½" long $25.00
Carving fork, steel with bone
handle, 2-tined, mid- to late-19th
century .... $8.00 to $12.00

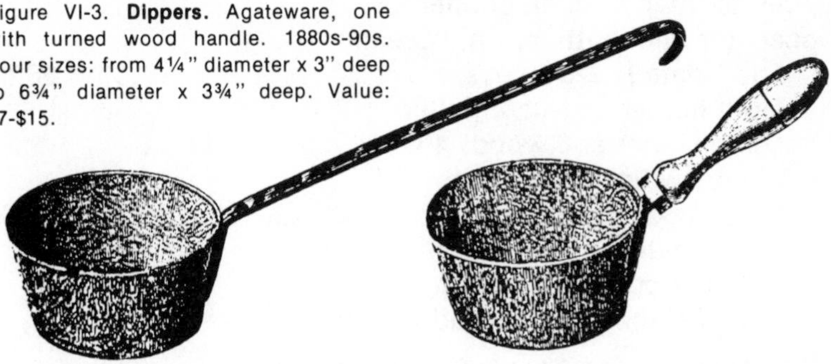

Figure VI-3. **Dippers.** Agateware, one with turned wood handle. 1880s-90s. Four sizes: from 4¼" diameter x 3" deep to 6¾" diameter x 3¾" deep. Value: $7-$15.

Dipper, gray graniteware, Windsor style, long tubular handle, quite handsome .... $10.00 to $15.00

Dipper, gray graniteware, bent handle, deep but small bowl .... $7.00 to $10.00

Dipper, wrought iron, 24" handle with hooked end, huge bowl with 2-quart capacity $50.00

Dipper, brown graniteware, 18" handle $12.00

Dipper, brass with wrought iron handle, 15¼" long, hooked end, late 18th or early 19th century $210.00

Dipper, wrought iron with rattail handle, 15" long $28.00

Dipper, tin, 14" long with 5" bowl $22.00

Dipper, tin with tubular handle, 2-cup capacity, 9½" long $20.00

Dipper, tin, 9" long tubular handle, cheap at $6.00

Dipper, mottled brown & white graniteware, 14½" long with 5¼" bowl, slight chipping $10.00

Dipper, ash burl, 3" deep bowl x 6" x 5½", unusual 13" long handle, beautiful patina $160.00

Dipper, burl, 3" deep bowl x 6¼" diameter, 4" long handle, early 1800s $115.00

Dipper, goard, 4 7/8" deep x 9½" long, straight necked handle $14.00

Dipper, goard, 3" deep x 8" long, curved neck handle, polished and in very good condition $16.00

Dipper, for maple sugar, copper $70.00
Dipper, for milk bottles, tin, "Cream
    Top," dated 1925 .... $8.00
Dishcloth holder and cork puller
    combo, wire and wood, 4 wire
    prongs which grasp cloth, 12"
    long, 1880s to 1910 .... $6.00 to $8.00
Dishcloth holder and vegetable
    skimmer combo, wire, prongs
    same as above, other end is wire
    spoon .... $7.00 to $10.00
Flour scoop, carved wood with
    fingerhold grip, primitive, very
    smooth and attractive $64.00
Flour scoop, carved from one piece
    of wood $20.00
Flour scoop, metal bowl with wire
    handles, handles stamped "Airy
    Fairy Kwik Bis-kit Flour" and
    "Airy Fairy Cake Flour", 7½" long $6.00
Fish slice, perforated tin with wood
    handle, 12½" long, 19th century,
    called a "slice" but not for slicing,
    it's for lifting cooked fish from a
    fish cooker. The word "slice"
    relates to the thin broad shape —
    as in a slice of bread or cheese .... $65.00 to $95.00
Forks, meat or flesh, iron or wire with
    wood or wire handles, 1900 to 1940s .... $2.00 to $8.00
Forks, meat or flesh, wrought iron,
    18th or early 19th century,
    depending on design and size .... $65.00 to $150.00
Fork, roasting, brass and steel, 3-tine,
    telescoping handle, probably
    English, 12" extends to 20" $34.00

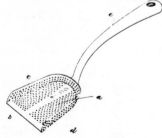

Figure VI-4. **Egg Lifter Patent Drawing.**
Pat'd August 5, 1890 by Ann E. Smith,
Springfield, Ohio. For poached eggs. "As
an article of manufacture, an egg-lifter
composed of a single piece of perforated
metal with a straight solid cutting-edge
and a perforated rim of substantially
uniform height . . .

280

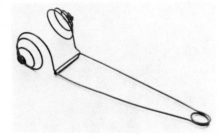

Figure VI-5. **Egg Lifter.** Wire, 12½" long, c. 1890-1920. Perfect for retrieving hard boiled eggs — or how about matza balls? Collection of Meryle Evans. Value: $8-$12.

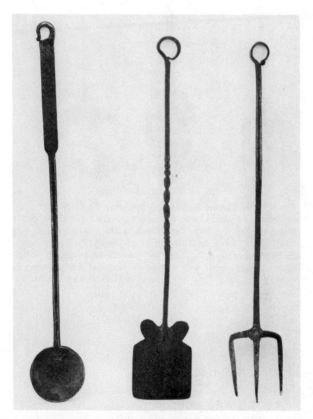

Figure VI-6. **Spoon, Spatula and Fork for Hearth Cooking.** Spoon: wrought iron with zigzag incised, whitesmith-finished handle. American, late 18th century, 18" long. Sold at auction for $125. Spatula or cake turner: wrought iron with great twisted handle and beautifully shrugged shoulders on the blade. Wonderful piece from late 18th century. American, 17" long. Sold for a well-deserved $600. Flesh fork: wrought iron with whitesmith-finished handle, 3 prongs, American, late 18th century. Sold at auction for $75. Picture courtesy of Robert W. Skinner Inc., Auctioneers, Bolton, MA.

281

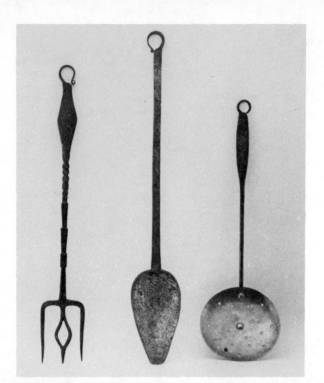

Figure VI-7. **Flesh Fork, Tasting Spoon and Skimmer.** Fork: 3-tined wrought iron with beautifully designed twisted and stepped handle with chevron, finished by a whitesmith. Beautiful hanging ring. Reticulated center tine. American, late 18th or early 19th century. 18½" long. Sold for amazingly low $175. Spoon: wrought iron with nicely finished loop for hanging. Late 18th century American. 21" long. Sold for only $50. Skimmer: brass bowl with riveted-on wrought iron handle. Early 19th century American. 16½" long. Sold at auction for $120. Picture courtesy of Robert W. Skinner Inc., Auctioneers, Bolton, MA.

Fork, wrought iron, 2-tine, 19" long,
    early 1800s $60.00
Fork, wrought iron with wooden
    handle, 3-tine, 55" long, early 1800s $95.00
Fork, iron with turned wood handle
    and brass hanging hook, 4 prongs
    forming a square, 26" long $155.00
Fork for toasting, iron tines, wood
    handle, 20" long, early 1800s $75.00
Fork, wrought iron with simple heart
    at handle end, 30" long, 2-tines $48.00

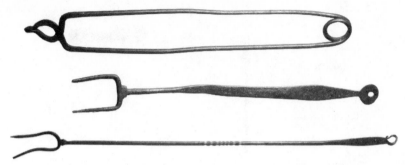

Figure VI-8. **Meat Forks and Tong.** Wrought iron, early 19th century. Picture courtesy of The Smithsonian Institution, Museum of History and Technology.

Fruit auger, see Sugar auger.

Ice cream servers, see FORM, MOLD, SHAPE.

Ice tongs, see CANNING, CHILLING, FREEZING, DRYING.

Jar lifter, see CANNING, CHILLING, FREEZING, DRYING.

Ladle, dark blue spatterware $13.00
Ladle, tin, for cream, dated 1924 .... $6.00
Ladle, "Sweet Clover Condensed Milk" $10.00
Ladle, iron and brass, end of 18th century $225.00
Ladle, brass with wrought iron handle,
    ring handle, dated "1835" which
    is partly why it cost $350.00
Ladle, brass bowl with wrought iron
    handle, 14½" long $90.00
Ladle, pewter bowl with socket-fitted
    turned wooden handle, 15" long,
    probably American, mid-19th century $60.00
Maple syrup taster, brass $27.50
Marrow spoon, carved wood, possibly
    cherry, 10" long, late 1700s, early
    1800s $90.00

283

Figure VI-9. **Pie Lifter** (top left), **Can Opener** with bull's head (top right), **Basin** of cast iron, **Candlesticks.** Pie lifter: wrought iron, c. 1840. Value: $125. Can Opener, c. 1880. Value: $45-$60. Basin, c. 1830. Value: $50. Picture courtesy of Georgia G. Levett, Levett's Antiques, Camden, Maine.

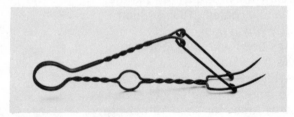

Figure VI-10. **Fork.** Wire with push-off action . . . stick it into a potato and press lever so it will push potato off onto plate. 9¼" long. 19th century. Collection of Meryle Evans. Value: $12-$18.

284

Figure VI-11. **Fish Slice.** Perforated tin with wood handle and hanging ring. Simple fish design. 12½" long. 19th century. Collection of Meryle Evans. Value: $60-$75.

Figure VI-12. **Fork and Taster.** Fork is wrought iron, c. 1796. Value: $65. Taster, iron and brass. C. 1800. Value: $75. Picture courtesy of Georgia G. Levett, Levett's Antiques, Camden, Maine.

Figure VI-13. **Ladle/Strainer** (top left): **Ladle** and **Peel** (crossed below). Ladle/strainer, tin with wooden handle, long pointed spout. 13¼" long. Brass ladle with steel handle, unmarked, 13" long. Steel peel, marked "Levi Lewis," 14¾" long. All early part of 19th century. Collection of Meryle Evans. Value in order: $100-$125; $70-$85; $50-$65.

Figure VI-14. **Dish Towel Holders** and **Vegetable Servers.** Fancifully bent wire, with ring-bound prongs. Longest is 13½" long. Left and center, author's collection. Right, collection of Meryle Evans. Value: $7-$10.

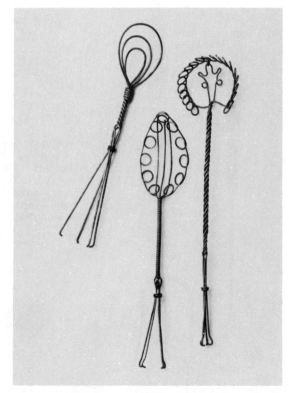

Figure VI-15. **Plate Lifter.** Wire and wood. "Triumph." From Montgomery Ward catalog, c. 1895. Original price: 13 cents. Value: $12-$15.

Marrow spoon, very fine-grained wood
with good patina, 11¼" long,
engine-turning on end of handle,
late 1700s, early 1800s $85.00
Olive or pickle fork, tinned steel,
2-prong, 8" long, 20th century
probably .... $1.00 to $2.00
Olive or pickle fork, twisted wire, 10"
long, probably 19th century $6.00
Peel, wrought iron, 22" long, early 1800s ..... $45.00 to $65.00
Peel, wrought iron, ram's head handle,
29½" long $60.00
Peel, wrought iron, knob handle, 51" long $50.00
Peel, wrought iron, ram's head handle
with beautiful curl to "horns," 45"
long, 18th century $150.00
Peel wrought iron, ram's head handle,
much shorter handle, 25" long $120.00
Peel, carved pine, 51" long $110.00
Peel, wood, probably pine, very short
5" handle, 13" long "blade" $35.00
Peel, wood, short handle, possibly Shaker $25.00
Pie lifter, wire with wood handle,
2-prongs, 17½" long $25.00
Pie lifter, wire and wood, "Triumph",
clamps around pie plate $15.00
Pie lifter, hexagonal tin platform to
support pie, green wooden handle,
adjustable side grips, "Sure-
Grip", 20" long, nifty $16.00

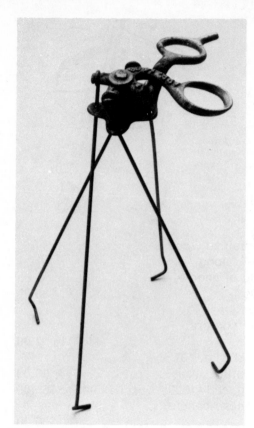

Figure VI-16. **Pie Lifter.** Scissor action. Pat'd April 14, 1908, but no other marks. Doesn't it look like a water strider or something from Disney movie, "Dark Crystal"? 8" high. Collection of Meryle Evans. Value: $30-$40.

Pie lifter, heavy wire with sliding
    hook, pat'd 1883 .... $28.00
Scoop, tin, strap handle, 3¾" long $6.00
Scoop, flour, tin with wood handle,
    7" long .... $6.00 to $10.00

NOTE: A very attractive old-style brass scoop, curved and with a riveted-on wooden handle, 16¾" long, is being produced and sold as a "coal scoop" by Brasscrafters of Syosset, NY. To the unwary, it might well appear to be an antique.

Sugar or dried fruit auger, also called
    a "Sugar Devil," wrought iron
    with wood T-handle, looks rather
    like a dancing post-hole auger,
    pat'd July 27, 1873(5?), 16¾"
    long to 17" long .... $90.00 to $150.00

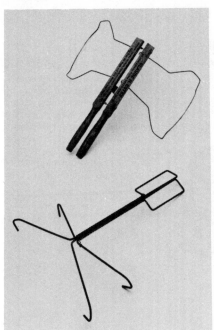

Figure VI-17. **Pie Lifters.** Top is wire and wood, very like the "Triumph." It serves as an advertising piece with words stamped on the wooden handle: "Claude H. Estee, Shepherd, Michigan. Beans, Grain, Farm Seeds, & Wool. We deal coal, flour, feed, mason's supplies, etc." "Hang Near the Range & Stop Burning Your Hands." Spring action, 13½" long. Bottom is all wire, looks like a dragonfly. 16" long. Located by the Primitive Man, Bob Cahn, Carmel, NY. He evaluates at $35-$45.

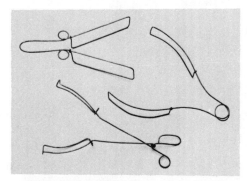

Figure VI-18. **Pie Lifters.** Wire. Top left has finger holes and works okay as long as the pie isn't too heavy. 14¾" long. Top right is slightly springier, not any stronger. 14¾" long. At bottom is the least trustworthy. I wouldn't carry a mud pie with it! 16½" long. Collection of Meryle Evans. Value: $12-$16.

Figure VI-19. **Peel or Spatula.** Wrought iron with wood handle. 19th century. Collection of Meryle Evans. Value: $55-$70.

289

Figure VI-20. **Dipper and Spatula or Cake Turner.** Wrought iron. 8" long dipper (or tasting spoon) and 8" long spatula, both late 18th century American. Rat-tail handles. Sold for $275 for the two. Picture courtesy of Robert W. Skinner Inc., Auctioneers, Bolton, MA.

Figure VI-21. **Peels** Wrought iron, 19th century. From 10½" to 14½" long. Estimated at 1983 Linden sale between $50-$100 for the lot. Realized: $242. Picture courtesy of Christie, Manson & Woods, International Inc.

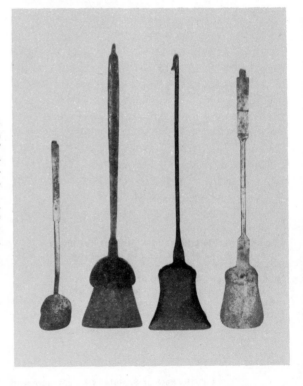

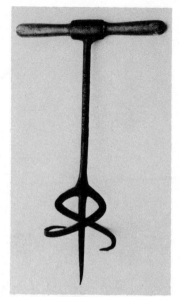

Figure VI-23. **Sugar or Dried Fruit Auger.** Forged iron with wood handle. Marked "Pat'd July 27, 1873" (or possibly '75). 16¾" long. Sometimes called a "sugar devil" — like a whirling dervish. Collection of Meryle Evans. Value: $100-$135.

Figure VI-22. **Skimmer.** Very simple sheet brass, marked "B.S. Porter." 13½" long x 5 1/8" wide. 19th century American. Picture courtesy of the National Museum of American History, Smithsonian Institution.

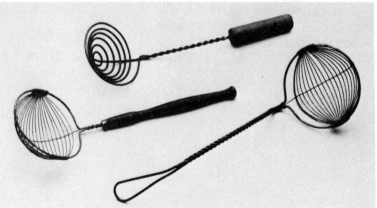

Figure VI-24. **Vegetable Servers or Skimmers.** Wire with wire or wood handles. All wire: 14" long x 5" wide. Long wood turned handle: c. 1870s-90s. 13" long x 4 3/8" wide. One with stubby wood handle: c. 1915-1920. 13" long x 3¾" wide. Author's collection. Value: $10-$20.

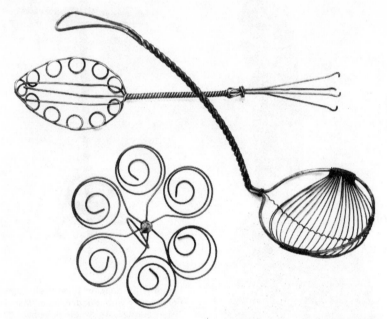

Figure VII-1. **Wirewares.** Bottom, folding 6-**egg rack**; right, **vegetable skimmer/serv-er**; left, combination **whisk or vegetable skimmer** and "grapple" for dishcloth to clean lamp chimneys. All late 19th century. Author's collection. Value: $8-$15.

Sugar auger, wrought iron, 2-prongs,
    T-handle, that looks for all the
    world like an old lawnmower
    handle, pat'd May 23, 1876 .... $125.00
Vegetable lifters or ladles, wire with
    long wire or wood handles,
    turn-of-century .... $8.00 to $15.00

MEASURE: WEIGHT, AMOUNT, SIZE & TEMPERATURE

Among the most important items in this category, as far as collectors go, are egg scales and measures. Egg scales are sought by collectors who specialize in patented items or mid-19th to 1940's things. Measures have a bit more "cachet" in the antiques world . . . mostly because of the beautiful copper graduated measures, many of which are English or Continental. This is not to play down the importance of other specialties. Some collectors go after nothing but scales — all kinds of scales. Probably the only things not collected, at least seriously, are butter triers and cake testers. I mean, how many long skinny wires with a ring at the end could you accumulate!

Bean sizing sieve, wood frame with
    wood slats, 18" x 18" square,
    adjusts down to exaggerated
    diamond shape, spaces between
    slats narrow $110.00
Candy thermometer, tin with brass
    face, J. Kendall & Co., marked
    "Spirit, Boil, Simmer, Heat,
    Temple, Freezing," 6½" long .... $22.00 to $30.00
Candy and jelly thermometer, metal
    with light green wooden handle,
    "Faylor," c. 1940s, mint $16.00

Clocks: see subsection at end of this category.

Dry measure, bentwood with tin
    binding, 1 quart size, 5¼"
    diameter, mid 1800s $40.00
Dry measure, bentwood with old red
    paint, bail handle $15.00
Dry measure, bentwood, copper nails,
    looks like a saucepan with
    exaggeratedly uptilted handle $45.00
Dry measure, bentwood, 8" diameter,
    with cover, Shaker, from Maine $80.00
Dry measures, set of 4 round
    graduated measures, 6", 7", 9"
    and 11" diameter $55.00

Figure VII-2. **Measure.** Tin quart size with wraparound lip. 19th century. Value: $12-$18.

Figure VII-3 **Measure.** With close-fitting lide (now shown). Copper, marked "Stevens & Duncklee, Concord, N.H." 5½" high x 5" diameter, holds 52 oz. Collection of Mary Mac Franklin. Value: $40-$55.

Figure VII-4. **Measures.** Copper with brass plates and handles. Tin-lined. ½ pint to 2-pint size, marked on plates. 19th century. Collection of Mary Mac Franklin. Value: $35-$50 each.

Figure VII-5. **Measures.** Tin with wraparound lip. Largest 2 gallon size has reinforced handle. Smallest is ¼ pint. From F.A. Walker catalog, c. 1890. Value: $15-$30 each.

Dry measure bucket, wood, old green
    paint, 2 gallons $43.00
Dry measure, bentwood, painted gray,
    handforged lap nails, 9¾"
    diameter, 19th century $35.00
Dry measure, oak bentwood, "Daniel
    Cragin, Wilton, N.H.," 11½"
    diameter, 19th century $30.00
Dry measure, same only 5¾" diameter $20.00

Figure VII-6. **Egg Scale.** Painted tin. Jiffy-Way, pat'd 1940. 7 1/8" long x 5¾" high. Author's collection. Value: $12-$22.

Egg scale, aluminum, "Acme Egg Grading Scale," Specialty Mfg. Co., pat'd June 24, 1924, 10½" long x 4½" high, marvelous soft slithery sound of the fulcrum as eggs are weighed .... $16.00 to $24.00

Egg scale, painted sheet metal, extremely simple with cast metal counterweight, c. 1910-1940 .... $12.00 to $15.00

Egg scale, painted sheet metal, "Jiffy Way," Owatonna, MN, pat'd 1940, 7 1/8" long x 5¾" high .... $12.00 to $20.00

Egg scale, painted cast iron base, balance & weight, aluminum egg pan & dial, brass pointer, "Zenith Egg Grader," Earlysville, NY, 8" high $28.00

Egg scale, metal, "Toledo" $16.00

Egg scale, stamped tin, marked "Oak's 'Sanitized' Equipment for every poultry need, "Oak's Mfg. Co., Tipton, Indiana, c. 1920s $18.50

Egg scale, metal, "Unique" $3.00

Figure VII-7. **Egg Glasses.** Wood and glass, or iron and glass. From F.A. Walker catalog, c. 1880. Value: $45-$60.

Figure VII-8. **Measures.** Tin. "Maryann's Accurate Measure," Chicago. Set of four graduated cups, ¼ to a whole cup. Author's collection. Value: $6-$10. Large 1 quart size, with wraparound lip and strap handle. Collection and picture of Lar Hothem. Value: $12-$18.

1 Qt.

1½ Pt

1 Pt.

½ Pt

Figure VII-9. **Quart Measure.** Tin with wraparound lip and strap handle. Picture from Matthai-Ingram catalog, c. 1890. 1 quart size. Value: $12-$18.

Figure VII-10. **Room Thermometer.** Red-painted stamped tin in teapot shape. Approx. 7" wide, c. 1920s-40s. "Tel-Tru" Thermometer Co., Rochester, NY. Value: $5-$6.

Egg tester/candler, pierced tin cylinder with strap handle, resembles a drinking cup, marked "The Family Egg-Tester. Patented March 13, 1876," 3" high, with hole in top for holding eggs to be candled $28.00

Ice cream scoops: See under FORM, MOLD, SHAPE & DECORATE.

Measure, brass, strap handle, 1 pint size, mid-19th century .... $60.00 to $70.00
Measure, copper, wraparound pouring lip, strap handle, 1 quart size $80.00
Measure, gray graniteware, wrap-around lip, 1 pint size $35.00
Measure, gray graniteware, 1 quart size $30.00
Measure, tin, "Kreamer," 4 cup size .... $5.00 to $7.00
Measure, tin, wraparound pouring lip, strap handle, 1 pint size, late 1800s ...... $14.00 to $18.00

Measure, tin, flared wraparound lip,
   strap handle with grip brace, 8
   cup size, 8" high $12.00
Measure, gray graniteware, 2 quart size $32.00
Measures, copper and brass combined
   elongated necks and widely-flaring
   bodies (like skirts), 1 quart and
   1 gallon size, the pair $225.00

NOTE: The above measures are liquid measures. See also "Dry measures."

Measuring cups, set of 4 Jadite cups $18.00
Measuring cup, green glass, "Kellogg's" ...... $9.00 to $10.00
Measuring cup, tin, embossed "Drink
   Barrington Hall Coffee," 1 cup size $3.00
Measuring cup, glass, embossed
   "Faultless Diamond Starch," 1 cup $4.00
Measuring cup, spun aluminum,
   "Swans Down Cake Flour Makes
   Better Cakes" embossed on side
   1 cup .... $7.00 to $12.00
Measuring cup, tin, deep wraparound
   lip, 5" high, 2 cup size, late 1800s .... $8.00 to $12.00
Measuring pitcher, tin, Dover, 1 quart $4.00
Measuring pitchers, copper, set of 6,
   signed "D.M. Smith," early 19th
   century, the set $500.00

NOTE: I don't hate to confess ignorance, fortunately. I wonder if "measuring pitcher" might not be the same as "measure with wraparound lip" to two different collectors?

Measuring spoons, tin, "Original,"
   marked ¼ teaspoon, ½ teaspoon,
   1 teaspoon, and in drops: 15, 30
   & 60, pat'd 1900, don't often see
   old measuring spoon sets .... $7.00 to $10.00
Scale, beam, cast iron, "Dearborn Patent" .... $30.00 to $40.00
Scale, candy, tin base with brass pan
   and white-enameled dial, "Hanson
   Brothers," 12" high $45.00

Figure VII-11. **Scales and Weights.** Balance scale with pan. From F.A. Walker catalog, 1890s. Value: $70-$95.

Scale, dial, "Perfection," pat'd 1906 .... $10.00
Scale, spring balance (the kind that "
hangs), "Landers #2" $6.00
Scale, spring balance, brass face,
"Eagle Warranted" $14.00
Scale, spring balance, for ice, iron
with brass face, c. 1900 .... $25.00
Scale, spring balance, "Frary's
Improved Balance #2," 50 pound
capacity $20.00
Scale, spring balance, "Chatillon,"
pat'd 1867 and 1891, 8" long, 25
pound capacity .... $10.00 to $15.00
Scale, spring balance, "L.F. & Co."
(Landers, Frary & Clark) $6.00
Scale, spring balance, brass face,
"Excelsior," 50 pound capacity $18.00
Scale, stillyard (sometimes called
"steelyard") with iron weight,
raised star cast on it, 25 pound capacity $14.00
Sorghum meter or faucet, fitted into
keg, pat'd 1878 .... $35.00
Spigot for cider barrel, wood with
pewter key, marked "John
Sommer's Best Block Tin Key" .... $7.00 to $15.00
Thermometer, for rooms, stamped tin,
shaped like an urn $5.00
Thermometer, for rooms, stamped
tin, shaped like a fat teapot, and
painted red, mfd. by "Tel-Tru
Thermometer Co.," Rochester, NY $5.00

Figure VII-12. **Scoop or Dry Measure.** Carved from one piece of wood. Marked "TOLLARD." 15¼" long. 19th century. Picture courtesy of Christie, Manson & Woods International Inc. Realized price, with 4 pantry boxes — shown elsewhere — $180.

MEASURING TIME

I could be argued with, but this seems a good place to put clocks and egg timers (hour glasses). I've only included the obvious kitchen clocks.

Clock, blue & white "Delft plate,
   Dutch scene, works $40.00
Clock, "Cookie Time" $18.00
Clock, tin, frying-pan shaped,
   Sessions, c. 1920s $18.00
Clock, real frying pan — a "Cold
   Handle" Acme, with key-wound
   clock, copyrighted 1899, made as
   souvenir for the Pan-American
   Exposition Company for the
   1901 fair .... $450.00 to $550.00
Clock, molded plastic frying pan with
   copper finish, Model 504, Herold
   Products Co., Chicago, c. 1950s .... $30.00 to $40.00
Clock and inkwell combo, brass made
   for the 50th anniversary of the
   Joseph Spidel Grocery Co.
   (1863-1913) mfd. by Mercedes,
   flour sacks, brooms, barrels/kegs
   and groceries, cast round face $130.00
Egg timer, wood, old red paint, 19th century $20.00
Egg timer, wood, old blue paint,
   19th century $75.00

TEA, COFFEE & CHOCOLATE

This category, a very popular one with collectors, comprises the vast numbers of tea and coffee pots and kettles, coffee mills and tea balls and infusers. Coffee grinders are probably the most popular as a special category. Some of the most splendiferous coffee mills were featured in an article in **Art & Decoration,** August/September 1982, published in Paris. I was unable to get any of the pictures to share with you because the pieces were all from unnamed private collections in France.

Chocolate pot, tin, side handle with
turned wood handle, small
"trapdoor" in lid to allow muddler,
c. 1870 .... $150.00
Chocolate pot, copper with steel
handle, with what could be the
original wooden muller (or
muddler), 7" high, English,
mid-18th century $180.00
Chocolate pot in its own nickel-plated
castor, brown and white
agateware with nickel-plated
collar, lid and spout, marked
"Manning Patent," 11" high $350.00
Chocolate saucepan, gray graniteware,
pouring lip, 9¼" diameter .... $9.00 to $12.00

Beneath the tropic sky there blooms a tree
Laden with fruitage and most fair to see.
Out of its fruit seeds is the **COCOA** made
Of **BLOOKER**, foremost in his branch of trade
Known through the world, its flavor rich and rare,
Each Housekeeper who buys finds past compare.
Rightly the tree, its source like it is fame,
Since "Theobroma", food fit for the gods,"
twas fitly named.

Concentrated and pure and yet not dear,
Once use it and you'll find it has no peer.
Doming with European fame to Western shores,
On all sides welcomed, genuine praise outpours,
Ah there! at all the principal grocery stores.
Advertisement in the New York Times, **January 4, 1890.**

Coffee boiler, tin, side spout, c. 1870 . . . . $20.00 to $28.00
Coffee boiler, white and blue enameled tin $50.00
Coffee boiler, white and brown
    speckled enameled ware, nickel
    plated base and lid, wood finial
    and handle, "Manning &
    Bowman," pat'd 1889, 9" high $185.00

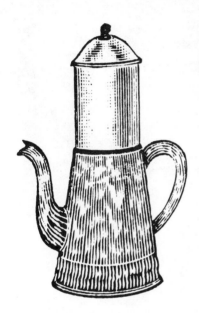

Figure VIII-1. **Biggin**, for coffee making. Graniteware and tin. From Matthai-Ingram catalog, c. 1890. Value: $75-$90. This is an early drip method, and was invented around 1800 by a Mr. Biggin. To quote from an 1884 cookbook, **Practical Housekeeping**, "Two cylindrical tin vessels, one fitting into the other; the bottom of the upper one is a fine strainer, another coarser strainer is placed on this with a rod running upwards from its center; the finely ground coffee is put in, and then another strainer is slipped on the rod, over the coffee, the boiling water is poured on the upper sieve and falls in a shower upon the coffee, filtering through it to the coarse strainer at the bottom, which prevents the coffee from filling up the holes of the finer strainer below it." Eat your heart out, Melitta!

Figure VIII-2. **Coffee Boiler.** Another style. Tin with side-strap handle, plus small strap "tipper" to ease pouring, 6, 8, 10 or 12 quarts. From F.A. Walker catalog, 1870s. Value: $20-$28.

Figure VIII-3. **Coffee Boiler.** Tin with bail handle and strap handle too. Seamless lip — body and lip made of one piece. Made in 2, 3, 4 and 6 quart sizes. This is the typical shape of coffee maker used in the "wild West," at least in the movies! From Matthai-Ingram catalog, c. 1890. Value: $20-$25.

303

Figure VIII-4. **Coffee Pot.** Tin, with fluted spout, delicate mushroom finial on lid, iron handle. C. 1895. Picture courtesy of The Smithsonian Institution, Museum of History and Technology.

Coffee boiler, gray graniteware, bail
    handle with wood grip, 1½ gallon
    capacity $18.00
Coffee boiler, white and sky blue
    marbleized enamelware, bail
    handle, 13" high $35.00
Coffee boiler, gray graniteware, 1
    gallon size $25.00

Figure VIII-5. **Coffee Pot.** Toleware with straight spout, strap handle, hinged lid with curled tin knob. 8 7/8" high. 19th century. Picture courtesy of the National Museum of American History, Smithsonian Institution.

Coffee boiler, blue agateware, wire
bail handle and fixed side handle,
10" high, 8¾" diameter at base
of tapered body, late 19th century $15.00

Coffee cup, graniteware, marked
"Dickinson's 'Pine Tree' Seeds" $45.00

Coffee grinder, wood box with hand
wrought iron bowl, "French style,"
c. mid-19th century $80.00

Coffee grinder, hand wrought iron
mill, mounts on wall, about 6"
high, early 19th century $160.00

Coffee grinder, wood box with pewter
hopper bowl, 7" x 7" x 5" box,
early 19th century $115.00

Coffee grinder, wood with ornate cast
iron top, "French style," bad
condition and still $55.00

Coffee grinder, wood with iron
hopper, 19th century $75.00

Coffee grinder, cast iron with original
red paint and pin-striping and
other decoration, marked "L.F. &
C." (Landers, Frary & Clark), New
Britain, CT, 19th century $175.00

Coffee grinder, tin and cast iron with
wood crank knob, "Universal
#109," Landers, Frary & Clark,
pat'd February 14, 1905, 5¼"
square x 5¼" high $55.00

Figure VIII-6. **Coffee Pots.** Toleware. Left to right: Tapering cylindrical body, straight
spout, strap handle, hinged lid. Black ground with fruit and leaves. 7 7/8" high.
Realized $600. Center: side spout, hinged lid. 8¾" high. Estimated $600-$1000;
realized only $420. Right: 8" high. Realized $600. Seymour sale, 1982. Picture
courtesy of Christie, Manson & Woods International Inc.

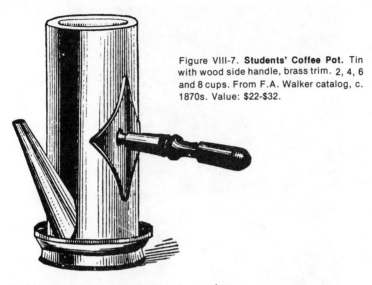

Figure VIII-7. **Students' Coffee Pot.** Tin with wood side handle, brass trim. 2, 4, 6 and 8 cups. From F.A. Walker catalog, c. 1870s. Value: $22-$32.

Coffee grinder, cast iron, store-size, "L.F. & C." Universal $60.00

Coffee grinder, wood and iron, "Home Coffee Mill #767," Mfd. by Arcade Mfg. Co., pat'd June 5, 1884, original paper label on box $55.00

Coffee mill, cast iron, double wheel store model, "Enterprise No. 12" $320.00

Figure VIII-8. **Coffee Pot.** Heavy tin with side spout, copper bottom. From Matthai-Ingram catalog, c. 1890. Made in 1, 1½, 2, 3, 4 and 6 quart sizes. Value: $20-$28.

Figure VIII-9. **Coffee Pot.** Graniteware with choice of graniteware or tin lid and wooden handle. One to 5 quarts. This was pictured twice in an 1880 Lalance & Grosjean catalog: once as a coffee pot, once — exactly the same — as the "Agate Belle" teapot. Value: $30-$50.

307

Figure VIII-10. **Coffee Pot.** A real tinsmith's work of art. Funnel top for making drip coffee. Hinged lid, strap handle. 19th century, possibly 1880s. 11" high. Picture courtesy of the National Museum of American History, Smithsonian Institution.

Coffee grinder, cast iron, huge — for
   store, single wheel, 6' high .... $400.00 to $450.00
Coffee grinder, all sheet metal..................... $40.00
Coffee grinder, wall type with original
   paint, "Arcade" .... $42.00 to $50.00
Coffee grinder, wood and iron, lap
   model, "Arcade" $75.00
Coffee grinder, glass, "Arcade #3" $100.00
Coffee grinder, "Arcade IXL," 11" high
   with 7½" square base $150.00
Coffee grinder, "Golden Rule," with lid $150.00
Coffee grinder, blue & white German
   "Delft" $125.00
Coffee grinder, wood and iron, clamps
   to table, "S.H. Co.," St. Louis $120.00
Coffee grinder, cast iron and wood,
   double wheel, painted blue, 13"
   high, "S.H. Co.," St. Louis $300.00

Coffee grinder, cast iron and wood, double wheel, "Enterprise," pat'd July 12, 1898, 11" wheel $275.00

Coffee grinder, wall type, "Regal" $40.00

Coffee grinder, cast iron with original paint and stenciled designs, "Enterprise No. 7," 17" double wheel, hopper surmounted by cast eagle, dated 1873 .... $425.00

Coffee grinder, sheet iron with tin drawer, box style, "Universal, Landers, Frary & Clark," pat'd February 14, 1905 .... $32.00

Coffee grinder, cast iron with badly alligatored original red paint, 18" high, 18" double wheels $295.00

Coffee grinder, brass with wood handle, box style, c. 1920s $28.00

Coffee grinder, electric, shaped like a coffee pot, 3' high and meant for store or restaurant $325.00

Coffee grinder, wood with cast iron hardware, lap type .... $45.00 to $55.00

Coffee grinder, cast iron cabinet side mount, folding handle, marked "Geo. W.M. Vandecrift," pat'd 1870 .... $75.00 to $95.00

Coffee grinder, cast iron, wood, "Parkers Columbia Rapid Grinder, No. 260," 1 pound size, side crank, 1890s .... $35.00 to $45.00

Coffee grinder, cast iron and wood tin drawer with wood front, "Challenge Fast Grinder," Sun Mfg. Co. 1 pound size, ornate casting .... $35.00 to $45.00

Coffee grinder, cast iron and wood, "French style" box with hopper & crank on top, very plain .... $25.00 to $45.00

Coffee grinder, painted and decorated cast iron, Enterprise "Family Mill No. 2," 4 ounce size, double wheel, drawer in base, this is the family-size version of the very

309

good-looking red and gold store
grinder, kept on the counter .... $65.00 to $90.00
Coffee grinder, stamped steel with
black enameled finished,
"Universal No. 109," sunken
hopper, crank in top, 6" high,
turn-of-century .... $20.00 to $30.00
Coffee grinder, japanned cast iron,
wood dovetailed box, "Parker's
Union Coffee Mill No. 25," 6¼"
high, c. 1908 .... $22.00 to $30.00
Coffee grinder, japanned cast iron,
side mill, type mounted on wood,
then the wall, "Sun No. 94," c. 1900 ...... $12.00 to $15.00
Coffee grinder, cast iron finished with
thin copper plating, wooden box,
sunken hopper, crank in
top, "Parker's National Coffee
Mill No. 430," 4½" high .... $35.00 to $50.00

**NOTE: Hammacher Schlemmer advertises a single wheel
grinder thus: "Exact replica of the coffee grinder used during
the turn of the century. Fire engine red body and black wheel,
topped with chrome hopper. Hardwood base drawer and handle.
12" high, 7" square base." It sells for about $35.00. Well, even if
it weren't for the chrome hopper, you'd never mistake this for an
old one, and I cannot, after diligent search, find what this one is
an "exact replica" of, but anyway, it works and it's fine as long
as you don't get misled.**

Coffee maker, tin with turned wood
handle, strainer inside, c. 1910-1915 ..... $12.00 to $18.00
Coffee percolator, light blue speckled
enameled ware, "Universal," pat'd
first in 1894 .... $25.00 to $30.00
Coffee percolator, yellow enameled
ware with green trim, glass top $18.00
Coffee percolator, dark blue spattered
graniteware $16.00
Coffee percolator, copper and brass,
urn-shaped with wood handles,
finial and spigot handle, footed
base, with stand, 13" high,
"Manning & Bowman," pat'd 1906 .... $95.00

310

Figure VIII-11. **Coffee Percolator.** Pale green enameled iron. (By the way, this is the green called "closet green" in some stove catalogs. Dunno why.) C. 1910. Value: $10-$25.

Coffee pot, 2-tone gray spotted
    graniteware, pewter spout, base
    trim, handle and crown collar and
    lid, 8¾" high $125.00
Coffee pot, red enamelware, nickel-
    plated lid, goose neck $25.00

Coffee pot, turquoise and white
   spatterware, deep blue trim, 7" high $25.00
*Coffee pot, agateware with colorful
   depiction of Miss Liberty, ornate
   pewter spout, domed lid
   and handle, Statue of Liberty
   Commemorative pot, c. 1886.
   Offered for sale in 1982 by those
   great dealers, AL & Nancy
   Schlegel of Willow Hollow,
   Penacook, NH. A bargain at $225.00
Coffee pot, dark blue graniteware,
   gooseneck spout, 8" high $22.00
Coffee pot, tin, very tall and thin —
   Shaker style, 12" high $45.00
Coffee pot, tin with brass plate
   marked "The Young America,"
   dated 1859 .... $65.00
Coffee pot, gray spattered graniteware
   tin lid, large size .... $28.00 to $36.00
Coffee pot, white and black enamel-
   ware, tall and thin $35.00
*Coffee pot, brown and white spattered
   agateware, domed "golden"
   pewter lid, spout and handle,
   golden-colored tin "skirt," 11 3/8"
   high, absolutely gorgeous $180.00
Coffee pot, green and white stripes,
   small size $38.00
Coffee pot, brown graniteware with a
   few chips, 12" high $25.00
Coffee pot, teal & white swirled
   agateware, 11½" high $40.00
Coffee pot, tole-decorated tin ware,
   decorations in perfect condition
   in red, yellow and green on black
   asphaltum ground $1700.00

Figure VIII-12. **Coffee Mill.** Wall-mounted
"English style," as opposed to boxy
"French" or "lap" mill. From F.A. Walker
catalog, 1880s. Value: $12-$18.

Figure VIII-13. **Coffee Grinder.** Cast iron and wood "French style." 19th century. Picture courtesy of The Smithsonian Institution, Museum of History and Technology.

Coffee pot, engraved tin, Pennsylvania German, designs include tulips, eagle, flag and the ever-popular peacock, 19th century, very rare and great $3400.00

Coffee pot, black and white enameled ware, large, c. 1910 to 1930 .... $35.00 to $40.00

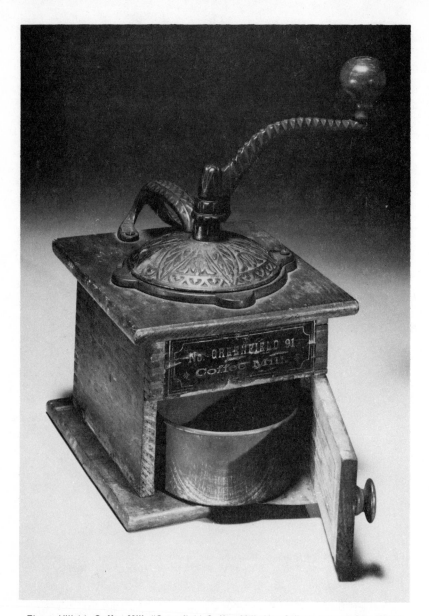

Figure VIII-14. **Coffee Mill.** "Greenfield Coffee Mill, No. 91" on paper label. Wood with cast iron grinding mechanism. The unusual feature is the tin pan that catches the grounds, and which — by the cooperation of an ingenious little swing-out platform, attached to the door — presents itself to the user. 19th century American. 9½" high. Picture courtesy of the National Museum of American History, Smithsonian Institution.

Figure VIII-15. **Coffee Grinder.** Wood with cast iron. Lap type. Late 19th century. Author's collection. Even with missing drawer knob, value: $35-$45.

Figure VIII-16. **Coffee Mill.** Wood and cast iron. Parkers Columbia No. 260, from Montgomery Ward, c. 1895. Value: $35-$45.

Figure VIII-17. **Coffee Grinder.** Wall-mount, English style. Cast iron. Late 1800s. Author's collection. Value: $12-$20.

Figure VIII-18. **Coffee Roaster.** "American Coffee Roaster," pat'd April 28, 1868 and November 7, 1863. Clockwork mechanism. Sets on 2 eyes of range. You load the heavy wire canister with coffee beans, set it into frame of cast iron, slip tin cylindrical cover over it, wind it up with its own key, and let 'er roll. 9" high x 18½" long. Collection of Meryle Evans. Value: $110-$150.

Coffee pot, gray graniteware, tin cover,
graceful shape, 9" high .... $25.00 to $30.00

Coffee pot, tin, conical shape with
side spout, 8¾" high, unusual
if simple .... $80.00 to $95.00

Coffee pot, tin, slanted sides, straight
spout, scroll-y handle with lid
rest, mid-19th century .... $55.00 to $65.00

Coffee pot, tin, 3-loop tin finial on
lid, 6" high, 1830s to 1850 .... $55.00 to $65.00

Coffee pot, blue and white enameled
ware with flower design, tin lid,
gooseneck spout .... $70.00 to $90.00

Coffee pot, copper with brass ferrule
and hinge, wood finial on lid,
wood handle, "James S. Shaw
Co.," gooseneck spout, 5½" high .... $50.00 to $65.00

Figure VIII-19. **Coffee Roaster.** Heavy cast iron, with crank to stir the coffee beans
with 4 "fingers". This is a pit bottom style, meant to sit down in eye of range. Looks
like a pirate's chest with iron hinges. 11" high x 8¾" diameter. Collection of Meryle
Evans. Value: $50-$70.

Coffee pot, painted tin with flowers,
   fruits, leaves on black
   background, tapered with
   gooseneck spout, domed lid,
   braced strap handle, 11½" high,
   mid-19th century . . . . $650.00 to $1000.00
Coffee pot, painted tin with scrolls
   and flowers on dark green ground,
   somewhat worn, tapering sides,
   nice scrolled strap handle, deep
   conical lid, 11" high, 19th century . . . . . $450.00 to $700.00
*Coffee pot, brown and white agate-
   ware, white metal lid, copper
   base, shell-and-column motif on
   throat of spout and handle, 10" high $300.00
Coffee pot, lavender/mauve enameled
   ware, tin spout and tin lid with
   turned wood finial, 9" high $95.00
Coffee pot, bluish-gray graniteware,
   tin top with wood finial, unusual
   in that it's a one-cuppa! $65.00
Coffee pot, robin's egg blue & white
   agateware, gooseneck spout . . . . $50.00 to $65.00
Coffee pot, peacock blue & white
   enameled ware, gooseneck spout . . . . $35.00 to $45.00
*Coffee pot, pink agateware with
   handpainted petunias, nickel-
   plated trim and base $175.00

**NOTE: Those items marked with an asterisk* were from the
stock of Willow Hollow Antiques, 185 South Main Street,
Penacook, NH 03301. This is a fabulous source for antiques of
all descriptions, and the Schlegels do a huge mail order
business along with their drive in trade. They put a great deal of
effort into their hand-illustrated catalogs, and it's well-worth
your effort and money to purchase them. Different lists are
different prices . . . either $2.00 or $3.00.**

Coffee roaster, iron, shaped rather
   like a frying pan with a lid, lid has
   small opening, also lidded, for
   adding coffee beans, crank is on
   top, c. 1870 . . . . $35.00 to $50.00

Coffee roaster, sheet iron and cast
    iron, "Griswold Mfg. Co.," fits
    over range eye, sliding door in
    side of can-like body, c. 1880 .... $35.00 to $50.00
Coffee roaster, tin cylinder with very
    long handle $200.00
Coffee server, Red Wing pottery,
    wood handle $8.00
Coffee urn, copper and brass,
    "Queen Anne" style, domed lid,
    late 19th century $300.00
Tea ball, spun aluminum with chain, 1930s ...... 4.00 to $6.00
Tea kettles, cast aluminum, Griswold,
    Wagner or Wear-Ever (The
    Aluminum Cooking Utensil Co.),
    1903-1915, if in good condition,
    any of these .... $20.00 to $30.00

Figure VIII-20. **Tea Kettle for Oil Stoves.** Tin. From Matthai-Ingram catalog, c. 1890. Value: $60-$75.

Figure VIII-21. **Tea Kettle.** Enameled cast iron, deep midnight blue. 19th century. Courtesy Darwin Urffer. Value: $30-$45.

318

Figure VIII-22. **Tea Kettle.** Galvanized cast iron with "pit bottom" — recessed base that fits into range eye. Note the heat dissipating "Alaska" handle. From Matthai-Ingram catalog, c. 1890. Value: $30-$40.

Figure VIII-23. **Tea Kettles.** Graniteware, both from a Matthai-Ingram catalog, c. 1890. One on right has the so called "pit" bottom for setting down into range eye. Value: $20-$45.

Tea kettle, cast aluminum, "Colonial Tea Kettle," Wagner Ware, pat'd 1902, lid swivels sideways, 6 quart size $28.00

Tea kettle, cast iron with swiveling or pivoted copper cover, gooseneck spout, 9" high .... $80.00 to $90.00

Tea kettle, tin with copper range-eye base, strap handle, domed lid, late 1800s .... $70.00 to $75.00

Tea Kettle, cast iron with tin cover, heavy bail handle, long gooseneck spout, 5½" high .... $55.00 to $70.00

Tea kettle, gray enamelware $30.00

Tea kettle, deep blue and white
    enamelware over cast iron,
    "Wrought Iron Range Co., St.
    Louis" on lid $65.00
Tea kettle, deep green agateware,
    white enameled interior,
    gooseneck spout, high domed lid
    with hinge, made in Yugoslavia $25.00
Tea kettle, nickel-plated copper, bail
    handle with black wood grip, "Rome" $38.00

NOTE: The above "Rome" is the kind of kettle that often has its nickel plating removed for cosmetic purposes. I would bet that this particular one, if the plating had been removed, would be twice as much money.

Figure VIII-24. **Tin Wares.** including **Tea and Coffee Pots.** Picture courtesy of Georgia G. Levett, Levett's Antiques, Camden, Maine.

Figure VIII-25. **Tea Kettle.** Cast aluminum with bail handle and wood grip. Swiveling lid. "Colonial Design, Safety Fill," mfd. by Griswold, Erie, PA. Pat'd September 9, 1913. Holds 4 quarts. 8½" diameter. Collection of Paul Persoff. Value: $20-$30.

Figure VIII-26. **Tea-kettle.** Copper with gooseneck spout. Made by Jacob Gable, Lancaster, PA., c. 1843, and marked on the handle "J. Gable 8." With the handle upright, the height is 14 3/8". Picture courtesy of the National Museum of American History, Smithsonian Institution.

Tea kettle, mottled green agateware,
 a bit of flaking $26.00
Tea kettle, cast iron, gooseneck spout,
 bail handle, three small feet,
 cover, its bulbous shape
 insured that it would fit most
 any range eye, as well as being
 useful in fireplace cookery,
 marked with initials in a heart,
 late 18th or early 19th century $300.00

321

Figure VIII-27. **Teapot.** Gray graniteware with tin spout, handle, lid, breast-band and base rim. 19th century. From the collection of Susan Kistler, Lenhartsville, PA.

Tea kettle, copper with brass finial,
  gooseneck spout, designed for
  range eye use, 6 quart size,
  almost undoubtedly original
  finish (ie. never nickeled) $200.00
Tea kettle, blue & white swirl agateware,
  white lining, swivel lid marked
  "Wrought Iron Range Co.," 4
  quart capacity $35.00
Tea kettle, cast iron, gooseneck, 3
  feet, 8" high, 10" diameter $110.00
Tea kettle, copper with iron whistling
  bird in spout $45.00
Tea kettle, cast iron, marked "Rhine
  Mfg. Co." $23.00
Tea kettle, copper, beautiful slender
  gooseneck spout, fixed handle,
  domed and ridged lid with high
  acorn finial, mid-19th century $145.00
Tea kettle, brown & white enamel over
  cast iron, small 2 quart size $36.00
Tea kettle, teapot and coffee pot set,
  sky blue enamelware with cobalt
  knobs, coffee pot has "Fry" glass lid $100.00
Tea kettle and teapot, shaded blue
  ombre enamelware, 6" and 6½" high $55.00

Teapot, gray graniteware with pewter
cover, spout, "belly" band and
handle, copper bottom, footed,
body is beautiful near-round form,
handle is scrolled, lid is domed
with pretty finial $165.00
Teapot, yellow graniteware with red
poppies and green trim,
gooseneck spout $35.00
Teapot, ceramic, Black Cat $15.00
Teapot, aluminum with wood handle,
chain in lid attached to tea
strainer, "Merit," c. 1920, this
one looks to me for all the world
like "The Little King" of comic
strip fame .... $12.00 to $18.00
Teapot, copper, wood finial and
handle, gooseneck .... $65.00 to $75.00
Teapot, gray graniteware, tin top, c. 1890s $22.00
Teapot, 3 metals — tin, brass &
copper, brass finial on lid, footed
and very graceful $85.00
Tea steeper, white graniteware with
blue trim .... $9.00 to $12.00
Tea strainer and stand, "Main Tool &
Mfg. Co." .... $4.00 to $6.00
Tea strainer, gray graniteware $12.00
Tea strainer spoon, silverplate,
"Tetley Tea" $28.00
Whistle for tea kettle, stamped and
pieced brass, bird with "stem" to
fit into spout, 3½" long, pat'd 1923 ...... $20.00 to $28.00

STOVES & STOVE TOOLS ALSO COOKERS

Stoves are undoubtedly the **least** collected objects in the Cooking & Preserving category, though only because of their size I'm sure. Stove parts **are** collected by some people. Recently someone revealed to me that he has in the past climbed into many a dumper (which dot the side streets of Manhattan as temporary dumps for construction or renovation wastes), intent on getting cast iron gas stove jet rings, which come in cast forms as varied as flowers in a garden. This is very like my old passion for saving porcelainized-iron drop pulls, knobs and handles from stoves I found in the street. The most popular collectible stoves are real working salesmen's samples, and second to them, toy stoves. They are found in the categories RELATED COLLECTIBLES and TOY KITCHEN COLLECTIBLES.

Ash shovel, wrought iron, ram's head
    handle, 18" long $60.00
Canal boat stove, cast iron, 2 burners,
    3-legged, only 18" high, late 1800s .... $300.00 to $400.00
Coal tongs, cast iron, small and decorative ... $18.00 to $22.00
Fire kindler, wire, screen and
    composition head, c. 1900 .... $3.00 to $5.00
Fire kindler, wire, composition, wood
    handle, in cylindrical tin box,
    "Smith's No. 1," pat'd 1871 .... $12.00 to $18.00
Fireback, cast iron, parrot design in a
    medallion, ornate scrolling $190.00
Fireback, cast iron, portrait of General
    Wolfe in medallion, surrounded by
    flags, etc $900.00
Fireback, cast iron, cupids and flower
    garlands $56.00

NOTE: The Country Iron Foundry has 11 fireback designs, "hand made originals and historic replicas in grey iron." I don't have one . . . if I can't fit in an old stove, I'm sure I've not got room for a 48 pound fireback! They will send a brochure/catalog for $1.00 [refundable]. 1792 Lancaster Pike, Paoli, PA 19301.

Figure IX-1. **Stove,** for use on **Fishing Vessels** or **Whaling Ships.** Cast iron with separate rack for supporting pot, iron bail, 3 legs, 9½" high x 13" diameter. Used in San Francisco, 19th century, and collected there by the U.S. Fisheries Commission. Picture courtesy of The Smithsonian Institution, Museum of History and Technology.

Fireless cooker, metal box with 3
    wells with original soapstone
    heaters $28.00
Fireless cooker, tin, 2 holes with
    soapstones, "The Ideal" $12.00
Portable stove, japanned tin, "Quick
    Meal" .... $65.00 to $75.00
Steam cooker, tin with copper base,
    Toledo Cooker Co., "The Ideal
    Steam Cooker," pat'd 1900, 16"
    high, tin domed lid with strap
    handle, nickeled-brass whistle .... $65.00 to $75.00
Stove, blue porcelainized iron, "Quick
    Meal" $1000.00
Stove, cast iron wood stove, "Oak
    Jewel No. 618" $395.00
Stove, beige enameled iron,
    Kalamazoo, 1927 .... $475.00
Stove, cast iron, "Imperial Clarion
    8-20," Wood & Bishop, Bangor, Maine $850.00
Stove, cast iron, "Home Clarion," also
    Wood & Bishop, but much simpler $800.00

Figure IX-2. **Camp Stove.** Wrought iron with turned wooden handle and hanging ring. Similar to stove for ships — see picture from Smithsonian Collection. American 18th century. 5¼" high x 12" long x 6" wide. Sold at auction for $375. Picture courtesy of Robert W. Skinner Inc., Auctioneers, Bolton, MA.

Stove, cast iron, "Atlantic Grand," Portland Stove Foundry, Maine, mid-19th century $1700.00

Stove, cast iron and nickel over copper, "Copper Clad," 6 burners, oven warming oven, hot water reservoir, all original accessory tools, 5' high $1450.00

Stove, baby blue & white porcelainized iron, "Windsor" gas cookstove $240.00

Figure IX-3. **"Quick Meal" Portable Stove, Tank and Burner Jets.** Japanned tin. No manufacturer or date shown. We assume this is but half of a portable stove; the other half would have been the burners. Fuel tank and filter at top; air valve for tank at far right of tank; underneath are 4 cocks, each with air intake valve at back. At right are 3 flues (?), perforated tin tubes inside each cylinder is heavily carbonized. Possibly rubber tubes connected cocks to the cooker's burners. if you know, please write in and explain to owner and me! 12" high x 18½" wide. Collection of Meryle Evans. Value: $60-$85.

Stove, cast iron, "Kalamazoo," 1936 .... $750.00
Stove, cast iron, table top gas stove,
    "Griswold," 3 burners $85.00
Stove, cast iron, table top gas stove,
    2 burners, porcelain knobs $18.00
Stove, cast iron, "Oven Parlor No. 7,"
    Newberry, Filley & Co., Troy, NY,
    also known as a "dining
    room helper" because the top is a
    small oven $200.00
Stove blacking in tin, red, white & blue
    label with a flag, "The Union Blacking" $10.00
Stove lid lifter, nickeled iron, coil
    handle to disperse heat $2.00
Stove lid lifter, cast iron with
    coiled wire handle, marked "STOVER" $2.50
Stove lid lifter, cast iron, in
    combination with a pot lid lifter at
    other end $20.00
Stove lid lifter, wrought iron, early 1800s ..... $25.00 to $30.00
Stove lid lifters, nickeled iron, pat'd
    designs, late 1800s .... $8.00 to $15.00
Stove ornament, painted cast iron,
    figure of George Washington in
    academic gown, paint not original
    47" high, 19th century, this one
    sold in 1980 .... $1750.00
Stovepipe ornament, painted cast iron,
    George Washington, indistinctly
    signed on rear of damaged base,
    46" high x 15" wide. Difference in
    height probably due to damage.
    Estimated to go at 1980 Christie's
    auction for $600/$900, but realized $550.00
Stove plate, cast iron, from early
    cookstove made up of plates —
    rather like a prefab house, this
    one depicts two tall men with
    guns and what look like Liberty
    caps, and two bearded men in
    frock coats shaking hands, from
    the Hudson River Valley,
    24" high x 25½" long $975.00

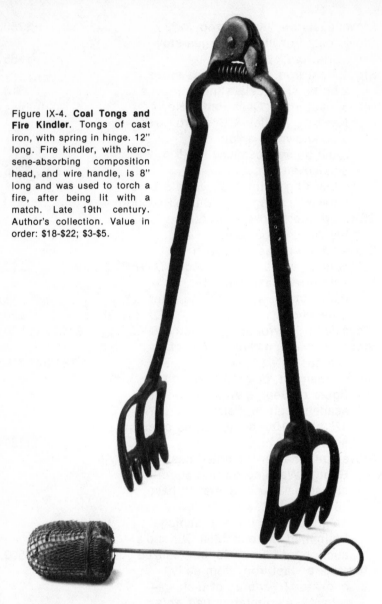

Figure IX-4. **Coal Tongs and Fire Kindler**. Tongs of cast iron, with spring in hinge. 12" long. Fire kindler, with kerosene-absorbing composition head, and wire handle, is 8" long and was used to torch a fire, after being lit with a match. Late 19th century. Author's collection. Value in order: $18-$22; $3-$5.

Stove shovel, cast iron, made from
   one piece with hook ended handle,
   18" long, probably Shaker $130.00
Stove tongs, wrought iron, 16" long,
   Shaker $50.00
Stove tools, wrought iron, shovel,
   poker and lid lifter (known as a

"Democrat" according to the
Schlegals of Willow Hollow
Antiques), Shaker manufacture $150.00
Stovetop oven, tin, "Princess," 1920s .... $10.00 to $12.00
Stovetop oven, tin with copper bottom,
2-door, "Conservo" $15.00
Stovetop oven, tin with iron bottom
and wire rack, "West Bend
Ovenette" with thermometer in
lid, 10½" diameter, c. 1940s $6.00

NOTE: Some people call stovetop ovens "Dutch ovens," but I've reserved that term for the rim-lidded pots listed in the "Utensil" section.

Figure IX-5. **Stove Pipe Figure of George Washington.** Painted cast iron, original paint. Indistinctly signed on rear of base, base damaged. Probably made in NY, definitely 19th century. 46" high x 15" wide. Estimated at Christie's Brooke sale, 1980, at $600-$900. Realized price: $550. Picture courtesy of Christie, Manson & Woods International Inc.

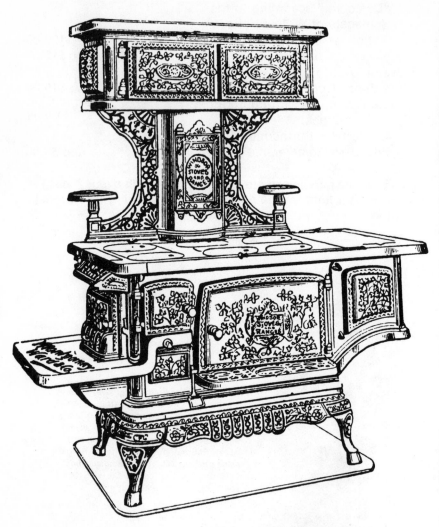

Figure IX-6. **Grand Windsor Stove.** Cast iron, 6-hole, water reservoir. From Montgomery Ward catalog, 1895.

CAMPSTOVES

Boy Scout round Coleman stove,
    original canvas bag $15.00
Coleman camp stove, round with
    brass reservoir $10.00

Figure IX-7. **Gas Range.** "Detroit Jewel," Detroit, Michigan and Chicago, Illinois, c. 1930s. Enameled iron. Motto is "They Bake Better." Stands just under 60" high. Picture courtesy of the National Museum of American History, Smithsonian Institution.

UTENSILS

For some of you, we've arrived at the heart and soul of the matter . . . the vessels, kettles, pots, pans, broilers, grills, etc. All those things as basic and essential to cooking as, well, as food itself! Which came first? The pot or the twig with which to stir? Probably the pot, although a sharpened branch spit undoubtedly predated that. Anyway, the forms of pots and kettles have hardly changed from the first ones made of clay or metal. So many of the early forms proved themselves so near perfect that they are being made today in almost exactly the same form as they were 100, 200, even 500 or 1000 years ago . . . only the technique of manufacture and sometimes the materials are different. What we cook **on** is different now, so we don't have tiny legs on our skillets to raise them off hot coals, nor do we have the bottoms of our utensils cast so that they will fit down into the eyes of woodburning ranges. But sloped and straight sides, bail handles, domed lids, heat-conducting handles, even rivets to hold the handles on, are still with us. A saucepan imported from France in 1980 by Kitchen Glamour of Detroit (tin-lined heavy copper with cast iron handle) is pretty much indistinguishable from its ancestor imported from France in the 1870s and '80s by F. A. Walker of Boston. A new cast iron Dutch oven will probably differ only in that it is less corroded than the one a century old.

At any rate, for establishing an attractive gleam and aura of old time grace to a kitchen, nothing can compete with a selection of useful copper, brass, iron, tin, and even aluminum utensils hung within reach as if they were in constant use (and aren't some of them?)

Ale boot, shoe-shaped, copper, strap
    handle, pushed into hot ashes to
    warm ale, 18th century .... $120.00 to $150.00
Apple butter kettle, copper, huge size
    with bail handle .... $200.00 to $400.00
Apple roaster, tin, reflecting oven with
    adjustable toasting tray, early
    19th century $250.00
Apple roaster, tin and iron, wood
    handle, 1870s (this is the kind
    that looks a bit like a silent butler
    or a dustpan!) .... $45.00 to $55.00

Figure X-1. **Baker with Multiple Roasting Pans.** Patent model. Tin and wire. Pat'd 1872 by T.J. Cummings. 13" long x 7 7/8" wide x 5" high. Picture courtesy of The Smithsonian Instittution, Museum of History and Technology.

Apple roaster, tin, half-round shape
    with feet, 2 tiers $350.00
Apple or bird roaster, sheet iron,
    domed with hooks $170.00

NOTE: Most apple, bird and cheese roasters are interchangable.

Army skillet, tin, World War I $10.00
Asparagus boiler, tin, Matthai-Ingram
    stamped decorative lid and pierced
    rack, ear handles, rectangular
    and tall, c. 1890 . . . . $30.00 to $35.00
Bain Marie pans, copper, set of 6 in
    sizes from 8 ounces to 24 ounces,
    c. 1830-1860 . . . . $650.00
Bain Marie, heavy tin, with 6 high-
    sided saucepans, all wit lids,
    2-eye size for cookstove $125.00

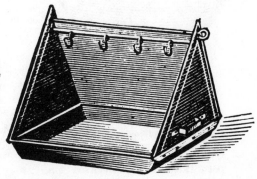

Figure X-2. **Bird Roaster.** Tin reflector oven for hearthside use. Hooks for 4 birds. From F.A. Walker catalog, 1870s. Value: $100-$150.

333

Baking pan, tin, stamped "Free 49
cent pan with your initial purchase
of new Py-O-My Pastry Mix,"
rectangular $3.50
Bean pot, gray graniteware, with lid,
large size, 7" diameter x 6" tall .... $15.00 to $20.00
Bean pot, white & pale green speckled
graniteware, ear handles .... $17.00 to $22.00
Bean pot, blue & gray glazed
stoneware, marked "Boston
Home of the Bean, Spirit of 76,"
Centennial item $65.00
Bean pot, blue & white stoneware, big
and bulbous $135.00
Bird roaster, tin, very simple arched
top with 4 hooks, no legs or feet,
10" high x 10" wide x 8" deep $135.00

See also: Apple roasters.

Bottle warmer, blue graniteware
covered saucepan that fits into
Sterno stove, 3¼" diameter,
overall height 7" $14.00
Bread raiser, stamped tin, ventilated
domed lid, 8 quart size .... $20.00 to $30.00

Figure X-3. **Bread Raiser.** Enameled
ware, footed. Sizes: 8, 10, 14, 17 and 21
quarts. From F.A. Walker catalog, 1870s.
Value: $45-$65, depending on size and
condition.

Figure X-4. **Bread Raiser.** Heavy tin. Note
ventilation holes in domed lid, near knob.
From Matthai-Ingram catalog, c. 1890.
Value: $20-$45, depending on size,
condition.

334

Figure X-5. **Broiler.** Possibly missing lid and base. Tin, wire mesh and turned wood. "American Broiler," S. Boyer's American Broiler Co., Proprietors. Pat'd July 21, 1868, October 19, 1869. Marked on brass identification plate. 11" diameter. Collection of Meryle Evans. Value: $25-$35.

Bread raiser, same as above, but
    largest size — 21 quarts! .... $35.00 to $45.00

NOTE: You see a lot of these badly dented and terribly crusted, and they still go for $10 or so.

Broiler, rotary, wrought iron, round
    grill with double serpentine
    design, 3-footed, 18th century .... $75.00 to $150.00
Broiler, whirling, wrought iron, quite
    simple, 18th or early 19th century ...... $55.00 to $150.00
Broiler, whirling, wrought iron,
    quite simple $120.00
Broiler, stationary, front legs with
    penny feet, back legs double
    "toed", beautiful long handle $420.00

Popcorn Pudding

"Pop some corn nicely, then roll it as fine as you can. One pint of corn to one quart of sweet milk; add a small piece of butter, one teaspoon salt, beat two eggs with enough sugar to sweeten the milk; mix all together. Bake 20 minutes."
"The Housewife," published in NYC, August 1904

Broiler, whirling wrought iron, tripod
    feet, long handle with hanging eye $150.00
Broiler/gridiron, stationary, wrought
    iron, 4 short feet with ram's head
    handle, 30" long x 17" side $95.00
Broiler, rotating, wrought iron, round
    wavy grid, small $230.00

335

Broiler/grill, whirling, hand wrought,
11" diameter x 24" long overall,
early 1800s $50.00

See also: Gridirons & Grills.

Candy kettle, very heavy copper, iron
ear handles, 17" diameter, 19th
century $300.00
Cauldron, cast iron with wire bail
handle with wood grip, pot-belly
style meant for setting in range
eye, marked "Erie" $35.00

NOTE: This seems as good a place as any to ask you all what is meant by "gypsy kettle" which I see advertised sometimes. Is it the same as above?

Chafing dish/hash dish, tin, oval with
Queen Anne style legs, 3-tube
camphene burner, 10" high
12" long, mid-19th century $125.00
Chafing dish/hash dish, copper,
"Empress Ware," pat'd 1907, 3 parts ..... $45.00 to $60.00
Chafing dish, enameled ware, lid and
stand, 1890s .... $80.00 to $95.00
Chestnut roaster, tin and wire, pat'd 1879 ..... $35.00 to $45.00

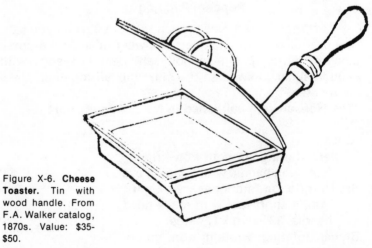

Figure X-6. **Cheese Toaster.** Tin with wood handle. From F.A. Walker catalog, 1870s. Value: $35-$50.

Figure X-7. **Chafing Dish.** Agateware, with wood handle. From Lalance & Grosjean catalog, 1890. Value: $80-$95.

Figure X-8. **Chafing Dish.** Hammered copper with wood handles and finial, 4 flared brass legs and other brass details. Designed by eminent Arts & Crafts Movement artist: Gustaf Stickley, c. 1910. 12¾" high x 15½" long. Estimated to sell at auction between $700-$900. Realized: $900. Picture courtesy of Robert W. Skinner Inc., Auctioneers, Bolton, MA.

Chestnut roaster, steel with decorative
    engraving, wood handle, 12"
    diameter pan, c. 1810-1830 .... $175.00
Chestnut roaster, copper pan, twisted
    wrought iron shaft and wooden
    handle, pierced design in cover,
    13½" diameter, estimated to go
    at 1981 auction for $150/$250, but realized $425.00

Figure X-9. **Cornpopper**. Wire screen with wood grip on handle, c. 1910. 25" long x 5 3/8" wide. Author's collection. Value: $10-$15.

Clam steamer, copper with a screen
    shelves, sliding door, 18½" high
    x 12" diameter $135.00
Cornpopper, wire and mesh, wood
    handle, wire mesh box with
    sliding metal lid, c. 1910 .... $10.00 to $15.00
Cornpopper, wire mesh, tin and wood,
    cylindrical hopper of wire mesh
    with tin at both ends,
    triangular support, 27" long,
    late 19th century .... $10.00 to $22.00
Cornpopper, tin with crank handle,
    shaped like a saucepan, raised
    bottom, "E-Z Corn Popper," 9"
    diameter, saw four of these in a
    few months between .... $10.00 to $17.50
Cornpopper, screen dome with litho
    tin Mickey Mouse, over tin pan, at
    Opfer toy auction, November
    1982, wonderful $65.00
Cornpopper, tin, cylindrical with
    twisted wire handle, pat'd 1897 .... $55.00

NOTE: There's an interesting early newspaper story about a cornpopper, that appeared in the "New York Times," August 3, 1890, "As reported in the Concord, New Hampshire "People and Patriot":

"The First Cornpopper Laughed At"

"In the winter of 1837, Mr. Francis P. Knowlton of Hopkinton, New Hampshire, purchased of Mr. Amos Kelley a sheet of wire netting from his manufactory on the main road, and constructed the first cornpopper ever made. The various parts were cut the required shape and sewed together with wire. Mr. Knowlton then made some for Judge Harvey and Judge Chase, which they sent to various parts of the United States as curiosities. Thinking he could see a field of usefulness for the newly-conceived article, Mr. Knowlton made several and took them to Concord to a hardware store, hoping to introduce before the public a useful utensil and to receive a reasonable remuneration. His production was scorned and ridiculed by the proprietors and they refused to have anything to do with it.

"He gave up and Mr. Amos Kelley began pressing them into shape out of wire and they slowly grew in favor."

Double boiler, enamelware, white
    porcelain knob on lid, large size $26.00
Double boiler, gray graniteware $20.00
Double boiler, medium blue enamelware $20.00
Dutch oven, cast iron, hand wrought
    bail handle, 3 legs, 14" diameter,
    early to mid-19th century $220.00

Figure X-10. **Double Boiler.** Inner copper kettle with bail handle suspended from "S" hook from fixed handle of outer iron pot. 1830s-50s. 16½" high x 13½" diameter. Formerly in the Keillor Collection. Value: $160-$210.

Figure X-11. **Dutch Oven or Tin Oven,** for hearthside use. Tin. From F.A. Walker catalog, 1870s. Value: $45-$65.

Figure X-12. **Dutch Oven.** Cast iron with bail handle and 3 short legs. Nice deep flange on lid. American, 18th century. 6¾" high x 9¼" diameter. Sold at auction for $375. Picture courtesy of Robert W. Skinner Inc., Auctioneers, Bolton, MA.

Dutch oven, cast iron, "Barstow Stove
    Co., No. 2", 7¾" high, 19th century ..... $30.00 to $45.00
Dutch oven, cast iron, 3 peg feet, deep
    flange, 11" high, 19th century .... $120.00 to $130.00
Dutch oven, cast iron, 4 feet, high-
    flanged rim, bail handle, mid-19th
    century .... $75.00 to $85.00
Egg holder, for boiling eggs, fits into
    saucepan, wire, folds up to fit in
    drawer, holds 6 eggs, 7" high,
    1900 to 1930 .... $5.00 to $10.00

Figure X-13. **Egg Poacher.** "Maryland" . . . can be used in an ordinary stew pan as well as a skillet. Heavy tin with steam vent handle. 3 egg size. From Matthai-Ingram catalog, c. 1890. Value: $18-$30.

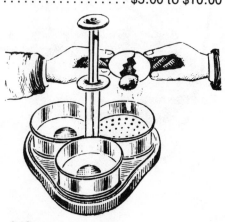

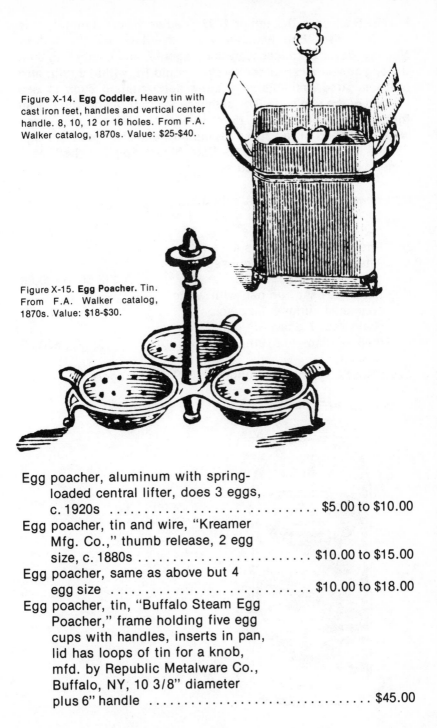

Figure X-14. **Egg Coddler.** Heavy tin with cast iron feet, handles and vertical center handle. 8, 10, 12 or 16 holes. From F.A. Walker catalog, 1870s. Value: $25-$40.

Figure X-15. **Egg Poacher.** Tin. From F.A. Walker catalog, 1870s. Value: $18-$30.

Egg poacher, aluminum with spring-loaded central lifter, does 3 eggs, c. 1920s .... $5.00 to $10.00

Egg poacher, tin and wire, "Kreamer Mfg. Co.," thumb release, 2 egg size, c. 1880s .... $10.00 to $15.00

Egg poacher, same as above but 4 egg size .... $10.00 to $18.00

Egg poacher, tin, "Buffalo Steam Egg Poacher," frame holding five egg cups with handles, inserts in pan, lid has loops of tin for a knob, mfd. by Republic Metalware Co., Buffalo, NY, 10 3/8" diameter plus 6" handle $45.00

NOTE: Back in a December 1897 "Ladies Home Journal" this Buffalo Steam Egg Poacher was advertised by the Sidney Novelty Works of Chicago, seeking agents, and combining with the egg cooker a cereal cooker that would fit, within a ring, into the pan. Also available were extra deep custard cups to use instead of the egg cups. The cost was $.50 for the poacher, $.50 for the cereal cooker and $.25 for the set of custard cups. These were described in the ad as aluminum, and it is possible that Sidney Novelty was using "Buffalo Steam Egg Poacher" as a generic description for their copy.

Egg poacher, tin, platform with 3 separate perforated cups, 3 short feet, tall center handle or lifter, which served as a "steam pipe," this was used for steam poaching, c. 1870 .... $18.00 to $30.00

Egg poacher, cast iron pan with white enameled surface; lid also enameled. 7 poaching cups cast in. 8¾" diameter, 19th century $60.00

See also: "Egg Cookers" under ELECTRIC category.

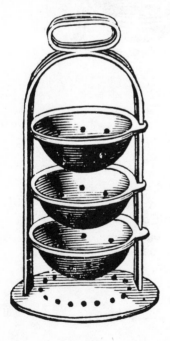

Figure X-16. **Egg Poacher**. Tin. From F.A. Walker catalog, 1870s. Value: $15-$20.

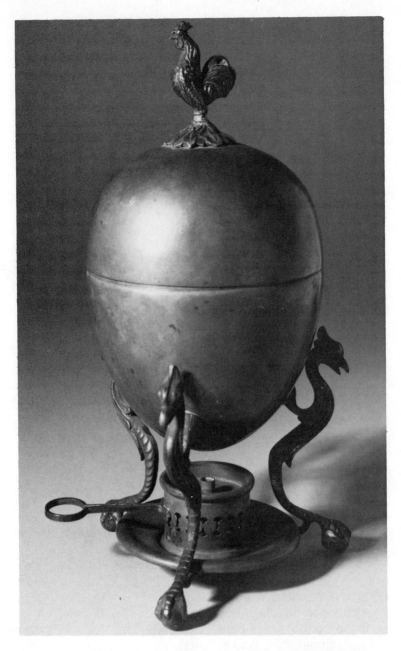

Figure   X-17. **Egg Boiler.** For table top use. Works like a chafing dish with little fuel stove under the egg-shaped boiler. Rooster finial. Just 6" high. 19th century. Picture courtesy of the National Museum of American History, Smithsonian Institution.

Figure X-18. **Farina Boiler,** like a double boiler. Tin with strap handle on lid. From F.A. Walker catalog, 1870s. Value: $15-$20.

Figure X-19. **Fruit or Cereal Steamer,** like a double boiler. "Pure White Porcelain Cereal and Fruit Steamers, with enameled wood handle on food jar, and tinned iron handle on half planished tin boiler; for cooking oat meal, rice, or any kind of fruit, they are unexcelled; nothing can burn in them. Capacity of food jar: 3 pints . . . 62 cents, 4 pints . . . 80 cents; 5 pints . . . 90 cents." From Montgomery Ward catalog, 1895. Value: $28-$40.

Fish roaster/broiler, wrought iron
   with wood handle, fits on fire
   bar in front of fire, 4 hooks, 16" long $250.00
Flan pan, fluted, "Dr. Oetker," made
   in Germany, 11¾" diameter $12.00
Frying pan, wrought iron, rat
   tail handle, 12" diameter, 14"
   handle, early 19th century . . . . $75.00 to $100.00

Frying pan, wrought iron, 5" long
    including handle, late 18th century .... $150.00 to $180.00
Frying pan, cast iron, 3-footed, 6"
    diameter, 19th century $18.00
Frying pan, cast iron, footed, 10½"
    diameter $20.00
Frying pan, cast iron, marked "Great
    Plains Gas," 5½" diameter $3.50
Frying pan, gray agateware, 13" diameter $35.00
Frying pan, cast iron, marked "Stuart,
    Ferancee-HP For Iron Deficiency
    Anemia," 4" diameter $10.00
Frying pan, gray graniteware $27.00
Frying pan, "Spry Shal-O-Fryer," $15.00
Griddle, cast iron, hinged, makes 3
    griddle cakes, fits over 2 range
    eyes, 1870s .... $35.00 to $50.00
Griddle, cast iron, 10" round $14.00
Griddle, cast iron, with heart design $45.00
Griddle, rotating fireplace style,
    wrought iron, heart-shaped end
    of handle, 3 peg feet, 25" long $150.00

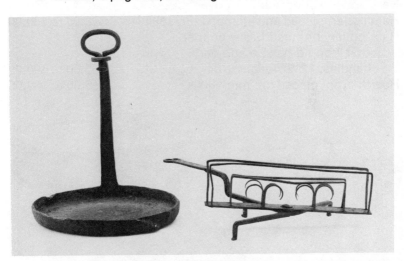

Figure X-20. **Griddle and Toaster.** Left: hanging cast iron griddle with trammel ring. Rather deep rim. Late 18th century American. 16" high x 13" diameter. Sold at auction for $175. Right: revolving toaster, wrought iron, ram's horn handle. American, 18th century. 17½" long x 13½" wide. Sold for $300. Picture courtesy of Robert W. Skinner Inc., Auctioneers, Bolton, MA.

Figure X-21. **Grid-iron**, portable with its own **suitcase**. Looks like the 20th century . . . traveling patio parties! From Androck catalog, 1936. Value $12-$18, maybe a bit more with suitcase in good shape.

Griddle or girdle plate, as they were
    called in the 18th century, wrought iron $110.00
Gridiron, wrought iron, 4 small peg
    feet, 10½" x 11" with 11"
    handle, early 1800s . . . . $110.00 to $130.00
Grill, revolving or rotary, wrought iron,
    fleur de lis design, 18th century,
    probably not American . . . . $200.00 to $350.00
Ham boiler, copper with tin cover $50.00
Ham boiler, pieced and stamped tin, 1890s . . . $20.00 to $30.00
Ham boiler, tin-lined heavy copper,
    cast iron lid handle and ear
    handles, 12½" long, 1870s . . . . $65.00 to $90.00
Hearth oven, pieced tin, mid-1800s . . . . $65.00 to $80.00

Figure X-22. **Ham Boilers.** Tin-lined copper with iron handles. Left: 10½" x 6½" x 7" deep. Right: 12½" x 7 5/8" x 7" deep. 1860s-1880s. Collection of Mary Mac Franklin. Value: $80-$110.

Figure X-23. **Kettle.** Cast iron with wire bail handle. The lid states "Dutch Oven," but it is a stove-top adaptation of the early cast iron Dutch ovens with deeply flanged lids to hold hot coals. All these, because they could be used to cook something in for many hours, are forerunners of the "Crock Pot." Author's collection. Value: $25-$40.

Figure X-24. **Kettle with Scraper.** Cast iron with wire bail handle. Note 3 short feet. Early to mid-19th century. Picture courtesy of The Smithsonian Institution, Museum of History and Technology.

Figure X-25. **Kettle.** Cast iron with 3 legs and bail handle twisted for extra strength. American, late 18th century. 6¼" high x 4¼" diameter. Ridge closest to bottom allowed this to be used later in eye hole of a range. Sold at auction for $275. Picture courtesy of Robert W. Skinner Inc., Auctioneers, Bolton, MA.

Hot dog steamer, brass and copper,
lined in zinc, "W.B. Berry," 2
hinged lids in top, c. 1900 .... $100.00 to $115.00

HOT TIP: Sunbeam has a wonderfully collectible product out now, a hot dog steamer in the shape of a dog house, 7" high x 7¾" long. The house is of white enameled metal and the peaked roof with steam vents is well-modeled heavy duty plastic. "The Dog House" is printed on the front. What makes me think this is a good future collectible is the fact that it's a "figural" piece, rather faddish but well-made.

Kettle, copper, 24" diameter x 12"
deep, 19th century $200.00
Kettle, cast iron, footed, with lid $65.00
Kettle, copper, with lid $75.00
Kettle, cast iron, Griswold #8, with lid $17.00
Kettle, cast iron, fixed handle, 22"
diameter x 12" deep, 19th century $42.00
Kettle, cast iron, with pouring lip, 9" diameter $8.00
Kettle, blue mottled graniteware, 2
gallon size, lid $35.00
Kettle, heavy cast metal, large, adv'g
"Forbes Coffee" $6.00
Kettle, cast iron, bail handle with
swivel hook for fireplace
cookery, footed, 14" diameter $42.00
Kettle, cast iron with pouring lip, 6"
diameter, 3 feet $18.00
Kettle, cast iron, footed with canted
sides, 11" diameter, early 19th
century $38.00
Kettle, cast iron, round bottom (for
range cookery) with feet (for
fireplace or hearth), 17" diameter
x 10" deep $35.00
Kettle, blue enameled ware, bail
handle, 1 quart size $28.00
Kettle, brass, wrought iron bail handle,
8" diameter, 19th century .... $125.00 to $150.00
Kettle, cast iron, bail handle,
"Holland's Mfg. Co.," small 5" diameter $22.00

Oyster Pie

Line a deep dish with a crust made as follows: To two quarts of flour add three teaspoonfuls of baking powder, four tablespoons of lard or butter and a little salt; mix with water as for biscuit; wash the oysters and strain the liquor; pour it over them; thicken a cup of water with a tablespoonful of flour; butter the crust on both sides; cut across in the centre; pepper and salt the oysters; bake well.

Scammel's Treasure-House of Knowledge, 1891

Kettle, cobalt blue and white
    enamelware, bail handle with
    wood grip, drain spout and clamp
    for holding lid on, 10½" high $38.00
Kettle, gray graniteware, wire bail
    handle with wood grip, 6" deep .... $10.00 to $12.00
Kettle, hammered copper with
    wrought iron swing bail handle,
    cylindrical body, 16" high $425.00
Kettle, spun bell-metal with wrought
    iron swing handle, 6" high,
    19th century $230.00
Oyster broiler, wire, double frame of
    twisted wire, looks like those
    toasters we used at camp to roast
    hot dogs and/or hot dog buns $20.00
Pancake maker, cast iron, makes 3
    pancakes at a time, fits over 2
    range eyes, 16" long .... $25.00 to $35.00

See also: Griddles.

Lemon Flapjacks

One pint milk; flour eggs; juice of one lemon; flour to make a light batter; a pinch of soda; fry in hot lard; serve with sugar and nutmeg.

Scammell's Treasure-House of Knowledge, 1891

Figure X-26. **Potato or Cruller Fryer.** Heavy tin. Pat'd July 8, 1879. From Montgomery Ward catalog, 1895. Value: $15-$25.

Figure X-27. **Milk Sauce Pan or Double Boiler.** Heavy tin with wood handle and iron handle, earthenware inside. 1, 2, 3, 4 and 6 pint sizes. From F.A. Walker catalog, 1870s. Value: $15-$30.

Posnet, bell metal, marked "Austin & Crocker, Boston," on long handle, 18th century, sold at Garbisch auction in 1980 for $3100.00

Potato baker with cover, cast iron with pale green enameled cover, "The Master Bake Pot," pat'd 1918 .... $22.00 to $25.00

Preserve kettle with lid, gray graniteware, bail handle and side tilt handle grip, 18" diameter, 13" deep ...... $30.00 to $35.00

Preserve kettle, gray graniteware, wire bail handle .... $15.00 to $18.00

Pressure cooker, heavy cast metal, "Windsor 'A' No. 10," Montgomery Ward Co., lid screws down with swivel clamps, gaskets on each steam cock, 10" high $18.00

Pressure cooker, or soup digester, heavy planished tin, clamp-on lid, bail handle, 1870s .... $30.00 to $40.00

Figure X-28. **Pots and Pans.** A new finish for aluminum cookware, that seems like a whole new material. A very hard, non-porous surface which is black. **"Calphalon,"** by Commercial Aluminum Cookware Company, 1980. These wares were introduced in 1966 for professional chefs. A future collectible. Picture courtesy of Commercial Aluminum Cookware Company.

Figure X-29. **Pressure Cooker.** Windsor "A" No. 10, Montgomery Ward Co. Heavy cast metal . . . a killer if it blew up! Has rack inside, no lid gasket, but each steam cock has gasket. Bail handle, 5 wingnut clamps that swivel and drop out of way to open lid. Photographed at Bonnie Barnes' Anteek Corner, Waynesboro, VA. Value: $18-$25. NOTE: Similar ones are mfd. now.

NOTE: A heavy polished cast aluminum pressure cooker, resembling the old style, is being made today in four sizes: 10½ quarts, 15½ quarts, 21½ quarts and 41½ quarts. There are 6 screw clamps; petcock and gauge are on the lid. They sell for between $40 and $130 or so.

Reflector oven, sheet iron, has a
  crank spit, grease spout and four feet $250.00
Reflector oven or "tin kitchen," as
  they used to be called, tin,
  cranked spit, door in back, 4 legs,
  pour-off grease spout at side
  bottom, 18" wide $250.00
Reflector oven, tin, with spit, 25" long
  x 17" high $80.00
Reflector oven, made of heavy tin
  plates, soldered together, spit,
  20" long x 16" high, 4 legs $220.00
Reflector oven, tin, spit and spout, 4
  legs, 19" wide x 17" high $180.00
Reflector oven, tin, 19" wide, late 1800s $65.00
Reflector oven, tin, meant for biscuits
  — has shallow shelves, 14" wide,
  c. 1840-50 .... $55.00 to $65.00
Reflector oven, tin, meant for biscuits
  but shelf broken off $45.00

Figure X-30. **Revolving Toaster.** Wrought iron with wood handle. Used hearthside. Early 19th century. Picture courtesy of The Smithsonian Institution, Museum of History and Technology.

NOTE: In 1797, a Tin Plate maker by the name of D. Crawley of New York City advertised in the newspaper that "a very capital improvement [has been made] on the tin roasting ovens so universally in use, by making easy what was thought the most difficult task in using them, [the former mode of basting] which by the improvement is done on the top by means of a hopper and strainer, which causes the fat to drip gradually on the victuals roasting." I assume this means he designed a tin kitchen with a hopper and strainer built right into the top above the spitted meat. At the time Crawley was working, tin was imported in plates, measuring 8" x 14", from Wales for the most part. This is why early tin kitchens, like one of the ones listed above, are made of pieced together plates. P.S. If you want to read a very old-fashioned but sweet storybook, featuring as a "character" one of these neat old reflecting ovens, look for "The Tin Kitchen," by J. Hatton Weeks, published in New York & Boston by Thomas Y. Crowell & Co., 1896.

Roasting pan, gray graniteware, high
    domed lid for big-breasted chicken ...... $12.00 to $15.00
Roasting pan, turquoise & white
    enamelware, 10" x 16" x 12" .... $12.00 to $20.00
Roasting pan, dark blue & white
    speckled agateware, repaired
    with a "Mendit," 13½" long .... $10.00 to $15.00
Roasting pan with cover, gray
    graniteware, original paper label
    "Nesco" .... $12.00 to $15.00
Roasting pan, gray graniteware, for turkeys $15.00

Figure X-31. **Revolving Toaster.** Wrought iron with unusual "corn sprout" supports for bread in addition to double arches. Late 18th or early 19th century. Picture courtesy of the National Museum of American History, Smithsonian Institution.

Figure X-32. **Revolving Toaster.** Wrought iron with two sets of double arches. Early 19th century. 19" long. Formerly in the Keillor Collection. Value: $135-$180.

Figure X-33. **Roaster.** Wrought iron with slightly damaged ram's-horn handle. Beautifully simple early 19th or late 18th century piece. 26" long. Formerly in the Keillor Collection. Value: $175-$225.

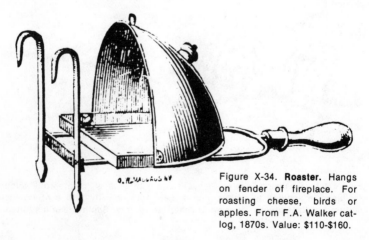

Figure X-34. **Roaster.** Hangs on fender of fireplace. For roasting cheese, birds or apples. From F.A. Walker catlog, 1870s. Value: $110-$160.

Figure X-35. **Saucepots.** Cast iron, with tin lids and wood handles. Foreground: marked "Baldwin No. 2", 1½ pints, base is 4½" diameter. Rear: "T. Holcroft & Sons No. 5" with a registery mark. 5" high, holds 4 pints. Both late 19th century. Picture courtesy of the National Museum of American History, Smithsonian Institution.

Roasting pan, turquoise & white
    enamelware, large $45.00
Roasting pan, gray graniteware, self-basting $20.00
Roasting pan, mottled green agateware,
    rectangular rather than oval,
    flat-top cover .... $9.00 to $12.00
Rum warmer or aetna, tin, footed,
    pierced lid, c. 1870 .... $75.00
Salamander, wrought iron, 18th century .... $180.00 to $220.00
Sauce pan, copper with tin lining,
    long steel handle, mid-19th
    century, lid missing $95.00
Sauce pan, copper with iron handle,
    copper lid with brass finial,
    dovetailed construction, 7" high x
    6" diameter $250.00

Figure X-36. **Skillets.** Cast iron, used sitting on raked coals in fireplace. 18th or early 19th century. Picture courtesy of The Smithsonian Institution, Museum of History and Technology.

Sauce pan, copper with iron handle,
    marked on both pan and lid "D.H.
    & M. Co., N.Y." 9½" diameter,
    19th century $75.00
Sauce pan, copper with iron handle,
    copper lid, marked "Duparouet,
    New York," 9" diameter, 19th century $100.00
Sauce pan, gray graniteware,
    2 quart size $17.00
Skillet, forged iron with long handle
    small size $82.00
Skillet, forged iron, long handle, 3 peg legs $45.00
Skillet, cast iron, "No. 4," 3¼" diameter $12.00
Skillet, cast iron, "Griswold," square
    for frying eggs (not that eggs are
    square, but most cake turners
    have square edges) $35.00
Skillet, cast iron, "Griswold No. 0," $35.00
Skillet, cast iron, "Griswold No. 4" $43.00
Skillet, cast iron, Wagner Ware chicken
    fryer #8, with cover $14.00
Skillet, cast iron, Wagner Ware, #8 .... $8.00
Skillet, stamped metal, advertising
    "Snow King Baking Powder," $15.00
Skillet, sheet iron, 3 legs 3" high,
    9" diameter with 13" handle,
    lightweight (which might seem
    some disadvantage today because

the heavy hold the heat better,
but a boon to a woman who
constantly, hour after hour, had
to lift heavy cast iron utensils) $65.00
Skillet, purple & white swirl enameled iron $40.00
Skillet, forged iron with pouring spout
and fixed arched handle with
trammel ring, 12" diameter x
12½" high (including arched handle) $150.00
Soapstone griddle, soapstone with
iron frame and handle .... $30.00 to $40.00
Soup pot/and cover copper with
iron handles dovetail construction,
marked on pot and lid with initials
"L.F.D. & H., N.Y.", 12" high $100.00
Spider, cast iron, 3 short peg legs, 9"
diameter with 5½" handle,
mid-19th century $135.00

Figure X-37. **Skimmer, Broiler, Basins, Posnet and Skillet.** Wrought and cast iron. Brass skimmer, iron handle shank with wood grip, c. 1800. Value: $125; broiler, c. 1800. Value: $150; small posnet, c. 1830. Value: $45-$65; skillet, c. 1830. Value: $75.00. Picture courtesy of Georgia G. Levett, Levett's Antiques, Camden, Maine.

Figure X-38. **Steam Cooker.** (Two views.) "The Arnold Automatic Steam Cooker," Wilmot Castle & Co., Rochester, NY, pat'd July 8, 1879, May 9, 1882 and September 2, 1882. Tin with a heavy copper plate on the bottom. The lid is missing. The bottom reservoir was filled with water and the steamer was placed over the burner. The steam rose through a hole in the exterior cylinder and cooked what was in the lift-out pan. Wilmot Castle also made a bottle sterilizer that held several small bottles. The steamer is 8¾" high. Pictures courtesy of the National Museum of American History, Smithsonian Institution.

Spider, wrought iron, "WHITFIELD"
  on handle, 14" diameter x 8"
  high, 17" handle $155.00
Still (!) copper with brass spigot and
  tinned inside, "The Sanitary Still
  No. 3," mfd. by A.H. Pierce Mfg.
  Co., 3 gallon size, 20" high,
  maybe I should have put this
  under "Canning & Preserving" ha ha ... $250.00 to $300.00
Tea kettle still, copper, funnel top
  and coils, c. 1870s $350.00
Toaster, pivoting, wrought iron and
  wire, 3 arches, early 1800s .... $100.00 to $150.00
Toaster, pivoting/swiveling, wrought
  iron, 2 arch, early 1800s .... $95.00 to $110.00
Toaster, swiveling, wrought iron, 4
  rectangular arches, late 1700s $170.00

Figure X-39. **Steamer.** Double boiler style. Tin and copper. "Woodward & Lathrop." 19th century. Picture courtesy of The Smithsonian Institution, Museum of History and Technology.

Toaster, swiveling, very decorative
wrought iron, late 1700s $265.00
Toaster, pivoting, wrought iron and
wire, 4 pairs of arches, arched
feet, 40" long, early 19th century $225.00
Toaster, rotating, wrought iron, 3
pairs of arches, penny feet, hole
in handle for hanging, 28" long $175.00
Toaster, rotating wrought iron, 2 sets
of 3 twisted arches, 13" long
toaster plus 13" long handle $195.00
Toaster, pivoting, hand-wrought,
quite a number of them at
Brimfield's huge flea markets, 1982 .... $180.00 to $225.00
Toaster, swiveling, wrought iron, simple $125.00
Toaster, hinged, for bannocks, horse-
shoe shape $400.00
Toaster, tin and wire, stove top style,
does 4 pieces of bread, 1930s .... $4.00 to $8.00
Toaster, tin and wire, "Pyramid" does
4 slices on top of stove $6.00

NOTE: The above are still being made for camping out.

Figure X-40. **Stove Set.** Wood box with various utensils. Note doughnut cutter lower center, fluted tart pan, tubed fluted cake pan, coffee boiler, even stove polish. Late 19th century. Value: $145-$165.

Figure X-41. **Stove Set.** All kinds of utensils, as advertised for setting up housekeeping. Late 19th century. If you could find such a trunk, filled with 50 or so items, value might be: $200-$300.

Figure X-42. **Stove-Top "Dutch Oven."** Tin with sliding door. There's a rack inside. 10¾" diameter x 6½" high. 19th century or very early 20th. Collection of Meryle Evans. Value: $20-$30.

Figure X-43. **Tin Kitchen with Clock Jack.** Sheet iron with superstructure to support a key-wound clock jack. Flywheel with 6 counterweights to operate as a governor. Vertical wrought iron spit with hooks. Propped up on wood support — indicates this piece was either customized to fit a particular hearthside or that one leg has broken. C. 1790-1840. Picture courtesy of the National Museum of American History, Smithsonian Institution.

Figure X-44. **Tin Kitchen.** Tin with 4 hooks, plus spit and crank. "Back door" for adjusting or basting food, while oven remains in place in front of fire. From F.A. Walker catalog, 1870s. Value: $115-$165.

362

Figure X-45. **Tin Kitchen.** Sheet iron, made from rectangles of tin soldered together, indicating early date — 18th or early 19th century. Wrought iron spit could be used at three different levels. Note tiny slots in it — these were used with skewers to fasten meat to the spit so that it could be cooked on all sides. Strap handles. 13¼" high x 18 5/8" long. Picture courtesy of the National Museum of American History, Smithsonian Institution.

Figure X-46. **Toaster.** Hand wrought iron, revolving toaster for use at the hearth. Early to mid-19th century American. 11" long x 7" wide x 3¾" high. Formerly in the Keillor Collection. Value: $140-$175.

Toaster, stove top, all wire in one piece $12.00
Toaster, wire and wood, the wire
    "hands" clasp the bread slice,
    leaving its pattern white and
    untoasted on the brown bread .... $12.00 to $18.00
Toaster, wire with wood handle,
    makes a "star" pattern $24.00
Whirling broiler, wrought iron, heart-
    ended handle, late 1700s, early 1800s $400.00
Whirling broiler, wrought iron, tripod
    base and long handle, 36½" long,
    early 1800s $200.00

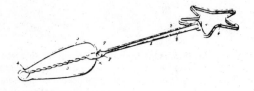

Figure X-47. **Toaster Patent Drawing.** Pat'd July 21, 1891, by William S. McMillan, of Avoca, PA. Twisted wire with star-shaped toast holder.

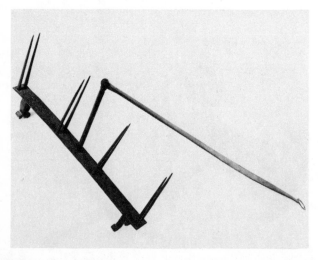

Figure X-48. **Toaster or Roaster.** Hand wrought iron, 19th century, possibly English. Pivots and can therefore be easily shifted so that both sides are broiled or toasted. 30" long x 13" wide. Formerly in the Keillor Collection. Value: $125-$160.

The following special article was written for this second edition of 300 YEARS OF KITCHEN COLLECTIBLES by two deservedly eminent graniteware collectors, Vernagene Vogelzang and Evelyn Welch, who have written the book. Published in 1981 by Wallace-Homestead, it is entitled GRANITEWARE, COLLECTOR'S GUIDE WITH PRICES. I'm very proud to have them join me and the other contributors and am thrilled with the special pictures taken for this book. If you would care to correspond with them about graniteware, please use a self-addressed stamped envelope and write either Vogelzang at 211 Lois Avenue, Modesto, CA 95350, or Welch at 11718 Warnerville Road, Oakdale, CA 95361.

THE GROWTH OF GRANITEWARE
By Veragene Vogelzang and Evelyn Welch

Every kitchen in the United States probably had at least one piece of graniteware thirty-five years ago and yet many people have forgotten what it is.

They will remember, though, when they visualize a scene from a Western movie in which a five-gallon coffeepot and its steaming black contents are heating over the campfire. Most likely that coffeepot was graniteware and it was what kept life from being so miserable on the open range at round-up time.

It had a stout bail that enabled it to be suspended from a pothook over the fire. A high handle was riveted to the side opposite the spout so that the heavy pot could be tilted forward for pouring without removing it from the pothook. That coffee pot became an institution in the West.

And graniteware became an institution in the United States. It was made in enormous quantities by a great number of companies. The Canton Stamping and Enameling Company operated twenty-four hours a day with a daily average capacity of 75,000 pieces and it was not one of the largest manufacturers.

The St. Louis Stamping Company, the Vollrath Company of Sheboygan, Wisconsin, and the Lalance and Grosjean Manufacturing Company, New York, were the first three and they became the largest.

Cookbooks published by the St. Louis Stamping Company, labeled "Patent Granite Iron Ware, Trademark Registered June 9, 1874," provide us with the earliest known mark. "Graniteware" was probably coined from this trade name.

It was made in a full range of colors and a tremendous variety of shapes and sizes. In some cases it was made for such a singular purpose that there are still controversies as to the intended use. An egg skillet is often mistaken for an egg poacher; an ant cup for a jello mold; and a round coffee flask for a canning jar. All these and thousands more may be properly identified from manufacturers' catalogs which contain pictures and descriptions of their products.

On July 25, 1848, a United States patent for the **Improvement in Enamels for Iron** was issued to Charles Stumer of New York. His patent was for a vitreous glaze to coat a piece of metal. The item would subsequently be fired at a temperature just below the melting point of the metal, thereby fusing the two. So we know that metal enameling began before 1850 in the United States. Graniteware, however, was not mass produced in the U.S. until the 1870's.

It was first manufactured in Europe where housewives quickly recognized its qualities. It was light weight, easy to clean, colorful and cheap. Many people were extremely poor. They had few conveniences and were thrilled with any aid to make life easier — a grater, a double boiler or a slotted spoon. The Sears catalog advertised a twenty-four piece set of cookware for $4.37.

Graniteware manufacturers, distributors and consumers prospered for almost sixty years even though there were some problems. Enamel cracked, rust formed and holes developed. To remedy this, repair kits were put on the market. They were known as **Mendets, Pecks Rivets,** or **E-Z-MEND-RS** and were composed of a nut and a screw, a couple of washers and a wrench.

In 1877, it became necessary for manufacturers to reassure the public that their products were not harmful. For some reason, people were afraid graniteware was poisonous.

Twenty cases of severe poisoning were reported in 1899. An investigation traced the source to a baker in a town near Boston who had cooked the cream for the cream cakes these twenty people had eaten, in an enameled kettle. The kettle contained antimony.

Perhaps a similar situation prompted the St. Louis Stamping Company to obtain a chemical analysis from F.A. Genth, Professor of Chemistry, University of Pennsylvania, in 1877. Genth analyzed Granite Iron Ware and found it "entirely free of lead, arsenic and other metals injurious to health" and he added that his family had seen it at the 1876 Centennial Exhibition in

Philadelphia, and had been using it with great satisfaction since. He wrote, "In my opinion there is no article in the market superior to it and none which combines to the same degree, the advantages of glass with the strength of metal."

But a superior article appeared on the market — aluminum — and by 1930, graniteware sales had noticeably declined.

They've picked up again, for, at the present time, rare old pieces are in demand by collectors. Manufacturers would be surprised that their '76, '77 date marks might lead to confusion as to the century when they were made. Almost every department store carries many brands of enamel cookware in a great assortment with a wide range of prices. Self-basting roasters, canners, plates and mugs, coffeepots and teapots are very popular.

Decorators use old graniteware to impart the Western look. One of the most unusual sales was to an American decorator in Japan who bought a dozen old battered pieces of gray graniteware for McDonalds in Tokyo.

Although most kitchens today may not have any graniteware, they probably do have a piece of contemporary enamelware.

NOTE: A good many graniteware pieces are to be found in the preceding "Tea & Coffee" and the "Utensil" sections.

Figure GW-1. **Graniteware Bowl and Pitcher.** Pitcher has footed base and strap handle with wraparound lip. Rare. Value: $75. Courtesy Vogelzang and Welch.

Figure GW-2. **Graniteware Comfit Pan.** Graniteware frame with metal mesh and turned wood handle. This pan was used on the stove to prepare sweetmeats. A piece of fruit or a nut was dipped in syrup, placed on the rack to be heated and the excess sugar that dripped off was recycled. Value: $47.50. Courtesy Vogelzang and Welch.

Figure GW-3. **Foot-warmer.** Enameled cast iron with bail handle with wood grip. Marked "Godin & Cie AUGUISE AISNE Bte S.G.D.B. No 5", made in France. A hot brick was placed inside this portable, energy-saving device. Value: $135. Courtesy Vogelzang and Welch.

Figure GW-4. **Big-gin.** Marked "Gran-ite Iron Ware, Pat'd May 30, '76 and July 3 '77." Pewter spout and top and handle. When the heavy pewter drip top and inserts are removed, this converts into a "Belle" teapot. Value: $375. Court-esy Vogelzang and Welch.

Figure GW-5. **Mold.** Enamelware. This white lion mold was probably lined with lady fingers and filled with a rich Bavarian mousse. Value: $55. Courtesy Vogelzang and Welch.

Figure GW-6. **Caster Set, Syrup Pitcher and Butter Dish.** Graniteware with pewter trim. Caster set has pressed glass bottles for salt and pepper, oil, vinegar and mustard. These sets are scarce, desirable and handy, and many people are returning to the custom of using them at table. Value: $400. Graniteware syrup pitcher with pewter trim and finial in shape of lady's head. Value: $167.50. Butter dish has pewter trim including rack for butter knife and ice compartment insert. Value: $200. Courtesy Vogelzang and Welch.

Figure GW-7. **Tea Set.** Graniteware with pewter spouts, collars, handles, lids, mint condition. Marked "Manning Bowman & Co." Complete set has a copper base. Teapot holds 3 cups. Tray: 13¾" diameter. Value for set: $675. Tray: $24. Courtesy Vogelzang and Welch.

Figure GW-8. **Roaster.** "Columbian." This covered pan was purported to tenderize meat because it kept the moisture in for self-basting. 8" high x 15" x 11" oval. Value: $37.50. Courtesy Vogelzang and Welch.

Figure GW-9. **Salt Shaker and Salt Boxes.** As far as we know, only two of these salt shakers have been found — one in Kentucky, one in Massachusetts. Value: $45-$100. The wall-hung boxes held salt for dipping into while cooking. The small one on the right is missing its wooden lid. Large box: $75-$120; small: $47.50. Courtesy Vogelzang and Welch.

Figure GW-10. **Scoops.** Small thumb scoop is marked "Granite Iron Ware, May 30 '76, July 3 '77", mfd. by the St. Louis Stamping Co. Center: confectioner's scoop with wood handle. Appears in Lalance & Grosjean catalog, 1903. Flat bottom scoop with wooden handle appears in same catalog. Scoops become obsolete with the advent of packaging and graniteware scoops are no longer made. Values, in order: $60, $60, $85. Courtesy Vogelzang and Welch.

Figure GW-11. **Tabletop Stove.** Graniteware with cast iron frames. The one-burner kerosene stove has 6 parts, including heavy tray to protect table top. Marked "George Haller Original Germany 259". 13" high. Value: $268. Courtesy Vogelzang and Welch.

Figure GW-12. **Strainers/-Drainers.** Graniteware over perforated tin. At left is a corner sink strainer. The square strainer at center fits over sink drain. Wedge-shaped strainer at right has three short feet. These were used primarily for washing vegetables and fruits under running water. Values: $24, $47.50, $47.50. Courtesy Vogelzang and Welch.

373

Figure GW-13. **Teapots and Coffee Pot.** Graniteware with cast iron handles that didn't burn like wooden ones. Teapot at left has reticulated handle to disperse heat. It is embossed "L & G" (Lalance & Grosjean). Tin lid has replaced knob. Teapot at right, with hinged lid, is shown in L. & G. Mfg. Co. catalog, 1894. Cast in handle is "Pat. Oct. 1889". Coffee pot at rear has pocket spout and was advertised in Iron Clad Mfg. Co. catalog, 1897, mfd. in NYC, NY. Values, in order: $72.50, $67.50, $60. Courtesy Vogelzang and Welch.

Figure GW-14. **Washboard and Gas Iron, with Trivet.** The wood washboard has a corrugated graniteware washing surface (shown) and a finer-ribbed wooden back. Mfd. in U.S. Natural gas iron is marked "DAVIS" in oval, flexible metal hose and wooden handle. Enameled iron trivet to match. Values: $33.50, $48, $17. Courtesy Vogelzang and Welch.

Figure GW-15. **Water Carrier.** Used for carrying hot water for the bath — the lid covers the spout to prevent spilling and heat loss. This is one in a 3-piece "King" or "Prince" toilet set, shown in the 1903 L. & G. Mfg. Co. catalog at only $2.50 each! Value now: $125. Courtesy Vogelzang and Welch.

CANNING

For the last few years the "old fashioned" necessity for putting up food in canning jars has enjoyed a revival. It has even — in these hard times — become something of a necessity again for many people. It is also a practical way to bring back some old-fashioned values (and flavors) to kitchens! Canning, or fruit jars, are far and away the most popular aspect of this field, although most of the early collectors (and maybe even the present ones) got into it through their interest in glass collecting. I would imagine that many collectors now get interested when they first discover fruit jar wrenches — of which there are many many patented designs.

Canner, tin and copper, "Mudge's
   Patent Canner," mfd. by Biddle-
   Gaumer Co., late 1880s $175.00
Canner, tin and copper, "Mudge's,"
   14" high x 13" long x 8" deep $165.00

NOTE: The Mudge Patent Processor, for Canning and Cooking Fruit & Vegetables was self-proclaimed as a "household necessity . . . the cheapest, most efficacious, most economical system of putting up high standard goods." It came in several models, which ranged in price from $3.00 to $12.00, and which differed in size, number of canners, quality and quantity of the "tin plate, cold-rolled copper bottoms, copper tops and steam whistles." It was patented July 27, 1886. The Mudge was used by putting the processor box on the range, putting water into it, then the carefully filled canning jars into the water with the covers placed over them. From the original instruction booklet come these directions: "Have water boiling to generate steam before using. Keep well boiling vigorously while using the canner as you must have sufficient steam to do good work. Put fruit or vegetables in the jar raw. Place jar on a dry folded towel while pouring in the hot syrup or water to prevent breakage. Pour in slowly. In cooking or canning dry, be careful to temper glass jars before subjecting to the action of the steam. Place wooden blocks on the canner under the jars to prevent breaking. Do not put the lids on the jars while processing . . . Be careful to sterilize lids and rubbers before sealing. Never allow water to boil away. If steam escapes through the whistle, it is time to refill [the well] to keep the bottom from burning . . . Be sure to wipe the canner dry after using before putting away. Read Mrs.

Rorer's directions carefully." Finally, in order to catch every possible purchaser, the booklet claimed "While this apparatus is called a cannery, it is an admirable contrivance for cooking vegetables, meats and making tea and coffee. It saves time and fuel and preserves flavor and color." Accompanying the canner was a jar holder: "Our adjustable jar holder will be appreciated by those who have burnt their fingers in lifting hot jars. They are leather lined, strongly bound by tin with wooden handles. The adjustment is made so they will fit any size jar. Handy for sealing and removing jar lids too." The original price for the jar holder was 25 cents! By the way, this instruction booklet [which itself would have collectible value] had recipes written by the famed Mrs. Sarah Tyson Rorer who often wrote on cooking.

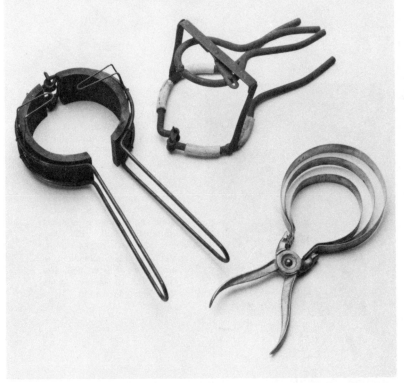

Figure XI-1. **Jar Lifters or Wrenches.** At left: wood with heavy wire handles. Top: wire with leather, double grip. Very unusual . . . the bottom one grips the jar and the top one, pivoting on its frame, unscrews the lid! 9½" long. Bottom right: copper wrench with 3 bands which can be clipped in to fit the circumference of the jar to be opened. Copper plate, handles. 9½" long. All located by the Primitive Man, Bob Cahn, Carmel, NY. His evaluations, in order: $55-$75; $28-$35; $45-$55.

Figure XI-2. **Canner.** (Two views.) "Mudge Patent Processor, for Canning and Cooking Fruit & Vegetables," John L. Gaumer Co., Philadelphia, pat'd July 27, 1886. Cold-rolled copper and tin. 14¾" high x 13¼" long x 8" wide. Box is 4" high. Included here is the jar wrench, all wood, 9" long, and Mrs. Sarah T. Rorer's instructions and recipes. Note steam whistle lower left corner of box top. Original prices ranged from $3-$12, depending on amount of copper and size. Collection of Meryle Evans. Value now: $160-$180.

Canning, or fruit, jar, stoneware,
  "Weir," gallon size, complete
  and good condition $25.00
Canning jar, aqua glass, "Mason
  Midget," 1858 .... $25.00
Canning jar, aqua, "Lightning Putnam
  #31," bail handle $12.50

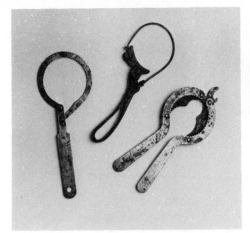

Figure XI-3. **Fruit Jar Wrenches.** Left: A.C. Williams, c. 1900; Best S. Co., pat'd 1917; jar and bottle opener, Author's collection. c. 1910. Value: $8-$10.

Canning jar, aqua, "Lightning," 1
quart size, bail handle $3.00
Canning jar, stoneware, glazed in
shades of brown, 12-sided,
Marked "Peoria Pottery," 7" high
x 4½" diameter $38.00
Canning jar, aqua, "Millville
Atmospheric," 1 quart, 1861 .... $55.00
Canning jar, stoneware, "Weir," with
amber glass lid, 1892, 1 quart size $20.00
Canning jar, aqua, "McDonald's New
Perfect, No. 1," bail handle $12.50
Canning jar, aqua, "Eagle," with iron
yoke clamp and glass lid $125.00
Canning jar, green, "Swayzee's Improved" $18.00

Figure XI-4. **Jar Rack and Jar Lifter.** Wire rack holds 4 jars for sterilizing. Basket part is 3¼" high x 10¼" diameter. Lifter works with one hand — your thumb goes through hole at top while fingers pull up on wood grip. 10" high. Early 20th century. Author's collection. Value: $15-$20.

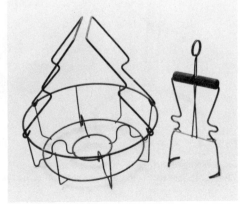

379

Figure XI-5. **Fruit Jar Funnel.**
Tin. C. 1890-1910. Author's
collection. Value: $4-$8.

Canning jar, aqua, "Mason's," pat'd
November 30, 1858, quart size $5.00
Canning jar, aqua, "Lafayette," glass
& metal stopper, quart size $118.00
Canning jar, amber, "Smalley & Co.,"
pat'd April 7, 1896, rectangular
with arched shoulders & tin lid,
2 quart size $36.00
Canning jar, amber, marked
"Putname," 1 quart $16.00
Canning rack, wire, rectangular, and
meant for use in a 2-hole boiler $9.00

Figure XI-6. **Jar Holders.** Wire and wood. One on right, 9" long. See picture of Mudge
Patent Processor. 19th century. Author's collection. Value: $3-$7.

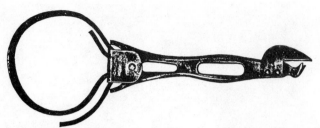

Figure XI-7. **Jar Sealer and Can Opener.** Leather strap and cast iron frame. "Mason Jar Sealer and Opener," from F.W. Seastrand catalog, c. 1912. Value: $7-$12.

Fruit jar filler funnel, mottled gray
    graniteware .... $18.00 to $22.00
Fruit jar funnel, pieced tin, ring
    handle, large mouth (all this kind
    of funnel have large mouths) .... $4.00 to $8.00
Fruit jar holder, wire, looks like a doll
    stand, 6" high .... $3.00 to $6.00
Fruit jar lifter, wire, long handle $8.00
Fruit jar lifter, iron, "E-Z Lift" $2.00
Fruit jar wrench, tinned iron, "A.C.
    Williams," 8" long, c. 1910 .... $3.00 to $8.00
Fruit jar wrench, iron and wood, cast
    iron and wire, "Best S. Co.," pat'd
    1917, 7¾" long .... $5.00 to $12.00

Figure XI-8. **Stoneware Crock.** Pale gray with shiny glaze, wire bail handle, c. 1900. Author's collection. Value: $20-$30.

Figure XI-9. **Canning Jars.** (Two pictures.) "The Gayner," "Columbia," "Ball Improved," "Mason's Improved Butter Jar," and "Millville Atmospheric Fruit Jar." The Gayner Glass-Top, Salem, NJ, is c. 1915. The Columbia, with glass lid held secure with a wire bail levered into place. It dates between 1896-1900. The Ball Improved has a metal screw-band seal and glass lid, c. 1910-1922. The Mason's Improved has a metal screw band seal and glass lid, and probably dates to the turn of the century. It is unmentioned in Julian Harrison Toulouse's **A Collectors' Manual: Fruit Jars.** I suspect it was not made by Mason. Last is the Millville, with a glass lid held by yoke and thumbscrew. It dates to about 1862. Pictures courtesy of the National Museum of American History, Smithsonian Institution.

Fruit jar wrench, cast white metal,
leather strap, 8½" long .... $7.00 to $12.00
Fruit jar wrench, iron with wood
handle, "teeth" hold the jar lid,
8½" long .... $6.00 to $10.00
Fruit jar wrench, iron, "C.A. Powell,"
mechanical $3.00
Fruit jar wrench, red rubber over wire,
"Daisy Jar Opener" $6.00
Fruit jar wrench, nickeled steel,
adjustable, "Winchester's of
Carthage," Carthage, Missouri $8.00
Fruit jar wrench, cast iron, "Wilson's" $8.00
Fruit jar wrench, cast iron and wire, c. 1910 .... $6.50
Fruit jar wrench, "Speedo," mfd. in
St. Louis, geared $6.00
Fruit jar wrench, iron, "Cunnard" $6.00
Fruit jar wrench, iron, "Cupples" $3.00
Fruit jar wrench, iron with red
rubber grippers $12.00

NOTE: It does seem a bit funny that everything in this category actually has to do with "jarring" not canning foods! But just to fill out the story, I'll add one tool, called a "tipping copper", that was used to solder closed the hole left in the top of the early cans. As I wrote in my first book, "Even the housewife could literally can her food. The cans were boiled, the hot food put in, and the top soldered on. A hole was punched in the lid and can boiled again — the steam escaped through the hole. The hole was then immediately soldered closed, using a tipping copper and solder. If a can was found with two holes, both soldered up, it indicated that someone had taken a spoiled batch of food, re-heated and re-sealed the cans." A tipping copper, with a long iron shaft and wooden handle, with a wedge-shaped copper head, would bring about $4.00 to $10.00.

ONE MORE NOTE: A peculiar but interesting sounding "new fruit jar" was discussed in the pages of the October 1880 "Scribner's Monthly" magazine: "A new device for preserving fruit in its natural condition consists of a glass jar or tumbler, having a cover with a rubber packing-ring, secured to the jar by a screw clasp. At the bottom of the jar is a hole, designed to be closed air-tight by a suitable stopper, and inside the jar is placed a layer of dried clay, to absorb the moisture that may escape from the fruit. The grapes or other fruits are hung up inside the jar, the cover is put on, and air is withdrawn by means of an air-pump, when the opening in the bottom is closed and sealed." Rube Goldberg, anyone?

CHILL & FREEZE, CURE & DRY

This is the category where are found ice boxes, ice cream freezers and the implements for shredding or breaking ice. Most people do not collect any but the small implements. The old ice boxes — many of them oak and as stylish as Mission furniture — are in great demand, but one or two is the limit for most people. And most people end up using them as bars. Pictured in this chapter is the most extraordinary ice box I ever saw: what fun to have a large old-fashioned kitchen to put it in!

The most popular kitchen collectibles having to do with freezing are ice cream molds and dishers; they are found in the FORM, MOLD, SHAPE & DECORATE section.

Ice box, oak, "Northey Duplex," 4
    doors, 6' 2½" high x 4' 1½" wide
    x 2½' deep $350.00
Ice box, ash, enameled interior, 57"
    high, 2 door .... $175.00 to $200.00
Ice box, oak, porcelain lining, lift top
    lid, 47" high, 27½" wide .... $160.00 to $190.00
Ice box, pine with zinc lining, lift top,
    42" high .... $125.00 to $140.00
Ice box, zinc, 2 door, high legs .... $150.00 to $170.00

NOTE: Every old ice box I've come across has a musty smell that does not readily go away, even with treatments of baking soda, soda pop, fresh paint, detergent, etc. Do you have a good hint to share in the next edition?

Ice chipper, steel with wood handle,
    "Crown," North Brothers, c. 1900,
    wicked-looking teeth .... $8.00 to $12.00
Ice chisel, steel with wood handle,
    "Crown Ice Chipper," American
    Machine Co., pat'd 1884 .... $8.00 to $12.00
Ice cream can, gray graniteware,
    1 quart size .... $35.00 to $45.00

Ice cream freezer, tin, "Kress," pat'd
    July 23, 1912 .... $25.00
Ice cream freezer, tin, "Acme" $20.00
Ice cream freezer, tin, "Acme," pat'd
    Feb. 15, 1910, July 3, 1912,
    2 gallon size $40.00
Ice cream freezer, wood with cast iron
    crank, dated 1858, 2 gallon size $95.00
Ice cream freezer," Liberty Can Co.,
    pat'd 1920, 1921, 2 quart size,
    clamps to table .... $55.00 to $65.00
Ice cream freezer, wood and
    galvanized metal, "Frost King" .... $40.00 to $50.00

Figure XII-1. **Ice Box.** Zinc. Turn-of-century. Collection of Robert and Mary Mac Franklin. Value: $150-$170.

Figure XII-2. **Ice Box.** (Two views) Handpainted metal with ice water spigot at side. Shelves revolve inside. This icebox came from New York state and was painted by hand around 1910 by a commercial artist for her parents. Photographed at the flea market booth of Howard Templeton, Sellersville, PA. Value: $300-$500.

Ice cream holder, tin, bail handle,
    "Thermopak," insulated $15.00

Ice cream molds and scoops: see FORM, MOLD, SHAPE & DECORATE.

Ice crusher, cream-colored painted
    cast metal, wood-handled crank,
    "National Ice-Crusher," pat'd
    #2048569 (1936), on a stand, with
    place for tumbler, 9" high $28.00
Ice cube crusher, iron hopper, green
    Depression glass bowl, "Lightning" ..... $38.00 to $45.00
Ice cube crusher, cast iron jaws and
    handle, "Stover 'Cube Kracker',"
    mfd. in Freeport, Ill., 7¾" long $15.00
Ice pick, wooden handle, "Stewart
    Ice Co." $6.00
Ice pick, all metal, "Coca Cola" .... $2.00 to $8.00

386

Figure XII-3. **Ice Box.** Decoratively finished wood, Eastlake style. Faucet and tumbler stand at left. Meant for use in parlors and dining rooms, not the kitchen. 54½″ high, c. 1880. Picture courtesy of The Smithsonian Institution, Museum of History and Technology.

Figure XII-4. **Ice Cream Freezer.** Japanned and stenciled tin, with imitation graining, gold and bronze decorations and label. Heavy porcelain knob with gilding on close fitting lid. "Automatic Ice Cream Freezer," Treman King & Co., "System Dr. Meidinger, Ithica, NY 1 & 3 East State Street." Inside lifts out — bayonet twist — to pack salt in. Galvanized insides. Long cone-shaped insert to hold ingredients. 3 pieces plus lid. 13½" high x 6" diameter. 1880s? Collection of Meryle Evans. Value: $55-$85.

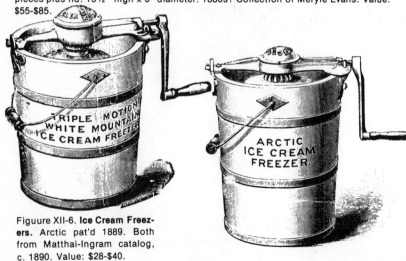

Figuure XII-6. **Ice Cream Freezers.** Arctic pat'd 1889. Both from Matthai-Ingram catalog, c. 1890. Value: $28-$40.

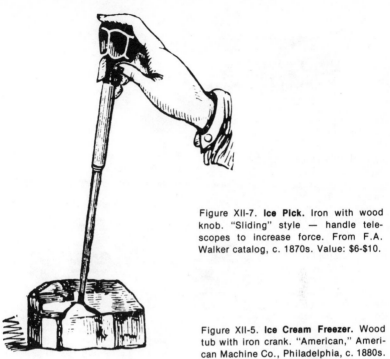

Figure XII-7. **Ice Pick.** Iron with wood knob. "Sliding" style — handle telescopes to increase force. From F.A. Walker catalog, c. 1870s. Value: $6-$10.

Figure XII-5. **Ice Cream Freezer.** Wood tub with iron crank. "American," American Machine Co., Philadelphia, c. 1880s.

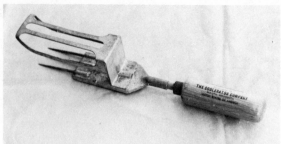

Figure XII-8. **Ice Pick and Scraper.** Nickeled iron with wood handle. Turn-of-century. Adv'g "Coolerator. The Air Conditioned Refrigerator," mfd. by the Coolerator Co., Duluth, MN, US of A. 12" long. Photographed at Bonnie Barnes' Anteek Corner, Waynesboro, VA. Value: $12-$16.

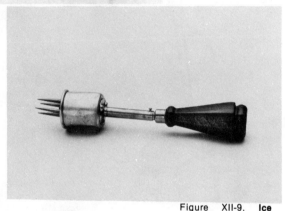

Figure XII-9. **Ice Pick.** Steel prickers, wood handle, aluminum housing. Reveal prickers by pushing up and twisting aluminum cup, bayonet lock. 8" long. Located by the Primitive Man, Bob Cahn, Carmel, NY. His evaluation: $18-$25.

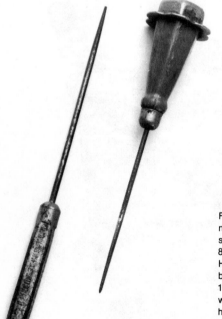

Figure XII-10. **Ice Picks.** Left: nickel steel and steel. The 4 sides read "John A. Schwaz-838-840 Broadway, Brooklyn, High Grade Furniture, Columbia Grafonolas." Pat'd 3/24/-14. 8¾" long. Right: steel, wood, nickel-plated crusher head. Probably Androck. 7 5/8" long. Author's collection. Value: $6-$10.

390

Ice pick, "Arcade" $10.00
Ice pick, wood handle with motto "Use
    Ice Year Around" $2.00
Ice picks, nickeled steel, all steel or
    steel with wood handle, all about .... $6.00 to $10.00
Ice picks, same as above but with
    advertising .... $6.00 to $12.00
Ice scraper and chipper, cast iron
    with wood handle, "White Mountain" ..... $10.00 to $12.0
Ice shaver, cast iron, "Gem" $7.50
Ice shaver, "Enterprise No. 33," pat'd 7/4/93 .... $40.00
Ice shaver and pick, nickeled iron,
    "Coolerator. The Air-Conditioned
    Refrigerator," mfd. by The
    Coolerator Co., Duluth, Minn.,
    has maw to catch ice shavings $14.00
Ice shaver, cast metal, "Mogan (or
    Morgan)-Strowbridge Iron Co.,
    #12," New Brighton, PA, big cup
    with adjustable and sharpenable
    blade $5.00
Ice shaver, nickeled cast iron, "Gem
    Ice Shave" North Bros. Mfg. Co.,
    Philadelphia, patent applied for
    (no date), hinged hopper,
    removeable blade, 6" long $15.00
Ice shaver, cast iron, "Arctic Ice Shave
    No. 33," Grey Iron Casting Co.,
    Mount Joy, PA $12.00

Figure XII-11. **Ice Scoop.** Galvanized tin with wood handle. C. 1890. Author's collection. Value: $7-$12.

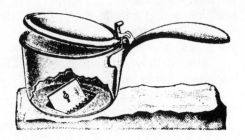

Figure XII-12. **Ice Shredder or Shaver.** Cast iron, sometimes nickel plated, sometimes tinned. Blade adjusts for coarse or fine. This is a cutaway view . . . the cup isn't transparent. Enterprise Hardware Co., 1902. Cost 50 cents or $1.25 then. Value: $10-$12.

Ice shaver or shredder, nickeled iron,
     "Enterprise Hardware," shaped
     like a saucepan with lid,
     replaceable blade .... $10.00 to $12.00
Ice shaver, cast iron base with steel
     shaving table, stands high on 4
     beautiful scrolled cabriole legs,
     mid-1800s .... $80..00 to $100.00
Ice shredder, plated iron, "Enterprise
     No. 43," cone-shaped, shaving
     blade in lid, used "upside down"
     to make snow balls, c. 1900 .... $15.00 to $20.00

Figure XII-13. **Ice Water Cooler.** Japanned tin with stenciled label, cast iron finial and faucet. 2, 3, 4, 6, 8, 10, 15 and 20 gallons. From F.A. Walker catalog, 1870s. Value: $45-$65. Also came porcelain-lined, 2, 3, 4, 6, 8 and 10 gallons.

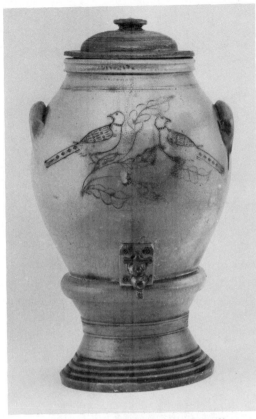

Figure XII-14. **Water Cooler.** Stoneware with 2 incised cobalt blue birds on branches. Ear handles, turned base. Metal spigot. Marked "4" on one side. Pennsylvania, mid 1800s. 21½" high. Estimated to sell between $400-$600. Realized: $500. Picture courtesy of Robert W. Skinner Inc., Auctioneers, Bolton MA.

Ice tongs, iron with wooden handle, adv'g "Dixie Gem Coal, Ice & Fuel Co.," 14" long $17.50
Ice tongs, simple wrought iron, used by ice man .... $25.00 to $45.00
Ice tongs, wrought iron, very decorative ...... $35.00 to $50.00
Ice tongs, iron, "Butler Ice Co.," 14" long $12.00
Ice tongs, iron (?), not very sturdy, 13" long $15.00
Refrigerator bottle, green glass, pat'd September 15, 1931 .... $15.00
Water cooler, crockery, Red Wing, 6 gallon size $270.00
Water cooler, stoneware, blue striped, 14½" high x 10" diameter $55.00
Water cooler, stoneware, blue and white, 3 gallon size $100.00

Figure XII-15. **Fruit Dryer.** Wood with galvanized tin base and wire mesh screening in each drawer. Used on top of range to dry sliced fruit or pitted, halved apricots, etc. Author's collection. Value: $100-$120.

Water cooler, stoneware with cobalt
    flower design, pewter faucet, 4
    gallon size, no lid $160.00
Water cooler, spongeware, marked
    "Avery & Winter Pottery Co.,
    New York," #6 size $300.00
Water cooler, Red Wing, 5 gallon size,
    with lid $275.00

CURE & DRY

Corn dryer, wrought iron, 20"
    long, hangs from ceiling hook,
    looks like a fish backbone, c. 1820s ...... $35.00 to $50.00
Corn dryer, wire, c. 1910 .... $8.00 to $15.00
Dryer, fruit, stovetop, wood box with
    wood and wire screen/mesh
    drawers .... $100.00 to $120.00
Meat curing pump, "Morton Salt," in
    original cardboard tube with
    instructions $25.00

ELECTRIC APPLIANCES

Until very recently there has been little collector demand for electric kitchen appliances, except for the very earliest things from the first decade of this century. Recently this has begun to change. There's even a book called **Electrical Collectibles** by Don Fredgant (see the Bibliography), which covers kitchen appliances along with many others.

The trend, however, is difficult to plot and I have very few prices to share with you — more than the first edition, but not many more. Many of the items might even be found still in use (perhaps by a Sunday driver of mixers, so to speak) and there are a few World War I appliances being brought into electrical repair shops or being sold at house sales.

Occasionally you read about people who have been depending on their GE monitor top refrigerators since the 1930s, or a Westinghouse counter-top oven, the very first, from the late 1920s, or a Mixmaster from 1918! This is even more heart-warming — and I mean this sincerely — than the news that someone is still using their grandmother's stovetop griddle or their great uncle's apple parer. I suspect that I feel this way because in this present age of appliances, when they aren't made very well to begin with and some cannot be repaired, it seems a minor miracle to turn on something electric and get the same magical thrill of the quiet hum that was felt 50 or 70 years ago.

The categories are varied, and all are potentially desirable collectibles. I believe that shortly there will be many collectors of early electric classics — toasters, coffee makers, juicers, mixers, waffle irons, frying pans, etc.

As far as pricing goes, I believe that for a while longer, early appliances will be priced as second hand, obsolete gadgets rather than collectible, curiously attractive objects. The exception (or at least one of them) is electric toasters, which have been edging up toward $30 for a while. When we went through the extended — and continuing — fashion for all Art Deco items a few years ago, the toasters from the 1930s, which resemble minor architectural feats, became very popular.

Butter churn, "Dazey" electric, with
    instruction booklet $15.00
Casserole, "Nesco Thrifty Cook
    Casserole #B40," National
    Enamel & Stamping Co.,
    Milwaukee, Wisconsin, tan,
    brown and black enameled body
    with chrome and red Art Deco
    design of woman serving steaming
    casserole dish on front, 2 Bakelite
    Deco black handles and lid knob,
    inner bowl, electric cord, "high"
    and "low" settings, no date,
    nifty looking $50.00

Figure XIII-1. **Electric Chafing Dish, Stove and Coffee Percolator. Dining Room Set.** General Electric, 1918-1919. Chafing Dish, Type ECD; Stove, Type ES; Percolator, Type ECP. Picture courtesy of General Electric. Thank heavens most of the big companies keep historical files and collections. Value for chafing dish or percolator: $45-$70. For stove: $15-$25. For full set: $60-$100.

Figure XIII-2. **Electric Coffee Percolators.** Left: chromium plated with ebonized wood handles and faucet handle. Mfd. by Royal Rochester Co., No. E639. "Pyrex" percolator lid. 15" high, works. Collection of Robert Franklin. Value: $25-$45. Right: silver-plated, "Automatic Percolator," Hot Point, Edison Electric Appliance Co., no date. 12" high. Photographed at Bonnie Barnes' Anteek Corner, Waynesboro, VA. Value: $50-$60.

Churn, "Gemdandy Deluxe Electric
    Churn," Albaner (?) Mfg. Co.,
    Birmingham, 18" high glass
    barrel with screw-on lid with
    motor, bail handle, no date $25.00
Coffee grinder, electric, original paint,
    c. 1920 .... $85.00
Coffee percolator, "Royal Rochester
    Company," chrome, ebonized
    wooden handles, faucet spout,
    Pyrex lid, 15" high .... $25.00 to $45.00

Figure XIII-3. **Electric Cookers.** Rival's "Crock-Pot," Model 3101 (front and right). Woodtone, 3½ quart size; "flame" or "avocado," 3½ quarts. Model 3102 (rear, 1971). Also Wood tone. These are first cousins, once removed, of the Naxon Beanery, and are classics for future collectors. 10 3/8" high. Picture courtesy of Rival Manufacturing Company.

Coffee percolator, "Hotpoint 'automatic percolator'," Edison Electric Appliance Co., silver plated, no date $50.00
Coffee pot, "Royal Rochester," floral-patterned Fraunfelter china, pat'd August 12, 1924, with chrome base and faucet, also matching creamer and covered sugar bowl $135.00
Coffee pot, copper, makes 4 cups $35.00
Coffee pot, chrome, large party size, mid-1920s $25.00
Coffee pot, "Forman" electric, chrome with tan handles and spigot, "football type" $18.00
Coffee pot, chrome, "Edison General Electric Hotpoint," with sugar and creamer to match $22.00
Egg cooker, ceramic, red, Fiesta Ware .... $30.00 to $35.00

Egg cooker, same as above only pale green $30.00
Egg cooker, yellow Fiesta, "Hanscraft"
    cooker but poaching rack missing $35.00
Egg cooker, orange Fiesta Ware $35.00
Eggbeater, electric, with Depression
    green glass bowl $28.00
Griddle, "Electrahot" Style 512,
    chromed metal, a small rectangle
    on legs $10.00
Juicer, "Sunkist Jr." .... $12.00 to $15.00
Juicer, "Dormeyer" $20.00
Milkshake mixer, "Thoromix," doesn't work $16.50
Mixer, "Lindstrom," with original
    glass bowl, 1920s $4.00
Popcorn popper, aluminum with wood
    handles, glass cover, "Knapp
    Monarch Co." .... $6.00 to $12.00
Toaster, "Handy Hot," 2 slices $10.00
Toaster, 2 slice, fancy grillwork, c. 1920s $25.00
Toaster, fancy Deco cutouts, chromed,
    makes 2 slices of 3" x 3" toast
    (for what? canapes?) $25.00
Toaster, wire, "General Electric Model
    X2", GE's first electric toaster, 1905 .... $75.00 to $125.00
Toaster, wire and hand-painted floral
    decorated porcelain base, "General
    Electric, Model D12", pat'd 1908 .... $60.00 to $85.00

Figure XIII-4. **Electric Slow Cooker.** Naxon Utilities Corporation, Beanery or Bean-Pot, Model 340, c. 1969. "Fast" or "Slow" settings. This bean-pot was the immediate predecessor of the Rival Crock-Pot slow cooker. Rival acquired Naxon in 1970, and thought that the Naxon was so "drab looking," so downright ugly — that it should be redesigned. Alas! Think how many simple enameled or metal finishes have been complicated with imitation plastic wood veneer, and the infamous decorator colors, "Pumpkin," "Harvest Gold" and "Avocado." Picture courtesy of Rival Manufacturing Company. Value: $20-$45 for this early model.

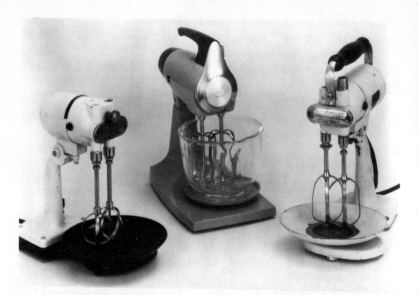

Figure XIII-5. **Electric Mixers.** Sunbeam. Left to right: 1930 model, 1967-1974; 1933. I saw the 1930, in so-called "closet green" — pale and chalky — with many attachments, in junk shop on Block Island for $8. A bargain. Picture courtesy of Sunbeam Corporation.

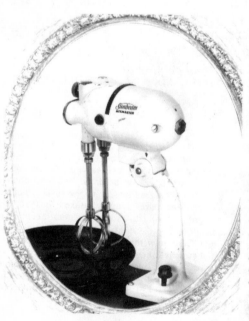

Figure XIII-6. **Electric Mixer.** Sunbeam Mixmaster, 1930. Picture courtesy of Sunbeam Corporation, complete with portrait oval. I have a 1933 booklet, entitled "Kitchen Tested Recipes" by the Home Economists of the Famous Sunbeam Mixmaster. From that booklet I learned that there were many attachments: a slicer and shredder, potato peeler, drink mixer, silver polisher, meat grinder, food chopper, coffee grinder, can opener and knife sharpener. Everything except a drill press. A Power Transfer Unit was needed to reduce the speed of the motor; it fastened to the drive shaft with a thumb screw. Other attachments included a sausage stuffer, grapefruit reamer, mayonnaise oil dropper, and juice strainer. If you find a Mixmaster complete with all 13 attachements, and the power transfer unit too, you truly have what Sunbeam called "a handsome thing in any kitchen." Value: $50-$75.

400

Figure XIII-7. **Electric Mixer and Juicer on Stand.** General Electric, 1919. Notice hinged frame. Picture courtesy of General Electric. Value: $65-$85.

Figure XIII-8. **Food Processor.** Cuisinart, Model CFP-4, 1973. This is the model first introduced to America at the National Hosewares Show in Chicago in 1973. Carl Sontheimer, an engineer who loves to cook, discovered in 1971 the "Robot-Coupe," invented by Pierre Verdun, at a French housewares show. He brought it back to Aemrica and refined the machine to his satisfaction. A collectible future classic. Picture courtesy of Cuisinarts, Inc.

Toaster, nickel-plated copper, "Electrex," United Drug Co., pat'd 1920, 1927 .... $20.00 to $30.00
Toaster, "Universal," pat'd 1913 to 1920 .... $22.00
Waffle iron, twins — stacking, "Manning-Bowman," Art Deco on 11" round stand, curved Bakelite handles $75.00

Figure XIII-9. **Electric Mixer.** Hobart Corporation's "KitchenAid" Model H 1918. This mixer, meant for home use, followed by three years the first commercial electric mixer — for restaurants and hotels — that was introduced in 1915. Picture courtesy of Hobart Corporation. Value: $65-$85. Hobart Corporation, founded in 1897, was innovative from the beginning. To quote from a short history of the company, "During the period from 1905 to 1910, peanut butter and hamburger were becoming popular items in the American diet, and Hobart introduced an electric meat chopper and a peanut butter machine. To build sales for these products, Hobart pioneered time-payment selling". In another publication, a **Newcomen Address** by President David Meeker, from 1960, the story is related of Hobart's dishwasher. Hobart and the Crescent Washing Machine Company joined in 1926. To quote: "The history of (Crescent) dates back to the 1880's when an imaginative and purposeful lady, Mrs. Josephine Garis Cochrane, built a machine for the purpose of doing her own dishes." What a story to pursue sometime!

Figure XIII-10. **Electric Hot Plate.** General Electric, c. 1919. Note huge thermostat on cord. Helical coil-mounted. Picture courtesy of General Electric. Value: $10-$15.

Figure XIII-11. **Electric Pancake Griddle.** Cord not shown. General Electric, Model PH52, 1922. Picture courtesy of General Electric. Value: $12-$20.

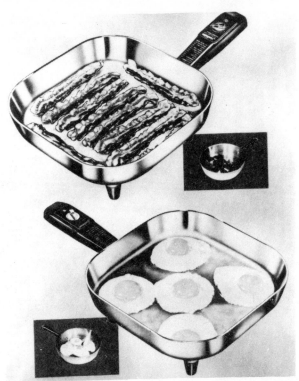

Figure XIII-12. **Electric Fry Pans.** Sunbeam. "Controlled Heat Automatic Frypan", 1953, medium size. A "Fry-Guide" on the handle. Submergable for washing up to control dial. This was supposedly the first electric frying pan, even though as far back as 1893 it was possible. At the Columbian Exhibition in Chicago, a working electric kitchen was installed. There was a saucepan, water heater, broiler and boiler, each connected to a separate outlet. It didn't catch on for a while — even in 1920 people were disgruntled because the electric cooking utensils burned out easily, and capable repairmen were very hard to find. This **frying pan,** in medium size, was followed in 1954 with large and super sizes, and finally in 1957 with the Standard Size. The first model of any of these sizes would be collectible future classics. Picture courtesy of Sunbeam Corporation.

Figure XIII-13. **Electric Kettle.** Note white porcelain feet. General Electric, early 1900s — even GE doesn't seem to have the exact date. Picture courtesy of General Electric. Value: $40-$75.

403

Figure XIII-14. **Electric Kitchen Appliances.** All General Electric, all highly collectible. Bottom left: toaster with white porcelain base decorated with flowers, 1908. Top left: 1923 toaster. At center is the charming "Angelus Campfire Bar-B-Q Mashmallow Toaster," which is undated but undoubtedly early. Note little forked sticks for the marshmallows. Top right is a pedestal-base waffle iron with porcelain insert in lid. Undated. Values: 1908 toaster, $50-$100; 1923 toaster, $25-$35; marshmallow toaster, $20-$35; waffle iron, $550-$100. Picture courtesy of General Electric.

Figure XIII-15. **Microwave Oven.** Amana Refrigeration, Inc. 1967. Seems hard to believe they've been around now for 16 years. Amana, a division of Raytheon, manufactured this first home microwave oven, 115-volts, for countertop use. It is a classic of the future, just as the newish convection ovens will be. Picture courtesy of Amana Refrigeration, Inc.

Figure XIII-16. **Refrigerator.** The famous General Electric "Monitor-Top" from 1927, Model R-5-2. The first GE electric 'fridge, a monitor-top that lacked the long legs of this one, was manufactured in 1926. To quote from Don Wallance's marvelous book, **Shaping America's Products,** 1956, "Even the panel at the bottom of the cabinet of the 1926 model, originally intended to conceal a pan for collecting drippings for the ice, was retained . . . The monitor top . . . was produced until 1935, with yearly changes and refinements. But public prejudice against the exposed refrigeration unit began to mount, undoubtedly spurred on by the ridicule of competitors. The characteristic appearance of the exposed condensor coils wound around the steel case of the unit soon earned it the nickname 'bird cage.' . . . Someday the monitor top refrigerator may become an exhibit in the Smithsonian Institution." Ah ha! Hear that, curators? Some monitor-tops came in highly-decorated versions with enameled floral designs. Picture courtesy of General Electric.

Figure XIII-17. **Electric Range and Dishwasher.** General Electric, 1924. This farm kitchen postdates the entire electric kitchen on display at the Columbian Exhibition in Chicago by 31 years! Picture courtesy of General Electric.

Figure XIII-18. **Electric Toaster.** with **Toast Rack.** Hand-painted porcelain base. General Electric, 1908. Picture courtesy of General Electric. Value: $60-$120.

Figure XIII-19. **Electric Toaster.** General Electric, Model X2, made in 1905. This is the **first** electric toaster, really elegant simplicity. If you have one, it is worth at least $75, and probably more. Picture courtesy of General Electric.

Figure XIII-20. **Electric Toaster.** General Electric Model D12, made in 1908-09. Porcelain base, undecorated. Picture courtesy of General Electric. Value: $50-$65.

Figure XIII-21. **Electric Toaster,** without rack that kept toast warm. Hand-decorated porcelain base. General Electric, 1908. Picture courtesy of General Electric. Value: $50-$100.

Figure XIII-22. **Electric Toaster.** Nickel plated, with blue wood knobs. Electrex, pat'd 1920, 1927, United Drug Co. Author's collection. Value: $20-$40.

Figure XIII-23. **Electric Toaster.** (2 views.) General Electric, 1940. Note that nifty spider web design. Author's collection. Value: $20-$35.

409

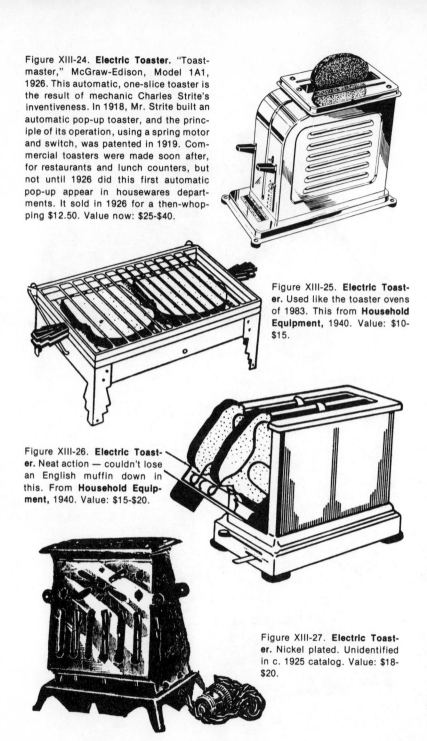

Figure XIII-24. **Electric Toaster.** "Toast-master," McGraw-Edison, Model 1A1, 1926. This automatic, one-slice toaster is the result of mechanic Charles Strite's inventiveness. In 1918, Mr. Strite built an automatic pop-up toaster, and the principle of its operation, using a spring motor and switch, was patented in 1919. Commercial toasters were made soon after, for restaurants and lunch counters, but not until 1926 did this first automatic pop-up appear in housewares departments. It sold in 1926 for a then-whopping $12.50. Value now: $25-$40.

Figure XIII-25. **Electric Toaster.** Used like the toaster ovens of 1983. This from **Household Equipment,** 1940. Value: $10-$15.

Figure XIII-26. **Electric Toaster.** Neat action — couldn't lose an English muffin down in this. From **Household Equipment,** 1940. Value: $15-$20.

Figure XIII-27. **Electric Toaster.** Nickel plated. Unidentified in c. 1925 catalog. Value: $18-$20.

Figure XIII-28. **Electric Waffle Iron.** General Electric, c. 1900. Cumbersome, and think of trying to wash it — ever so carefully and fearfully. Note heat-dissipating handles, just like the stove-lid lifters used on old wood-burning stoves. Picture courtesy of General Electric. Value: $45-$65.

Cans, jars and bottles: they all have to be opened. In this category are many of the ingenious devices used to gain entry to cans, jars and bottles! The most elegant group can be found among the corkscrews. Corkscrews may still be holding their own as most popular collectibles in this category, but I am sure it's a close tie with can openers.

One of the most select of all collector societies is devoted to those clever metal pigtails: The International Correspondence of Corkscrew Addicts, which limits its international membership to 50. Some of the corkscrews pictured here are part of the fabulous collection of Brother Timothy Diener, Cellarmaster of The Christian Brothers in California, and a retired "Right" (as in, "I'd rather be right than president") of the Correspondence.

In a corkscrew collection, as elsewhere among kitchen and cookery items, the patient and patented search for improvement is evident. Therefore, while handmade and one-of-a-kind corkscrews are valuable additions to any collection, it is perhaps the patented examples that excite the most interest. The Englishman William Lund was probably the most prolific inventor of corkscrews and his screws vary considerably in design and mechanical principle. Two important corkscrew auctions were held in New York City during 1982, at Phillips, in September and December. Some nice expensive Christmas presents were undoubtedly bought then.

Can openers are the other big collecting area in this category. I know that many of my readers have a special fondness for the sometimes absurd, always ingenious, examples of a tool that all of us take for granted.

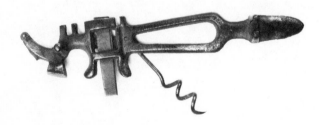

Figure XIV-1. **Can Opener.** Multiple use, with corkscrew and glass cutter, also knife sharpener. No marks. C. 1900. Author's collection, Value: $12-$16.

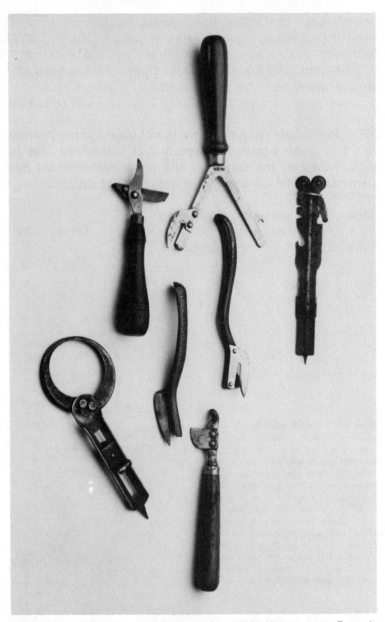

Figure XIV-2. **Can Openers.** Most unusual is the "V" for Victory at top. Turquoise wood handle, 7½" long. Combo at right has a knife sharpener at end, also cuts glass, opens cans and jars. "The Improved Peerless," Austria, U.S. Patent Pending. Other combo, lower left, opens cans and jars. "J.C. Forster & Son, Pittsburgh." Pat'd September 13, 1910. 6¾" long. Bottom: Cassady-Fairbanks, Chicago. Curved handle of cast iron and simple cutting blade, center inside right, is the "Delmonico," pat'd February 11, 1890. To its left: cast iron, has gritty casting on handle to improve grip. Unmarked. Collection of Meryle Evans. Value: $8-$22.

413

Bottle opener, cast brass, fish figural,
with corkscrew, made in Germany $12.00
Bottle opener, cast iron, lamppost drunk ..... $15.00 to $18.00
Bottle opener, cast brass, lamppost drunk .... $20.00 to $25.00
Bottle opener, cast iron, drunk with
palm tree .... $20.00 to $28.00

NOTE: Personally I don't care for the drunkard bottle openers. I think too much humor is made out of something that isn't funny. However, the lamppost and palm tree drunkard bottle openers are quite common, and widely collected.

Bottle opener, cast iron, clown with
moustache and 4 eyes .... $25.00 to $60.00
Bottle opener, cast iron, horseshoe
figural $20.00

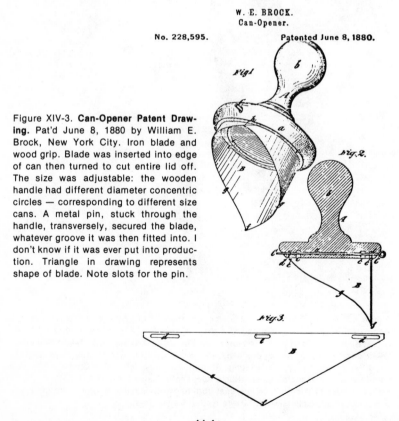

W. E. BROCK.
Can-Opener.

No. 228,595.

Patented June 8, 1880.

Figure XIV-3. **Can-Opener Patent Drawing.** Pat'd June 8, 1880 by William E. Brock, New York City. Iron blade and wood grip. Blade was inserted into edge of can then turned to cut entire lid off. The size was adjustable: the wooden handle had different diameter concentric circles — corresponding to different size cans. A metal pin, stuck through the handle, transversely, secured the blade, whatever groove it was then fitted into. I don't know if it was ever put into production. Triangle in drawing represents shape of blade. Note slots for the pin.

Bottle opener, cast iron, parrot
(another popular figural because
the beak is such a natural) .... $15.00 to $20.00
Bottle opener, cast iron, alligator .... $20.00 to $50.00
Bottle opener, brass, dachsund figural $50.00
Bottle opener, flat nickeled iron,
shaped like a dachsund, marked
"Medford Lager Beer" $40.00
Bottle opener, chromed metal,
reclining nude $35.00
Bottle opener, cast iron, steer head
form, very cubist sculptural form,
opener at muzzle end, no marks,
7" long, an opener to die for it's
so terrific looking $25.00
Bottle opener, iron, in shape of
pointing hand, marked "Effinger
Beer, Baraboo, Wisconsin $15.00
Bottle opener, painted cast iron,
pelican shaped .... $15.00 to $20.00
Bottle opener, double-ended, adv'g
"Stone Malt Co.," 7½" long .... $3.00 to $5.00
Bottle opener, tinned iron, red
lettering "Coca-Cola" .... $10.00 to $15.00
Bottle opener (cap lifter) and cake
server combo, wire and sheet
metal, pat'd November 24, 1914,
11 5/8" long $20.00
Bottle cap lifter and slotted spoon,
wire and sheet metal, pat'd
February 23, 1915, 10½" long $12.00
Bottle opener & spoon combo, iron,
adv'g "Firestone" $1.50
Bottle opener, wrench, meat cleaver,
iron, "Kitchen Klever Kleever" $8.00
Bottle opener, knife sharpener & glass
cutter combo, cast iron, "Apex" $6.00

**NOTE: Doesn't it make you wonder sometimes, the strange
combination tools? The above, for example; who was the
person who needed to cut glass and open a bottle too? A thirsty
burglar? What about the bottle opener and spoon combination?
For stirring beef bourguignon with beer?**

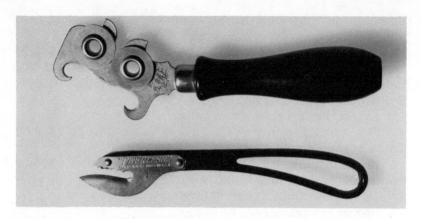

Figure XIV-4. **Can Opener and Knife Sharpener/Bottle Opener.** Top: "Sharp Easy", pat'd 1922, combo knife sharpener and bottle cap opener. Wood handle. Bottom: "Peerless" can opener, pat'd February 11, 1890. Cast iron with steel blade. Picture courtesy of the National Museum of American History, Smithsonian Institution.

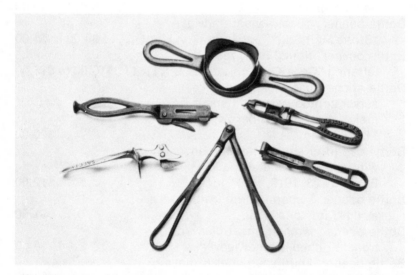

Figure XIV-5. **Can Openers.** Top: cast and sheet iron, two handles, cut the whole top off. C. 1890. 10" long. Second down, left: cast iron, little knob at end for pounding into jar. 7 5/8" long, unmarked. Third down left: nickel plated iron, "The Safety," pat'd May 12. 1914, 6½" long. Bottom: cast iron with pivoting handles. Poke tip in, swivel it around. Says only "patent applied for." 7¾" long. Next up on right: "U.S. Can Opener, Made in Pittsburgh PA, Pat'd May 7, 1895." 6" long. Sliding adjustment for different size cans. Next up: cast iron, "World's Best, Pittsburgh, PA," 6¾" long. Sliding adjustment. All located by the Primitive Man, Bob Cahn, Carmel, NY. His evaluation, in order: $28-$35 at top; $45-$65 all others.

Figure XIV-6. **Can Opener.** Cast iron with missing knife sharpener. Peerless, pat'd 1902 and 1903. Author's collection. Value: $8-$12.

Bottle opener, cast iron, donkey .... $30.00 to $48.00
Bottle opener, cast metal, swordfish $65.00
Bottle opener, figural in shape of rhino.
    A collector in Irving, TX, named
    Mike Jordan, wants to buy this
    one and will pay a whopping $100.00
Can opener, cast iron, "Champion,"
    an iron ring with a ratchet clamp
    to hold the can, separate cutter
    on another pivoting ring, long
    handles, pat'd 1873 .... $80.00
Can opener, cast iron, "Yankee" $2.00
Can opener, cast iron, "Peerless," pat'd 1890 .... $10.00
Can opener, iron, "Indestro" $3.00
Can opener, iron with wood handle,
    "Clean Cut" $6.00
Can opener, iron, pat'd 1892 .... $12.00
Can opener, iron, geared, "Enbay" $7.00
Can opener, wall mounted, "Dazey" $5.00
Can opener, iron, "Bully" (bull's head end) .... $20.00 to $30.00
Can opener, cast iron with attached
    blade, bull's head, 6" long $25.00
Can opener, "A & J" .... $2.00 to $10.00
Can opener, iron, "King", pat'd 1895 .... $5.00
Can opener, "A & J Miracle", 1930, 6¼" long $7.00
Can opener, cast iron, "Vaughn's
    Safety Roll Junior" $1.50
Can opener, cast iron, "Vaughn's
    'Open-All'" $1.00
Can opener, iron, marked "JWP" $8.00
Can opener, iron, "The Jewel" $12.00
Can opener, cast iron, "Hopper's",
    pat'd 1896 .... $35.00 to $45.00

Figure XIV-7. **Can Opener.** Shelf-clamp "Blue Streak," Turner & Seymour Mfg. Co., pat'd 1921, 1922 and 1923. Author's collection. Value: $12-$15.

Can opener, cast iron, alligator and
  black, in stereo-typical and
  obnoxious racist portrayal . . . . $25.00 to $35.00

NOTE: Most of us find the stereotypes and overt racism of the many so-called "Black Collectibles" very offensive. Surprisingly the most ardent collectors of such things as the can opener above and other examples [found on postcards, in toys and other supposedly innocuous objects] are relatively young blacks themselves. It is true that we cannot escape the implications or the present-day effect of those items from the past, nor can we ignore them and make them go away. i don't really believe they should be destroyed; but I do feel they should be recognized for what they are. I had planned when first beginning this edition, to put in a special "Black Collectibles" section, but I've changed my mind. Suffice it to say that for those who do collect such things, there are a number of kitchen items: for example, Aunt Jemima and Uncle Mose celluloid salt & peppers [around $20.00 to $25.00]; the Aunt Jemima "Memo Mammy" of molded composition, manufactured by Hamden Novelty Mfg. Co., Holyoke, MA, for around $30.00 to $45.00; celluloid cookie jars [around $100.00] and condiment sets [around $65.00].

Can opener, cast iron, rearing horse . . . . $15.00 to $20.00
Can opener, cast iron, crowing rooster . . . . $15.00 to $20.00
Can opener, cast iron, 2 parts, the
  "hands" move around like clock
  hands to cut a hole in the top of
  the can, pat'd 1889 . . . . $18.00 to $25.00

418

Figure XIV-8. **Can Opener.** Cast iron, with eagle on top. Mounted to piece of wood. This is a double opener — small short cans cut on side facing camera; taller cans in the back. Lever works small blade in the front to open a tuna fish size can. The blade in back is large and rather heart-shaped. 7½" high. Lever 12" long. Eagle makes me suspect this is an Enterprise product. C. 1880s-90s. Collection of Meryle Evans. Value: $80-$120.

Figure XIV-9. **Can Openers.** Top to bottom: multiple use with wood handle, c. 1930; small "Norlunds 3-in-1" with knife sharpener, c. 1915; wide nickel plated "Ten-in-One" by New Jersey Patent Novelty Co., c. 1910, that scales fish, opens bottles, slices carrots, etc. etc. Bottom: cast iron single use Peerless, pat'd 1890. Author's collection. Values: $8-$15.

419

 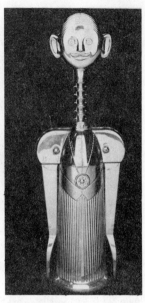

Figure XIV-10. **Corkscrew.** (Two views.) "Pierre the Sommelier", corkscrew manufactured in Italy and imported to the U.S. by Landes Marketing, NYC. A wonderful figural corkscrew from 1982, and certainly a future collectible. 8" high, silverplate or goldplate. Pictures courtesy of Landes Mkt'g. Inc.

Can opener, cast steel with wood
handle, "Vulcan Cut Can & Bottle
Opener," pat'd 1910, 8 7/8" long .... $10.00 to $12.00
Can opener, cast steel with wood
handle, "Midget," pat'd 1904,
adjustable for different sizes of cans ...... $7.00 to $15.00
Can opener, cast steel and tin, or iron
and tin, "fishtail" in style, includes
small replaceable sharpening
stone for knives, pat'd 1902/03,
and again around 1910 .... $10.00 to $12.00
Can opener, nickeled iron, wood knob
handle, "Blue Streak," mfd. by
Turner & Seymour Mfg. Co., pat'd
1921, 1922, 1923, clamps to shelf
edge or table .... $12.00 to $15.00
Can opener, steel, "Ten-in-One," New
Jersey Patent Novelty Co., c.
1910; this combination tool scales
fish, opens cans, opens bottles,
peels vegetables and drive screws! .... $8.00 to $12.00

Can opener, wood and steel, "Edlund Jr.," pat'd 1925, 1929, 6¼" long .... $8.00 to $12.00

Can opener, bottle opener and knife sharpener, metal with wood handle, "Boye," mfd. by The Boye Needle Company, pat'd September 10, 1912. Flyer that came with it states "Cuts the entire top from the can. Salmon, asparagus, tender fruits can be removed without breaking" .... $12.00 to $15.00

Cork driver, all wood, "Best Star of Bottling," John Sommers, pat'd 1885 .... $15.00 to $25.00

Cork driver, maple, 11¾" long x 2¼" diameter $30.00

Cork driver, maple, "Redichs" $35.00

Cork extractor, iron and wood, "B.J. Greely," T-handle, looks awfully like a button hook, c. 1880 .... $8.00

Cork press, painted ornately-cast iron, levered action, this implement sizes water-soaked corks to fit different size bottles, 1870s .... $20.00 to $35.00

Cork press, cast iron, "Whitehall-Tatum" (mostly for pharmaceuticals) $27.00

Cork press, cast iron, 4 sizes $30.00

Corkscrew, folding, "The Davis," pat'd 1891 ... $12.00 to $15.00

Corkscrew, cast iron with brass maker's plate, lever action, "The Royal Club," a Charles Hull patent, 1864 .... $280.00 to $325.00

Corkscrew, engine-turned steel with Bone or ivory handle, brush in T-handle, screw is in cylindrical barrel that fits over bottle top, pat'd by Edward Thomason, London, 1802 .... $100.00 to $125.00

Corkscrew, similar to above but a double-action type with side-mounted mechanism and a hermaphrodite screw, pat'd by Thomason in 1802 .... $110.00 to $140.00

Figure XIV-11. **Brother Timothy and Corkscrew Collection.** Cellarmaster of The Christian Brothers Winery, St. Helena, California, Brother Timothy is shown here with part of his vast collection of corkscrews, on display to the public in the Wine Aging Cellars at St. Helena. Picture courtesy of Christian Brothers.

Corkscrew, forged steel, compound
lever type (the criss-crossed
"arms" have 4 lever points) also
known as "lazy tongs," Wier,
pat'd 1884 .... $65.00 to $80.00

Corkscrew, forged steel, "Zig-Zag,"
another lazy tong compound lever
type, 1870s .... $45.00 to $65.00

Corkscrew, forged steel, 2 parts: the
screw, with rounded T-handle,
and a lever to lift out the screw
after it was inserted, pat'd by
Lund in 1855 and subsequently
copied by others .... $45.00 to $65.00

Corkscrew, steel in wooden tube,
advertising printed on tube is for
"Chamberlain's Pure Extracts",
small and meant for use with
flavoring extract bottles .... $6.00 to $10.00

Corkscrew, cast iron, side crank,
brush in T-handle which is wood,
cap fits over mouth of bottle, 1870s ...... $20.00 to $25.00

Corkscrew, steel and wood, W.
Williamson, pat'd 1887, cap fits
over mouth of bottle, 5¾" long .... $10.00 to $18.00

Corkscrew, tin, painted yellow with
"Listerine" litho'd on it; very
small and flimsy folding type
used with early corked Listerine
mouthwash .... $3.00 to $8.00

Corkscrew, turned wood handle,
English design, c. 1830 .... $65.00

Corkscrew, adv'g "Forbes Coffee" $8.00

Corkscrew, cast iron with wood
handle, shape of hatchet $20.00

Corkscrew, cast brass, sailing ship design $24.00

Corkscrew, heavily turned wood handle,
large, mid-1800s $55.00

Corkscrew, steel with boar's tusk
handle, with silver and ivory trim $95.00

Corkscrew, turned wood handle, steel
screw, brush in extremely poor
condition, nevertheless $65.00

Corkscrew, molded plastic clown
    head handle, 4½" long $65.00
Corkscrew, cast aluminum, shape of
    Shriner's cap, 6" long $48.00
Corkscrew, sterling silver and horn
    handle, 20th century $54.00
Corkscrew, turned ivory handle,
    black bristles, Thomason $685.00
Corkscrew, turned ivory handle, white
    bristles, Thomason $585.00

NOTE: I tried to get from the dealer handling the last two listings what was the reason for the high price, but he smiled as if to say "If you have to ask . . ." Consequently, I can't tell you. They were extremely handsome, and the brushes were in great shape [as if they'd never wiped away a cobweb in a hundred and fifty years!] and they had the brass plates. But . . . !

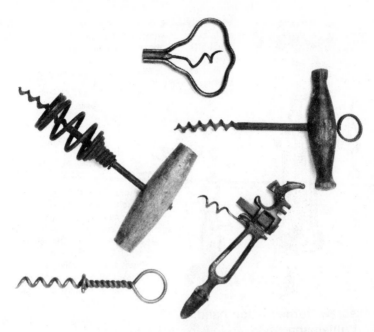

Figure XIV-13. **Corkscrews.** The two largest, with wooden handles, have the "Archimedean screw" and the others have "helical screws." Top is a folding screw. Bottom left probably had simple wooden protective sheath. Oldest is probably upper right. All 19th century. Commonly found. Author's collection. Value: $8-$15.

Corkscrew, heavy cast brass, shaped
 like ornate door key, marked
 "G E A Bochum," this was
 probably a sommelier's corkscrew
 . . . the key signifying his control
 of the locked door to the wine cellar $22.00
Corkscrew, brass with red faceted
 glass eyes, nude "bionic" man figural $12.00
Corkscrew, cast iron, tomahawk style
 with wood handle $20.00
Corkscrew, cast iron, Viking ship figural $20.00
Corkscrew, antler tip handle with
 sterling fittings, smallish: 3" long,
 19th century $25.00
Corkscrew, carved wood, formally-
 dressed man $40.00
Corkscrew, cast brass, form of a cat,
 marked "Israel & Hakuli" $25.00

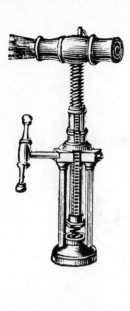

Figure XIV-14. **Corkscrew.** Probably steel with bone or wood handle fitted with brush. This is the King's style, ratchet wheel and a turning handle. From F.A. Walker catalog, 1870s, which has many imported items. Value: $100-$125.

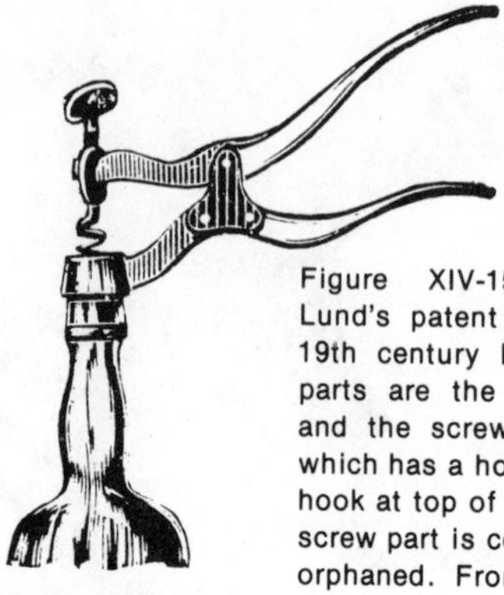

Figure XIV-15. **Corkscrew.** Lund's patent 2-part opener. 19th century English. The 2 parts are the plier-like lever and the screw, the shaft of which has a hole that fits over hook at top of plier/lever. The screw part is commonly found orphaned. From F.A. Walker catalog. Value: $70-$120.

Corkscrew, turned wood handle, "W. Williamson & Co.," Newark, NJ, pat'd August 10, 1887, 5¾" long $12.00

Corkscrew, carved bone, Uncle Sam bust, very unusual and very nifty $80.00

Corkscrew, steel frame with turned wood handle, brush intact, "London Rack," "Lund Maker Cornhill and Fleet Street London," rack & pinion action, mid-19th century $150.00

Corkscrew, steel, "Weir's Patent," September 1884, English concertina compound lever style with ring handle .... $90.00 to $125.00

Corkscrew, "The Utility," English manufacture $85.00

Corkscrew, brass with turned bone handle, brush intact, Thomason type with engraved brass cylinder housing Archimedian screw, early 1800s .... $110.00 to $140.00

Corkscrew, steel frame with Archimedian screw, stamped Diamant J P Paris" (J.H. Perille) c. 1900 .... $100.00

426

Corkscrew, cast brass, baby's upper
torso figural handle, French
turn-of-century $85.00
Corkscrew, steel, pump lever style
that works sort of like the handle
of a water pump, pat'd September
3, 1878 by W. W. Tucker, American .... $550.00 to $650.00
Jar opener, iron and wood, "Top Off
Jar & Bottle Screw Top Opener,"
Edlund Co., 1933 .... $3.00 to $7.00
Jar opener, metal with rubber, works
like pliers, "The Cunnard Co.,"
pat'd 1936 .... $5.00 to $7.00
Jar and bottle opener, metal, "4-in-1,"
J. C. Forster & Son, pat'd 1910 .... $5.00 to $8.00
Milk bottle paper-cap opener, wire,
embossed with dairy name, like a
cross between a pick and a button hook .... $3.00 to $7.00
Milk bottle opener, metal with wood
handle, adv'g "White Lily Milk,"
5" long $10.00
Milk can opener, "Carnation Sanitary" $10.00

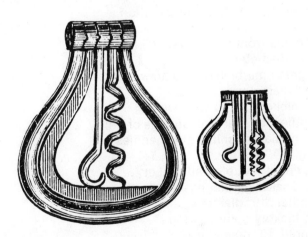

Figure XIV-16. **Corkscrews.** Combination folding tools, for the pocket. Big one has corkscrew, button hook and a hooked blade(?), steel frame. Other has two corkscrews, button hook and pick. From F.A. Walker catalog, 1870s. Value: $15-$20.

CARRY, CONTAIN, STACK, RACK & HOOK: FOR STORAGE

Containers are very popularly collected items in this category, comprising boxes, tins, cans, bottles, jars, crocks, jugs, baskets and much more. The very specialized things — like tins, bottles and baskets — are represented here only with the merest mention . . . just so you can feel you have some handle on the subject! You will find many collector books to guide you if these are fields of interest to you.

Some containers are open, and are made to hold and carry objects such as bottles or cutlery. Others are open ahd hold food or liquids — like pails or pitchers. Others are meant to be kept closed, and sometimes even locked — like bread boxes and tea caddies. Cookie jars are among the more popular containers, and many people have colorful rows of figural jars, made from every conceivable material, on display in their homes. Cookie jars make a nice complementary collection for cookie cutters and rolling pins.

Apple tray, painted tin (tole), square
    bottom with widely-slanting
    arch-topped sides, good condition
    with original paint in red, green
    and yellow — usually on dark
    background .... $135.00 to $160.00
Apple tray, tole, very worn condition
    of paint .... $35.00 to $65.00
Barrel, made from tree trunk, 30" high
    x 19" diameter $40.00
Basin, green marbleized enamelware,
    8½" diameter $18.00
Basket, hickory splint with wood
    handles, bushel size, storage or utility $45.00
Basket, miniature splint, two handles,
    only 3½" x 3" $28.00
Basket, splint, double wall basket $175.00
Basket, Shaker garden basket, 2
    handles, 19" diameter $115.00
Basket, hickory splint, swing
    handle, 13" diameter $165.00

See also: Cheese baskets under SEPARATE, STRAIN & SIFT.

Bottle carrier, green enamelware,
   holds 6 bottles, bottle opener is
   on the hinged lid .... $45.00 to $75.00
Bowl, bird's-eye maple, 11" diameter $62.00
Bowl, cast iron, 9" diameter x 7" deep $45.00
Bowl, burl, 16" diameter x 7½" high,
   fine condition $950.00
Bowl, burl, lathe-turned bands on
   outside, cracks fixed long ago
   with solder, 15" diameter, handsome $375.00
Bowl, burl, small crack in rim, very
   good patina, 10" diameter x 5" deep $165.00
Bread box, green graniteware $35.00
Bread box, enameled white with
   stencil "BREAD" $30.00
Bread box, hinged lid, green & white
   enamel, 19" long $45.00
Bread box, japanned tin with stenciled
   leaf design on hinged lid, ear
   handles of wire, 12" wide .... $25.00 to $35.00
Bread box, japanned tin in imitation
   graining, wire handles, stenciled
   "BREAD," c. 1890s .... $18.00 to $35.00

Figure XV-1. **Market or Garden Basket.** Dyed straw. 1930s-40s. Collection of Mary
Mac and Robert Franklin. Value: $18-$25.

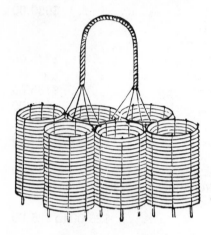

Figure XV-2. **Beer Pot.** Graniteware. Looks almost exactly like a coffee boiler except bottom is not as wide in diameter. Reinforced strap handle. From Lalance & Grosjean Mfg. Co. catalog, 1890. Value: $20-$35.

Figure XV-3. **Bottle Carriers.** Wire, sizes for 2, 4 or 6 botles. From F.A. Walker catalog, 1870s. Value: $20-$30.

Bread and cake box, enameled tin, white porcelain knobs, roll-top with cake drawer, 16" wide x 14½" wide .... $20.00 to $35.00

Bucket, fibreware, wire and wood, "Indurated Fibre Ware," pat'd 1883/84/85/86, bail handle 9¼" high, rare because the pressed wood pulp from which they were made was easily cracked $35.00

Butter box, bentwood, original blue milk paint, 14¼" diameter $55.00

Butter box, bent pine, bentwood handle with iron hardware that locks when box is picked up! 12" diameter .... $75.00 to $100.00

Butter box, blue painted bentwood, wire bail, lid $140.00

Butter box, bentwood, painted recently with daisies and strawberries (!), 9½" diameter, and because it's no longer original, surprisingly high at $40.00

Figure XV-4. **Burl Bowl.** Oval, with small ear handles. Late 18th century. Picture courtesy of Georgia G. Levett, Levett's Antiques, Camden, Maine. Value: $350-$450.

Figure XV-5. **Burl Bowl.** Elliptical with tapering sides. 24¼" long x 6½" high. American 19th century. This is a large one, and apparently in perfect condition. Estimated to go at Brooke auction, 1980, between $800-$1200. Realized: $1200. Picture courtesy of Christie, Manson & Woods International Inc.

Butter crock, gray stoneware with blue bands, original lid, wire bail handle, 8½" diameter, late 19th century .... $28.00 to $35.00

Butter crock, blue and cream stoneware, lid and wire bail handle, mid-19th century $85.00

Butter crock, blue and gray stoneware, lid missing, 8½" diameter x 6½" high $85.00

Butter crock, brown "Rockingham" glazed pottery with original lid $50.00

431

Butter crock, blue and gray stoneware,
in relief on the side is "BUTTER,"
original lid $70.00
Butter crock, yellowware, with lid $45.00
Butter crock, apricot stoneware, bail
handle, original lid, 9" diameter $175.00
Butter crock, spongeware, original lid $60.00
Butter crock, Red Wing pottery, 5
pound size, red and gray $175.00
Butter crock, blue spongeware $42.00
Butter dish, gray graniteware with
pewter insert and lid, 19th
century, unusual $175.00
Butter pail, Red Wing pottery, with
lid, 5 pound size $200.00
Butter pail, Red Wing pottery, with
lid and advertising in blue on
gray, 3 pound size $220.00
Butter pail, wood, 11" diameter, with lid $18.00
Cake box, japanned tin, stenciled
"CAKE," 12" diameter, lid with
hasp closing, c. 1890 .... $22.00 to $30.00
Cake box, stenciled tin, red, black and
gold, "CAKE BOX," Schepp's
Cocoanut advertising inside
slant-front lid, which has a
porcelain knob: "The object of
this can is to serve as a Cake Box
— the convenience of which will
be readily seen at a glance. The

Figure XV-6. **Cake Box or Safe.** Japanned
and stenciled tin with iron handle. 3
shelves with or without locks. 3 sizes
available. From F.A. Walker catalog,
1870s. Value: $25-$45.

cover opening in front and letting
down, does not necessitate the
trouble of pulling the box out
from under the shelf and
almost any Lady would cheerfully
pay twice the price of one in
preference to the unhandy old
style box. PRICE 60 CENTS" . . . . $65.00 to $100.00
Cake box, painted tin, 2-shelf, Schepp's $35.00
Cake box, painted tin, blue & gold,
    with "CAKE" on front, 12" x 15" $30.00
Cake box, round tin with lid, color
    printed with fruit cake with big
    missing slice, "Paradise Fruit
    Cake," 11" diameter x 3½" high,
    c. 1930s, nifty $15.00
Cake box, lithographed tin with
    designs including leaves and
    sailing ship and lamps, 3 shelves,
    21" x 16" $75.00
Cake carrier, heavy tin, adv'g
    "Jewel Tea" . . . . $25.00 to $35.00
Cake stand, steel top platform on four
    cast iron legs formed like bamboo
    poles, masonic signs engraved
    on top, 18th century, extremely unusual $595.00
Candle box, tin with traces of black
    paint, 10¾" long x 6¼" high,
    cut-out hangers, hasp lid $210.00

Figure XV-7. **Cake Boxes.** Japanned and stencil-decorated tin. Hinged and
hasp-closed lids. From F.A. Walker catalog, 1870s. Value: $25-$40.

Figure XV-8. **Candle Box.** Japanned tin, wall hooks for hanging. 13¾" long. American 19th century. Estimated to go at 1983 Linden sale between $80-$120. Realized: $286. Picture courtesy of Christie, Manson & Woods International Inc.

Candle box, wood with early grain
  painting, slanted sides, old cut
  nail, cut-out half moon in
  arched back board, 11" long, 6" high $245.00
Canister, japanned tin, stenciled
  "TEA," hinged dome top, 6" high .... $22.00 to $28.00
Canister, japanned tin, stenciled
  "COFFEE" on side, hinged lid .... $18.00 to $25.00
Canister set, tin with red and gold
  paint, 6 pieces, hasp closings on
  hinged lids, nice condition, late
  19th century .... $80.00 to $90.00
Canteen, oak staves with iron hoops,
  painted gray over old red paint,
  small size, mid to late 1700s $100.00
Cheese box, bentwood, staved sides,
  Shaker manufacture, 15" diameter $175.00
Cheese box, bentwood bass, painted
  in shades of yellow, 15¾"
  diameter x 9" high $42.00
Cheese box, bentwood, 16" diameter $13.00
Cheese box, varnished bentwood
  with lid, 12" diameter $25.00
Cheese box, red-painted bentwood,
  12" diameter with lid $65.00
Cheese crock, "Hasselbeck Cheese
  Co., Buffalo, NY," half-gallon size $40.00
Cheese tray, tole with unrestored
  original paint, fair condition $350.00

Figure XV-9. **Canisters.** Left, stamped tin with stylized overall mums. Close-fitting lid. Japanned. 6¼" high. Right: japanned tin, stenciled "COFFEE" Hinged lid. 5¾" high. 19th century. Author's collection. Value: $15-$22.

Coffee bin, tin with paper label, "Rand & Watson Coffee," 19" high x 13" wide .... $60.00 to $80.00

Coffee safe, wood, slanted bin top, "Lion Coffee" paper label, late 19th century $310.00

Coffee tin, litho'd tin, "Breakfast Call," Independence Coffee & Spice Co., 3 pounds $45.00

Condiment shaker, turned wood, 4½" high, 1800s $25.00

Cookie jar, ceramic, McCoy, in shape of coffee grinder .... $15.00 to $20.00

Figure XV-10. **Coal Vase.** Japanned and stenciled tin with iron feet. Bin pulls open to reveal small supply of coal for parlor heating or kitchen cooking stove. Self-closing. Patented. Probably English. From F.A. Walker catalog, 1870s. Value: $45-$60.

435

Cookie jar, ceramic, McCoy, shape of
pot-bellied stove .... $18.00 to $25.00
Cookie jar, ceramic, McCoy, puppy $26.00
Cookie jar, ceramic, McCoy, kissing
penguins, less than perfect or
even fine condition $15.00
Cookie jar, same as above, fine condition $32.00
Cookie jar, ceramic, McCoy, basket of fruit $35.00
Cookie jar, ceramic, McCoy, dog $32.00
Cookie jar, ceramic, McCoy, rabbit $17.00
Cookie jar, ceramic, McCoy, rooster $45.00
Cookie jar, ceramic, McCoy, basket-
weave with duck $22.00
Cookie jar, ceramic, McCoy, fireplace $36.00
Cookie jar, ceramic, Abington, money bags $32.00
Cookie jar, ceramic, RAP Co., hen
with chick $10.00
Cookie jar, ceramic, Leeds, Mickey &
Minnie 1940's turnabout .... $32.00 to $38.00
Cookie jar, Red Wing, gray line, with lid $30.00
Cookie jar, 1965, Popeye $110.00
Cookie jar, ceramic, Hull, Red Riding Hood $35.00
Cookie jar, turnabout boy & girl bears $38.00
Cookie jar, embossed glass, says
"Dad's Cookie Co." $60.00
Cookie jar, celluloid Aunt Jemima $110.00
Cookie jar, Red Wing pottery, with adv'g $45.00
Cookie jar, ceramic Aunt Jemima $26.00
Cookie jar, ceramic, Katzenjammer
Kids' "Captain" $45.00
Cookie jar, plastic, Kellogg's cereal,
Tony Tiger $30.00
Cookie jar, ceramic, Red Wing, blue monk $28.00
Cookie jar, Red Wing, yellow monk .... $30.00 to $45.00
Cookie jar, Red Wing, yellow Dutch Girl $45.00
Cookie jar, Red Wing, beige baker $42.00
Cookie jar, ceramic, pink brick cottage
with wicker bail handle, 9" high $18.00
Cookie jar, Red Wing, sponge band $285.00
Cookie jar, ceramic, Shawnee, pig
with bandana, 11" high $16.00
Cookie jar, ceramic, Shawnee, Puss & Boots $40.00
Cookie jar, ceramic, Shawnee, pig
w/bandana, 11½" high $16.00

Cookie jar, blue and white stoneware $165.00
Cookie jar, "Fluffy U.S.A.," kitten and
    bow, 13" high $23.00
Cookie jar, ceramic, "Jewel Tea"
    autumn leaf design, tab handles $75.00
Cream can, tin, 5½" high with lid $8.00
Cream can, gray graniteware, bail
    handle with wood grip, cover $18.00
Cream can, embossed tin, lid with
    bail handle, 12 quart size $13.00
Crock, Red Wing, 15 gallons $45.00
Crock, Red Wing, 2 gallon size $35.00

NOTE: The cutlery trays [or knife boxes or silverware trays as they are variously called] are among my most favorite of the non-mechanical kitchen collectibles. Perhaps it is because of the many styles and decorations. I'm delighted that the one I like the best is mine [gosh! that sounds selfish], but if I had the room I think I'd satisfy my fancy for many more. I don't believe I've ever seen one of the old ones divided into three parts, as the cutlery boxes we use in our kitchen drawers are today; nor have I ever seen an explanation for this, though certainly knives, forks and spoons were all in wide use during the 18th and 19th centuries. In the 17th century, you may recall from reading, forks were extremely rare, and people used the point of their knives to stab morsels that couldn't be eaten with spoon or fingers.

Cutlery tray or knife box, variegated
    wood in light and dark colors,
    Shaker manufacture, center
    handle, 12" long x 8" wide, x 2½" high $40.00
Cutlery tray, bentwood with turned
    wood handle, probably Shaker,
    center handle, 4¾" high at
    handle, 13" long $100.00
Cutlery tray, variegated wood,
    center handle $60.00
Cutlery tray, variegated wood, Shaker
    12" long x 9½" wide x 3" deep $35.00
Cutlery tray, chestnut wood, straight
    sides and fancy cutout handle,
    11¾" long x 7½" wide x 2" high $18.00

Figure XV-11. **Coffee Bin and Mocha Bin.** Painted and stenciled tin, nice eagle and shield design. Roll top style. "Bacon Stickney & Co. Albany, NY." Marked "MOCHA" and "COFFEE". 19" high x 13" wide x 13" deep. Late 19th century. Estimated to go between $200-$300 at 1981 Bellamy sale. Realized: $350 for the pair.

Cutlery tray, natural finish wood,
    slightly canted sides, 3¾" high
    central cutout handle, 12" long x
    7¾" wide x 1 7/8" high $16.00
Cutlery tray, unpainted wood, well-
    slanted sides, 4" high cutout
    handle, 12¾" long x 8½" wide at
    top edge, 2¾" high $16.00

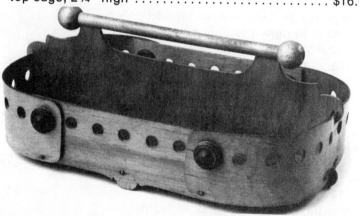

Figure XV-12. **Cutlery Tray.** Cutout bentwood, turned wood grip, green baize lining. C. 1890. Author's collection. Value: $35-$50.

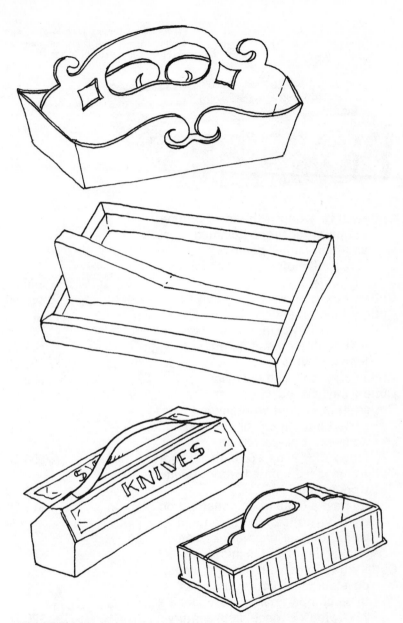

Figure XV-13. **Cutlery Trays or Knife Boxes.** At top is scroll-sawn walnut, varnished, late 19th century. Center is primitive but sculptural box made of thick pine, mid-19th century. Bottom left is japanned tin with reinforced strap handle and pair of hinged lids. Late 19th century. Bottom right is box with simple cut-out handle, variegated pieces of wood in light and dark colors. probably Shaker. 19th century. Also found with flared sides like one at top. Values: $40-$75; $35-$60; $45-$75; $55-$100.

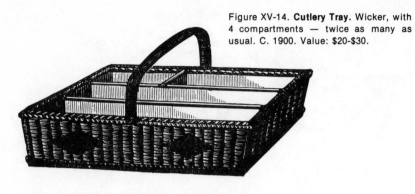

Figure XV-14. **Cutlery Tray.** Wicker, with 4 compartments — twice as many as usual. C. 1900. Value: $20-$30.

Cutlery tray, wood with old or original red paint, scalloped slanted sides and high center board with a "broom handle" grip, 14" long x 5" wide $40.00

Cutlery box, bentwood, probably Shaker $65.00

Cutlery tray, pine with original dark green paint, center board handle with high arch and cutout, 13" long x 7" wide $55.00

Cutlery tray, oak with red paint $12.00

Cutlery tray, carved wood with high handles $35.00

Cutlery tray, walnut with slanted sides carved into "tiles" or "quilted" squares, rope-carved grip, 10" long x 5½" wide x 5" high at handle $50.00

Cutlery tray, red painted wood, open work handle $20.00

Cutlery tray, simple wood construction $18.00

Cutlery tray, tin, painted green and white, tubular handle (like some Shaker items, but is this?) $45.00

Cutlery tray, pine with straight sides, dovetail construction, this has three compartments, 10½" long x 7¼" wide x 2" deep, 20th century $20.00

Cutlery tray, miniature painted wood, 5" long x 2" wide $10.00

Cutlery tray, butt-jointed wood with only very slightly-canted sides, very high centerboard handle with

heart cutout, handsomely painted
with leaves and tendrils, late 18th
or early 19th century $450.00
Cutlery box, unfinished pine, slanted
sides set on base with slight lip,
high arched handle with cutout,
the fabulous feature of this is a
well-constructed drawer
lengthwise in the bottom, early 1800s $450.00
Cutlery tray, pine with geometric
pattern pressed into sides and
ends (probably done like the
steamed and pressed-wood
chairs), cut out handle, 11¾"
long x 7¼" wide x 2¼" high at
sides, early 1900s $25.00
Cutlery tray, pine, dovetailed corners,
simple cutout in center handle
board, 11" long x 7" wide $12.00
Cutlery tray, painted pine with
imitation graining in several
shades of ochre and brown, 13"
long x 6¼" wide, mid-19th century .... $120.00 to $150.00
Cutlery tray, painted pine with imitation
graining, very fanciful with knots
and extreme graining, described
accurately as "folk art" $95.00

Figure XV-15. **Dinner Pail.** Tin.
Stacking compartments. From
F.A. Walker catalog, 1890s.
Value: $18-$25.

NOTE: Folk art is a catch-all term meant to describe a certain naivete, but is too often used to lend distinction and extra value to many things better described simply as "handmade" or "crude" or "old magazine craft project style." Folk art is the exceptional not the ordinary work of "folk." I'm not going to go to great lengths to describe or define folk art here, or what I think it is. It is practically impossible to come up with an all-purpose definition. If you want to start developing your own taste for it, conjure up a vision of all the handmade objects you have [or have seen] which were made by people who considered themselves craftsmen or artists but whose work does not fall into the mainstream of academic art of the period in which they worked. Then sift out what you believe to be the very best examples — the pieces that are definably "art," which have something about them you may not be able to describe in words — and you probably have a few pieces that qualify as "folk art." The secret is to refine your own taste even if you can never satisfactorily define it outloud, and please don't let someone else — like me! — tell you what is or isn't folk art.

Cutlery box, painted wood, scroll-cut
    centerboard handle with heart
    cutout, lids on both sides, 4
    small peg feet, Pennsylvania
    German, late 18th century $550.00
Cutlery tray, tin, with stenciled design,
    center grip handle, 14½" long,
    turn-of-century .... $40.00 to $55.00
Cutlery tray, fancy veneered cut-out
    bentwood, lined with green baize,
    turned feet, 1890s or so .... $35.00 to $50.00
Cutlery tray, pine, deeply-canted
    sides, centerboard with simply
    carved handle, mid-19th century .... $45.00 to $55.00
Cutlery tray, oak, machine-dovetail
    construction, turned handle grip,
    late 19th century or early 20th .... $45.00 to $55.00
Cutlery tray, wicker, fixed basket
    handle, unusual 4 compartments,
    turn-of-century .... $20.00 to $35.00
Dish covers, heavy tin with cast iron
    knobs, oblong or oval to fit over
    serving dishes and platters, 19th
    century .... $10.00 to $20.00

Figure XV-16. **Dish Cover.** Wire screening with japanned tin edging and black wood knob. Meant to keep flies off the food. 1880-1890. Possibly Matthai-Ingram. Author's collection. Value: $7-$15.

Dough box, pine, rectangular box with
 slanting sides, cover with
 "inchworm"-like carved handles,
 23" long x 8½" high, 19th century $280.00
Drink dispenser, metal and glass, in
 original cardboard box, "Orange
 Crush," 1950s .... $65.00 to $80.00

NOTE: See also the dough mixers under MIX, BEAT, STIR, CHURN & BLEND

Dutch crown or meat hook, wrought
 iron, 4 hooks, 18th century .... $150.00 to $250.00
Dutch crown, wrought iron and wood,
 very simple .... $65.00 to $90.00
Egg basket, wire, square, 1920s to 1940s ...... $6.00 to $12.00
Egg basket, folding wire, holds 1 dozen $14.00
Egg basket, twisted wire $25.00
Egg basket wire, collapsable, 20th century ..... $8.00 to $15.00

Figure XV-17. **Egg Carrier or Stand.** Wire, This one holds eggs — they made them tiered that would hold eggs in two or three levels! Wirewares, by the way, are a real specialty with some people — very sculptural like Calder. Dover Stamping Co., c. 1870s-90s. Author's collection. Value: $18-$30. A 2-tiered one might be $40-$60.

Egg carrier, wood, "Gardner," dated 1889, holds 1 dozen $35.00

Egg carrier, "Star," 1906, 1 dozen $30.00

Egg carrier, "Humpty Dumpty," 12½" square x 12" high, 4 dozen eggs $24.00

Egg carrier, same as above only 7" high, 2 dozen $20.00

Egg carrying box, aluminum, compartments for each of 24 eggs $20.00

Egg carrying box, wood painted yellow green, 12" square, wire bail handle $75.00

Egg carrier, "Star Egg Carriers & Trays," mfd. by John G. Elbs, Rochester, NY, pat'd 1903/05/08, 1 dozen size $42.00

Egg carrier, wood with wood lid, "Dannen Quality Eggs," 1 dozen size $14.00

Egg stand, wire, like a basket with a vertical twisted wire central handle, 8 egg cups, 1870s to 1890s ...... $18.00 to $30.00

Egg stand, wire, 2-tier version of above, holds 14 eggs .... $40.00 to $60.00

Egg stand, pewter, pedestal base with a vertical handle looped at end, holds 4 boiled eggs, 19th century $55.00

Firkin, wood with dark green paint,
finger lapped construction, 12" high $35.00
Firkin, tapered sides, bail handle, 12" high $80.00
Firkin, mocha painted wood, finger
lapped, 9½" high $50.00
Firkin, for sugar, hinged lid, bail
handle, 8" high $62.00
Flour bin, white enameled tin $28.00
Flour bin and cornmeal bin, pine
with slant-front lids, unpainted
wood, 32" wide $90.00
Fly screens or dish covers, wire mesh,
japanned tin edge in green, blue,
red and asphaltum brown, domed
covers with wooden knob on top,
late 19th century, various nesting
diameters .... $7.00 to $15.00
Fruit basket, wire, footed with handle,
trifoil wire pedestal base, 14"
high, handsome $175.00

Figure XV-18. **Flour Container.** Japanned and stenciled tin. This one has a popularization of the then very popular Japanese motifs on it, c. 1880s. Value: $45-$75.

Figure XV-19. **Flour Canister.** 3-part, with sifting tray inside. Tin-lined copper. 7" high x 6¾" diameter. 19th century. Collection of Mary Mac Franklin. Value: $55-$75.

445

Fruit cake tin, decorated lid, 1930's
    Deco design . . . . $10.00 to $15.00
Ham hook, braided wrought iron, late
    17th or early 18th century, meat
    hung in smokehouse on this $95.00
Jelly pail, spun brass, #13 . . . . $75.00
Jug, stoneware, blue eagle on gray,
    shield body, NY origin, 2 gallons $210.00
Jug, Ft. Dodge stoneware, beehive,
    3 feet high $185.00
Lard jar, gray stoneware, funnel top,
    ½ gallon size $16.00
Lunch box, tin, "Federal Sweets &
    Biscuit Co." $18.00
Lunch pail, tin, "Sensible Tobacco" $15.00
Lunch box, bentwood, lidded, 8" long
    x 5" wide $12.00
Lunch bucket, tin with wire bail
    handle and wooden grip,
    cup fits onto lid, tray inside,
    7" high, 1880s $42.00
Lunch bucket, tin with two inner trays,
    cup fits onto oval domed lid,
    marked "Lisk," 9½" x 6 3/8" oval,
    wire bail handle with wooden
    grip, late 1800s $45.00
Lunch bucket, deep cobalt enamelware,
    cup fitted onto lid, 2 inner trays,
    bail handle, very fine condition $70.00
Lunch box, brown pasteboard with
    leather strap handle, "Sensation"
    tobacco box $25.00
Lunch box, embossed and japanned
    tin, book-shaped box, "Larrabee's
    Lunch Box," 8½" high x 5½"
    wide x 3" deep, wonderful $48.00
Lunch pail, gray graniteware, the
    "miner's type" $65.00
Lunch pail, litho'd tin, Girl Scout,
    4" x 6" x 3" $45.00
Lunch box, tin, "Patterson's Seal Cut Plug" $30.00
Lunch box, blue with litho'd Scottie
    dogs, 2 handles $12.00
Lunch box, litho'd tin, Peter Rabbit, worn $15.00

Lunch box, Archie's, with thermos, 1969 .... $5.00 to $8.00
Lunch box, tin, Tom Corbett Space
     Cadet, with thermos, 1952 .... $12.00 to $15.00
Lunch box, tin, Roy Rogers & Dale
     Evans Chuck Wagon $12.00
Lunch box, tin, Patterson tobacco
     basketweave design $18.00
Lunch box, tin, Batman and Robin,
     with thermos $12.00
Lunch box, Steve Canyon, 1959 .... $18.00
Lunch box, tin, Disney's schoolbus $7.00
Lunch box, tin, Gomer Pyle, 1966 .... $7.00
Lunch box, tin, North Pole, lid in poor
     condition, otherwise pretty good $225.00
Lunch box, tin, Hopalong Cassidy,
     thermos has plastic lid $15.00
Lunch box, tin, George Washington $40.00
Lunch box, "Winner Cut Plug"
     tobacco, tin $85.00
Lunch pail, "Just Suits" plug tobacco, tin $30.00
Lunch pail, round tin, Disney's
     Pinocchio, 1940 .... $18.00
Lunch box, "Pedro" tobacco, tin $38.00
Lunch pail, "Seal of North Carolina"
     tobacco, tin $40.00
Lunch pail, tin, Lone Ranger with
     missing thermos $12.00
Lunch pail, "Winner Cut Plug" $78.00
Lunch pail, "Plowboy" tobacco, tin $45.00
Lunch pail, gray graniteware, 6"
     diameter x 4" high .... $25.00 to $35.00
Lunch box, tin with wire handle and
     hasp, divided compartments, 8"
     x 8" x 4" deep .... $25.00 to $35.00
Lunch box, enameled tin, two bail
     handles, oval shape with close
     fitting separate lid, c. 1920s .... $12.00 to $18.00

NOTE: Read Bob Carr's introduction to lunch boxes following this CONTAINER category. And, if you're interested, at press time for this book a newsletter for collectors of children's lunch boxes was being started by Lee and Helen Garner, 3608 Chelwood N.E., Albuquerque, NM 87111. It is to be a quarterly, projected cost $10 a year, with the name "The Paileontologist's Retort."

Figure XV-20. **Match Box Holder.** Painted tin with decal apples. 1940s. Author's collection. Value: $5-$10.

Maple syrup jug, tin with japanned
woodgrain decoration, tin strap
handle .... $40.00 to $55.00
Matchbox holder, brass, round
pedestal base, 2¾" high .... $28.00 to $35.00
Matchbox holder, red painted tin,
hangs on wall, embossed
"MATCHES" .... $15.00 to $20.00
Matchbox holder, white painted tin
with apple or rooster, etc., decal, 1940s ... $5.00 to $10.00
Match safe or holder, embossed
aluminum, wall hung .... $10.00 to $15.00
Match safe, cast iron, frog shaped,
adv'g "Pointer Stoves and Ranges" $45.00
Match safe, adv'g "Universal Stoves" $45.00
Match safe, adv'g "DeLaval Separator" $30.00

NOTE: There are several DeLaval cream separator collectibles, some of them cut out of paper or tin in the shape of a cow and the separator. All interesting and fairly valuable.

448

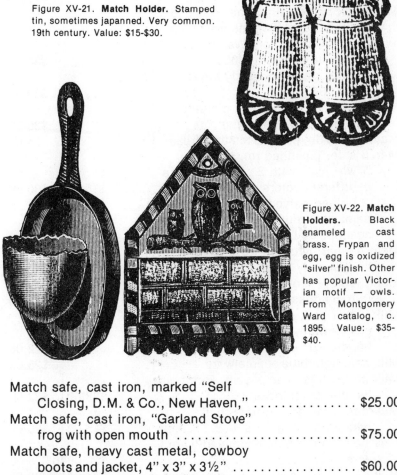

Figure XV-21. **Match Holder.** Stamped tin, sometimes japanned. Very common. 19th century. Value: $15-$30.

Figure XV-22. **Match Holders.** Black enameled cast brass. Frypan and egg, egg is oxidized "silver" finish. Other has popular Victorian motif — owls. From Montgomery Ward catalog, c. 1895. Value: $35-$40.

Match safe, cast iron, marked "Self
Closing, D.M. & Co., New Haven," $25.00
Match safe, cast iron, "Garland Stove"
frog with open mouth $75.00
Match safe, heavy cast metal, cowboy
boots and jacket, 4" x 3" x 3½" $60.00
Match safe, cast iron, bin with lid,
marked "IDEAL" on lid, embossed
flowers on sides, spring dispenses
matches, 5" x 3" .... $35.00 to $40.00
Match holder, cast iron, "Anchor Stoves" $35.00
Match holder, cast iron, 2 black boys
and watermelon, 1884 Cotton
Exposition item $65.00
Match holder, adv'g "The Pet of The
Dairy," Sharples Separators,
with mother, child and the cows $175.00

Matchbox holder, wood, hangs on
wall, for strike anywhere matches
— no striker, 7½" x 3½" x 2½" $10.00
Matchbox holder, tin, "The Best Old
Hickory Farm Wagons are Made
By the Old Hickory Wagon Co.",
Louisville, KY, late 1800s $30.00
Match safe, tin, embossed "MATCHES",
dated 1878 .... $30.00
Match safe, cast iron, grape cluster
and leaves, wall hanging $30.00
Match safe, tin, painted red and cream, 1930s $4.00
Match safe, japanned tin, marked
"Twin" . . . with 2 pockets, came
in different colors .... $15.00 to $30.00
Match holder, carved wood with blue
paint, wall hung, heart and
scallops on back board, 11" high $55.00
Meat hanger, wrought iron, 6 small
hooks, early 1800s $85.00
Meat hook or crown, wrought
iron, 6 hooks on chains, early 1700s $250.00
Milk jug or pail, gray enameled
graniteware, tin lid, wire bail
handle with wood grip, 3 cups, 7" high $22.00
Milk pail, light blue enamelware $25.00
Milk pail, white enamelware, wire bail
handle, cover locks .... $28.00 to $32.00
Milk pail, gray graniteware, bail
handle, 2 quarts .... $15.00 to $20.00
Milk pail, blue ombre enameled ware,
wire bail .... $20.00 to $28.00
Milk pail, same as above but green ombre .... $24.00 to $30.00
Milk pan, gray graniteware, 12" diameter .... $5.00 to $7.00
Milk pan, handmade tin, 15" diameter
at top, 3½" deep $4.50
Milk pan, lap-constructed of several
pieces of tin, 12" diameter at rim,
slopes to 9" diameter,
3" deep, early to mid-19th century $12.00
Milk pan, navy and white enamelware $12.00
Milk pan, redware with yellow slip glaze $80.00

NOTE: The milk pans are sometimes called Skimming Pans.

Figure XV-23. **Milk Pail.** Blue ombre enamelware, bail handle with wood grip. Collection of David Arky. Value: $20-$28.

Milk pitcher, mottled gray graniteware ....$20.00 to $24.00
Milk pitcher, china, with Mickey
    Mouse design from 1930s $125.00
Pail, gray graniteware, lid and bail handle ....$20.00 to $25.00
Pail, copper with wire bail handle and
    zinc or tin lining $40.00
Pail, deep blue and gray enamelware,
    cover, bail $22.00
Pail, marbleized midnight blue and
    white enamelware $16.00
Pail, white enamelware, wire bail
    handle, cover $16.00
Pantry box, wood, painted soft green,
    close-fitting lid, 7" diameter ....$35.00 to $50.00
Pantry box, poplar, Sabbath Day
    Lake Shaker $75.00
Pantry box, bentwood, 6" diameter ....$20.00 to $25.00
Pantry box, oval bentwood, 4" x 2¾" x 1½" $65.00
Pantry box, brown-painted bentwood,
    copper nails, stenciled "Slippery
    Elm," 8" diameter, c. 1870 ....$100.00
Pantry box, round bentwood, painted
    old red $125.00
Pantry box, green painted wood,
    finger laps, 3" x 6" x 5" deep, oval,
    marked "B. Sprague" $125.00

Figure XV-24. **Pantry Boxes.** Blue-painted round boxes. Small one is 6¼" diameter; far right: 9¾" diameter. American 19th century. Value: about $50 each. Picture courtesy of Christie, Manson & Woods International Inc.

Pantry box, oval bentwood painted
very dark blue, stitched laps, 11"
long, late 1700s $125.00
Pantry box, bentwood painted robin's
egg blue, 2 finger laps, 5½" long, oval $90.00
Pantry box, varnished wood, 11" diameter $95.00
Pantry box, 7" diameter, bentwood
with deep green paint, 3-finger lap
box with 1-finger lap lid $500.00
Pickle jar, stoneware, "The Weir," bail
clamp on lid, 14" high x 8" diameter $30.00

Figure XV-25. **Pie Rack.** Twisted wire, holds 4 pies, for cooling or storage. 19th century. Collection of Mary Mac Franklin. Value: $25-$30.

Figure XV-26. **Pickle Jar.** Green glass in the so-called "Cathedral" shape with gothic arched hexagonal sides. 13" high. American 19th century, blown-mold. 13" high. Estimated to go at recent auction between $200-$250. Realized: $350. Picture courtesy of Robert W. Skinner Inc., Auctioneers, Bolton, MA.

Picnic basket, wicker, fitted out with
    knives and forks, tumblers,
    napkins, collapsing cup, tin
    canister, tin plate, wine bottle
    and pickle jar, has lock and key,
    12" long x 8" wide x 7" deep $115.00
Pie rack, twisted wire, stacks 4 pies .... $25.00 to $30.00
Pie rack, iron, mounts on wall, dated 1874 .... $70.00
Pie rack, tin $20.00
Pitcher, white enamelware, 9" high .... $7.00 to $12.00
Pitcher, spatterware in green/yellow/tan,
    stenciled "Ridgeway Dairy" .... $30.00 to $45.00
Plate warmer, japanned tin with bronze
    decorative trim, cast iron cabriole
    legs, claw fee, 30" high x 15" wide $200.00

Figure XV-27. **Pitchers.** Tin, with wonderfully inventive handles and shapes — aided here, perhaps, by the naivite of the catalog artist. From F.A. Walker catalog, 1880s. Value: $50-$125.

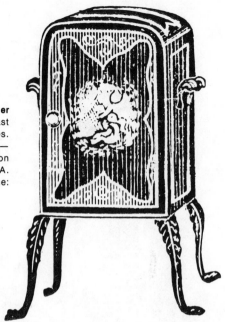

Figure XV-28. **Plate Warmer Cabinet**. japanned tin with cast iron legs and side handles. Back open to fire or stove — plates and dishes heated on shelves inside. From F.A. Walker catalog, 1870s. Value: $125-$200.

Plate warmer, japanned tin, cast
iron legs, 1870s $135.00
Plate warmer, tin and cast iron, 3 legs,
early 1800s .... $135.00 to $175.00
Plate warmer, wire and forged iron,
concentric wire platform, meant
to hang in fireplace, 15" diameter $125.00
Potato basket, wire, large and old,
bushel size, 20" diameter $165.00
Salt box, glass with wood lid, "SALT"
molded on side, lid has
moisture-absorbing sponge fixed
to it, 3¾" deep .... $28.00 to $45.00
Salt box, gray graniteware, wood lid $32.00
Salt box, wood with wood lid, 5" wide x
6½" high at front (slanted lid
raises to 8½" high at back) x 6"
deep front to back $25.00
Salt box, apricot colored crockery,
wood lid $95.00
Salt box, Red Wing, hanging box with lid $400.00
Salt box, pottery, wall-hung, no lid $42.00

Figure XV-31. **Pottery Jug.** Dark brown glaze. Wooden plug. Author's collection. Value $30-$45.

Figure XV-29. **Potato Field Basket**. Wire, a bit jaywopper-ed. Bail handle. 19th or 20th century. Author's collection. Value: $15-$25.

Salt box, gray and cobalt stoneware,
hanging, round with flattened
back, the German "SALTZ" on front $50.00
Salt crock, stoneware, wood lid, 6"
diameter .... $25.00 to $35.00
Salt trencher, treen (turned wood),
footed base with fitted lid, only
2¾" high .... $65.00 to $90.00
Salt & pepper shakers, painted cast
metal in shape of coffee pots,
small size .... $6.00 to $8.00
Salt & pepper shakers, painted (one
white, one black) cast white-metal,
pot-bellied stove shape, 2¾" high .... $7.00 to $10.00
Salt & Pepper, white china with gold
trim, in shape of old GE monitor-top
refrigerator from the 1930s,
"Made in Japan" .... $8.00 to $10.00
Salt & Pepper, white "milk" glass, GE
monitor-top fridge .... $12.00 to $22.00
Salt & Pepper, china painted blue,
black and red, in shape of boy
chef, adv'g "Tappan Ranges" .... $10.00 to $15.00
Salt & Pepper, ceramic, green and
yellow, ears of corn, 4½" high $6.00

Figure XV-32. **Salt Crock.** Green-glazed crockery. Knob on lid, as usual, hard to grasp — particularly with buttered fingers. Why'd they make 'em like that? Wall hung style. Picture and collection of Lar Hothem. Value: $35-$55.

Figure XV-33. **Salt Box.** Wood, constructed like a piggin, with one long stave forming hanger. Iron hoops. From the South, 19th century. 12" high x 4¾" diameter. Picture courtesy of the National Museum of American History, Smithsonian Institution.

Salt & pepper, glass, in shape of Ball
Mason jars, metal caps $22.50
Salt & pepper, ceramic cactus plants
on cactus "wood" base, souvenir $12.00
Salt & pepper, Toonerville figurals $50.00
Salt & pepper, "ESSO" gasoline pumps(!) $15.00
Salt & pepper, heavy cast metal,
painted white with red and green
decoration, coffee pots, 1¾" high $8.00
Salt & pepper, cast metal, "Friskies"
adv'g: dog is salt and cat is
pepper, mfd. in Dayton, Ohio .... $20.00 to $24.00
Salt & pepper, glass, figural milk
"Sealtest" bottles $18.00
Salt & pepper, Orphan Annie and Sandy $30.00
Salt & pepper, Little Red Riding Hood,
5½" high $25.00

Figure XV-34. **Salt and Pepper Shakers.** Molded plaster, painted green, with red flowers on one, yellow on the other. Cactuses, 2" high, sit in base made of real cactus wood. Souvenir of Benson, Arizona, c. 1940s. Author's collection. Value: $12.

Figure XV-35. **Salt and Pepper Dispenser.** Glass containers in green plastic frame. Imperial Metal Mfg. Corp., pat'd August 5, 1939, #1,772,041. Wonderfully imaginative thing — push the black button, pepper shakes out, the white . . . salt. 2" high x 2 3/8" wide. Author's collection. Value: $8-$15.

Salt & pepper, glass, "Esslinger's"
   beer bottles $20.00
Salt & pepper, ceramic, John Kennedy
   and rocker, with original box $35.00
Salt & pepper, "Gunther Beer" bottles,
   metal caps $7.00
Salt shaker, souvenir of Balance Rock,
   Bar Harbor, ME $12.00

NOTE: The above is in here because I've got a thing about balanced rocks, but I don't know what real S & P collectors think of buying single shakers.

Spice box, 6 cans, japanned heavy
   stamped tin, cast iron handle on
   hinged lid, hasp closing, c. 1890s .... $30.00 to $50.00
Spice box, tin with brass handle on
   domed lid, 6¾" diameter, holds 6
   small containers .... $35.00 to $50.00
Spice box, 8 cans, varnished bentwood
   stenciled "SPICES" on lid, each
   bentwood spice container inside
   has name stenciled on lid, 9"
   diameter, 1870s .... $65.00 to $90.00

Spice box, bentwood, 8 canisters of
bentwood $150.00
Spice box, painted tin, 6 cans $58.00
Spice box, painted tin, 6 cans, some rusting $45.00
Spice box, tin, 6 small boxes inside,
all labeled $45.00
Spice box, japanned tin with gold and
red pinstripes on asphaltum
background, 6 square cans
(nutmeg, cloves, mace ginger,
allspice, cinnamon) and nutmeg
grater inside lid, 9" long x
6 1/8" wide $80.00
Spice box, tin, stenciled cans for
cloves, mace, cinnamon and
nutmeg, lid missing latch $28.00

NOTE: In the ad for the above listing, the wording was "needs latch," but I'm not confident that anyone could ever replace the latch successfully. Although for many many years I just bought whatever turned up, including things in poor, incomplete or broken condition. I don't advocate this practice for the regular collector. Most of my collection is what is known as a "study collection" — that is, I add things to it so that I have some material evidence of an item.

Figure XV-36. **Spice Box.** Turned wood, lovely patina. Stacked containers screw one on the other. "Nutmegs," "Cinnamon," "Allspice," "Cloves" and one that's unlabeled. Each container is 1½" deep and 2½" diameter on inside. Total height: 9½". 19th century. Collection of Meryle Evans. Value: $75-$100.

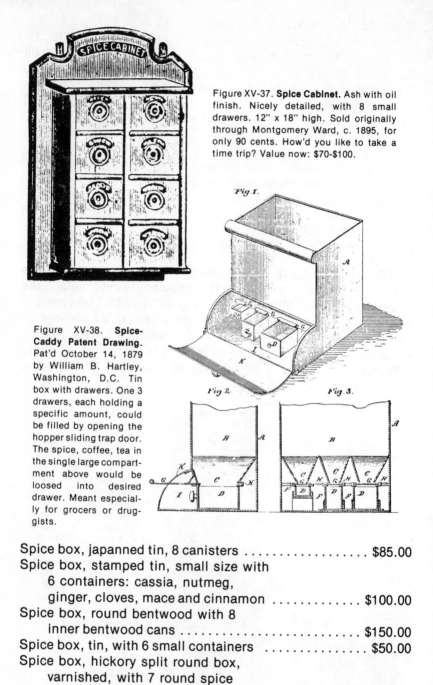

Figure XV-37. **Spice Cabinet.** Ash with oil finish. Nicely detailed, with 8 small drawers. 12" x 18" high. Sold originally through Montgomery Ward, c. 1895, for only 90 cents. How'd you like to take a time trip? Value now: $70-$100.

Fig. 1.

Fig. 2.   *Fig. 3.*

Figure XV-38. **Spice-Caddy Patent Drawing.** Pat'd October 14, 1879 by William B. Hartley, Washington, D.C. Tin box with drawers. One 3 drawers, each holding a specific amount, could be filled by opening the hopper sliding trap door. The spice, coffee, tea in the single large compartment above would be loosed into desired drawer. Meant especially for grocers or druggists.

Spice box, japanned tin, 8 canisters $85.00
Spice box, stamped tin, small size with
     6 containers: cassia, nutmeg,
     ginger, cloves, mace and cinnamon $100.00
Spice box, round bentwood with 8
     inner bentwood cans $150.00
Spice box, tin, with 6 small containers $50.00
Spice box, hickory split round box,
     varnished, with 7 round spice
     containers inside, 8" overall
     diameter $135.00

Figure XV-39. **Spice Box.**. Japanned tin with hinged hasp-closing lid and iron finial. In round box, 7 containers, all stenciled: "Ginger," "Cloves," "Pepper," "Allspice," "Mace," "Nutmeg," and "Cinnamon." From F.A. Walker catalog, c. 1880s. Value: $85-$100.

Spice box, tin with asphaltum japanning, domed lid with brass finial, inside partitioned into "wedges" for 6 spices, nutmeg grater fitted in centerhold, 6½" diameter .... $50.00 to $65.00

Spice cabinet, wood, 6 small drawers with one wide drawer at bottom, celluloid drawer labels (could be written on with pencil and washed off for changes), late 19th century ..... $120.00 to $150.00

Spice cabinet, oak, 8 small drawers with set-in knobs, arched back board with 2 hanging holes, 1880s to 1890s $225.00

Spice cabinet, oak, 16 drawers $155.00

Spice cabinet, various woods with original yellow paint, 6 drawers labeled: bay leaf, allspice, cinnamon, ginger, cel. seed, mus. seed, wonderfully shaped backboard hanger, early 1800s $550.00

Spice cabinet, 4 drawers, adv'g "Meyer Brothers" $375.00

Figure XV-40. **Spice Cans and Tray.** Japanned tray and japanned canisters in reddish brown asphaltum finish. Strap handle, c. 1890s. Tray: 5½" x 4¾" and canisters: 2 7/8" high x 1¾" diameter. Author's collection. Value: $15-$22.

Spice cabinet, japanned tin, imitation
    graining, 6 spices $45.00
Spice cabinet, pine, 8 drawers, late 1800s ... $90.00 to $110.00
Spice chest, maple, 6 drawers with
    white porcelain knobs and
    whitish pewter-like labels which
    could have penciled words
    washed off, 19th century .... $150.00 to $165.00
Spice chest, dark green-painted wood,
    8 drawers, dovetail construction,
    meant for countertop not wall-
    hanging, 19" high x 27½" long 320.00
Spice chest, dovetail wood with old,
    dark finish, 12 drawers with nice
    knobs, 17" high x 19" wide x 6½"
    deep, countertop or could be hung
    from wall $480.00
Spice chest, tin painted red, 8 drawers,
    scalloped top edge, wall hanging $120.00
Spice containers, Blue Onion china,
    set of 6 .... $75.00
Spice containers, glass with shaker
    tops, McCormick & Co. spices,
    set of 6 .... $10.00

Spice containers, tin with Dutch scene
      litho'd in blue & white, 3" high
      x 2½" square, only five $20.00
Spice containers, Blue Onion china,
      set of 6 . . . . $95.00
Spice container, Silas Pierce nutmeg tin $15.00
Spice container, bentwood with
      stencil (like those fitted in round box) $15.00
Spice rack, tin with fancy tinwork on
      arched handle, holds 6 canisters,
      early to mid-19th century $275.00
Spice rack, wire in shape of crossed
      spoon and fork with 4 hooks for
      hanging 4 china chefs with painted
      faces, paper labels and hanging
      loops on top of chef caps. Made
      in Japan. 9" long x 3½" high;
      chefs are 3½" high, c. 1950s, super $28.00
Spice rack with 12 milk glass shaker
      jars with black metal lids, marked
      "Griffith Laboratories," Chicago,
      IL, patent #2,107,697 (1938),
      each jar square in shape
      and 4 3/8" high . . . . $25.00 to $35.00
Spice rack, carved pine with round
      wooden canisters for 7 spices,
      late 1800s $225.00
Spice rack, towel rack, bowl shelf, red
      painted pine, probably
      Pennsylvania German, 19th century $65.00
Spice shaker, green Depression glass,
      metal screw-on lid, "Cloves"
      paper label intact . . . . $14.00 to $16.00
Spice shaker, bulbous blownmold
      glass, metal shaker lid, flat back $28.00
Spice tray, "Grand Union" spice set in
      handled tray $48.00
Spice tray, japanned tin, strap handle,
      6 small cans, late 19th century . . . . $15.00 to $22.00
Spill holder, Pennsylvania redware
      with yellow/green/brown/tan glaze
      in squiggly bands top and bottom,
      6" high, hangs on wall $185.00

Spoon rack, carved tulip poplar,
    painted red, carved with pinwheels
    and geometric designs, holds 5
    spoons, 18th century New England $950.00

Tomoto Pie — A Crust Filled With Tomato Butter

Peel and cut 25 pounds of tomatoes into halves and
press out the seeds. Allow eight pounds of apples, peeled
and cored and quartered. Weigh the whole mixture and to
each pound allow one-half pound sugar and the juice of
one-half lemon. Boil the tomatoes and apples together
stirring until you have a thick, smooth paste. Add the
sugar and lemon juice, boil 20 minutes and it will be ready
to can. (Use to fill a baked pie shell.)
Mrs. S. T. Rorer, "Ladies Home Journal," May 1900

Store barrel, wood, "Davis Baking
    Powder" on paper label on side,
    23½" high x 15" diameter.
    Imagine what a dipper full of
    pickle juice would have done to this! $150.00
String holder, cast iron, beehive shape $40.00
String holder, cast iron, fish $65.00

**CAUTION: Lots of cast iron string holders in the antique forms
have been reproduced over a long period of time.**

Sugar bowl, painted tin, double
    stepped foot ring, slightly domed
    lid with 3 small tin cylinders for
    the knob, black ground with red,
    yellow and green flowers, 3¾"
    high x 4" diameter, super $300.00
Sugar bucket, japanned tin, stenciled
    "SUGAR", late 1800s .... $15.00 to $25.00
Sugar bucket, wood, lapped
    construction, cover, bail handle,
    probably Shaker, 8" diameter $40.00
Sugar bucket, pine with wire bail, cover $35.00
Sugar firkin, bentwood with original
    red paint, pegged wood handles,
    14" high .... $55.00 to $65.00

See also: firkins.

Figure XV-41. **Soup Tureen.** Tin with cast iron ornate finial and handles. Lid has "bite" opening in edge for ladle. Came in sizes for 3, 4, 6, 8 and 10 quarts. From F.A. Walker catalog, 1870s. Value: $75-$110.

No. 10.
Oval Soup Tureens.
Nos. 2, 3, 4, 5, 6.
Qts. 3, 4, 6, 8, 10.

Figure XVII-42. **Soup Tureen.** Tin, with cast iron handles and lid finial. C. 1870s. 15½" long x 9½" wide oval, 10" high. American. Formerly in the Keillor Collection. Value: $75-$110.

467

Figure XV-42 **Sugar Bucket.** Wood with bentwood hoops and handle. From Massachusetts, 19th century. 9¾" high x 10½" diameter at base. Picture courtesy of the National Museum of American History, Smithsonian Institution.

Sugar shaker, "Cleminsons Girl" $15.00
Syrup pitcher, hammered copper with
 brass fittings, dovetail
 construction, Arts & Crafts
 movement, late 19th century $30.00
Syrup pitcher, gray graniteware $145.00
Syrup pitcher, pink Depression glass,
 metal lid .... $12.00 to $18.00
Tea bin, tin, "Lee & Cady Green Tea,"
 90-pound size, lanted lift-up lid .... $90.00 to $125.00
Tin can, "Black Beauty Stove Polish" $6.00
Tin can, "The Union Blacking," red,
 white and blue design picturing
 flag, 3½" diameter $10.00

Tin can, "Peter Pan Peanut Butter" on
 paper label, 11 ounce size $40.00
Tin can, "Postum Cereal", small .... $12.00 to $15.0
Tin can, embossed "Rumford Baking
 Powder," small or large .... $6.00 to $10.00
Tin can, "Zanzibar Brand Sausage
 Seasoning," hinged lid $40.00

Aristocratique Sauce

Green walnut juice and anchovies, equal parts; cloves,
mace, and pimento, of each, bruised, 1 dram to every
pound of juice; boil and strain; add to every pint one pint of
vinegar, one-half pint of port wine, one-quarter pint of soy,
and a few shallots; let the whole stand for few days; decant
the clear liquor.
Scammel's Treasure-House of Knowledge, 1891

Towel rack and comb case, gray graniteware $125.00
Utensil rack, carved wood with heart
 designs, late 18th or early 19th century $300.00
Utensil rack, blue and white graniteware $70.00

PERFECT
KITCHEN RACK

EACH SET PACKED IN CARDBOARD BOX THAT WILL CARRY ANYWHERE

PERFECT KITCHEN SET.
THE Handsome Japanned Rack on which the
cutlery, etc., is hung, is over 23 inches long
and 5 inches high. The Rack is so made that
the top sets out away from the wall, leaving ample
space for all the lids and covers to rest. Rack has
ten hooks as shown, on which the articles are hung.
All the articles shown are household conveniences
and necessities. Handles are black and all well
finished. All of regulation size and length.
 This Kitchen Rack and equipment have been
specially designed and are exclusive and supply the
housewife with articles long wanted, and that will
be a daily source of comfort. On account of the
combination, the conveniences of over 20 articles
are supplied in this set.
OUR PERFECT KITCHEN SET consists of the following:
1 Perfect Kitchen Rack. 1 Cleaver, 7-inch blade.
1 "Right Shape" Paring Knife. 1 Basting and
Utility Spoon. 1 Corundum Knife Sharpener. 1
Patent Strainer Spoon and lifter. 1 Bread Knife.
1 Carver Knife, 8-in. blade. 1 Combination Can-
Opener and Cap Extractor. 1 Cake Turner and
Egg Lifter. 1 Kitchen or Flesh Fork.
 Retail Price, Complete Set, $2.00.
Perfect Kitchen Rack when sold separately.
 Retail Price, 25c.

Figure XV-44. **Utensils: Kitchen Set and Rack.** Japanned tin with 10 implements.
Turn-of-century. Value: $75-$100 with all tools.

Utensil rack, white agateware, wall-
mounted, 21¼" tall, matching
small and large ladles and 2 skimmers $175.00
Utensil rack, gray graniteware, some-
what shield-shaped, 19" tall, with
spoon, dipper and skimmer .... $85.00 to $110.00
Utensil rack, gray graniteware $68.00
Utensil rack and pastry sheet, tinned
sheet iron, holds rolling pin in
curved bottom edge, 16" x 23",
late 1800s $150.00
Utensil rack, heavy metal with rooster
form, adv'g "Moorman's Feed,"
wall-mounted, 1 hook $10.00
Utensil rack, same as above only a
cow's head $12.00
Vegetable bin, newly-painted tin,
small size, with 2 pierced tin doors
enclosing 2 shelves, lid on top
covers shallow bin, late 1800s or
early 1900s $15.00
Wire basket, for fruit, nifty twisted handle $35.00

The following article is a reprint courtesy of the "Antique
Trader" — a paper with what seems to be a special fondness for
things to do with kitchen collectibles and related subjects. It
first appeared June 27, 1979. Collector and writer Robert J. Carr
has had pictures taken especially for this book — including a
great color picture in the color section. Bob, who is involved
with the Garners' new newsletter, "The Paileontologist's Re-
tort," would be glad to hear from other collectors. Please
enclose an SASE when you write him, at 7325 Cornell Avenue,
St. Louis, MO 63130.

CHILDREN'S CHARACTER LUNCH BOXES
By Robert J. Carr

When I went to elementary school, my classmates carried
their lunch in one of two kinds of packages. The first was the
ever present brown bag; the second was a large, black, domed
lunch box. These black lunch boxes were originally designed for
working men and are still on the market today. Neither of these

packages was particularly suitable to the world or interests of children. Beginning in the mid-1930s, a lunch box was designed which appealed more to kids and which heralded the marketing of lunch boxes designed specifically for children.

In searching for the origins of the character metal lunch box I discovered that the Geuder, Paeschke and Frey Company of Milwaukee produced a "Mickey Mouse Lunch Kit" in 1935. This lunch kit consisted of an oval shaped lunch box which contained a small tray but no thermos. A picture of it appears in the color section of this book. Mickey Mouse and other Disney characters, including Minnie, are prominently displayed on the cover and sides of the kit. In 1937 the Libbey Glass Company and the Owens-Illinois Glass Company marketed a Snow White and the Seven Dwarfs lunch box and in 1940 followed with a Pinocchio lunch box. Although I have been collecting lunch boxes for 10 years, I have only the Mickey Mouse box. My guess is that because all three picture Disney characters, they are highly sought after and have been scooped up by collectors of Disneyana.

In chronological order, the next character lunch box that I found was the Joe Palooka lunch box, dated 1948. Joe, Humphrey and other characters from the famous Ham Fisher comic strip are pictured on the sides and top. It is a difficult box to find, but occasionally turns up at collectors' shows and flea markets.

1950 was the advent of the character lunch box as we know it today. In that year, Aladdin Industries, Inc., of Nashville, Tennessee began to market character kits. Incidentally, Aladdin is the same company that has manufactured the highly collectible Aladdin lamp since 1908. Aladdin's first character was Hopalong Cassidy. Hoppy was a popular movie and TV hero at the time and there was an instant demand for these lunch kits. It was not fully cartooned but rather had a decal that pictures Hopalong on the side of the box. The half-pint vacuum bottle inside was not cartooned. In 1952, Aladdin brought out the Tom Corbett Space Cadet kit which, again, was not fully cartooned. The vacuum bottle however was of improved quality and was fully decorated. Both Hopalong and Space Cadet boxes are extremely popular with collectors, and turn up sometimes at flea markets and in "Antique Trader" ads. Later Aladdin kits, fully cartooned and containing a cartooned vacuum, include such TV and movie heroes and heroines as Annie Oakley, Wild Bill Hickok, Daniel Boone, Robin Hood and Zorro.

In 1953, the King-Seely Thermos Company began to manufacture school lunch kits similar to those made by Aladdin. Some early examples are the Roy Rogers, Davy Crockett and Trigger boxes. A third manufacturer of character boxes during the '50s was the Adco Liberty Manufacturing Corp. I have a Lone Ranger and a Davy Crockett and the Alamo box made by Adco. Apparently Adco dropped out of the competition early on, but both Aladdin and King Seely-Thermos continue to market a new line of lunch kits each year.

Although most I have mentioned so far are less than 30 years old, they are quite difficult to find. After all, they were expendable items subject to daily use and abuse by children. In fact, it is amazing that so many of the early boxes have survived in such good condition. The other factor adding to the difficulty of collecting the character boxes is that they fit in with other categories of collecting.

If you collect or plan to collect lunch boxes, try to buy them in excellent condition, complete with thermos. The thermos makes a nice go-with that helps make your collection more interesting and complete. Sometimes dealers sell the cartooned thermoses separately.

At present, not too many people collect character lunch boxes. It is often possible to buy a lunch box for a few dollars. I suspect that this will change as collectors become more aware of how colorful and graphically interesting these lunch boxes are. In addition, character lunch boxes serve as a record of a generation's heroes and heroines and are thus an important part of our cultural history.

Editor's Note: The last paragraph was written four years ago. I spoke with Lee Garner in April 1983 about this newsletter, and apparently an article in "Collectibles Illustrated" early in '83 drew over 125 responses around the country. The time that Bob Carr speaks of — when prices go up and collectors recognize the appeal of lunch boxes — has come!

Figure LB-1. **Beatles Lunch Box and Thermos Bottle.** Made by Aladdin Industries, 1966. Tin, satchel handle. Box: 7" high x 8" long x 3¾" wide. This pair is difficult to find because of the strong demand for Beatles' collectibles. Picture and collection of Robert Carr. Value for pair: $75.

Figure LB-2. **VW Bus Lunch Box**, designed by Omni-Graphics, Yonkers, NY, no longer in business. Tin, with molded plastic satchel grip and catches on hinged lid. 10¾" long x 7" high x 5" wide, c. 1960. A rare lunch box. Picture and collection of Robert Carr.

473

Figure LB-3. **Lunch Box with Train and Plane.** Tin with swinging strap handles. 4 1/8" high x 7¾" long x 5 3/8" wide, c. 1930. This box has extremely fine graphics depicting an early passenger plane and a train with a full head of steam. It was made in at least three different color combinations. Picture and collection of Robert Carr. Value: $35.

Figure LB-4. **Mickey Mouse Lunch Kit.** Color litho'd tin with "Bull Dog" wire handles, mfd. by Geuder, Paeschke and Frey, Milwaukee, in 1935. 4¾" high x 8¼" long x 5" wide. This is the earliest known comic character lunch box and was made by a firm that had specialized in tinwares for at least 55 years. Picture and collection of Robert Carr. Rare, and value at least: $100.

Figure LB-5. **Peter Rabbit Lunch Box.** "Peter Rabbit on Parade." Tin with single strap handle, oval with close fitting lid. This small lunch box pictures characters from Peter Rabbit, as ill'd by Harrison Cady. Mfd. by Tindeco in the 1920s. A similar, more commonly found Peter Rabbit lunch box has square corners. 2¼" high x 4½" long x 3½" wide. Picture and collection of Robert Carr. Value: $45.

FURNITURE & FURNISHINGS

Every kitchen had some basic furniture — if nothing else, a cupboard or cabinet and a work table. The romanticized view of the kitchen with rocking chair, spinning wheel, pipe stand, sleeping cat on a cushion, etc., has some basis in reality because the very early kitchens were actually keeping rooms, where many of a household's activities took place. In the 19th century, however, kitchens became much more specialized, and the furniture in them was related to the preparation of food.

Old kitchen furniture is in great demand today, though not necessarily by collectors of kitchen things. The "country look" — which may be dying out even as I write — is responsible to some degree for the increased popularity of old kitchen things — utensils and furniture. Do you remember when a Hoosier or Hoosier-type cabinet could be bought at a yard sale or estate auction for about $25.00? In the original condition, with all the fixin's? I bet you wish, as I do, that you'd bought one then. I think I could keep up my interest in baking if I had a cupboard where everything was in one place, and where there was a nice working surface too.

Another popular item are wallhung cupboards, late 18th and early 19th century. These are usually painted — in dark greens, deep blues and wonderful rich reds. They are also often quite worn, but it is my very firm belief that they've earned the scars and should remain in the condition in which their long-ago owners left them. How I hate to read the word "refinished" in connection with the old painted furniture. Friends of mine in Wilbraham, Massachusetts — just a few miles from the gloriously infamous Brimfield, where collectors and dealers do deals three times a year — have a collection of varied old wallhung cupboards in their home, which was once a wayside inn. How wonderful they look.

Baker's cupboard, very like a pie safe,
    pine with one large door, slatted
    shelves and screened sides, for
    cooling fresh-baked bread loaves $450.00
Butcher block, deep solid maple on
    turned legs, 20" square, 19th century $300.00
Cabinet, oak, with roll front and flour bin $250.00
Cabinet, maple, bottom has 2 bins, 2
    drawers and 2 molding boards for
    rolling out dough; top section has

8 drawers flanking a small
cupboard with door, 48" wide,
late 19th century .... $180.00 to $250.00
Cheese safe, glass and wood, meant
for a 19th century store, wavy old
glass on 3 sides $750.00

Clocks: see the MEASURING section.

Cupboard, walnut, 2 pieces, 12 small
glass windows and 3 spice
drawers of tiger maple in top; 3
tiger maple drawers for cutlery
in 2-door base, Pennsylvania
German, 19th century $3000.00

Figure XVI-1. **Built-In Storage Plan.** This was probably the first "high tech" kitchen design, and it was done by those famous daughters of the Reverend Henry Ward Beecher: Catherine Beecher and Harriet Beecher Stowe. Appeared in their book, **"The American Woman's Home,** published in 1869.

Figure XVI-2. **Kitchen Cabinet Table.** Elm with maple top, cast iron handles. Zinc bin drawer at bottom held 100 pounds of flour! 2'8" high x 4'4" long x 2'4" deep. From Montgomery Ward Catalog, c. 1895. Value: $75-$90.

Cupboard, oak, 19th century, simple $100.00
Dry sink, dovetail construction, 2
    doors, painted in old red over
    original imitation graining $375.00
Dry sink, pine with cast iron liner to
    well, traces of old paint, very plain $50.00
Hanging cupboard, pine with grayish
    blue paint, 1 simple paneled door,
    no molding, brass keyhole and
    simple door latch, 1830s to 50s $400.00
Hanging cupboard, simple pine
    painted with blue milk paint, 2
    door, probably Pennsylvania
    German, 1870s or '80s $275.00
Hanging cupboard, old green paint
    over pine, 3 shelves with one
    door, simple latch, Maine $225.00
Hoosier-type cabinets — most range
    considerably in price, with those
    at the low end either very plain or
    in poor condition; the most
    expensive are either large, with
    bins and a built-in sifter, or have
    unusual original decoration. Try
    for one that hasn't been extensively
    refinished to suit the "modern"
    taste; it looks wrong and is less
    valuable. Mostly .... $120.00 to $400.00

Hoosier cabinet, varnished wood, porcelanized iron counter top, sifter, revolving spice rack for 7 containers with shaker tops, flour and sugar containers, perfect condition $430.00

Hoosier cabinet, all original finish, double doors above, flanking flour bin with oval glass window, slightly arched top, bins below, 4 drawers, sifter, spice rack, etc. $1000.00

Hoosier cabinet, oak in original finish, flour bin and sifter, roll front that really works well $275.00

Larkin cabinet, cutback hutch top with two doors above, 2 utility drawers over bin, nice legs $595.00

Figure XVI-3. **Meat Safe.** Wood with screening. No reason this couldn't be a pie safe too. From L.H. Mace catalog, 1880s. Value: $90-$120.

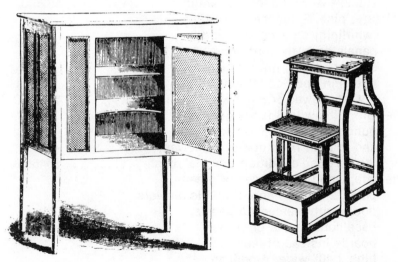

Figure XVI-4. **Utility Steps.** Wood, nicely made. Steps slid in under frame. From F.A. Walker catalog, 1870s. Value: $35-$45.

Hutch table, pine in original finish,
   c. 1730s $2100.00
Hutch table, pine and maple in original
   red stain, circular top above bench
   base, 27" high, 45¼" diameter
   top, late 1700s, New England.
   This was estimated to sell at
   auction in 1982 for between $4500
   and $6500, but for unexplained
   reasons was withdrawn from sale.
Milk cupboard, wood with original
   mustard colored paint, 6 shelves,
   open back and front for air
   circulation, 70" high, Pennsylvania
   German $1000.00
Pie safe, pine, punched tin in star
   and side panels, unexceptional
   geometric pattern, 2 door, 37" wide
   x 58" high $265.00
Pie safe, pine with handmade pierced
   tin front and sides, stars and
   crescent moons, 2 door, 55" high $380.00
Pie safe, pine punched tin in star
   design on doors only, closed on
   sides, 4 very long legs, 50" high $325.00
Pie safe, pine, 3 punched tin panels
   (whirligig) on each side and 3
   panels on both front doors, 3
   shelves, clean, not refinished,
   4 legs in good condition (that is,
   not rat chewed or water weakened) $465.00
Pie safe, pine with 3 fancy geometric
   punched tin panels on each side
   and in both front doors, 3 shelves,
   legs in good condition, original finish $545.00
Pie safe, wood with traces of green
   paint, 2 shelves above double drawers,
   doors with pierced tin panels,
   base constructed of cutout
   boards instead of legs, 53"
   high x 40" wide, American
   mid-19th century $150.00

Figure XVI-5. **Portable Pantry.** Japanned tin with wheat design stamped in the tin. So worn that the maker's name is illegible, but some mark was originally on right side, under coffee grinder crank. Possibly a "Perfect Pantry." At top is what appears to be a frame for a clock or mirror? Approx. 50" high x 36" wide. Drawing taken from dim Polaroid taken at booth of dealer Forest Evick Jr., Staunton, Virginia. Value: $575. (NOTE: for a photograph of another make, see p. 118 of **Antique Tin & Tole Ware** by Mary Earle Gould.)

Portable pantry, japanned tin with
   stenciled flowers and words,
   "PERFECT PANTRY," pat'd 1904,
   bins for flour and coffee, coffee
   grinder on right, white porcelain
   knobs on doors, 6 spice canisters $950.00
Portable pantry, japanned tin, wheat
   design stamped in the tin, so
   worn and rubbed it is impossible
   (except perhaps with infrared?) to
   read maker's name, big bins on
   top for coffee, flour and corn
   meal, coffee grinder on right side;
   flour sifter works by moving lever
   back and forth, 6 spice canisters
   with double lids, including shaker
   lid, 2 heavily encrusted
   compartments at bottom —
   almost as if used as oven, but
   that couldn't be $575.00

Portable pantry or "security safe",
    painted tin, bins for staples,
    lockable compartmentss, coffee
    grinder $1600.00

Spice cabinets & chests: see CONTAINER section, just preceding this category.

Table, enamel top, drop leaf and
    extension, 1910 to 1940s if in
    good condition with nice design on top .. $50.00 to $70.00
Table, birch with single wide birch
    plank top, 2 side drawers, turned
    legs, late 19th century .... $150.00 to $250.00

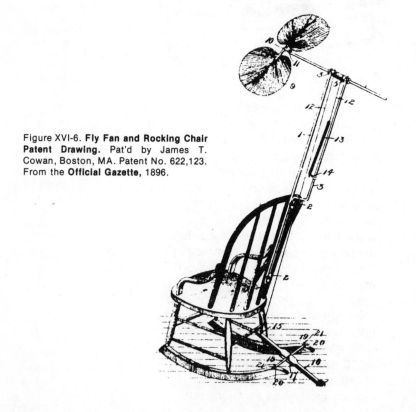

Figure XVI-6. **Fly Fan and Rocking Chair Patent Drawing.** Pat'd by James T. Cowan, Boston, MA. Patent No. 622,123. From the **Official Gazette**, 1896.

CARE OF UTENSILS & TOOLS

CLEAN, SCRUB, WASH, DRAIN & SHARPEN

My favorites here are the brushes and the dish drainers. Who'd ever think — after the last 40 or so years with rubbercoated wire dish drainers — that they used to be made in so many fanciful and interesting ways? My most favorite, at least in my collection, is the wooden peg one, found at Renninger's indoor market, Adamstown, PA, as the only treasure in 12 hours of scouring.

Brush, iron handle, "People's" for
    blacking stoves $18.00
Brush, natural fiber, wood handle,
    bottle washer with cranked
    handle! 1920s .... $8.00 to $15.00
Brush, tin, wire and wood, marked
    "Y-R," fan-shaped pat'd 1900,
    for cleaning sinks and pots .... $7.00 to $10.00
Dish drainer, pine with woven wire
    screen and wood dividers, 1880s $30.00

Figure XVII-1. **Bottle Washing Brush.** Turned wood handle, nice bottle-bottom black bristles. Nickeled brass crank. 10¾" long. 1910-1930s? Author's collection. Value: $8-$15.

Figure XVII-2. **Dish Drainer.** Water and soap-bleached wood with dowel pegs. 17¾" x 11½" x 2¾" deep. 1890s. Author's collection. Value: $20-$30.

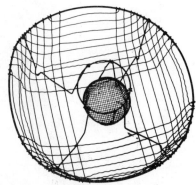

Figure XVII-4. **Dish Drainer.** Wire with mesh cutlery drainer in center. 15" diameter x 5¼" high. C. 1890-1910. Author's collection. Value: $12-$20.

Figure XVII-3. **Dish Drainer.** Blackened tin and wire, with fold-down cutlery drainer. Androck, No. 199. 19½" x 12" x 3 7/8" high. About 1890-1910. Author's collection. Value: $12-$20.

Figure XVII-5. **Dish Drainers.** Wire. "Loop Weld," by Marlboro Wire Goods Co., c. 1910. 18¾" x 12" x 3 7/8" high. At right is child's version, made just as well. This had original cardboard identifying it. 6 1/8" x 3 5/8". Author's collection. Values: $8-$12 and $12-$18.

Dish drainer, wire, round with flatware
    basket suspended in center, 15"
    diameter, turn-of-century .... $12.00 to $20.00
Dish drainer, wire, "Marlboro Wire
    Goods," meant for 12 plates,
    flatware trough at end, 19" long,
    c. 1910 .... $8.00 to $12.00
Dish drainer, all wood and beautifully
    water worn, pegs set into narrow
    pieces of wood, white rubber
    feet, 18" long, probably 1880s
    to 1900 .... $20.00 to $30.00
Dish drainer, blackened tin and wire,
    "Androck No. 199," tin fold-out
    flatware rack, 19½" long, rusts
    like crazy! 1936 .... $12.00 to $20.00
Dish or plate scraper, hard white
    rubber, "Daisy," Schact Rubber
    Mfg. Co., 5¾" long .... $3.00 to $4.00
Dish or plate scraper, rubber with
    wood handle, "A & J" (Edward
    Katzinger Co.), 1940 .... $3.00 to $5.00

Figure XVII-6.
Dough Scraper. Cast steel. 3¾" long x 3" wide. 19th century. Collection of Mary Mac Franklin. Value: $25-$35.

Dish pan, gray graniteware.................. $10.00 to $12.00
Dish pan, dark blue and white
    agateware, ear handles, 12" diameter $9.00
Dish pan, gray graniteware,
    12" diameter $13.50

To Wash Dishes

Dishes should be rinsed in clear, hot water after having been washed in soap suds. It is necessary from a sanitary point of view; the caustic alkali is corrosive and unwholesome, and the grease often impure. A rack made of narrow strips of half-inch board is a device frequently used for draining dishes, thus saving the trouble of wiping them. This rack placed on a shelf inclining towards and adjoining the sink holds the dishes securely while they are drying. Milk is a substitute for soap in the kitchen. A little put into hot water will soften it, give the dishes a fine gloss, and will not injure the hands. China and glass (when very dirty) are best cleaned with finely powdered fuller's-earth and warm water, afterwards rinsing it well in clean water. All china that has any gilding upon it may on no account be rubbed with a cloth of any kind, but merely rinsed, first in hot and afterwards in cold water, and then left to drain till dry. Cups and saucers which have become stained with coffee or tea can be easily cleaned by scouring them with baking soda.

Scammell's Treasure-House of Knowledge, 1891

Dough scraper, wrought iron, looks
like a small hoe with a very short
handle, 19th century .... $25.00 to $35.00
Dough scraper, iron blade with short
wood handle, quite primitive $35.00
Dough scraper, wrought iron, like a
hoe but with hollow handle
(probably missing a wooden
handle of whatever length useful
to the cook who owned it) $28.00
Dough scraper, forged iron, ring
handle, 15" long $75.00
Griddle greaser and scraper, cast iron,
tin and cloth lard pad,
"W.H. Bixler," pat'd 1873 .... $16.00 to $20.00
Knife board, painted wood with bath
brick, heart cutout at top end,
Pennsylvania German, 1860s .... $100.00 to $135.00
Knife scouring box, pine with original
green paint on outside, simple
box attached to footed scouring
platform, mid-1800s .... $135.00 to $150.00
Knife scouring box, pine, very simple $65.00

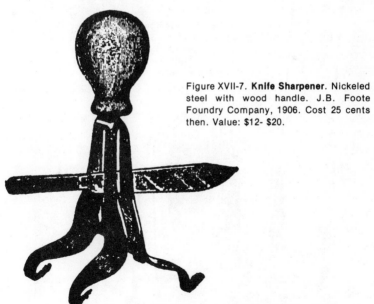

Figure XVII-7. **Knife Sharpener.** Nickeled
steel with wood handle. J.B. Foote
Foundry Company, 1906. Cost 25 cents
then. Value: $12- $20.

Knife sharpener, adv'g "Crescent Hill
Milk," 1920s $8.50
Knife sharpener, "Sharpeit," Dazey
Churn Co., pat'd 1925 .... $20.00
Knife sharpener, iron with wood
handle, "Eversharp" $1.50
Pot cleaner, wire rings like chain mail,
late 1800s, I've seen these for
about $16 in last couple of years,
but I heard from my Texas
connection that out there they
may go much much higher .... $16.00 to $40.00
Pot scraper, tin, adv'g "Mount Penn
Stove Works" .... $25.00 to $28.00
Pot scraper, litho'd tin with picture of
woman and cream separator,
"Sharples Tubular Cream Separator" $28.00
Pot scraper, tin, triangular with hang-
up hole, no advertising — possibly
scoured off long ago $10.00

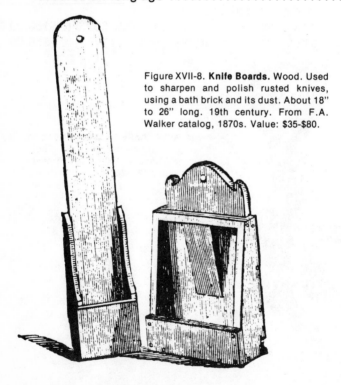

Figure XVII-8. **Knife Boards.** Wood. Used to sharpen and polish rusted knives, using a bath brick and its dust. About 18" to 26" long. 19th century. From F.A. Walker catalog, 1870s. Value: $35-$80.

Figure XVII-9. **Knife Cleaner.** Wood and leather, with iron fittings. Bath brick or othe fine pumice-like material was sprinkled on and rubbed with leather between two levered parts. 19th century. 10¼" long x 5½" wide x 4½" high. Formerly in the Keillor Collection. Value: $45-$75.

No Model.)

H. F. W. LEMKE.
KETTLE SCRAPER.

No. 522,794.   Patented July 10, 1894.

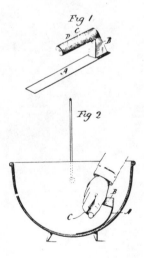

Figure XVII-10. **Kettle Scraper Patent Drawing.** Pat'd July 10, 1894 by Herman F.W. Lemkie, Clinton, CT. Flexible metal blade sharpened both sides, with wood tiller handle.

489

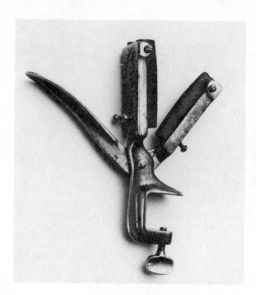

Figure XVII-11. **Knife Sharpener.** Nickel plated cast metal, H.L. Johnson, pat'd July 24, 1888 and September 2, 1890. Screw clamps to table edge. 2 sharpening stones worked by lever. 6 7/8" high. Located by The Primitive Man, Bob Cahn, Carmel, NY. Value: $45-$65.

Figure XVII-12. **Plate Scrapers.** Left: White rubber, tin with wood handle. Marked "WB/W." 5¾" long, c. 1925. Right: All rubber, white with painted handle. "Daisy," Schacht Rubber Mfg. Co., Huntington, Ind., c. 1932. 5¾" long. Author's collection. Value: $3-$5.

490

Figure XVII-13. **Sink.** Porcelainized cast iron with unusual built-in corner drainer for washing vegetables. Shown here with strainer resting in it. Drainboard at right side. Fastened to wall and has 2 front legs. Picture taken in 1920's mansion on Ossabaw Island, off Savannah, Georgia.

Figure XVII-14. **Sink Brushes.** Wire with wood handles. Top: Pat'd February 27, 1900. Marked "Y-R." (Get it? First time I ever got it in 10 years!) 9¼" long. Other with bent wire for corners. 4" long. Collection of the Disshuls. Value: $9-$20.

Figure XVII-15. **Soap Saver.** Wire with mesh holder for soap scraps. Swish this through water in dish pan and get lots of suds. From a turn-of-the-century unidentified flyer. Value: $8-$15.

Soap saver, wire mesh box, wood handle ..... $10.00 to $20.00
Soap saver, wire with twisted wire handle $15.00
Soap saver, perforated tin box with
    wire handle, pat'd September 14, 1875 ... $12.00 to $18.00
Soap shaker (canister to hold scouring
    powder), tin, screw-on lid $6.00
Soap shaver, pierced tin with wire arch
    handle, embossed "Sunny
    Monday — Saves Soap & Labor,"
    looks very much like a grater, but
    woe to the person who gets soap
    shavings in their parmesan! $10.00

See also the section on Household Chores.

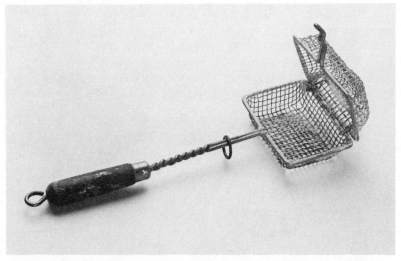

Figure XVII-16. **Soap Saver.** Mesh box with wood handle. 10" long, c. 1920-1940. Collection of the Disshuls. Value: $-$15.

ADVERTISING POT SCRAPERS
By Karol Atkinson

NOTE: Some references are to scrapers in color section.

"Pot what?" This is the standard answer received in the search for these elusive little kitchen helpers of the past.

The tin advertising pot scraper is not to be confused with the circular chain mesh version which is relatively easy to find.

Most examples found are in the shape of the Dove brand below. The Junket shape is seen less frequently. Actual measurements are 3" wide x 2 9/16" high for the Junket.

Dating the scrapers is difficult. Only one of my scrapers has the year of issue on it — the Sharples Cream Separator with a date of 1909. An approximate date can be assumed on the Admiral Coffee scraper (see color section) owing to the spelling of "Pittsburg" with the "H" at the end. The last time in history this spelling was in effect was 1890 to 1911. An estimate of manufacturing dates would be 1900 to 1925. All but one of the scrapers illustrated would fall between these dates with most of them dating between 1900 and 1910. The chrome-like finish of the Big Diamond Flour (see color section) indicates a much later manufacture date plus a bottle opener replaces the traditional round hang-up or finger hole.

The Cleveland Co-Operative Stove Co. issued scrapers illustrating their various stoves and ranges. The earliest of their three known examples is one with a pot belly stove. Next is the combination range and finally one with a gas range.

Some of the scrapers have advertising on both sides informing the user everything there is to know about the product advertised. The reverse of the Sharples Cream Separator, World's Best as well as a Sharples, 1909, is cobalt blue and depicts the separator. The two different varieties of the Junket also have advertising on both sides. Besides scraping pots, the Junket scraper also scraped the mixing bowl, cake pan, rolling pin and moulding board.

Comical phrases, illustrations and-or verses are printed on scrapers such as the Dove Brand Ham & Bacon.

The Ward's Better Butter and Fairmont Creamery are examples of a stock pot scraper which could be ordered and personalized with the company's name. A similar practice was used with advertising trade cards.

The familiar red wing logo of the Red Wing Milling Co. seen so often on their crocks and jugs is also present on their colorful pot scraper. For collectors in the Midwest and Northwest anything bearing the red wing is highly desirable.

Most commonly seen of the pot scrapers in the eastern United States are Mt. Penn Stove Works (see color section) and Henkel's Flour. As with other collectibles, the examples cited may differ in availability according to areas.

Very few metal ware manufacturing companies chose to sign their product. Out of all my scrapers only two: Passaic Metal Ware Co., Passaic, New Jersey and the H.D. Beach Co., of Coshocton, Ohio. Both companies are better known for their high quality tin lithograph trays.

No firm price guidelines exist to date on pot scrapers. All the scrapers in this writing have been purchased for between $2.00 and $45.00 each. I believe that these prices reflect a hobby that is still affordable in today's spiralling collectibles field.

At present there are perhaps only a half dozen or so avid collectors of pot scrapers. After one becomes acquainted with these little pieces of tin it is difficult not to be attracted to them.

Some other pot scrapers available but not in my collection are Nesco Enamelware, Royal King Gas Heaters, Delco Light, American Cup Coffee and Arnold's Twin Bread.

EDITOR'S NOTE: If you wish to correspond with Karol Atkinson about these colorful scrapers, write to her at home at 903 Apache Trail, Mercer PA 16137. Please be sure to enclose a self-addressed stamped envelope if you wish an answer.

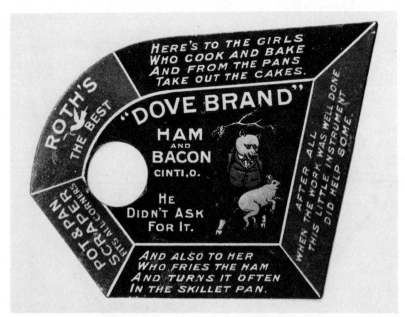

Figure PS-1. **Pot Scraper.** Picture courtesy of Karol Atkinson.

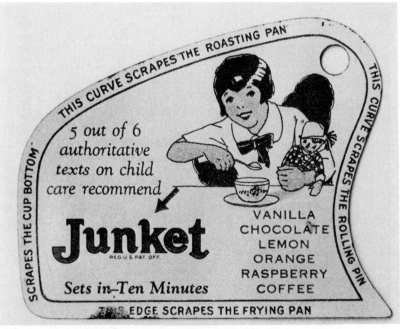

Figure PS-2. **Pot Scraper**. Picture courtesy of Karol Atkinson.

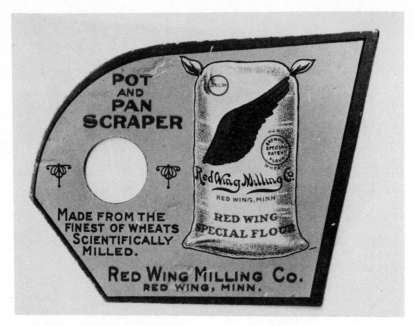

Figure PS-3. **Pot Scraper.** Picture courtesy of Karol Atkinson.

Figure PS-4. **Pot Scraper.** Picture courtesy of Karol Atkinson.

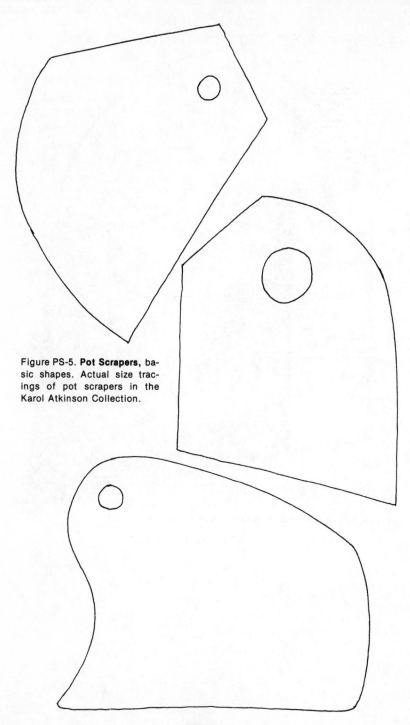

Figure PS-5. **Pot Scrapers,** basic shapes. Actual size tracings of pot scrapers in the Karol Atkinson Collection.

RELATED COLLECTIBLES
COLLECTIBLES RELATED TO KITCHENS & COOKING

This is one of my favorite categories — probably because it is a catchall place for me to indulge my fancy for things that seem like other things, or objects that have some connection in form or subject to something else. A bit of foolery. Perhaps it's just that I can't let go of the subject, and begin to see "kitchenalia" (as someone ill-advisedly termed the subject once, and in print yet!) everywhere I look. Certainly, the "related" stuff has been the saving of my collecting instinct. When I ran out of room for the big stuff, often what I looked for and bought was quite small . . . I mean, how many more Heinz pickle pins and stove advertising mirrors you can get into a one-room apartment, compared to Cathedral pickle jars and stoves!

You'll probably have fun with this area too; it also allows easy egress into other collecting fields. Go from kitchen gadgets to old photographs of people in kitchens to old photographs, perhaps on to old cameras . . . or who knows!

Advertisements, color magazine ads
    or black/white ads, showing
    kitchens, housewives, etc., 1900
    to 1950s .... $5.00 to $15.00
Advertising mirror, color litho with
    picture of range, "Dockash Stove,"
    Scranton, PA $35.00
Advertising trade cards, colorful
    chromolith cards, generally about
    playing card size or smaller,
    showing — often in great detail
    — stoves, enamelware, people
    (or animals) cooking, still-lifes of
    food, all from 1870s to 1890s .... $1.00 to $10.00
Advertising tray, litho'd tin, swans in
    a pond with a red ribbon on
    border, "White Swan Flour," with
    "To the users of the celebrated
    White Swan Flour, with best
    wishes of the manufacturer" on
    the back, 16½" x 13½" oval, terrific $85.00
Apron, coverall advertising "Mother
    Hubbard Flour, Worth the Difference" $12.00

NOTE: Aprons make a wonderful collection, but old ones are hard to find. Look carefully in boxes at yard sales, estate sales, thrift shops. Your mother or grandmother probably has a few old ones stashed too . . . aprons don't seem to enjoy the de rigeur status they used to have. How I wish I still had some of those fluttery pinafore aprons, some in printed calicos, that I remember my mother wearing in the 1940s! After I learned to iron napkins, I graduated to aprons . . . and usually ironed [as I remember it], with the breakfast room door open, letting in the sun, with the charmed voice of Arthur Godfrey soothing the strokes of my iron.

Ashtry, stamped metal, marked
    "Sheridan Stove Mfg. Co.,
      Quincy, Illinois" $4.00
Bank, cast metal, "A & P" $8.00
Bank, metal, model of a "Westinghouse"
    roasting pan $22.00
Bank, figural of "Electrolux" refrigerator $18.00
Billhook, "Black Cat Stove Polish" $7.00
Blotter, advertising "Morton's Salt" .... $1.00 to $4.00
Calendar and notebook, "National
    Yeast Co.," 1887 .... $17.50
Card game, "Lion Coffee" $10.00
Charm, 14k gold, coffee grinder .... $35.00 to $50.00
Chocolate figurals used for display,
    foils in different colors, animals,
    Easter, etc. .... $6.00 to $8.00
Comb case, embossed tin, with
    Japanese fans and ribbons, 3
    pockets and a mirror, hung on
    wall, sometimes simply called
    a "tidy" .... $25.00 to $35.00
Cookie container, hinged glass top,
    adv'g "Sunshine Biscuits," $60.00
Daily reminder, "Hoosier," meant for
    Hoosier cabinet $22.00
Envelope, with printed picture of little
    boy sitting with loaf of bread,
    "Ceresota Flour," 1903 postmark $10.00
Envelope, 3 color picture of 2 cans,
    "White House Brand Tea and
    Coffee, George L. Curtis & Co.,
    wholesale distributor," 1909 postmark $15.00

Figure XVIII-1. **Flue Covers.** Stamped metal, often brass-plated. Cheap litho'd pictures. Value: $8-$18.

Figure XVIII-2. **Fly Trap.** 3-parts: wooden base where you put bait, wire inteior cone of screening, only 4" high with small hole at apex, then the bigger upper compartment, from which there is no escape. 9¼" high x 5½" diameter. 19th century. Collection of Meryle Evans. Value: $25-$40.

Envelope, 2 color picture of a box of
cinnamon, "Royal Brand Spices,
Mustards, Herbs, Etc., George L.
Curtis," 1908 postmark $20.00
Envelope, 2 color picture of coffee
can, "White House Coffee,
George L. Curtis," 1906 postmark $20.00
Envelope, 3 color pictures of pepper
and mustard boxes, "Slade's
Pepper, Mustard," 1907 postmark $40.00
Envelope, same as above but 1908 postmark $20.00
Envelope, 4 color picture, "Kennedy's
Champion Biscuit," no postmark,
but first decade of 20th century $25.00
Envelope, black and red picture of
meat grinder, "The Pennsylvania
Meat Cutter," no postmark $7.50
Envelope, blue ink, picture depicting
jar holder in use, "The Boss Jar
Holder & Top Wrench," c. 1900 .... $25.00
Envelope, 2 color picture of meat
grinder on table, "Great American
Meat Cutter," no postmark $20.00

The Improved Keyless Fly Fan.

A GREAT HOME COMFORT.

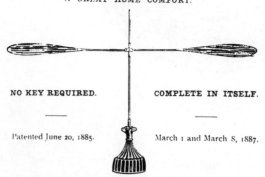

NO KEY REQUIRED.   COMPLETE IN ITSELF.

———   ———

Patented June 20, 1885.   March 1 and March 8, 1887.

The most attractive, convenient and durable Fly Fan in the market.

Figure XVIII-3. **Fly Fan.** "The Improved Keyless Fly Fan,: pat'd June 20, 1885 and
March 1, March 8, 1887. 29½" high x 48" wingspread . . . "It drives all flies away by
the shadow and movement of the wings while revolving." Pat'd and mfd. by
Matthai-Ingram. Value: $125-$150.

Envelope, blue ink, "The Rising Sun
and Sun Paste Stove Polish,"
no date $15.00
Envelope, blue ink, Columbian
Exposition cover depicting
gigantic stove that was on display
at the 1893 Expo . . . the stove
was 25' high x 30' long x 20' wide!!!
"Mammoth 'Garland' World's Fair, 1893" $65.00

**NOTE: Whoo boy! Do I wish I knew where that stove was today!
Just imagine it!**

Figurine, "Polly-Put-the-Kettle-On,"
Royal Worcester porcelain .... $85.00 to $90.00
Flask, gray graniteware, cork stopper,
6½" long .... $50.00 to $60.00
Flask, silverplate with rebus message
"Birds of a Feather, Flock
Together" on side, 1890s, 7" long $45.00
Flour sacks, colorfully printed pictures
and advertising, 2 pound to 25
pound size, approximately 12½"
x 26" down to 6" x 9", these may
still be available from Paul Van
Vactor, 300 Stilx Avenue,
Louisville, KY 40206. He advertised
a wonderful collection of 11
different bags some time ago in
"Antique Trader Weekly" —
each ranging from .... $2.00 to $4.75
Flour bags, colorfully printed paper,
many varieties . . . these available
from Industrial Revolution, Box
25615, Chicago, IL 60625. Also
some cloth bags. Selected groups .... $4.95 to $50.00
Flue cover or "chimney hole cover"
cast iron, very decorative $25.00
Flue cover, stamped tin, painted in
oils with picture of child feeding cat $50.00
Flue cover, stamped and painted tin
with color litho'd farm scene (on
paper) in center .... $8.00 to $10.00
Flue cover, cast iron $18.00

Flue cover, metal frame with picture
of 2 girls in bonnets under glass,
chain to fix it over stove hole $18.00
Flue cover, brass frame, English
countryside, 5" diameter $15.00
Flue cover, tin, litho'd picture of
garden girl with red roses, 8"
diameter, spring clips $1.50
Flue cover, glass in brass frame with
reverse painting on the glass,
sylvan scene $8.00
Fly fan, cast iron base with muslin
wings, National Enameling &
Stamping Co. (Matthai-Ingram),
pat'd 1885/87, clockwork wind-up
action, keeps wings revolving for
75 minutes per wind, 48" high .... $125.00 to $160.00
Fly killer, wick type, "Seiber Magic
Fly Killer," 1913 .... $12.00
Fly trap, tin and wire screen, 9" high,
1880s .... $18.00 to $25.00
Fly trap, wood base and wire
screen, round base and
demispherical screen dome,
"Harper's Patent 1875 Balloon
Fly Trap" $85.00
Fly trap, wood base and screen
"quonset hut"-shaped top, inner
dome has small hole at top, end
of trap has bung hole and plug for
inserting bait, 11" long, 1870s,
quite primitive, although
probably manufactured not homemade $23.00
Grocery box, folding wood box marked
"Maas Grocery," 12" x 15", pat'd
late 19th century $45.00

Labels: see separate listing further on in this book.

Lamp, embossed china wall plate with
black chef at the stove, brass
fixture, 6½" x 6½", Occupied Japan $35.00
Letter opener, metal, adv'g "Shatten's
Coffees, Teas & Spices $18.00

Letterheads, printed pictures, "Quaker
Oats," "Chase & Sanborn Coffee,"
"Checkers Popcorn Confection,"
1921, each $4.00
Measuring tape, adv'g "General
Electric" refrigerators $12.00
Measuring tape, "Frigidaire" $25.00
Measuring tape, in shape of tea kettle $10.00
Measuring tape, figural of champagne
bottle in cooler, wind-up, c. 1880 .... $165.00
Needlecase, cardboard in shape of
salt box, "Worcester Iodized Salt"
in black on orange, 3" long x 1¾" wide $7.50
Needlecase, cardboard diecut, shape
of kitchen range, "Buy a Household
Range," 3" x 4" $12.00
Paper doll, Nabisco "Cookie Man," uncut $8.00
Paperweight, adv'g "Lyons Best Flour" $22.00
Pencil box, wooden, shape of rolling
pin, screws apart, 8" long .... $17.00 to $22.00
Pencil clip, tin, adv'g "Morton's Salt,"
blue/white .... $5.00 to $7.00
Pencil sharpener, "Baker's Chocolate"
girl in waitress outfit .... $28.00 to $50.00
Pencil sharpener, cast iron, figural of
Coca-Cola bottle $30.00

Figure XVIII-4. **Pot Menders.** "Mendets," — metal patch, tiny "bolt," and the small
triangular wrench, mounted on color-printed card. Collette Mfg. Co., c. 1940.
Author's collection. Value: $3-$5.

Photograph, hand-colored Wallace
Nutting interior scene of "Woman
Churning Butter" $60.00
Photographs, showing interior kitchen
scenes, posed or candid,
pre-World War I .... $5.00 to $15.00
Picture, cotton applique and
embroidery, motto picture in
frame, "A cheerful kitchen . . . ,"
1940s, 10" x 12" $30.00
Pin, Heinz pickle pin, green plastic .... $3.00 to $6.00
Pin, buffalo in skillet, Pan American Expo $12.50
Pinback, adv'g "Ceresota Flour" in
ornate brass frame $13.50
Pinback, adv'g "Use Bell's Coffees" $12.00
Pinback, adv'g "Scovill Stoves" $5.00
Placemats, "Campbell Kids," 5 mats
& napkins $25.00

**NOTE: The Campbell Soup Company's Campbell Kids have had
a long and interesting life, beginning back in 1904 when they
were created by the illustator Grace Wiederseim Drayton. They
were chubby because Grace, as she said later, had been a
chubby little girl. Then in 1921, an effort was made to make the
Campbell Kids over into animated soup cans . . . cans with arms
and legs . . . but the public apparently hated them. In the 1950s
they were modernized and slightly slimmed, then slimmed
again in the 1970s with the new line of lighter soups. Now,
according to a newspaper report, the Kids will have to lose even
more weight because they will soon be the "mascots" [when
Campbell's sponsors the team] of the United States Figure
Skating Team for the Olympics! By the way, a great buy about
three years ago was the molded plastic soup cup in the shape of
a Campbell Soup Kid. They were sold for about 79 cents at the
grocery store. I'm glad I bought several; they're bound to go up
in value. This is the object lesson of this long digression: you
can add contemporary things to your collection, and while you
should buy what you like, there's no telling the investment
value!**

Pocket mirror, adv'g "Copper Clad
Ranges" .... $20.00 to $25.00
Pop gun, cardboard, "Clover Ice
Cream," 1914 .... $10.00

Figure XVIII-5. **Paper Envelope for Madam Blumer's Egg Saver.** Lincoln Chemical Works, Chicago. 3½" x 2¼". Turn-of-century. Egg substitute: one pinch equals one egg. Value: $1-$2.

Figure XVIII-6. **Post Card.** Cooking related subject — invitation to buffet dinner, 1947. Value: $1-$2.

Poster, chromolithograph view of the
    St. Louis Beef Canning Co.
    ("Choice Canned Cooked Meats")
    factory, ice house, steamboat,
    railroad, and scenes of people
    eating the canned meat, St.
    Louis, MO, c. 1880, 10½" x 12½" $45.00
Potholders, appliqued cloth with
    hearts and diamonds, red, green
    on white, rings for hanging, each $5.00

THE WARM WEATHER — *Terrific explosion of a Ginger Beer Truck.*

Figure XVIII-7. **Pen and Ink Drawing.** "The Warm Weather — Terrific Explosion of a Ginger Beer Truck," drawn by K. Gregory (?), c. 1880. 11 1/8" x 8¼". Notice the corkscrew in the vendor's hand, and the exploding ceramic ginger beer bottles. Those are the tan and ochre thick stoneware bottles, about 7"-9" high, seen often at sales. Value: $50-$75.

Figure XVIII-8. **Die-Cut Invitation.** Obverse side. Pasteboard with engraving. For Boston Tea Party Centennial celebration at Faneuil Hall, December 1873. Picture courtesy of the National Museum of American History, Smithsonian Institution.

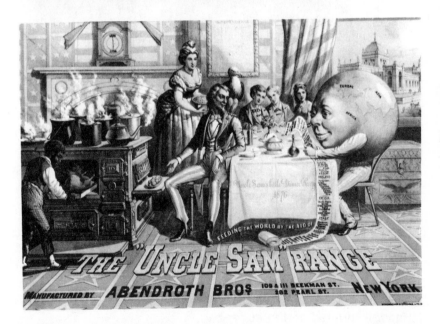

Figure XVIII-9. **Advertising Poster for Uncle Sam Stove.** Fabulous color lithograph. Picture courtesy of Bruce Barber.

Figure XVIII-10. **Kettle Scraper Patent Drawing.** Pat'd July 10, 1894 by Hermann F. w. Lemke, Clinton, CT. Flexible metal blade, sharpened both sides, with wood tiller handle.

Potholder, appliqued cat's head, very
    fanciful $6.00
Ragdoll, printed cotton sugar bag,
    "Miss Supreme," printed with
    directions, 100 pound bag $15.00

NOTE: Instead of listing Salesman's Sample Stoves and other items here, I'm going to put them with Toys and Miniatures following this section. I realize that salesman's samples and toys, even those that work, are different, but without a great deal more study than I can give the subject, I'd rather follow along in the state of benign confusion that exists for most of us. The difficulty is not in telling which is a miniature or toy that doesn't **work, but which — among the things that do work — what was an adult salesman's selling piece and what was a clever toy.**

Shaker can for Ovaltine, "Orphan
    Annie," with decal, 1936 .... $45.00
Sign, red and green enameled
    embossed tin, "Kerosene Electrolux
    Refrigerator installed here,"
    1930s, this was fridge used in
    1934 to keep milk for the Dionne
    Quints up in the Canadian wilds,
    a warehouse find, sold each at $35.00
Sign, colorful tin, "Marrows Ice
    Cream," printed both sides, 20" x 28" $65.00
Sign, tin, shaped like coffee cup,
    "Golden Girl Cola," 54½" x 40 3/8" $60.00
Sign, copper, shaped like huge tea-
    kettle, 19th century English shop
    sign, sold at auction in 1982 .... $4750.00
Sign, folding cardboard, "Beech Nut
    Bacon," shows 2 women in
    kitchen, 35½" x 25½", c. 1915 .... $275.00
Sign, tin, "Nappanee Dutch Kitchenet,
    The World's Finest Kitchen
    Cabinet," shows Dutch girl,
    17½" x 7½" $45.00
Sign, red scrim or lawn cloth,
    painted to advertise "Garland
    Stoves," meant for hanging in
    store, 20" x 21½" $55.00
Sign, tin, "Rumford Baking Powder" $35.00
Statue, metal, Indian advertising
    "Doe-Wah-Jack" oak stoves, 10" high $60.00
Stickpin, "Doe-Wah-Jack" Indian
    head, round $30.00

Figure XVIII-11. **Stove Token or Medal.** Such cast metal medals were produced for a variety of products. This happens to be for a Gem City heating stove, but others were made for cookstoves. 2" diameter, c. 1890. Private collection. Value: $7-$12.

Stickpin, red pennant, "Libby Food
Products" $10.00
Stickpin, "Swift's Silver Leaf Lard,"
shape of leaf $21.00
Stove advertisement, iron, in form of
hatchet, adv'g "Laurel Stoves &
Ranges" $30.00
Tablecloth, cotton damask, turkey red
with fringe $26.00
Tablecloth, linen cutwork damask,
white with green floral border,
85" x 55", 12 napkins to match $115.00
Tablecloth, red and white woven
checked cotton, 12' long — good
for church picnics $45.00
Tablecloth, cream Quaker lace, 70" x 55" $50.00
Tablecloth, navy and white Jacquard
weave cotton, 90" x 90" $45.00
Tablecloth, filet lace, 55" x 72" $30.00
Tablecloth, cotton printed with
poinsettias and other Christmas
motifs, 72" x 56" $15.00
Tablecloth, cutwork linen, pale green,
74" x 55" $75.00
Tablecloth, floral lace on netting,
ecru, 64" x 48" $25.00
Tablecloth, blue damask, flowers and
ribbon bands, 48" x 48" $15.00
Tablecloth, printed cotton, map of
Florida, 1940s $12.00

Tablecloth, printed cotton, map of
 California, 1940s $10.00
Tablecloth, handwoven linen, two 30"
 x 120" bands sewn together,
 side-by-side, mid-1800s $25.00

Tape measure: see Measuring Tape

Thimble, blue plastic with black
 lettering, "Sunbeam Bread with
 a Bonus" $1.50
Thimble, aluminum, "Frigidaire" $4.00
Thimble case, "Mrs. Love", wood
 rolling pin, early 1800s $50.00
Top, "Esskay Frankfurts" spinning top $10.00
Watch fob, adv'g "Malleable Ranges" $40.00
Watch fob, adv'g "Rock Island Stove Co." $37.50
Watch fob, adv'g "Jermer Stove Co." $37.50
Watch fob, adv'g "DeLaval Cream
 Separator" $22.50
Watch fob, adv'g "Copper Clad
 Malleable Ranges" $25.00
Whistle, "Oscar Mayer" figural weiner $7.00

Until you get introduced to the world of miniatures — as a child, reading **The Borrowers,** or as an adult indulging in the age old fancy for tiny things — you might not be aware how many household items have been introduced in very small sizes. In this category are things relating to cookery; later in the book there's a new section on other household collectibles, and a special section of household toys and miniatures.

As I wrote a few pages back, I am not equipped to sort out the differences between working toys, salesman's samples, and — I might add — patent models. Many of the things listed in this price guide have not actually been seen by me, and sometimes I must rely on incomplete descriptions.

"Miniature" in the strict sense is something made to scale, 12":1". Many miniatures were made for adults, as parlor decorations. Dollhouse objects are sometimes made to the miniature 12:1 scale, but more often are not. Dollhouses come in many sizes. Toys are generally meant to be played with by a child and are perhaps half the size of the real object. Some toys actually work. Models are made to scale too, but not necessarily 12:1, and most served a serious function — as a guide or representation of a full-size object to come. As far as I know, salesman's samples were also built to scale, and — like the models — work.

Dollhouse sink, stove, refrigerator,
    cardboard, "Built-Rite," in
      original box, mint condition $30.00
Dollhouse table of natural-finished
    wood with stencil, "Monitor Top"
      fridge, sink $28.00
Dollhouse "electric" stove and sink $12.00
Dollhouse, wood, 2 tables, cupboard,
    bowls, plates, buckets, 24 pieces in all $65.00
Dollhouse, stove, sink, china, 1930s $25.00
Dollhouse, stove, sink, cupboard,
    metal, "Tootsietoy" $30.00
Dollhouse icebox, cast metal,
    "Alaska," 3 doors, painted white
      with gold trim, 7" high x 4½" wide $75.00
Doll's angel food pan, aluminum $2.50

TOY TOWN COOKING SCHOOL

A very attractive outfit for the little girl who wants to cook just like mother does. It has about all the utensils that mother uses, such as a bread board, rolling pin, cookie cutter, tins, etc., but best of all, there is a bag of flour, not make believe, but real, a perfect miniature of the great big bag that mother has. There are packages of real soda, salt, cocoa, cotolene, etc. all put up in miniature of the well-known brands that every housekeeper is familiar with. There is also a cook book that any little girl can follow, and by which she can make real cookies, etc.

Figure XIX-1. **Advertisement for Toy Cooking Utensils.** "Toy Town Cooking School" in cardboard box, with rolling pin and pastry board, plus real packaged ingredients. From **Little Folks** magazine, c. 1916. Collection of Mary Mac Franklin.

Miniature baking dish, redware with
    yellow glaze, 1" x 2½" $65.00
Miniature rotating broiler, iron, 3 legs,
    nicely formed handle, 4¾" long
    x 2¾" diameter $50.00
Miniature coffee pot, tin, hinged lid,
    strap handle, long straight spout,
    2¾" high $60.00
Miniature picnic hamper, stenciled
    and litho'd tin, blue and white
    Dutch scenes in panels (boys
    playing ball, girls in posy ring),
    2 swinging strap handles, 2
    spring-loaded lids $85.00

Figure XIX-2. **Ice Cream Freezer.** Possibly a toy or a salesman's sample. Wood and metal, late 19th century. Cast into top is "Peerless Iceland Freezer." 7½" high. Picture courtesy of the National Museum of American History, Smithsonian Institution.

Miniature mortar and pestle, brass,
    engine turned on outside $18.00
Miniature kettle, cast iron, bail handle,
    3 feet, 1½" high x 3" diameter $20.00
Miniature teakettle, brass, bail handle
    and lid, 1½" diameter, c. 1950s $18.00

NOTE: A line of 14 miniature copper utensils are being sold in gift shops now as tree ornaments! They retail for between $2.00 and $5.00 . . . not much for nicely made little things, some with lids, two with working bail handles. There's a footed colander, basin, saucepan, teapot with gooseneck spout, measure, cooler, stewpot and some unidentifiable pieces. B.I.A. Cordon Bleu at 375 Quarry Road, Belmont, CA 94002 should be able to answer inquiries, but not orders.

Salesman's sample stove, cast iron
    with tin pipe, Abendroth, "Uncle
    Sam," dated 7/3/1885, weighs
    75 pounds, 24" wide x 14" high x
    11" deep, all eyes have lids, 7
    workable doors, 2 frying pans,
    griddle, lid lifter, sad iron,
    courtesy Bruce Barber $1650.00

Salesman's sample stove, cast iron
pot bellied, "Raven No. 66" $350.00
Salesman's sample stove, cast iron,
"Quickmeal Stove Co., No.
407-16," 26" high x 18" wide x 15"
deep, working doors, 2 kettles $1500.00
Salesman's sample stove, cast iron,
"Eternal Range," Excelsior-
Matthews, with many many
accoutrements, including curling
irons, teakettle, shovel, kettles,
flatiron, etc. $2600.00
Salesman's sample stove, nickel
plated cast iron, "Rival," pat'd
July 30, 1895 .... $450.00
Salesman's sample ice creeam freezer,
"White Mountain Jr." $125.00

**NOTE: I suspect that this might have been one of the small
exact versions of an adult item, advertised in magazines for
children [who could send away for such things with 25 cents or
so], used to encourage sales of the real thing to the parents.**

Souvenir, lard pail in miniature size, "Naphey's Lard," Philadelphia Centennial, 1776-1876 .... $35.00

Toy stove, tin, 5" x 6½", with kettle and cover, plus 3 hanging molds on back $35.00

Toy stove, cast iron, "Crescent," with utensils $45.00

Toy stove, cast iron, "Rival," only the range, no back plate or shelf or pipe $145.00

Toy stove, cast iron, "Favorite," 12" high, very ornate $950.00

Toy stove, cast iron, "Crescent" $100.00

Toy stove, cast iron, "Venus," 6¾" x 8", with 2 utensils $100.00

Toy stove, cast iron, "Eagle," with 4 lids, lifter, pot and griddle, very fancy casting, 6" wide x 5¼" high x 4¼" deep .... $50.00 to $60.00

Figure XIX-4. **Miniature Cookery Utensils.** Copper with brass handles, mfd. in Italy and distributed in the U.S. by B.I.A. Cordon Bleu, Inc., Belmont, CA. Very carefully and charmingly made, with good details — rolled edges, handles and spouts brazed on. 1" to 2" in height. Definitely a future classic collectible. Picture courtesy of B.I.A. Cordon Bleu.

Figure XIX-5. **Salesman's Sample Stove.** Cast iron with sheet iron stovepipe. "Uncle Sam," by Abendroth, dated 7/3/1875. Notice the color lithographed poster in preceding chapter. Picture courtesy of Bruce Barber. Value: $1650.

Toy stove, cast iron, "Arcade," parts
    missing $125.00
Toy stove, cast iron, "Royal Coal",
    10" x 6" high, missing the range-
    eye lids $50.00
Toy stove, cast iron, "Venus," 8" long
    x 5" high, with 3 old utensils .... $75.00 to $90.00
Toy stove, cast iron with tin sides and
    back, "Royal," 7" x 4¾" high x
    5" deep $15.00
Toy stove, cast iron, "The Queen," works $120.00
Toy stove, tin, litho'd to look like old
    tiled range, paw feet, 2 range
    eyes, 1 door in front $60.00

Figure XIX-6. **Toy Stove with Utensils.** Sheet tin, colored, 2 ovens, 4 covered stew pans, covered tea kettle, 5 assorted dishes, long-handled stew pan, 5 hooks on back plate. 6½" high x 4½" wide; overall height 7½". These came to store packed in sixes — 4 of which were red. Original cost was $1.00 for the 6, can you believe it? A slightly larger one with more utensils was only $2.00 for 6. Value now: $75-$100.

Toy stove, cast iron, "Little Fanny,"
Philadelphia Stove Works $115.00

NOTE: One "Little Fanny" at auction got $80, after $200 estimate.

Toy stove stamped tin, with red/black
chimney $15.00
Toy stove, cast iron, "Eagle," much
scrolled decoration, 7¼" long $90.00
Toy stove, cast iron, "Bluebird,"
4¾" high $50.00
Toy stove, cast iron, "Pet," 10¼" high $100.00
Toy stove, cast iron and embossed
tin, "Venus", 5" high x 4½" x 6½" $30.00
Toy stove, electric, chromed steel,
2 ovens, only 1 burner, 14" high
x 16" wide $75.00
Toy stove, red & white painted metal,
"Kingston Little Lady Range,"
oven marked "Cold", "Bake" and "Hot" $45.00
Toy stove, electric, "Empire," 1930s $20.00
Toy stove, electric, "Little Chef,"
10½" high x 13¾" wide x 7" deep $95.00
Toy stove, electric, "Empire" $60.00

Figure XIX-7. **Toy Kitchen Set.** Cardboard backing with 15 japanned and plain tin utensils sewn on. Little fish mold, grater with wire handle, ring molds, dust pan. I'd love to find one! Value: $5-$15 individual pieces; value on original 13¼" x 11" card: $100-$120.

Toy stove, electric, "Orphan Annie,"
with double oven .... $28.00 to $75.00
Toy muffin pan, tin, 5½" x 4", makes
6 muffins $12.00
Toy food chopper, cast metal $12.50
Toy sifter, tin $6.00
Toy cookwares, egg beater, spoons,
etc., aluminum, 8 items $24.00
Toy eggbeater, tin with wood handle,
"A & J" $10.00
Toy implements, metal with red wood
handles, ladle, cake turner,
masher, strainer and spoon,
1930s or 1940s $32.00
Toy food grinder, cast metal $45.00
Toy coffee pot, tin $10.00
Toy tea pot, tin $6.00
Toy food chopper, cast iron $15.00
Toy balance scale $15.00
Toy kitchen sink $15.00
Toy sink, litho'd tin, "Wolverine"
Snow White, 12" x 12½" $10.00
Toy refrigerator, "Wolverine," 17" high,
with milk bottles, sliding racks,
ice tray, food containers, in
original box $65.00

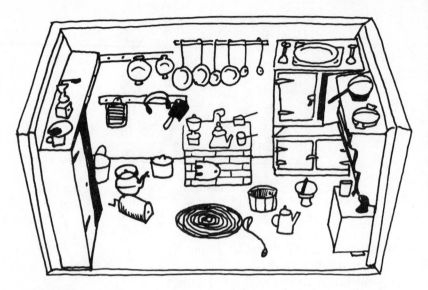

Figure XIX-8. **Toy "Nurenberg Kitchens."** Top one is fitted in wooden box, approx. 15½" high x 30" wide x 17" deep. Fitted out with kettles, pie board, fry pans, range and range kettles, coal hod, coffee roaster, plus much else not sketched in here. Cupboards of wood. This was formerly in the Keillor Collection, and was auctioned by Richard A. Bourne, Hyannis, Massachusetts in 1979. Below is a stamped tin kitchen, much simpler, but full of charm. Has working pump at right (as does other example), with recirculating water. Painted red, blue, gold and green. 7½" high x 12" wide x 5" deep.

Toy kitchen cabinet, wood
painted white, 2 doors, 11" high
x 11" wide x 4¾" deep $25.00
Toy implements, metal with red wood
handles, scoop and measuring cup $6.00
Toy potato masher, metal with red
wood handles, scoop and
measuring cup $6.00
Toy potato masher, metal with red
wood handle $4.00
Toy kitchen, white painted wood,
fridge, counter, table and 2
chairs, all for only $12.00
Toy rolling pin, wood with red handles,
8" long $5.00
Toy tea kettle, cast iron $65.00
Toy waffle iron, cast iron $65.00
Toy kettle, cast iron, swivel cover,
bail handle $45.00
Toy serving set, "Three Little Kittens,"
40 pieces including coffee pot
and coffee percolator, cups,
saucers and flatware, embossed
tin with litho'd kittens, in original
box, a wonderful nostalgia trip . . .
cheaper than any travel agent
could find for you $65.00
Toy food grinder, cast iron, clamp
on, 3" long .... $12.00 to $20.00
Toy fry pan, cast iron, "Favorite," 7"
long with handle $25.00
Toy meat grinder, cast iron, "Pony,"
clamps to table, 5" high .... $20.00 to $25.00
Toy rolling pin, handmade walnut $15.00
Toy waffle iron, cast iron, "Stover
Jr.," 4" diameter $25.00
Toy baking set, "Fire King" glass,
bowls, measuring cup, rolling
pin (wood), and pastry board, 1940s $35.00
Toy kitchen set, white-enameled tin,
"Playhouse No. 40," range, sink,
icebox and Hoosier-type cabinet $120.00

NOTE: How the word "playhouse" brings back memories! Back in the 1940s, when our family lived on a farm in Toledo, Ohio, my ingenious father built my brother and me a wonderful playhouse . . . complete with pitched roof and shingles, front porch with columns, two or three working sash windows and a door that fitted and swung on hinges. Sometimes I think the whole thing was a dream: my avid picture-taking family never took a single picture of our playhouse, and how sorry I am.

Toy "Hoosier" cabinet, green and
white painted wood, zinc counter,
35" high, marvelous looking $295.00
Toy cabinet, metal with white and red
paint, 2 parts: 10" high x 10½" x
17" table plus cabinet top, 10½"
high x 4" deep, with two doors $50.00
Toy kitchen appliances, metal, working
doors, "Marx" stove, refrigerator,
sink with cupboard underneath,
dishwasher "Beauty Maid" $250.00
Toy kitchen, of the sort known as a
"Nurenberg Kitchen," early 19th
century, grain-painted wood
with black and white painted "tile"
floor, complete with built-in
goose cage under one counter,
coffee mill, washtub, coal scuttle
with shovel, copper kettle, graters,
colander, cupboard, blue & white
china, ceramic molds, pots and
pans, potato mashers, 2½" long
jagger, copper pots, wooden cutting
board, spoons, whisks, ladles,
basins, table with drawer. This
is simply marvelous, and was
deaccessioned from Yesteryears
Museum, Sandwich, Massachusetts,
and was for sale at a 1982 antique
show in Connecticut for $5500.00

NOTE: Others of these "Nurenberg Kitchens" are occasionally for sale. They are truly extraordinary toys, perfect dollhouse rooms, and are always filled with great varieties of utensils and implements . . . sometimes braided rugs, chairs, coffee

roasters, stoves, food choppers in addition to what's listed above. Others of these kitchens are wonderfully made of stamped and painted tin, featuring a range and chimney along the back wall, sometimes a working water pump and sink. They vary in width from approximately 12" up to 24" or so, and most are between 7" and 14" deep.

Windup toy, "Cheery Cook," celluloid,
in box $25.00

HOUSEHOLD CHORES
WASHING, IRONING & CLEANING TOOLS

Almost every collector of cookery tools I know also has a few washboards or carpet beaters or clothespins too. Years ago, my mother, in an effort to fall in with my desire to stop at the rather grungier "antique" stores, when we were out on the road antiquing, tried to start a collection of carpet beaters. She never got very far, but the few she has are attractive. I think I might go for a clothespin collection — patented, handmade and Shaker manufacture — if I had the money and time. I've seen clothespins for $20 and $30 each! You'd have to be mighty conscious of what you hung up with such pins . . . if you used them.

For the next edition, I will add many pictures in this section, so I'd love to hear from specialized collectors.

The section following this one will be the **toys** connected to household chores, and "Related Collectibles."

Broom, wood splinters, early 19th
    century $45.00
Broomstick holder, cast iron with 3 slots $35.00
Carpet or rug beater, wire, green wood
    handle, "Bat Wing," wire almost
    pretzel shaped, Johnson Novelty,
    Danville, PA, pat'd October 4, 1927 ...... $12.00 to $17.00
Carpet beater, wire, turned wood
    handle, "Whisk" like twist to
    wires, 30" long $12.50
Carpet beater, wire, turned wood
    handle, long twisted 4-wire shaft
    opening into bulbous onion
    shape, 31" long $15.00
Carpet beater, wicker, 33" long $20.00
Carpet beater, wicker, intricate "knot"
    design, 35" long $13.00
Carpet beater, twisted wire, wood handle $9.00
Carpet beater, wicker, small $22.00

NOTE: A brand new wicker beater, about 25"long, might easily be mistaken for old.

Figure XX-1. **Electric Iron.** General Electric's first electric iron, produced in 1904, a year before their first electric toaster! Picture courtesy of General Electric.

Carpet beater, twisted wire, wood handle $9.00
Carpet beater, wire, fancy loopings $20.00
Carpet sweeper, "Clipper Tidy Sweep" $14.00
Carpet sweeper, Bissell "Silver Streak" $14.00
Carpet sweeper, oak, "Bissell" from 1910 .... $25.00
Carpet sweeper, oak and cast iron,
    original paper label $24.00
Charcoal iron, "Peerless," John W.
    Lufkin, Boston, 11" long x 10" high $65.00
Clothes plunger, tin and wood, brass
    plate states "Little's Champion
    Washer, 1891" $45.00
Clothes plunger/dasher/agitator,
    wood with X frame and vertical
    handle, 18" long, 8" x 8" X dasher $35.00
Clothes plunger/dasher, tin cone with
    wood broomstick handle, star
    stamped on tin $5.00
Clothes plunger, "Little Champion
    Washer," dates 1897 .... $40.00
Clothes plunger/agitator, tin funnel
    with wood handle, marked "Rapid
    Washer, made by C.T. Childers,
    Galesburg, Illinois," 28" long $10.00

See also: Wash stick and washers.

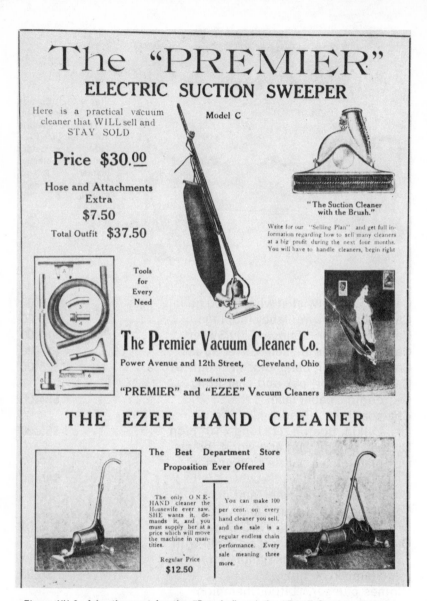

Figure XX-2. **Advertisement for the "Premier" and the "Ezee" Suction Cleaners.** February 1912, **"The House Furnishings Review."**

Clothes sprinkler bottle, moldblown
glass, extreme bulbous shape $12.00
Clothes sprinkler bottle, blue and
white cat $12.50

Clothes sprinkler bottle, girl with
blonde hair, white blouse and
green pants $10.00
Clothes sprinkler bottle, sad iron shape $10.00
Clothes sprinkler bottle, Chinese
man, blue and white $10.00
Clothespin bag, embroidered cotton $6.00
Clothespin bag, embroidered and
appliqued linen, "Saddlebag" style $8.00
Clothespins, handcarved wood, 3 of
Shaker manufacture $65.00
Clothespins, original package of wood
and metal, mfd. in West Paris, Maine $8.00
Crumb sweeper, celluloid, "Fuller
Brush Co." $15.00
Dust bellows, all wood, cylindrical
shape, "Universal Dust-Bellows,"
Aug. Kraushaar's U.S. Trade Mark
No. 39301, eagle and shield,
flowers and scrolls, 23" long $60.00
Dust mop container, tin, round, "Ward's" $3.00
Duster, painted tin, "Black Flag", plunger $7.00
Dusting brush, horsehair with wood
handle, Shaker, 9" long $70.00
Dusting brush, white and black
horsehair, wood with leather
hanging strap, "No. 14," 14½"
long, Shaker? $10.00
Dusting brush, variegated wood
handle, 20" long, Shaker $40.00
Dustpan, tin, Shaker style with
distinctive tubular handle, 8"
wide, pan quite deep $140.00
Dustpan, japanned (asphaltum) tin, Shaker $45.00
Dustpan, tin, adv'g "S.H. Curtis &
Sons Hardware, Waverly, Iowa" $15.00
Electric iron, nickel plated, with trivet,
"Universal Landers, Frary &
Clark, #E-909," 106/114 volts, 7" long $28.00
Electric iron, "Hotpoint Model R,"
Edison Electric Appliance
Company, pat'd October 25, 1910,
June 11, 1918, May 26, 1925, 6½" long $12.00

Figure XX-3. **Lacework Dolly.** Turned wood. A small hand washing machine, in a way. Used for very dainty things like handkerchiefs, which were put inside with soapy water and gently agitated with dasher. 11" high x 4½" diameter. Early 19th century. Formerly in the Keillor Collection. Value: $100-$150.

Fan, electric, cast iron base with brass blades and guard wires, "Westinghouse" $35.00

Fly swatter, fan-shaped splints, long handle, Shaker $65.00

Ironing board, wooden, 30" long $10.00

Ironing board, wooden, pat'd September 20, 1921, 8" wide x 30" long, adjustable and folds quite flat $12.00

Lamp funnel, copper, embossed "Coleman Lamp & Stove Co.," with paper label for "Steve's Furniture" $30.00

Lamp funnel, tin, "Coleman" $2.00

Pleater, tin, "The Simplicity," in original box with instructions $6.00

Polishing iron, cast iron, "M. Cook #1," Pat'd December 5, 1846, oval 2½" x 5¼" $52.00

Sad iron, "Mrs. Potts #3," 1870-71, detachable wood handle $20.00

Sad iron, cast iron, case type $18.00

Sad irons, "Enterprise," 3 irons and one handle $35.00

Sad irons, "A.C. Williams Co., Ravenna, Ohio," #1, #2, #3, one handle, 3 base irons $32.00

Sad iron, nickel plated, small size
"Asbestos," 4¾" long,
detachable cover and handle, just
under 2 pounds $35.00
Sleeve iron, "Grand Union Tea Co." $30.00
Soap grater, "Super" $1.00
Soap saver, tin frame, twisted wire
handle with hanging loop, wire
mesh container, 3½" x 2½" with
7" handle $15.00
Soap saver, wire mesh with wood handle $5.00

See also under earlier category: CLEAN, SCRUB, WASH, Etc.

Soap shaver, tin, "Fels Naptha" .... $3.75-$7.00
Trivet for iron, cast iron, "E" for
"Enterprise" $8.00
Trivets, various designs of cast iron, each $12.00
Trivet, cast iron, double point, "I
Want U" with depiction of iron
in center, for the Strauss Gas Iron,
Philadelphia, PA $30.00
Vacuum cleaner, "Old Victor" $100.00
Vacuum cleaner, "Winchester" $65.00
Vacuum cleaner, tin pump type with
wood handles, painted dark green
with "National Eagle" and shield
in gold, 1911 with manual .... $22.00 to $65.00
Wash stick, 2 prong, 32" long $25.00
Wash stick, 36" long $8.00
Wash stick, handcarved wood,
pivoting handle grip, early 19th to
mid-19th and nice wear $80.00
Wash stick, 38" long, charred at one end $18.00
Washboard, wood frame with stenciled
scene of Pilgrims, brass scrubber,
"National," 24" high x 12½" wide .... $12.00 to $16.00
Washboard, wood frame, brass
scrubber with tin soap saver at top $18.00
Washboard, wood frame, tin scrubber
and soap saver $12.00
Washboard, wood frame and zinc
scrubber, "The Zinc King" $7.00
Washboard, wood frame, "Shapleigh's" $5.00

Washboard, wood frame, partly
   obliterated lettering reads
   "Du—Handi" $8.00
Washboard, all wood, "Columbus," large $15.00
Washboard, all glass, "Midget-Washer,"
   8½" x 6", original label $7.00
Washboard, "Little Monarch," 16" x 7" $12.00
Washboard, wood frame, brass
   scrubber, 24½" x 12" $12.00
Washboard, wood frame with glass
   scrubber, soap saver, 23" x 12" $5.00
Washboard, wood frame, glass
   scrubber, 18" x 8¼" $3.75
Washboard, wood frame, zinc scrubber $3.00
Washboard, wood frame, wood frame
   with stencil of tree stump, glass
   scrubber, 18" x 8¼" $16.00
Washboard, wood frame, glass
   scrubber, "Atlantic No. 15," $12.00
Washboard, wood frame, blue graniteware $45.00
Washboard, wood frame, "Junior," tin
   scrubber and soap saver $10.00
Washboard, all wood, handcarved,
   early 19th century, recess at top
   for soap, quite handsome and
   beautiful patina $300.00
Washboard, wood frame stenciled
   with picture of the Capitol
   building, zinc (?) scrubber, "Capitol" $12.00
Washboard, all wood (for the War
   Effort metal drive), 18" x 12", 1940s $14.00
Washboard, wood frame, tin scrubber
   and soap holder, "Bangor" $10.00
Washboard, dovetailed wood frame,
   wood scrubber and soap holder,
   20½" x 12" $28.00
Washboard, "Scanti Handi" $6.00
Washboard, wood frame with brass
   scrubber, "Best Made" $15.00
Washboard, wood frame, tin, "sunrise" $10.00
Washboard, wood frame, tin scrubber,
   tin soap saver, "National Knickerbocker" $10.00
Washboard, wood frame with brass
   scrubber, "Standard Family" $7.00

Washer, wood box with iron crank,
    box on 4 legs, slide-out tub rack
    has 2 legs to rest on ground,
    "Columbia Hand Washer," pat'd
    December 3, 1895, 14" high x 12" x 10" $210.00
Washer, "Sunny Susie," worn brown paint $20.00
Washer, copper bottom tub with wringer $110.00
Washing machine, portable electric,
    aluminum body with iron handles,
    clip-on wringer, tub 14½" diameter
    x 10½" high, wringer 9½" x 3 7/8" $65.00
Washing machine, copper with wood
    dasher and copper cone $22.00
Washing machine, tin tub, wood
    dasher, iron crank, 1883 .... $145.00
Washing machine pamphlet, "Western
    Electric," 1908 .... $4.00
Washtub, 12-stave wood, 11½" diameter
    x 5" deep $45.00
Whisk broom, "Mammy," 4½" long .... $11.00 to $20.00

HOUSEHOLD TOYS, MINIATURES & SALESMAN'S SAMPLES

Please read the introduction to the toys and miniatures of cooking. The same holds true here, although there is a genuine patent model listed here. These toys, probably more than those for cooking, certainly played their part, over a hundred year period, in creating thousands of little practiced housewives, many of whom were undoubtedly of great help to their mothers.

Dollhouse set, cast iron, "Arcade,"
    step ladder, ironing board, carpet
    sweeper $30.00
Dollhouse vacuum cleaner $3.00
Dollhouse wringer washer $10.00
Patent model wash boiler, tin, patent
    model #80651, 1868, with official
    tag, nicely made $150.00
Salesman's sample wash tub, wood
    with wire rings, wringer bolted
    on, "Horse Shoe Brand,"
    "Warranted for Family Use," $125.00
Salesman's sample bed warmer,
    copper pan with brass ring and
    wood handle, 9" long $85.00
Salesman's sample washing machine
    wringer $75.00
Toy carpet sweeper, oak, "Bissell's
    Little Daisy," 1910 .... $25.00
Toy electric iron, "Wolverine No. 25A" $12.00
Toy iron, tin with plastic handle,
    "Wolverine," Booneville, Arkansas,
    7" long $8.00
Toy laundry basket, wicker, 1940s $8.00
Toy ironing board, wood, 17" high
    x 24" long $25.00
Toy sad iron, detachable wood handle .... $35.00 to $45.00
Toy sad iron, cast iron, cross rib grip,
    3" long $18.00
Toy sad iron, "Asbestos Sad Iron,"
    Dated May 23, 1900 .... $37.50
Toy sad iron, "Massingil" $20.00
Toy sad iron, "Asbestos," 4" long, 2 parts $18.00
Toy trivet, cast iron, 1884, 3" long $32.00

SUNNY MONDAY WASHING SET

For the little girl who loves to wash and keep her dollies' clothes neat and clean. This is a complete laundry outfit, all put up in an attractive box. There is a wash tub to wash dollies' clothes in and a washing board and a wringer. There is a clothes line for drying the washing, and clothes pins for hanging them up with. After the clothes are dry they may be ironed on the ironing board with the little iron provided in the set. Several well-known kinds of soap, washing powder, borax, and starch are included. Little girls who love to wash when mamma does will certainly enjoy this outfit.

Given for two new yearly subscriptions to LITTLE FOLKS. Cash price $1.00. Sent postpaid.

Figure XXI-1. **Advertisement for Toy Washing Set.** About 15 washing tools, plus a number of clothespins. Picture from **Little Folks** magazine for children, c. 1916. Collection of Mary Mac Franklin.

Toy washboard, tin with wood frame,
"Wolverine," 7" x 3½" $12.00
Toy washboard, "Daisy," 15" x 7" $15.00
Toy washboard, all wood $5.00
Toy washboard, wood and zinc, 1930s .... $12.00 to $18.00
Toy washboard, all glass, "Midget
Washer," 6" x 8½" $15.00
Toy washing set, washboard, metal
tub, cranked wringer, clothespins
and clothesline, "Wolverine",
1920s to 1930s $24.00
Toy washtub and washboard, tin, tub
8½" diameter $12.00
Toy wringer, folding tub rack, 16" high
x 15" long $150.00
Toy wringer, white painted wood with
wire handle, 3¾" wide x 5¼" long $12.00
Toy wringer, natural wood finish, 4¾"
x 6¼" $12.00
Toy wringer, wood, rubber and iron,
"Little Princess," mfd. by Anchor $45.00
Toy wringer, wood, rubber and iron,
"Super Anchor Brand No. 5
Domestic," in original box $50.00

HOUSEHOLD: RELATED THINGS

Candy container, glass, electric iron $20.00
Candy container, glass, carpet sweeper $125.00
Measuring tape, figural sewing
     machine, windup, 1880s $65.00
Measuring tape, figural Hoover vacuum,
     plastic, spring $45.00
Measuring tape, figural sad iron $125.00
Salt and pepper, Westinghouse
     washer & dryer $10.00

NOTE: As you know by now, I've got a great interest in looking around for things of contemporary manufacture that relate to the antiques, etc., in this book. At the grocery store in April, I bought a super pencil sharpener, made in the shape of a sad iron, 2¾" long x 2" high. It is described on the blister pack as "antique-finished zinc-alloy" [which means a coppery bronze tone], was made in Hong Kong and is distributed by Super Market Service Corp., 2 Paragon Drive, Montvale, NJ 07645. It is beautifully made, comes apart for emptying, and has moving parts besides. Also available are a platform scale from 1876, a coffee grinder from 1874 and various non-kitcheny things. And only $1.19 at this writing! I'd say these are definitely collectibles of the future.

PAPER STUFF

TRADE CATALOGS

A little over 20 years ago, a bookseller in Middleboro, Massachusetts — Lawrence B. Romaine — shared the fruits of a quarter century of pleasure and dedication with the public. R.R. Bowker Company published his 422 page **A Guide to American Trade Catalogs, 1744-1900.** Over 10,000 catalogs are listed, beginning with Benjamin Franklin's two — dated 1744 — one for stoves and one for a library of books for sale. In the introduction to his wonderful pace-setting book, Romaine says that he hopes a movement to locate trade catalogs "may eventually sweep the country. This means that at long last these lowly give-aways will be acknowledged as historical records from coast to coast." Apparently something of the sort did sweep the country, because it is terribly difficult now to find catalogs in certain subject areas, including kitchen and cookery wares.

There are several outstanding dealers specializing in old trade catalogs, Two of them — Robert C. Bailey of Hillcrest Books and Edgar Heyl — have been sending out catalogs from which I've bought for over 12 years. Like many of the catalog dealers, they are mail order only — see the listing on the next page.

Bailey has been in business since late 1959. Apparently he and Romaine were on the same wavelength. In a listing sent out not long ago by Mr. Bailey, he writes "Locating and purchasing desirable old catalogs for resale is becoming more and more difficult as the public becomes more aware that old catalogs are valuable items of Americana, the best tools available for industry research as well as being collector's items. Not only are we being asked much higher prices for what is available, but the available supply is apparently diminishing." Adding to this demand but at the same time bringing unexplored caches out of hiding are members of two national organizations. The Ephemera Society of America, based in Bennington, Vermont, and P.A.C.(Paper and Advertising Collectors) in Pennsylvania have collectively attracted over 2500 members. This formalized collecting field has encouraged many new dealers in paper Americana too, but we must face the discouraging reality: attics, barns and basements can only disgorge so many more 19th and early 20th century paper collectibles before being emptied.

If you wish to receive a dealer's periodic list, expect to buy regularly or to pay something for the privilege of being on their mailing lists. These detailed bibliographic listings are expensive to compile and mail, and become a fine record worth a good deal of money. When you write a dealer for information, or to tell them your wants, **do not forget to enclose a self-addressed stamped envelope.** You would be surprised how many people don't — whether they're writing for advice, information, offering something for sale, or offering to buy. Those of us on the receiving end cannot afford to respond — even 10 letters a week amounts to $2.00 . . . and postage rates go up.

SOURCES OF OLD CATALOGS

I have tried to find out where dealers who specialize in trade catalogs, or who put out special lists from time to time, are lurking about around the country. Without doubt, I've missed some, and would love to know about more for the next edition. Will you please drop me a line if you know of dealers other than the ones listed here?

Edgar Heyl*
11 W. Chase Street
Baltimore, MD 21201

Harold R. Nestler, Inc.
13 Pennington Avenue
Waldwick, NJ 07463

Hillcrest Books*
Route 2, Box 162
Spring City, TN 37381

Fortunate Finds Bookstore
Mildred E. Santille
16 W. Natick Road
Warwick, RI 02886

Francis Patrick Antiques
P.O. Box 833
Gaithersburg, MD 20760

Peter L. Masi — Books
P.O. Box B
Montague, MA 01351

*Trade catalogs exclusively

THE CATALOGS THEMSELVES

A great variety is available. Sizes range from folded broadsides and small folders to large, hardbound catalogs of several hundred pages. All the items listed below are illustrated catalogs — some of them have hundreds of linecuts and engravings. I am especially interested in early catalogs, and like the first editions from some of the more renowned companies, but this is because of a practical reason. I can date objects in my study collection. However, I believe that any and every edition is worth having. They all tell a story, and all are irreplaceable. Early catalogs, just like the ones today, caution the customer (whether he be a prospective salesman, retailer or customer) that the latest catalog supersedes all others. Some old catalogs even advise that all previous editions be discarded to avoid confusion.

New catalogs — which arrive in the mail every week or month — may not seem like collector's items as they pile up on the breakfast table. But think of them 10 or 20 years from today — filed away for your consultation as a collector! My mother began saving certain mail order catalogs about 15 years ago; they really are like money in the bank. I started saving housewares and kitchen utensil catalogs when my first kitchen book went to the printer. Now I've got half a file drawer full of them, and those from 1972 and 1973 have the multiple fascination of all "dated" things.

Below are a number of catalogs and flyers from before 1940. For the most part the condition is good or better. This means intact, unmarked (except with a contemporary price change noted by a purchaser), and sound (little chipping, crumbling or disintegrating). But as these catalogs get even more scarce, I buy them in fair, even poor condition, if I can get a good photocopy or photo from the pages.

I have divided them up into several categories — including **Churns & Creamery Supplies, Gadgets** (things with working parts), **Implements** (things like cake turners and slotted spoons), **Utensils** (pots, pans, hollow wares, bins and tins), and some combinations.

Bakers & Confectioners
H. Heug & Co., "Book of Designs for
Bakers and Confectioners." 1896.
48 pages with illustrations of
fantastical decorations for cakes
and candies $28.00
Sethness Co., "The Sethness Candy
Maker." 1925. Large catalog of
candy-making equipment, mostly
commercial .... $18.00 to $25.00
Wood & Sellick, "Confectioners
Machinery & Utensils." 1915.
183 pages including photographs $25.00

Camp Cooking
David T. Abercrombie, "Complete
Outfit for Campers, Hunters,
Surveyors, Prospectors." 1908.
Large catalog with many things
besides cookstoves and utensils .... $30.00 to $40.00
Sterno Corporation. 1930. Small catalog .... $6.00 to $7.00

Churns & Creamery Supplies
Diamond Balance Churn Company.
1891. Folder with a few simple
engravings .... $5.00 to $7.00
A. H. Reed, "Creamery Supplies."
1889. 38 pages $20.00

Furniture
Acme Kitchen Furniture Company.
1910. 20 pages of oak cupboards,
safes, tables, etc. .... $12.00 to $25.00

Gadgets
The Acme Pea Sheller Company, c.
1895. Folder .... $3.00 to $7.00
The American Machine Company, c.
1890. 100 page catalog with
"Perfection" meat chopper,
"American" cake mixer, "Gem"
cake pans, etc., plus many recipes ...... $10.00 to $15.00
Enterprise Manufacturing Company of
Pennsylvania and Iron Founders.
1881. 32 page catalog .... $22.00 to $30.00

"The Griswold Erie Cook Book." c.
1890. 32 pages, with illustrations,
of recipes ". . . made from left-
overs . . . made with the Griswold
Erie Food Cutter." .... $8.00 to $12.00
Hibbard, Spencer, Bartlett &
Company. 1884. Catalog of apple
parers, slicers, choppers, etc. .... $15.00 to $25.00
C. S. Osborne & Company, c. 1890.
Catalog .... $15.00 to $20.00
F. W. Seastrand, c. 1913. Small
catalog for traveling salesmen,
with all sorts of gadgets .... $8.00 to $12.00
F. A. Walker & Company. 1886. 4 page
folder picturing many gadgets of
American and foreign manufacture .... $7.00 to $10.00
F. A. Walker. 1890s. Flyer for
Vienna Cake Mold .... $3.00 to $5.00
F. A. Walker. 1890s. Flyer for Russian
Coffee Pot .... $3.00 to $5.00
F. A. Walker. 1890s. Flyer for French
Steam Coffee Pot .... $3.00 to $5.00
X-Ray Raisin Seeder, c. 1895. Flyer,
in full color .... $5.00 to $6.00

Gadgets & Electric Appliances
Landers, Frary & Clark. 1920s. 32 page
catalog-booklet with "Universal"
electric appliances and hand-
operated gadgets .... $12.00 to $17.00

Ice Tools
Gifford & Wood Co. 1911. 48 pages of
picks, tongs, scales plus
commercial machinery such as
conveyors $40.00

Implements
Lewis Dean Company. 1875. 8 pages
of wire goods $15.00
Gilbert & Bennett Manufacturing Co.
1887. Small catalog of wire goods,
sieves, etc. .... $12.00 to $22.00
Sargent Co. 1902. "Gem Chopper." 92 pages $15.00

The Washburn Company, "Androck
    Balanced Kitchenware." 1936.
    56 page catalog .... $17.00 to $22.00

Institutional Cookery
"Food & Small Equipment for Bakers,
    Hotels, Camps, Restaurants,
    Institutions." 1932. 181 pages
    with illus. $15.00

Refrigerators & Ice Boxes
Alaska Oak refrigerator. Catalog $22.00
Frigidaire Corporation (subsidiary of
    General Motors). 1927. Booklet .... $3.00 to $6.00
Kelvinator Corporation, "Kelvinator
    Refrigerates without Ice."
    Undated (c. 1920). 14 pages with illus. $8.00
Lockwood & Hall, "Refrigerators,
    Blacking Cases & Commodes."
    1885. 40 page catalog with
    many illus. $20.00
G. M. Shirk Manufacturing Company,
    "North Star Refrigerators." 1893.
    48 pages of oak ice boxes .... $10.00 to $20.00

Soda Fountains
Benedict Silver. 1932. Catalog of
    many soda fountain supplies $8.50
The Liquid Carbonic Company, "Soda
    Fountain Specialties & Supplies."
    1915. 96 pages of the whole
    shebang: from ice cream tables
    and chairs to pumps and cabinets $50.00

Stoves, Etc.
Bramhall Deane Company. 1906. 40
    page catalog .... $18.00 to $22.00
Broomell, Schmidt & Co., "The
    Heatencook Range." 1899. 32
    page catalog $15.00
The William Campbell Company, "The
    Rapid Fireless Cooker." 1915.
    64 page booklet .... $7.00 to $8.00

Excelsior Stove & Manufacturing
Company. 1926-27. Large catalog
of stoves .... $18.00 to $25.00
Fuller & Warren Company, "The
Matchless Oak." 1909. Folder .... $5.00 to $8.00
General Electric, "The Matchless
Kitchen." 1917. 35 pages with
photographs ... electric kitchens $8.00
H. E. Hessler Company, "The Palace
Andes Range." c. 1910. Folder .... $6.00 to $8.00

Utensils
The Aluminum Cooking Utensil
Company, "Wear-Ever." 1903.
Booklet .... $8.00 to $10.00
—. 1915. 32 page catalog of "Wear-
Ever" goods .... $10.00 to $15.00
Buehler, Bonbright & Company. 1872.
12 pages of tinware, enameled
iron wares, waffle irons, etc. .... $30.00 to $35.00
Cleveland Metal Products. 1920. Small
catalog of aluminum products .... $6.00 to $8.00
Cordley & Hayes, "Indurated Fibre
Ware." c. 1886. 48 pages of wares .... $8.00 to $12.00
Crandell & Godley Manufacturing
Company, c. 1886. 260 page
catalog of wares for commercial
and home kitchens .... $50.00 to $65.00
J. B. Foote Foundry Company. 1906.
32 page catalog for traveling salesmen .... $7.00 to $12.00
Gage & Company. 1888. 16 page
catalog of bowls, woodenwares .... $15.00 to $20.00
Geuder, Paeschke & Frey Company,
"Cream City Ware." 1926. 256
page catalog, including some
color pictures, of enameled
wares, copper and tin wares .... $35.00 to $60.00
Janney, Semple & Company. 1887.
Catalog of enameled wares, iron
wares, gadgets .... $30.00 to $45.00
Lalance & Grosjean Manufacturing
Co. 1890. 360 page catalog,
flexible cloth cover, full of utensils ...... $40.00 to $60.00

Matthai-Ingram & Company, c. 1890.
277 pages of all types of sheet
metal wares, great illus. .... $40.00 to $60.00
C. B. Porter Company. 1920s. 82 page
catalog of tinwares, enameled
tin, water coolers, bread bins, etc. .... $25.00 to $40.00
St. Louis Stamping Company. 1890.
316 page catalog of enameled
wares, tinwares, wire goods, etc. .... $40.00 to $65.00

Utensils, Gadgets & Implements Combined
Butler Brothers. December 1918.
General merchandise along with
lots of kitchen things .... $45.00 to $60.00
Butler Brothers. 1922. 422 pages of
general merchandise with lots of
kitchen things .... $40.00 to $55.00
Haslet, Flanagen & Company, c. 1886.
100 page catalog of tinware,
enameled tin, apple corers, etc. .... $25.00 to $50.00
Edward Katzinger Company. 1940. 50
page catalog of "A & J," "Geneva
Forge" cutlery, "Ovenex," "Ekco"
and "Katzinger" implements .... $20.00 to $35.00
Ketcham Company. 1888. 250 pages
of tinware, lamps and lanterns,
coffee mills, ice cream freezers
and much more $65.00
F. A. Walker & Company. 1870s. Any
of these wonderful, huge catalogs,
depicting all kinds of imported
and domestic tinwares, brass and
copper items, wooden wares,
etc., would command at least
$75.00 and probably more, at
least for those with 100 pages
or more .... $75.00 to $110.00

NOTE: Look for other general merchandise catalogs [like the
Butler Brothers listed here] which have sections on kitchen
wares. Old Sears Roebuck, Montgomery Ward, Larkin Company, Wanamaker, Stores, Siegel Cooper Company catalogs are
good bets. Some catalog dealers offer these humongous
catalogs "broken up" into sections so that collectors can
choose their specialty at an affordable price!

Housewares

The Marietta Manufacturing Co., "The
New Crescent Electric Fans."
1899. 32 pages with many illus. $15.00
The "1900" Washer Company, "The
'1900' Gravity Washer." No date,
but turn-of-century. 12 pages $8.00

COOKBOOKS

The first "receipt" books were handwritten, laborious copyings-out of favorite tasty ways to fix food, passed on from generation to generation; flour dusted, butter spotted, patted and mended and wiped off. The treasured recipes within are still treasures — for collectors and cooks alike. Many collectors start with a few modern cookbooks, and soon find themselves searching for old ones. Among the most popular, which have been neglected until recently, are the giveaway cookbooks that were prepared by the home economists employed by food and appliance companies. Many of these can still be found for under $3.00 — particularly at garage sales and church bazaars.

American housewives used English cookbooks for many years. Then American editions of the same books were published, although they pre-date the country's independence. Finally, purely American cookbooks were written. These are very valuable to collectors now, even in rather poor condition. Original owners had a very intimate and practical relationship with their precious few cookbooks, and today the rules that govern most of the book-collecting world are relaxed for the special field of cookbooks. Among early ones are **The Frugal Housewife; or, Complete Woman Cook** by Susanna Carter, published in Philadelphia in 1796; and Amelia Simmons' **American Cookery, or the Art of Dressing Viands, Fish, Poultry and Vegetables, and the Best Modes of Making Puff-Pastes, Pies, Tarts, Puddings, Custards and Preserves, and All Kinds of Cakes, from the Imperial Plumb to Plain Cake — Adapted to This Country and All Grades of Life,** published in Hartford, Connecticut, also in 1796. Both books, in their titles, offer a capsule study of social history of the time; many old cookbooks do, and are often hilariously sub-titled. Such books, when found in good condition, bring a lot of money. The Simmons, for example, was sold at an auction in 1977 for an astounding $3,000.00!

America was the home of Fannie Farmer, who is probably the most well-known name in cookery, even today. All of her cookbooks are collectible, to some degree. I once knew a mynah bird, that belonged to a charming couple who ran a shop in New York City that specialized in old cookbooks, who had in his vocabulary the name "Fanny Farmer," plus various other words like "pumpernickel bread" and his own name, "Cookie." I was crazy about that bird, and loved to drop in the shop just to hear him. One of his most charming tricks, which he taught himself, was humming in a bemused way. Apparently he picked the habit up from the owners, who — when the shop wasn't open — would hum and sing to themselves while working on the stock.

One more rarity to look for: the famous **Joy of Cooking** by Irma Rombauer. The first edition was privately printed in 1931 by the A.C. Clayton Printing Company in St. Louis. Quick! Go check your shelves . . . you may have that very edition.

Ames, Mary Ellis, ed. **Balanced Recipes**, Minneapolis. Pillsbury Flour Mills, 1933. This spiralbound book has aluminum covers! $38.00

Astor, Mrs. Jane. **The New York Cook-Book, Being the Art of Cooking in a Palatable, Digestable and Economical Manner,** New York: 1880 .... $30.00

Atlas Book of Recipes and Helpful Information on Home Canning & Preserving, Wheeling, WV: Hazel-Atlas Glass Co., 1943. Giveaway booklet $5.00

Baker's Chocolate, 1925. 60 pages with color $12.00

Barrows, Anna. **Eggs: Facts and Fancies about Them,** Boston: D. Lathrop, 1890 .... $20.00

Beecher, Catharine E. and Harriet Beecher Stowe, **The American Woman's Home: or, Principles of Domestic Science. . .,** New York: 1869 .... $55.00

Bradley, A. **For Luncheon and Supper Guests,** Boston: 1922. Recipes and menus $6.00

Canova Peanut Butter. **Peanut Butter 28 Ways** $6.00

Collingwood, Francis and John Wollams. **The Universal Cook and City and Country Housekeeper,** London: 1801 .... $75.00 to $100.00

Cornelius, Mrs. (Mary Hooker). **The Young Housekeeper's Friend; or a Guide to Domestic Economy and Comfort, Boston:** 1846 .... $75.00

—. Same, but published in Boston: 1865 .... $30.00

Detroit Jewel Stove, 32 pages,
operating instructions and recipes $9.00
D-Zerta cookbook, 1930, 4 pages $4.00
Dr. Price's Baking Powder, 1915 .... $8.00
Experienced American Housekeeper,
or, Domestic Cookery: Formed
on the Principles of Economy,
for the Use of Private Families,
New York: 1823 .... $115.00
Fairbanks Cook Book of Tested
Recipes, Fairbanks, AL: Ladies of
of the Presbyterian Church, 1913.
132 pages $40.00
Farmer, Fannie Merritt. **A New Book**
of Cookery, Boston: 1912. First edition $20.00
Farrar, S. D. **The Homekeeper:**
Containing Numerous Recipes for
Cooking and Preparing Food in a
Manner Most Conducive to Health,
Boston; 1872 .... $35.00
French's Mustard, 1921 Junior edition $6.00
Frigidaire, 1926, 16 page recipes $5.00
Gail Borden Eagle Brand, 208 recipes $8.00
Gebhardt's Deviled Dainties, 1924 .... $6.00
Gebhardt's Mexican Cooking, chili
powder booklet, 44 pages, 1930 .... $6.00
Gem Chopper Cook Book, New York: 1902 .... $8.00
Gerber Baby Food, 1930 .... $8.00
Gillette American Cookbook, 1889.
521 pages $10.00
Harland, Marion. **The Comfort of Cooking**
and Heating by Gas, New York:
1898. This has display ads for gas
stoves at the back $28.00
Harland, Marion **Dinner Year-Book,**
New York: 1878. 713 pages with
menus and recipes for the entire year $40.00
Hearn, Lafcadio. **La Cuisine Creole,** 1885 .... $850.00

**NOTE: The price of the above has much to do with its famous
author, who was noted for his exotic taste. He in fact moved to
Japan five years after this book was published, where he wrote a
number of books on that country.**

**The Housekeeper's Book . . . with . . .
Receipts . . . for the Use of American
Housekeepers,** Philadelphia: 1837.
First American edition. 217 pages $55.00
**House-Keepers Cook Book, Containing
a Great Variety of Unknown and
Valuable Receipts,** Philadelphia:
1838 .... $250.00 to $275.00
**House-Keeper's Guide and Indian
Doctor: Containing the Very Best
Directions for Making All
Kinds of Ice Creams, Preserves,
Jellies . . . ,** New York: 1855 .... $50.00
How Famous Chefs Use Marshmallows,
Campfire Co.: 1930 .... $8.00
**How the Shakers Cook and the Noted
Cooks of the Country,** NYC: A.J.
White, 1889. This is a funny
combo of Shaker recipes and
nostrums, almanac information,
plus non-Shaker famous chefs . . .
"as will be seen by the amounts
paid these cooks . . . their incomes
exceed those of Senators of the
United States. And the cooks get
'tips' besides. Senators are
supposed not to get 'tips'." Politics
and food $28.00
How to Be Happy, Use Spry, 48 pages $6.00
Jack Benny Jell-O Recipe Book $10.00
Jarrin, G. A. **The Italian Confectionery,
or Complete Economy of Desserts . . . ,**
London: 1820 .... $165.00
Jell-O recipe books, illustrated with
the Jell-O girl, woman with serving
tray, party people, 2 pix by Norman
Rockwell, 1922 to 1935, various
prices from .... $4.00 to $15.00
Johnson, Helen Louise. **The Enterprising
Housekeeper,** 1898 .... $15.00 to $25.00
Judson, Helena. **The Butterick Cook
Book,** NY: 1911. 359 pages, with
recipes to use with fireless cookers $20.00
Karo Syrup New Suggestions $4.00

Knox, Mrs. **Food Economy.** 30 pages $8.00
Knox Gelatine. 1936. 52 pages $8.00
Liebeg Company's Practical Cookery
    Book, London: 1893 .... $10.00
Lincoln, Mrs. D. A. **Frozen Dainties,**
    Nashua, NH: The White Mountain
    Freezer Co., 1899 .... $3.50
Lincoln, Mrs. D. A. **Boston Cook Book,**
    What to Do and What Not to Do in
    Cooking, Boston: 1883 .... $70.00
—. Same, published in 1894. 536 pages $25.00
Lorain Cooking, St. Louis: American
    Stove Co., 1926. Cooking with
    American's Lorain Stoves $15.00
Marvin. **Bon Appetit. The St. Louis**
    Cook Book, 1947 .... $5.00
Minute Tapioca, 1926. 16 pages $6.00
Morris, H. **Portrait of a Chef. The Life**
    of Alexis Soyer, Cambridge: 1938 .... $8.00
New Art of Buying, Preserving and
    Preparing Foods. Cleveland, OH: General
    Electric Kitchen Institute, 1934,
    giveaway booklet $6.00
New Family Receipt Book, Containing
    Eight Hundred Truly Valuable
    Receipts . . ., Philadelphia: 1818 .... $165.00
New Perfection Oil Cook Stove, 1914,
    27 page cookbook $15.00
Mrs. Putnam's Receipt Book; and
    Young Housekeeper's Assistant,
    Boston: 1849 .... $55.00
—. Same, but published Boston: 1854 .... $45.00
Pye, Mrs. Julia A. **Invalid Cookery,**
    Chicago: 1880 .... $20.00
Raffald, Elizabeth. **The Experienced**
    English Housekeeper, for the Use
    and Ease of Ladies, Housekeepers,
    Cooks, Etc. . . ., 1807 .... $85.00
Ralston Purina Mothers Manual, 1928,
    30 pages $8.00
Randolph, Mary. **The Virginia Housewife,**
    Baltimore: n.d. (c. 1831) $65.00
Rorer, Mrs. S. T. **Home Candy Making,**
    Philadelphia: 1889 .... $18.00

Royal Gelatine, 1942, 48 pages $6.00
Rumford Baking Powder, 1931 .... $12.00
—. Another, showing Rumford elves,
    1929, 12 pages $6.00
Sanitarium Bran, booklet $4.00
Savory Prize Recipe Book 1 for the
    'Savory' Roaster, Buffalo, NY: The
    Republic Metalware Co., 1922.
    A cookbook with pictures of
    Republic's wares $5.00
Story of Crisco, 1914, booklet $18.00
Swan's Down Cake Secrets, 1931 .... $8.00
Tschirky, Oscar. **The Cook Book by**
    'Oscar' of the Waldorf, Chicago:
    1896, 907 pages $20.00
Tulsa Cook Book. Favorite Recipes of
    Tulsa Ladies. Compiled by the
    Ladies' Aid Society of the First
    Presbyterian Church of Tulsa,
    Indian Territory, 1904 .... $40.00 to $50.00
Women's Temperance Kitchen Wall
    Temperence Cookbook, 1888, 27 pages $45.00
Wright, Mary M. **Candy Making at Home,**
    Philadelphia: 1920. 188 pages $20.00

NOTE: Regional cookbooks, like the Fairbanks Alaska one or the Tulsa one, above, especially those originating in one town or with one women's group, are increasingly valuable. They have been printed at least since the 1880s, as fundraisers, and offer a charming look at charity ladies of another age. I don't know why, but a good number seem to be Presbyterian . . . and from personal family experience I happen to know Presbyterian ladies cook awfully well!

LABELS

I don't know if it's because my own attention is focused on paper collectibles, but it seems that ephemera is growing very rapidly in popularity. Because the subject is food, the colorful lithographed labels used on fruit crates and cans seem a natural complement to collections of kitchen things.

These labels are usually priced one of two ways: a single price for a large grouping, dealer selects the group, or a price for warehouse finds — quantities of the same label, which I assume are bought by dealers rather than collectors, although if a label is particulary interesting, a collector might do well to corner the market and use it for trading. A third market is growing . . . sales of individual labels, sometimes at surprisingly hefty prices, by dealers at the specialized paper shows. Most sales are still mail order. **When inquiring of dealers what they have, send a S.A.S.E. along with your letter.**

The following is a listing of dealers who have advertised labels, etc. My apologies to those not listed: I'll be glad to include new dealers in the next edition.

Cairns Antiques, Box 445, Woodlake, CA 93286. 25 cents plus double-stamped #10 envelope for list.

Bonnie Bull, 63 October Lane, Trumball, CT 06611. S.A.S.E.

R. W. Bouldin, Route 2, Hohenwald, TN 38462. S.A.S.E.

Audrey Glenn, 66 Stoney Brook Road, Montville, NJ 07045. S.A.S.E.

Max Hazzard, 3711 Francis, S.E., Wyoming, MI 49508. S.A.S.E.

Industrial Revolution, Box 25615, Chicago, IL 60625. S.A.S.E.

Larry's Labels, Box 296, Philo, IL 61864. S.A.S.E.

Leonard Louis Lasko, "Mr. 3-L," P.O. Box 35, Soudersburg, PA 17577. S.A.S.E.

L. Lowther, 1010 "G" Street, The Dalles, OR 97058. S.A.S.E.

Orange Grove Cottage, Box 3392, Manhattan Beach, CA 90266. S.A.S.E.

Pacific Label Archives, P.O. Box 15445, Santa Ana, CA 92705. S.A.S.E.

The Paper Pile, Box 337, San Anselmo, CA 04960. S.A.S.E.

Phillips, P.O. Box 32, Ventura, CA 93002. Single stamp.

P. Smith, 2904-17 Street, Everett, WA 98201. S.A.S.E.

Staub's, Box 5233A, Coralville, IA 52241. Two stamps.

Stu's Place, RR L, Box 100, Greencastle, IN 46135. S.A.S.E.

Tom's, Box 6211, Santa Barbara, CA 93111. S.A.S.E.

Bill Wauters, 700 Clipper Gap, Auburn, CA 95603. S.A.S.E.

Walden, Box 424, Wadsworth, OH 44281. S.A.S.E.

The following is an adaptation from a talk that David Arky made before a collectors' group called Early Tools and Trades Society of New York. Mr. Arky is one of the two most experienced photographers of collectibles in the country today. He and Steven Mays, also of New York, photographed the thousands of photographs for the 16-volume "Encyclopedia of Collectibles" done by Tree Communications for Time-Life Books. Mr. Arky photographed the kitchen collectibles article for the "Encyclopedia," and his work has appeared in such different periodicals as "Craft Horizons," "Esquire," "Connoisseur" and "Lampoon"! I'm very proud to have him as a friend, and as the photographer of most of the pictures in this book.

PHOTOGRAPHING YOUR COLLECTION
By David Arky

Any camera can be used, but a 35mm single lens reflex or one of the Polaroid SX-70 models are especially well suited to the job. You may need a few inexpensive accessories if your interest is in taking close-ups of manufacturer's or maker's marks, or other details, but most modern lenses focus close enough to fill all of the picture area with an average-sized kitchen implement.

You should choose the right film for the natural or artificial light available to you. Natural light or daylight can be ideal, but I suggest that you shoot in an area or on a surface that is in shade, or else wait for an overcast day to give you less harsh shadows.

Using Color Film

You can use any of the following color films, all of which are balanced for daylight; Kodachrome 25 or 64, Agfachrome, and Ektachrome 64. The 200, 400 and 1000 ISO/ASA films are not recommended for our purposes. The numbers after the films indicate their relative speeds; the higher the number, the faster the film, which means that they need less light or exposure. Faster films are also grainier — that is, they have more texture and don't give as fine a result as slower film.

Artificial Light for most non-professional purposes, is Tungsten light, and that means special 250- or 500-watt lamps (bulbs) that will match the color qualities of Tungsten films. Fluorescent light requires special correction filters and is more difficult to work with. Standard light bulbs, like those found in table lamps or lighting fixtures, can be used with color film, but will result in a redder picture. The 250-watt ECA bulbs and

500-watt ECT bulbs, which can be bought at a camera store, are used with either Ektachrome 50 or Ektachrome 160.

Since Polaroid color film comes only in a daylight type, you have two alternatives when using Polaroid: you can place a filter over the lens — an 80A filter — which will correct the color of the light to match the film; or you can use Blue Tungsten lamps, which are the same color that the 80A filter is. The 250-watt lamp is coded BCA; the 500-watt is BCT.

Using Black and White Film

The same principles hold true for black and white films. The faster the speed of the film, the grainier the picture will be, and the less detail will be recorded. Panatomic-X (ISO/ASA 32) is the best bet for black and white film, especially if the camera is on a tripod. This film has very fine grain and yields good enlargements. Plus-X (ISO/ASA 125) is a fine grain film also, and can be used when faster speed is essential. If the camera is to be hand-held, then Tri-X (ISO/ASA 400) is the appropriate choice. It has good resolution with fine grain, but the size of the enlargements will be limited, say to 5" x 7", depending on the tones of the photograph. Medium gray tones tend to accentuate the grain, whereas very light or dark tones tend to hide the grain structure so that it becomes less apparent. Lighting for black and white pictures is somewhat easier than for color because any light source can be used — it is only the amount of light given off, not the light's color that counts.

Close-ups

For moderate close-ups you can purchase an inexpensive set of three lenses which thread onto the front of your normal lens. They are called close-up lenses, but you should take your camera to the store to get the right thread size. For even closer work, such as capturing fine details of maker's marks, you can use extension tubes which go between the camera body and the lens. These tubes allow you to get 1:1 magnification, which means that something ½" wide would be exactly that size on the slide, ie. lifesize.

Lighting

Proper lighting is really the most important part of taking a good photograph — that, and reading the correct exposure. The 'soft' light you get on an overcast or cloudy day is ideal for photographing a variety of things outdoors, and will work well indoors too if your windows aren't blocked by adjacent buildings or big leafy trees. In using window light you should place the object to be photographed on a table, as close to the window as possible. With the light coming from either the left or right side, place a white cardboard on the opposite side to reflect additional light back onto the subject. Otherwise very dark shadows on one side will result. (**See Diagram A.**)

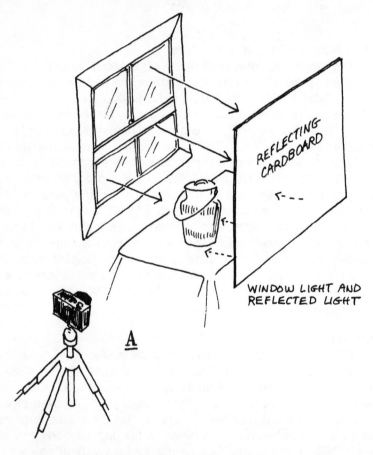

REFLECTING CARDBOARD

WINDOW LIGHT AND REFLECTED LIGHT

A

The Tungsten lights can be used in the same way, in the same general position as the window. I suggest putting tissue paper over the lights (though not touching as the lamps get extremely hot and could ignite the paper). This 'softens' the light — again, the purpose is to avoid harsh shadows. You can purchase inexpensive clamp-on light fixtures with reflectors at most hardware stores. These are adequate for the 250-watt lamps.

Regardless of the type of light being used, your main objective is to place the light at the appropriate angle to the subject. In order to best capture the texture in a grater, or to show a stamped mark on a handle, a strong side light is needed, without the bounce-back cardboard. The light should be placed so that it 'skims' across the surface. (**See Diagram B.**)

When photographing large implements or utensils, you will need two lights, so that the lighting will be evenly distributed, will show off the form and will fill in any dark areas. The reflecting cardboard in the first diagram does the same thing as an additional light but not as well.

One light should be placed at a 45-degree angle to the object being photographed, and the second light should be placed on the other side and slightly behind to give some depth to the lighting. (**See Diagram C.**)

Shiny Surfaces

You may encounter some problems when trying to photograph very reflective or shiny objects. If you place the item on a dark background there will nothing to reflect in its shiny surface and the metal will look dead. But when a shiny piece of brass, tin or pewter is put on a white or cream-color background, and if the camera is tilted down at a slight angle, the metal comes to life. It reflects the light areas that surround it, and gives off the glow you expect. It may be necessary to place white cardboards all around the object to reflect on each surface, and you will probably have to adjust the angles of the cards to catch the light. For this type of set-up you want the light to be as indirect as possible. Bounce it off the ceiling or an adjacent wall, if they are

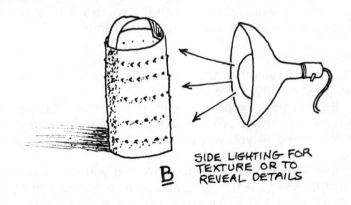

SIDE LIGHTING FOR TEXTURE OR TO REVEAL DETAILS

B

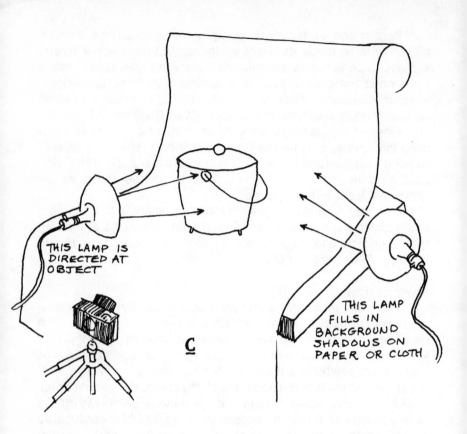

THIS LAMP IS DIRECTED AT OBJECT

C

THIS LAMP FILLS IN BACKGROUND SHADOWS ON PAPER OR CLOTH

light in tone, or off a large piece of white cardboard. (**See Diagram D.**)

Be careful to shield light so that it doesn't shine directly into the lens of your camera. Especially if you are using Tungsten lamps, anything aimed directly into the camera will spoil the quality of the image and wash out the rich color.

Most Valuable Tips

There are three other professional hints that will help you achieve good quality photographs:

1. Bracket your exposures. Film is relatively inexpensive, and by making several exposures at different settings — which is called bracketing — you will be assured of at least one good picture.

2. Use a tripod, even if you think that you can hold your camera still enough. A tripod helps you keep your composition as well as your focus. Lighting can be a time-consuming process, with much checking of the image in the viewfinder or lens, and a tripod will help you keep your position and get sharp, clear, well-composed results. The slower the film, the more you need a tripod, because the lens must remain open longer.

3. Use a cable release if the exposure is 1/15 second or longer. Especially when the camera is on a tripod, use of a cable release prevents the camera from shaking at the time of exposure. Or, try decaffinated coffee!

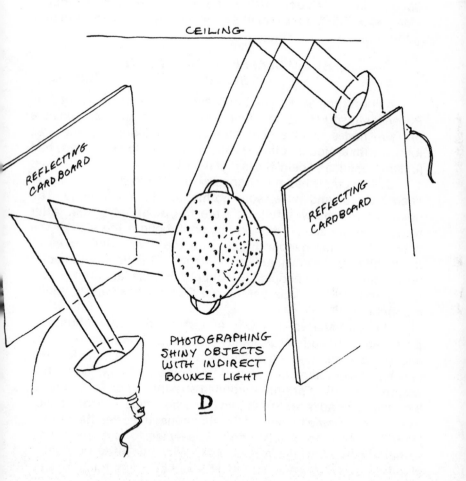

PHOTOGRAPHING SHINY OBJECTS WITH INDIRECT BOUNCE LIGHT

D

What follows is another exuberant piece written for 300 Years of Kitchen Collectibles by a dealer you're probably familiar with because of his colorful and regular advertisements in "The Antique Trader." It's pure coincidence that ol' Arkie, his self, and my friend David Arky, the photographer, have like-sounding names. Arkie's Antiques, Route 5, Chillicothe, Missouri 64601, offers complete mail order service, and a cheery greeting from Arkie, Emily, Punkin, Mickey, ol' Beemis and the horses, Pearl, offers complete mail order service, and a cheery greeting from Arkie, Emily, Punkin, Mickey, Ol' Beemis and the horses, Pearl, Sugar, Jimmy, Spook, David and Tiny. Send him a double-stamped S.A.S.E. for a recent list, which'll take you some time to wade through.

THE BIG CLAPPER ESTATE AUCTION
By Arkie

A short time back, wife Emily and ol' Arkie drove up into the Poosey, Missouri hills, to attend one of them auctions. This here ol' farm had seen five generations of the Clappers, and was loaded with antiques. Linnie Clapper, an old widow woman, had just deceased, and bein' the last of her tribe, an estate sale it was.

Ol' Mz. Linnie had run strangers off with the shotgun fer over twenty years, and never sold nothin' 'ceptin some eggs. The house and barns was full, as were the bloomin' sheds. After arriving on the scene, ol' Arkie couldn't believe the size of the crowd. They was people diggin' thru the sheds, an' boxes of items, all over the lawn, an' on the wagon. This here farm hadn't never seen so many people all at once! Why, the last time people had gathered here, was before Jud Clapper got caught sellin' moonshine!

The sale started promptly at 11AM, and the auctioneer's pace was fast and furious. Many times a person didn't bid fast enough, and another of the Clapper's prize possessions found a new home with someone else. After some tools had sold off a wagon, they sold a primitive wooden shaving bench for $75.00; a barrel maker's adze for $18.00; an iron wheel measure for $27.50, as a sample. Some boxes of miscellaneous, unsorted items sold from 50 cents to $18.00, and it seemed everybody found something worthwhile in each box. Why this little ol' man a standin' next to ol' Arkie bought a 50 cent box, and found one of the neatest ol' primitive kitchen can openers. Needless to say, ol' Ark done bought it from him. Here's a short list of some things found in boxes. A lady's fancy silver mesh purse, early and primitive kitchen utensils including pot scrubbers with iron rings, mechanical spatula, pie crust crimpers, a large sterling silver man's ring and lady's brooch, a wood and tin nutmeg grater, etc. It sure paid to buy them box fulls!

After the tools and boxes, the sale moved on to the primitive early furniture. A Shaker pine flour bin table with two tilt-out drawers sold for $50.00; an old icebox, rotted on base, $1.00; and a tall oak kitchen cabinet with tilt-out flour bin in base, $245.00. Then we moved on to a long table of early glassware, etc. Here a china shaving mug with elk scene sold for $18.50; a child's miniature 3 drawer wooden chest, $15.00; a glass kerosene sweetheart lamp with beaded hearts, $147.50; two gizzard split-oak baskets, $42.00 the pair; straight razors $5.00 to $7.00 each; a stereoviewer with a large lot of cards, $65.00; and from here the auctioneers moved to some nice handstitched quilts. These sold between $25.00 to $80.00. Then back to furniture, where a walnut marble top dresser sold for $240.00; a large dovetailed cherry blanket chest with handforged hardware, $160.00; a highboy oak chest, $185.00; and an oak bed for $90.00. At this time the crowd moved on to a large table of pots and pans.

Ol' wife Emily stared over at Arkie with her one good eye and she say, "Hey, ol' man! You best be for a loadin' up our furniture while I go pay! We gots a long drive home and the chores to do after we gits there!" Ol' Arkie say, "Hey, ol' woman, what time you got?" Wife Emily looks up at the setting sun an' say it's half past six, ni' on seven. This here upsets ol' Arkie causin' him knows how his ol' black and tan hound frets while a helpin' Arkie do the chores after dark. Ol' Arkie knows better than make the ol' hound mad, causin' coon season's jest a few weeks off.

Now just a final word to y'all fine folks out there from ol' Arkie. Does your life seem to be in the same ol' rut? Do you feel tired and listless? Can't sleep at night, and even food doesn't taste all that good? Well friend, this week check the newspaper under auctions, fill the car with gas, and when the weekend comes, head out! Even if you don't buy a thing, you can still enjoy watching the people with antique fever. Who knows, you might even catch the bug and go crazy like ol' Arkie done jest 22 years ago!

By the way, Linda, ol' Lem Sneden done tol' me ta tell ya abouts his watermelons. Seems they sent him some seeds that got crossed with a punkin. Once ya get inside one of them there melons, they has yellow meat, an' large white seeds, the kind thet gets caught in your throat before ya see's them. Outside they looks just like any ol' green watermelon.

Why, jest last week, at the Pine Ridge Church Social, ol' wife Emily done got one of them seeds caught in her throat, an' tryin' to be polite, she jest set there, didn't cough or nothin'.

Well, this here ol' gal a sittin' across the table from us says, "Hey, Emily, what you think 'bout Crosser Loney's coon hound a havin' eleven pups?" Ol' wife Emily don't answer and the ol' gal across the table sez, "Hey, Arkie, why don't wife Emily talk?" I done turned, and ol' wife Emily's face was blue, and I figures her eye shadow done run or something. 'Bout this time ol' Preacher Timken comes up and slaps ol' wife Emily on the back, an' says, "What y'all think of my sermon this evenin'?" This here slap on the back dislodges the seed in Emily's throat, an' with a large belch, the seed done sailed across the room, a hittin' one of the kids in the Spelling Bee. This here kid starts a squallin' and a raising all kinds of hell. Preacher Timkin is all upset, causin' him figures the ol' Devil's got the boy fer shur. With all this confusion a goin' on, I sneaks out behind the church ta talk coonhuntin' and drink Bubble Up with the boys.

So that's the story 'bout how ol' wife Emily and the yellow-meated watermelon broke up the Pine Ridge Church Social an' caused the devil to take possession of one of them poor, poor children.

BIBLIOGRAPHY

The following listing is of books of particular interest to collectors of old kitchen things. For a fuller, somewhat more esoteric listing, see my **Bibliography of Antiques and Collectbles in the English Language**, published in 1978 by Scarecrow Press, Metuchen, NJ 08840, which is available in many libraries.

[n.d. means no date; u.p. means unpaginated]
n.p. means no place of publication mentioned]

The American Hearth: Colonial and Post-Colonial Cooking Tools. Exhibit catalog. n.p.: Broome County Historical Society (NY state), 197-? Illustrated. u.p.

Beck, Doreen. **Collecting Country and Western Americana.** London: Hamlyn, n.d. Illustrated, 128pp.

Bull, Donald. **A Price Guide to Beer Advertising Openers and Corkscrews.** Trumbull, CT: Donald Bull, 1981. Illustrated. 40pp.

Celehar, Jane. **Kitchens and Gadgets, 1920-1950.** Des Moines, IA: Wallace-Homestead, 1982.

Coffin, Margaret. **The History and Folklore of American Country Tinware, 1700-1900.** Camden, NJ: Thomas Nelson & Sons, 1968. Illustrated.

The Cooks' Catalogue. Edited by James Beard, Milton Glaser, Burton Wolf, and Associates of the Good Cooking School. NY: Harper & Row, Publishers, 1975. Illustrated copiously, 565 pp.

The Cook's Store: How to Buy and Use Gourmet Gadgets. By the editors of "Consumer Guide". NY: Simon & Schuster, A Fireside Book, 1978. Illustrated, 192pp.

Consentino, Geraldine, and Regina Stewart. **Kitchenware: A Guide for the Beginning Collector.** NY: Golden Press, 1977. Illustrated, 128pp.

Curtis, Will, and Jane Curtis. **Antique Woodstoves.** Ashville, ME: Cobblesmith, 1975. Illustrated, 63pp.

DeVoe, Shirley Spaulding. **Tinsmiths of Connecticut.** Middletown, CT: Wesleyan, 1968.

Dover Stamping Co. 1869. (Facsimile catalog reprint.) Princeton: The Pyne Press, American Historical Catalog Collection, 1971. Illustrated, 205÷ pp.

Franklin, Linda Campbell, **From Hearth to Cookstove: An American Domestic History of Gadgets and Utensils Made or Used in America from 1700 to 1930.** Florence, AL: House of Collectibles, 1976, 1978. Illustrated, 271pp.

Fredgant, Don. **Electrical Collectibles, Relics of the Electrical Age.** San Luis Obispo, CA 93406: Padre Productions, 1981. Illustrated, 160pp.

Gould, Mary Earle. **Antique Tin and Tole Ware: Its History and Romance.** Rutland, VT: Charles E. Tuttle, 1958, 1967. Illustrated, 136pp.

— **Early American Wooden Ware and Other kitchen Utensils.** Rutland, VT: Charles E. Tuttle, 1962. Illustrated, 243pp.

Gray, Dorothy **Gone with the Hearth.** Millbrae, CA: Celestial Arts-Les Femmes, 1976. Illustrated, 225pp.

Greaser, Arlene and Paul H. Greaser. **Cookie Cutters and Molds.** Allentown, PA: 1969. Illustrated, 171pp.

The Handwrought Object, 1776-1976. Exhibit catalog. Nancy Neumann Press, Curator. Ithaca, NY: Herbert F. Johnson Museum of Art, Cornell University, 1976. Illustrated, 53pp.

Hankenson, Dick. **Trivets.** Maple Plain, MN: Author, 1963.

Harris, Gertrude. **Pots & Pans, Etc.** San Francisco, CA: 101 Productions, 1975. Illustrated, 96pp.

Harrison, Molly. **The Kitchen in History.** NY: Charles Scribner's Sons, 1972. Illustrated. 142pp.

Heck, Anne. **The Complete Kitchen: Where to Get Those Hard-to-Find Kitchen Utensils.** NY: Scribner's Sons, 1974. Illustrated 86pp.

Jones, Joseph C., Jr. **American Ice Boxes.** Humble, TX: Jobeco Books, 1981. Illustrated, 100pp.

Kauffman, Henry J. **American Copper and Brass.** Camden, NJ: Thomas Nelson, 1968. Illustrated, 288pp.

— **Early American Ironware, Cast and Wrought.** Rutland VT: Charles E. Tuttle, 1966; NY: Weathervane Books, n.d. Illustrated, 166pp.

— **The American Fireplace: Chimneys, Mantelpieces, Fireplaces & Accessories.** NY: Galahad Books, 1972. Illustrated, 352pp.

Kness, Darlene. **The Butterick Kitchen Equipment Handbook; An Illustrated Consumer's Guide to Cookware, Appliances and Utensils.** NY: Butterick, 1977. Illustrated, 192pp.

Lantz, Louise K. **Old American Kitchenware, 1725-1925.** NY: Thomas Nelson Inc. and Hanover, PA: Everybodys Press, 1970. Illustrated. 289pp.

— **Price Guide to Old Kitchenware.** Hydes, MD: Author, 19—. Illustrated, about 40pp.

Lifshey, Earl. **The Housewares Story: A History of the American Housewares Industry.** Chicago, IL: National Housewares Manufacturers Association, 1973. Illustrated, 384pp.

Lindsay, J. Seymour **Iron and Brass Implements of the English American House.** Bass River, MA: C. Jacobs, 1964. Illustrated, 88 + pp.

L.H. Mace & Co. 1883. Facsimile catalog reprint. Princeton, NJ: The Pyne Press, American Historical Catalog Collection. 1971. Illustrated, 69 + pp.

Matthews, Mary Lou. **American Kitchen Collectibles: Identification and Price Guide.** Gas City, IN: L-W Promotions, 1973. Illustrated, 81pp.

Maust, Don, ed. **American Woodenware and Other Primitives; a Collection of Essays on Woodenware, Treen, Tin, Brass, Copper, Iron, Pewter, and Pottery; a Practical Reference.** Uniontown, PA: E.G. Warman, 1974. Illustrated, 159pp.

Moore, Jan. **Antique Enameled Ware; An Illustrated Value Guide,** Paducah, KY: Collector Books, 1975. Illustrated, 78pp.

Norwalk, Mary. **Kitchen Antiques.** NY: Praeger Publishers, 1975. Illustrated. 135pp.

Objects for Preparing Food. Exhibit catalog. Introductions by Curator Sandra Zimmerman and Mimi Shorr (Sheraton). Washington, DC: The Renwick Gallery of the National Collection of Fine Arts, Smithsonian Institution, and the Museum of Contemporary Crafts of the American Crafts Council, 1972. Illustrated, u.p.

Perry, Evan. **Collecting Antique Metalware.** London: Hamlyn, 1974. Illustrated, 191pp.

Phipps, Frances. **Colonial Kitchens, Their Furnishings, and Their Gardens.** NY: Hawthorn, 1972. Illustrated, 346pp.

Porter, Enid M. **The Hearth and the Kitchen.** Cambridge, England: Cambridge & Country Folk Museum, 1971. Illustrated, 19pp.

Powell, Elizabeth A. **Pennsylvania Butter Tools and Processes.** Doylestown, PA: Bucks County Historical Society, 1975. Illustrated, 28pp.

Punchard, Lorraine. **Child's Play.** (Play dishes, kitchen things). Bloomington, MN 55431: Author, P.O. Box 20543, 198-? Illustrated, 281 pp.

Reid, Joe, and John Peck. **Stove Book.** NY: St. Martin's Press, 1977. Illustrated, 107 ÷ pp.

Russell, Loris S. **Handy Things to Have Around the House: Oldtime Domestic Appliances of Canada & the U.S.** Illustrated, 176pp.

Sandon, Henry. **Coffee Pots and Teapots for the Collector.** NY: Arco, 1974. Illustrated, 128pp.

Smith, Elmer Lewis, ed. **Early American Butter Prints; A Collection of Rural Folk Art.** Witmer, PA: Applied Arts, 1971. Illustrated, 32pp.

— **Tinware: Yesterday and Today.** Lebanon, PA: Applied Arts, 1974. Illustrated, 40pp.

Sonn, Albert H. **Early American Wrought Iron.** NY: Charles Scribner's Sons, 1928; NY: Bonanza Books, 1979. 3 volumes in 1. Illustrated, 263 + pp; 205 + pp; 263pp.

Tefft, Gary, and Bonnie Tefft. **Red Wing Potters and Their Wares.** Menomonee Falls, WI: Locust Enterprises, 1981. Illustrated, 192pp. Separate **Price Guide**, 14pp.

Toulouse, Julian Harrison. **A Collectors' Manual: Fruit Jars.** Everybodys Press, 1969. Illustrated, 542pp.

Everyodys Press, 1969. Illustrated, 542 pp.

Trice, James E. **Butter Molds; An Identification & Value Guide,** Paducah, KY: Collector Books, 1980. Illustrated, 176pp.

Vogelzang, Vernagene and Evelyn Welch. **Graniteware, Collector's Guide with Prices.** Des Moines, IA: Wallace-Homestead, 1981. Copiously illustrated.

Walker, Mary. **200 Years of Reamers.** Sherman Oaks, CA 91423: Muski Publishing, 198-. Illustrated. Separate price guide.

Watney, Bernard, M., and Homer D. Babbidge. **Corkscrews for Collectors.** Totowa, NJ: Sotheby Publications, 1981. Illustrated.

Wills, Geoffrey. **Collecting Copper and Brass.** NY: Bell Publishing Co. (Crown), 1962. Illustrated. 157pp.

Yena, Louise, **The Handbook of Antique Coffee and Tea Collectibles; Price Guide.** San Antonio, TX: Author, 1971. illustrated.

INDEX

Page numbers can refer to a price listing, picture or essay.

Linda Campbell Franklin's
KITCHEN
COLLECTIBLES
NEWS For Collectors of Antique Cooking Tools, Housewares & Cookbooks

Edited and published by
Linda Campbell Franklin

* **Six 16pp issues** each year. Many illustrations, valuable research and identifications. "I didn't know it would be so jam-packed!" wrote one excited subscriber.

* **Special rate** for readers of 300 YEARS: $17.00 a year. Second or gift subscriptions: $16.00. $3.00 per sample. All subscriptions go January 1-December 31 because the newsletter does not depend on events, calendars and other dated material for fill-up.

* **All checks in U.S. funds,** payable to L.C. Franklin. All letters to P.O. Box 383, Murray Hill Station, NYC, NY 10016. Add a note, please, about your specialties.

Regular Columns & Features
* Old Patent Papers   * Future Classics Advisory   * Trend-Spotting
* Classifieds   * Book Reviews   * Letter Column   * Dollhouse Kitchens
     * Paper Ephemera   * Collectible Cookbooks   * More!!

Subscribers include hundreds of collectors and dealers, and many museums and restorations all over North America.